HERO'S WAY

*Contemporary Poems
in the Mythic Tradition*

PRENTICE-HALL INTERNATIONAL, INC. London
PRENTICE-HALL OF AUSTRALIA, PTY. LTD. Sydney
PRENTICE-HALL OF CANADA, LTD. Toronto
PRENTICE-HALL OF INDIA PRIVATE LIMITED New Delhi
PRENTICE-HALL OF JAPAN, INC. Tokyo

HERO'S WAY

Contemporary Poems in the Mythic Tradition

edited by

John Alexander Allen

Department of English
Hollins College

PRENTICE-HALL, INC., ENGLEWOOD CLIFFS, N.J.

Library of Congress Catalog Card Number 78-137896

Printed in the United States of America

13-386862-1

Current Printing (last digit):

10   9   8   7   6   5   4   3   2   1

To my students
at Hollins College
whose keen interest and insight
served as Lady
at every crossroad of this
Hero's Way

Contents

Section Two: Stagnation, 57

Section Three: Intimations, 79

PART III: THE JOURNEY, 97

Section One: The Setting Forth, 103

Section Two: The Road of Trials, *123*

Section Three: The Beast, *149*

Section Four: The Double, *169*

PART IV: THE LADY, *189*

Section One: Her Nature, *195*

Section Two: The Meeting, *213*

Section Three: The Rescue, *241*

PART V: THE FATHER, *269*

Section Two: Conflict, *299*

Section Three: Atonement, *321*

Section Three: The Boon, *391*

Preface: To the Reader

Hero's Way is a collection of poems, mostly contemporary, and an account of a journey as ancient as the human race itself. The poems presented here are arranged in sequence, thematically, to correspond with the successive stages of the traditional Hero's Quest. Such an arrangement of poems is a novel one, and the Quest itself may be unfamiliar, in detail, to many readers. Therefore an explanation here at the outset is very much in order. The remarks which follow are intended to supply preliminary answers to the questions, what Hero?, and what Way? They should also serve to introduce the plan and purpose of the anthology and to prepare the reader for putting that plan to work. Most importantly, he is invited to adopt the rôle of Hero for himself and, in doing so, to convert the reading of poems from the rather perfunctory spectator sport that it sometimes is into the active enterprise that it can and should be. He can accomplish this by using the poems and the commentary which accompanies them as a guide for assembling, from his own experience, an individual version of the Quest. In the process, he may expect to learn a number of interesting things about himself as well as about poetry; and, if all goes well, he should acquire, somewhere along the road, a growing sense that poems are of immediate, real, and vital concern to himself personally.

Who, then, is the Hero? In some of the poems that follow, his identity is established from the start, because his name is well known from a familiar myth, or fairy tale, or episode in scripture. He is

Jack the Giant Killer, Perseus, the Prince in the tale of Sleeping
Beauty, or Lazarus. Knowing his name, we also know, in general,
what his story is and what to expect of him. Yet, when he is
brought to life and put into action by a particular poet, he usually
turns out to surprise us in some way. For instance, the title figure
in "Jack," by Randall Jarrell, is not the plucky (and lucky) farm
boy turned adventurer whom we remember from the fairy tale.
Instead, he is the man that the boy has unaccountably become. Old,
weary, and disillusioned, he reflects upon his past and wonders what
went wrong with it. The giant's wife protected him when his life
was endangered, and, as a result, he ran off with the prizes: the goose
that laid the golden eggs and the singing harp. How could he
have known that his retreat from Giant Land, which turned out just
as he wished, in fact betrayed a princess and left his actual task un-
done? Or take Graham Hough's "Andromeda." In this version of
the mythic rescue, when Perseus arrives to save the lady from the
sea monster, he finds that she is not prepared to fall in with his plan.
She has grown so accustomed to the beast she lives with, dreary
though he is, that she has passed the point of caring to be freed from
him. This turnabout maneuvers the reader into seeing a familiar
situation in a novel way: His expectations about the ideal relation-
ship between lady in distress and hero to the rescue are disappointed.
It occurs to him that there is something familiar about the habitual
stodginess which makes Hough's Andromeda invulnerable to libera-
tion. And he finds something a bit ridiculous about the hero in his
"gold helm," sulking because his "attitude was spoiled." Perhaps
it is at least in part the hero's fault that he sees the lady as nothing
more than a household drudge whom he can find little point in
rescuing. In short, Hough successfully uses the mythic material to
dramatize, in a humorous way, the difference between the spirit's
self-congratulatory aspiration and the dullness of the workaday
world which frequently is what it settles for.

In many poems, the protagonist is presented, not as the mythic
hero in his own person, but as someone whose experience is parallel
to his. For example, in Winfield Townley Scott's poem, "William
Primrose Gets His Guarnerius," the references to the story of Sleep-
ing Beauty are indirect. Neither the hero nor the heroine, as such,
appears. Nevertheless, their presence in the poem is necessary and,
on a second reading if not the first, quite unmistakable. Here, the
Prince is not a king's son but a Scottish musician of humble origin;

and his princess is a Guarnerius viola which can be awakened adequately, in a musical sense, only by the skillful touch of a master violist: "To awaken this / Required / No ordinary prince." May Sarton's title figure, Lazarus, on the other hand, is the poet herself on an occasion when her "buried self" arises, as from the dead, and makes its presence known by the impulse which she feels to begin the composition of a poem. In all of these instances, the Hero is a metaphoric figure upon whose nature and circumstances the poet plays his variations, turning him this way and that to suit his purpose, correspond to his emotion, make his point.

The Hero also may be Everyman, someone not unlike ourselves. Often he has no name and can claim no particular distinction. Yet his experience, even when it does not recall that of a specific Hero, has reference to heroic action. Such reference sometimes takes a negative form. The anonymous protagonist of "Perdita," by Louis MacNeice, like Jarrell's Jack, is the victim of an overwhelming sense of loss. The journey he has planned to make has been canceled by default before it ever began. The train which might have carried him on his way has never left the station. He has failed his traveling companion, Perdita, just as Jack has failed the "strait princess" whom he never found. Quite the opposite is true of the girl who tells her story in Yeats' poem, "Her Triumph." Like Andromeda, she is a captive who attains her freedom. When a champion appears to rescue her, she has only to be convinced that he is worthy of the task. Happily for her, he passes the test, and, breaking free from the dragon's coils, she looks out upon a world transfigured by her love. No dragons or derring-do of any kind appear in Josephine Miles' "A Meeting." In the plainest of language, the poem states the fact that a certain girl and a certain boy have at last been drawn together from opposite ends of a city. It is an adventure which seems anything but heroic. Yet, "Miraculous life! that in its brief and mortal / Progress achieves this union of intents." Although Miss Miles does not make the reference, the nameless boy is like the Prince in Grimm's tale, for he has a mission, whether he is aware of it or not, and it will be fulfilled in his meeting with the nameless girl whose rôle is essentially that of Sleeping Beauty. Many poems which are not explicitly associated with mythic heroes are nevertheless mythic in pattern. It is not difficult to see why this should be so. Myth can be defined in many ways, but in the literary context it is the distilled essence of human experience, expressed as metaphoric narrative. Literally, the old gardener in Richard Wilbur's "He Was" simply passes away; but he is resurrected when spring comes and the trees which he planted with such care unfold their leaves to the reviving year, for then his "found voice" rises "in the sparrowy air." Through metaphor, he has become another Lazarus.

The mythic heroes who are directly or indirectly associated with the protagonists of poems in *Hero's Way* may seem at first glance to have little relationship to ourselves. However, the poems themselves should soon persuade the reader that, for instance, the experience of Adam (or of Eve) and of Ulysses (or of Circe) is not as foreign to his own concerns as he had imagined. This discovery may well be the beginning of pleasure and understanding for any reader of poetry; and once it has been made, he will find that he is well on his way to learning a great deal not only about poems but also about myth and human nature, especially his own.

As one might expect, the mythic adventure that receives the greatest emphasis in poetry concerns the relationship between the Hero—as man or woman, god or goddess—and a figure of the opposite sex. It will not surprise the reader to be told that this motif, in myth and poetry, provides an infinitely various metaphoric expression of all that is most potently and constantly at work, informing, changing, and conditioning the human spirit to make us what we are. This complex subject can best be approached by means of a somewhat detailed consideration of two representative poems—one written from the masculine point of view, and the other from the feminine. The mythic episodes which will concern us here are Ariadne's rescue of Theseus from the labyrinth of the Minotaur, and the seduction of Danaë by Zeus in the form of a shower of gold.

Thomas Merton, in "Ariadne at the Labyrinth," presents a portrait of Ariadne, waiting beside the "starwhite wall" of the labyrinth for "the bold adventurer," Theseus, to emerge after his conquest of the Minotaur. We know that he could never find his way from the center of the maze back to the light of day if it were not for the thread which Ariadne has provided for him. Her crossed hands hold one end of that thread, and the hero is even now winding his way to safety at the other. And what do we know of Ariadne? She is patient, "a Barbadian flower." She is "calm as coral, / Silent as some plant of undersea." Her "eyes are lakes." Her "wild and gentle wisdom" is like "the Caribbean midnight," a darkness in which she paradoxically "foreknows / And solves the maze's cruel algebra." She is associated with the flowers which are the fruit of spring, with the depths of the sea with its mysterious life, with a darkness which brings forth her lover into "white morning." Her strength is no greater than that of the cotton thread she holds, yet it is very great, for it preserves the life of Theseus and draws out to her "The Bravest Soldier, the Wisest Judge, / The Mightiest King"—a man who is like a god. In a sense, Ariadne is giving birth to Theseus. Delicate as she is, she shares the life-giving properties of the teeming sea and the burgeoning earth. And her wisdom is like that of the spirit or the unconscious mind—mysterious, inscrutable, not to be learned or bargained for but only to be accepted, when it is offered, as a gift. In short, she is not only a girl but an incarnation of the mythic Lady, she who, in Richard Wilbur's phrase, is "the subject goddess of the dreams of men." If we, like Theseus, have ever been rescued from darkness, it is she who has rescued us. And, in saying that, we recognize her in every woman, real or imaginary, in our waking lives or in our dreams, whom we have ever loved. Although she remains a stranger, we know her intimately; and although she belongs to a whole which we cannot imagine in its entirety, she is a part of us.

When the relationship typified by the Ariadne-Theseus episode is reversed—that is, seen from the feminine point of view—the mortal woman becomes the beloved of a man who is also a god. An incident in the amorous history of Zeus provides the metaphor on which Julia Randall's "Danaë" is based. The setting of the poem is local and particular—a room in a "summer town." Here, the protagonist, like Danaë in her prison cell, is visited by an immortal lover: "I call his name a god." But the shower of gold which fell upon Danaë is sunlight here, or "finches in flight," or "the great / Acacia falling over me." The mortal lover is not present, has never been in this particular place; but the god is everywhere: "He comes glittering small, / Coining the air bright." Being "laved / In radiance" is like a waking dream—one of seduction. But the notion of sexual conquest, carried over from the myth, is used here to suggest the quality of an intuition or emotion: a sense of surrender to a loving presence, greater than the speaker's identity and essential to it. Its source is within her ("This love I make / Alone, and for my sake"), yet it transcends and encompasses her as sunlight does. But the god is also incarnate in a man, the "you" to whom the poem is addressed. The speaker brings the divine and mortal lovers together when she imagines herself, at some future time, a wife, whose "little son / Crawls on his mother's breast." She chatters over her chores. Then there is "a sudden glint" in her eyes, as from the reflected light of the declining sun; and the presence of the other lover comes upon her. At such a time, she says, the "softening / Of habit-hard attendance," the visible sign of her inner experience, should not be attributed to a "soft dream." It is a reality more real than herself, or the husband, or the real love which exists between them. It is the *cause* of reality, "that by which I love you, and I am." In its presence, husband and god, time and eternity meet; and they are seen as single and inseparable, one and the same.

Perhaps enough has now been said to link the Hero on the one hand with the great figures of myth, and on the other with the ordinary human being whose experiences everyone can share. We turn now to a consideration of the heroic Quest—the *way* of *Hero's Way.* The metaphor that supplies the overall design of this anthology derives from the traditional correspondence between the experiences of life as we live it and incidents which might befall a traveler on a journey. Such a journey, like our lives as they unfold, progresses from the known into the unknown, from the familiar into the mysterious and incalculable. The traveler who is fortunate enough to survive the dangers of the road may be rewarded by attaining the goal of the Quest, which is essentially the Boon of understanding. According to his capacity, he learns what is enduring and life-sustaining in a time-bound world; ideally, his individual being merges with and participates in the inexhaustible energy of the source of life. The discovery which crowns the Quest cannot, by definition, be passed along to others like a body of factual knowledge or a skill. It must be experienced to be known. But in myth, poetry, and fiction, it finds expression through the agency of metaphor. The fictional journey is instructive in a particular way: It provides a pattern into which the reader's experience can be fitted; and, ordered in that way, the jumble of perceptions and emotions which constitutes our daily life can yield a glimpse of wholeness which is imaginative but not imaginary.

Every reader shares with the questing Hero a disquieting ignorance of who he is and what lies in store for him; and he shares the fear, hope, and desire which that ignorance makes acute. Bound by time, he has no choice but to make a journey which, if it arrives at no other destination, may be relied upon to bring him to the grave. Everyone is presented with a continuing dilemma simply by the circumstance of being born; and thereafter, every stage of life—the attainment of adulthood, marriage and parenthood, old age and the imminence of death—adds new and infinitely trying complications. Regarded in this way, the Hero's journey may turn out to be no more than the highway to oblivion; and every incident along the way may only thwart the traveler's aspiration, torment him with loss upon loss, grief upon grief; tempt him with despair; and leave him at last, fixed in the image of his powerless ego, one more illustration of the view that life is only the fool of time. Yet the common story of mankind is also one of stubborn courage, sacrifice, and magnanimity—qualities which are the more touching for being offered freely in what must, in the context of time alone, be viewed as a losing cause. Under these circumstances, the Hero may appear comic or pathetic, yet he can never finally be dismissed as merely an object of contempt.

A dominant theme in the poetry of our time has been the tendency of mankind, mired in a dreary and short-sighted selfhood, to retreat from life rather than to meet it boldly and with redeeming touches of imagination. For this reason, the reader should not be surprised that *Hero's Way*, after presenting an introductory survey of Versions of the Quest, offers a group of poems which deal not with heroic exploits on however modest a scale, but with a sense of loss. The poems in Loss are associated with nostalgic frustration, a state in which the Hero makes his journey, if he sets forth at all, not forward into the unknown but backward into a past in which he imagines himself to have been more fully responsive to life, more gifted with potentialities, than he can be in these latter days. By contrast with these real or imagined former glories, his life has become a matter of time-bound routine. Time is the enemy, he its victim—a mood which is potently suggested, for example, by Louise Bogan's "The Cupola," where a mirror in an uninhabited room reflects the passing season in the images of airborne leaves outside the window—devoid of form, cut off from the source of life, disassociated, transient.

In the following section, Stagnation, the Hero is not visited by reminiscence of past splendors but is characteristically discovered trudging along on an aimless journey to he knows not where, or in some way imprisoned while he awaits the certain coming of death and oblivion. This is the Hero who has failed in his response both to the unavoidable dangers and to the attainable rewards of the active Quest. His state of being is one which one naturally associates with the jaded and cynical, whose lives wear on toward physical and spiritual impotence. The condition is not peculiar to any single stage. The young, for all the freshness and vigor which properly belong to them, are not exempt from apathy—a sense that meaning has drained away not only from themselves but from the persons, customs, institutions, daily preoccupations that fill and condition their days. The idiot image of himself as child which haunts the protagonist of Robert Penn Warren's "Original Sin: A Short Story" is not a product of worldly disillusionment. His unredeemed corruption has accompanied him from his earliest days. It was with him when he first left home, it followed him to college—unconvinced by his idealism, not to be left behind by frequent changes of ideology or address.

The Hero's Call to action sounds insistently in Intimations, though whether he will respond to it remains a question. It is as though his attention were being called to a rôle which he could play if he dared—one which he has never filled or has abandoned. A moment's vision breaks through his cloudy consciousness like the sun, and in that moment he apprehends the world in its immense complexity—beautiful, charged with potentiality, mysterious; and he has a sense of an incalculable energy, working through himself to some incalculable end. In such a moment, losing himself, the Hero paradoxically becomes far more than himself. His adventure may last no longer than a single heartbeat, but it will assure him that he is living still, that, at any hour of the day or night, his life—that circumscribed domain—may be in violence, or love, or terror altogether shattered and perhaps transformed.

As the reader continues through the successive parts of Hero's Way, he will find that the powerless protagonist of Loss and Stagnation reappears in every sector of the Road of Trials which stretches between the threshold of adventure and the goal of the Quest. Howard Nemerov's predecessor of Perseus ("all guts, no glass") will never reach that goal. He is always with us as a reminder that to be no more than one's self is to cut a pathetic figure—to be cast in stone by a Medusa who will always triumph with insulting ease over a would-be Hero who dares to confront her without the aid of a power more potent than his own.

Actually, the way of *Hero's Way* is a double one. At each
stage of the journey, if one cuts an imaginary cross section, he finds
one Hero blindly treading the maze of unredeemed mortality and
another catching a glimpse of immortal life, uncircumscribed, en-
lightened, and victorious. If one goal of the Quest both is and must
be death, the other is immortality; and the master paradox which is
reflected everywhere in myth, religion, and literature is that the two
goals, when they are understood, are not incompatible. The career
of the mythic hero ideally ends with his apotheosis; that is, with his
identification with the inexhaustible source of life. When Heracles,
or Christ, or Buddha has completed his labors on earth, he assumes
the nature and the powers of a god. He has found the Way; and
Everyman as Hero tries, according to his lights, to follow that same
road and to share the Boon of understanding which has been won by
those who have traveled it before him.

What kind of reality can the Hero's journey, conceived of as
the Quest for immortal life, possess for Everyman, whose limitations
are so painfully apparent? In order to provide a useful answer to
this essential question, we must first make a number of assumptions:
(1) Everyman can share in immortality only from the vantage point
of time. What happens after death is beyond the scope of the heroic
Quest, as the Quest is a metaphor for experience, and nothing which
transcends experience can have a part in it. (2) Immortality, in the
context of the Quest, must be conceived of not as an infinite exten-
sion of life in time, but as a glimpse or glimpses into timelessness;
that is, immortality is not quantitative but qualitative. (3) The
human psyche is mysterious, and all manner of curious and inex-
plicable phenomena occur within it, thus presenting us with ex-
periences which exceed our powers of understanding. (4) As
Howard Nemerov has suggested, one can say that the subject of
poetry is the reconciliation of opposites: time with eternity, life
with death, body with spirit, male with female, human with divine;
and poems which suggest such reconciliation do so in the only
possible way—through the agency of metaphor. (5) All of the in-
cidents of the heroic Quest and of poems which are associated with
them involve the reconciliation of opposites and correspond to
moments of insight which all of us experience and for which we can
therefore supply a counterpart in reality as we know it.

Earlier in this essay, poems by Thomas Merton and Julia
Randall were used to illustrate the metaphoric rôles which male and

female characters assume in poems of mythic pattern. For the male as Hero, a woman, particularly when she is the object of his love, tends to take on the attributes of Earth, Venus, Athene, the mythic Lady in any one of her guises or in all of them simultaneously. And conversely, for the female protagonist, the conception of a man is associated with the sun, Zeus, Apollo—the source of light and life and the ruler over them. Because this is true, the relationship between man and woman in poetry can be used to dramatize, with infinite variation, the aspiration of the Hero not only to love and be loved in return but to be whole, complete, immortal. The union of man and woman, however transitory and imperfect it may be, has power to suggest the bringing together of all things that are divided in the temporal world, the restoration of Eden, in which man and God are harmoniously at one.

The heart of the heroic Quest lies in the Hero's crucial encounters with certain deeply ambiguous beings, all of whom provoke in us a strong emotional response. These, in *Hero's Way*, are represented by poems that deal with Beasts, the Double, the Lady, and the Father. They are the Hero's enemy and his friend; they threaten to destroy him, and yet have the power to bring him safely to his journey's end. Of the Lady and the Father, suffice it to say that they appear not only in poems and in our dreams, but are incarnate in our parents, lovers, rulers, idols—every human object of love, fear, reverence, hatred, rivalry, and desire which reflects and conditions what we are, what we do, and what we may, in the fullness of time, become. What of the Beast and the Double? They also are familiar to every reader, if not from poems, then from fairy tales, legends, and contemporary novels. Everyone knows the story of St. George and the dragon, and the dragon lives again in Tolkien's Smaug, the goal of Bilbo's quest in *The Hobbit*. The emergence of a metaphoric Beast in the midst of a group of former choirboys is the subject of William Golding's *Lord of the Flies;* and Golding has said that his purpose in writing that book was to keep alive the memory of the Beast whose menace was so fearfully fulfilled in World War II. Yet the Beast is not necessarily an adversary. When King Darius ordered Daniel thrown into the lion's den, the beasts would do him no harm. Friendly animals as guides and counselors abound in fairy tales. And quite recently Peter Beagle has restored its proper significance to a Beast of good omen in his novel, *The Last Unicorn*. Like the Beast, the Double usually is sinister and has immense potential for destruction. We have met him in Conrad's *Heart of Darkness* and *The Secret Sharer*, Stevenson's *Dr. Jekyll and Mr. Hyde*, and Wilde's *The Portrait of Dorian Gray*. He belongs to the unknown or rejected side of ourselves, a creature whom we sometimes project into society as the outcast, the inferior race, the persecuted minority. Yet here again there is another side to the coin. The Double also can be recognized in the voices that spoke to Joan of Arc, the visions of Bernadette, the prince who was like a pauper, and the pauper who was like a prince. The persecuted and despised themselves can become the agents of atonement between antagonists. A message which is acutely relevant to our time is to be found in "The Savages," by Josephine Miles. She imagines the "Indian problem" being solved once and for all by Indians who respond to the white man's "act of love" by showing their native magnanimity: "We cannibals must help these Christians."

The Hero's reconciliation with any one of the beings mentioned above would constitute an epitome of the successful Quest; and it can hardly be coincidence that each of them has its analogue in psychiatry, where the patient's inner dilemma also must be reckoned with. The table of equivalents would include the following: for the Beast, Freud's *id;* for the Double, Jung's *shadow;* for the Lady, Jung's *anima;* and for the Father, Freud's *ego* and *superego* and Jung's *animus*. The episodes of the heroic Quest are well known to most of us not only from the psychological research which has influenced our way of thinking but from everyday experience: for example, falling in love, going to sleep concerned about a seemingly insoluble problem and awakening to find that it has somehow solved itself, writing a poem without consciously choosing a subject or words with which to convey it, spontaneously launching out upon a course of action without having the slightest notion why we do so. Above all, if we attend to our dreams and do not merely forget or dismiss them, we find that they often take the form of journeys which markedly resemble the Hero's progress on the Road of Trials. The annals of psychiatry present an immense body of commentary upon the significance of dreams. So consistently do they repeat certain events, details, and rôles which interact with that of the dreamer, that a psychologist like Jung can construct from the dreams of his patients a coherent and meaningful story; and we should not be surprised to learn that this story corresponds, in its essentials, to that of the Hero's Quest as it has been recounted from the most ancient times. It would seem that we possess an inner faculty, quite apart from the conscious mind, which speaks in metaphor, using as naturally as we do our native tongue the language of the journey into the unknown, the hazards of the road, the final goal.

The universal story of the Quest has a daunting and often terrible reality which myth reports unflinchingly, and which poets may seek to transcend but never to deny, ignore, or wish away. In view of what may seem at times to be an oppressive uncertainty and frustration in accounts of the Hero's journey, it is to be hoped that the reader will take particular pleasure in the poems collected here under the heading of the Boon. All are associated with love, from Jerome Rothenberg's "A Bodhisattva Undoes Hell," where "the white sun / carries love / into the world," to James Wright's "A Blessing," where a chance encounter with two Indian ponies causes a man to say with conviction, "Suddenly I realize / That if I stepped out of my body I would break / Into blossom." Such poems have a quality of vision which is best appreciated on the far side of the Road of Trials. They have an earned reality, one no less genuine than that of the anguish in adversity from which their vision springs. Fortunately, these, like all good poems, are their own best advocates. We believe them because we have ourselves experienced what they show us, though never before, perhaps, with comparable force and clarity. To understand a poem is to understand some part of one's self, and that can be disturbing indeed. Nevertheless, to share a vision which is authenticated from within will seldom fail to yield the reward of understanding—and that is simply pleasure.

The pleasure which comes from reading poetry with good understanding is a necessary and perhaps sufficient reason for persevering in the face of difficulties which everyone must overcome in learning how to do so. However, pleasure is not the only inducement, or even the most important one, for learning to read poetry. If *Hero's Way* fulfills its purpose, it will convince the reader that much contemporary poetry springs from and serves to maintain a venerable tradition—that of the heroic Quest in myth and literature. The Quest itself, in all of its complexity, provides a pattern by means of which the full range of human experience has long found expression. Through this pattern, the wisdom and vision of many centuries of observation and reflection have been brought to bear upon the unavoidable problems and unlimited potentialities that are the heritage of Everyman. These essentials of human experience can best be studied in a perspective which can be provided only by an inclusive metaphoric structure. Such a perspective can be found in certain single works of literature; for example, *The Odyssey*, *The Divine Comedy*, and *The Faerie Queene*. Or it can be found in the works of certain single authors, taken together; for example, the poems of Chaucer and the plays of Shakespeare. Knowledge of such authors and such works is indispensable for a comprehensive understanding of the mythic tradition in literature and of its significance as a record of Everyman's journey and a guide for all who undertake it. The mythic tradition is a living one which continues to give meaning to contemporary poetry and to derive meaning from it. We live in an age when many of the traditional guides of Everyman have weakened, lost authority, and ceased to be effective: religions, codes of behavior, institutions, and customs of the family and society. William Golding has said that a society which has no living mythology is doomed. And surely he is right. The dangerous confusion which we see around us on every hand finds Everyman more desperately than ever in need of a knowledgeable guide. Who will go with him and be at his side if not the poet, whose responsibility it has always been to keep mythology alive? The poet still provides, if we will let him, that slender and essential thread which allows the adventurer to meet and conquer the Beast at the center of his inner labyrinth, and then to find his way back through the dark and winding passages that lead him finally into the light.

Preface: To the Teacher

I

Hero's Way is a collection of contemporary poems, selected *first* because they are representative of the best work which has been produced by younger poets in recent years, and *second* because they are directly or indirectly related to some part of the age-old Quest of the Hero, in myth and literature, for the Boon of enlightenment. Each of these poems in its own way provides dramatic testimony to the unconscious urge of Everyman for creation or re-creation into a world of experience transformed by hard-won understanding of the human condition as it relates to eternal life and its inexhaustible source.

The collection of poems in *Hero's Way* is open-ended, and readers are invited to add to it their own selections of poems drawn from the many good contemporary authors who are not represented here and from the work of older American and English poets. A number of poems in the latter category—for example, several anonymous ballads and shorter works by Browning, Whitman, Shelley, Donne, Tennyson, etc.—have been included to suggest the possibilities for extending this collection backward in time. Poems in the mythic tradition are, of course, also to be found in abundance in the literature of countries other than America and England. These have been excluded from *Hero's Way* only because they would necessarily be offered in translation, which would lessen their value for purposes of critical analysis.

In the brief essays that introduce the several parts and sections of *Hero's Way*, the editor has made constant reference to works of literature, both poetry and fiction, which are too long and in many instances too well known to be included here. Many of the great landmarks of western literature are cast in the form of heroic Quests: *The Odyssey* and *The Aeneid, The Canterbury Tales, The Divine Comedy, The Faerie Queene, Paradise Lost*. And a multitude of works of almost equal significance in the history and development of our literary tradition contain mythic elements: *Beowulf; The Morte d'Arthur;* Shakespeare's *Lear, The Winter's Tale,* and *The Tempest;* Blake's prophetic books; Coleridge's *The Ancient Mariner;* Wordsworth's *The Prelude;* Goethe's *Faust;* Eliot's *The Waste Land*. The prefatory essays also refer at appropriate points to versions of the Quest which appear in the myths of many lands and ages, but in particular in those with which our literature and religion have made us most familiar—the hero tales of Greece and Rome and those of the Judeo-Christian scriptures: the adventures of Theseus, Heracles, Demeter, Jason, Prometheus; and those of Adam and Eve, Noah, Abraham, David, the Magi, Lazarus, and Christ himself. For the instructor's and student's convenience, a four-part bibliography is appended to the book, presenting the principal figures of Greek and Roman mythology referred to in the text; relevant biblical materials and works of literature; and works of particular interest in the fields of literary criticism, psychology, and anthropology. These lists are intended to be suggestive rather than exhaustive, and all of them can readily be extended.

II

In addition to providing a large selection of contemporary poems for class analysis, *Hero's Way* opens up an inexhaustible supply of possibilities for student projects for which the materials are available either in the text itself, in any college library, or in relatively inexpensive paperback editions. The suggestions that follow can no doubt be greatly augmented by the instructor.

Use of Supplementary Texts

Hero's Way lends itself readily to use in conjunction with supplementary texts in literature, psychology, and anthropology.

For example, the teacher may wish to combine the study of contemporary mythic poetry with the reading of one or more of the great mythic works of antiquity. The editor has used *The Odyssey* in a course in myth and literature to provide a pattern for the Heroic Quest in its entirety. The student's perspective upon contemporary versions of the Quest cannot fail to gain immensely from fresh acquaintance with the trials and ultimate success of Homer's deepdevising hero. Each of the principal adventures of Odysseus finds its parallel in poems included in *Hero's Way*. A list of the most notable of these might well include the following: "Nearing again the legendary isle" (C. Day Lewis), "The End of a Journey" (A. D. Hope), "Ulysses" (Tennyson), "Odysseus" (W. S. Merwin), "Circe" (A. D. Hope), "Maiden with Orb and Planets" (Howard Nemerov), "The Sirens" (Donald Finkel), "Ulysses and the Siren" (Samuel Daniel), "Proteus" (W. S. Merwin), "Leda and the Swan" (W. B. Yeats), "Choric Song" (The Lotos Eaters, V–VIII, Tennyson), "Ulysses" (John Ciardi), and "μῆτις . . . οὖτις" (W. D. Snodgrass). And one could cite many other poems whose relevance to *The Odyssey*, though less direct, is equally apparent. Comparison of such poems with the corresponding Homeric episodes illuminates both Homer and the modern works which at the same time carry forward and enrich the Homeric tradition. As class or written exercises, analyses of this kind serve to focus attention upon the meaning and utility of specific myths and metaphors and also to develop accuracy in reading and sensitivity to nuances of emphasis, tone, and mood in particular poems.

Collections of Poems

Many of the poems in *Hero's Way* were collected by students in literature and writing classes. They were asked, in the course of a semester, to submit ten poems which would be appropriate to the anthology, with the following stipulations: (1) Poems were to be taken from volumes by individual authors and not from anthologies. (2) Poems were to be by living authors. (3) Poems were to be copied (accurately!) by the student. Xeroxing, of course, guarantees complete accuracy, but copying by hand has the advantage of requiring the students to pay close attention to every word of a poem. (4) Each poem was to be accompanied by a short essay which explained its relevance to the section of the anthology for which it was submitted.   (5) Full bibliographical information was to be supplied for each poem.

Many variations on the collecting procedure can be devised. For example, instructors may wish to permit or require inclusion of poems from earlier periods of American and English literature; to ask students to specialize in a certain area of the Quest, or to *avoid* specializing; to encourage students to concentrate on a single poet of their choice; to suggest collections of poems which employ a certain metaphor that has its parallel in myth (*e.g.*, the pattern of emergence from *down under*), deal with a certain myth or mythic figure, or employ a special point of view (*e.g.*, that of the dreamer, the incompetent hero, the female protagonist).

Written Exercises

The poems in *Hero's Way* are arranged in a way which points up possibilities for variations upon similar materials; and therefore essays, when they do not deal with single poems, may well be devoted to the study of poetic technique by means of comparison and contrast. The following kinds of exercise are suggested: (A) A critical analysis of a poem or group of related poems, concentrating on exegesis, on a certain aspect of poetic technique, or on the characteristics of a particular poet's work. (B) A critical introduction to a group of poems included in *Hero's Way* or collected by the student. (C) An essay analyzing a certain myth or element (character, incident) of a myth, and/or of the use which a poet or certain poets have made of it. (D) An analysis of a major work of poetry (or of some part of it) from a mythic or archetypal point of view.

Research Papers

Here, reading in works of psychology, anthropology, mythography, and archetypal criticism of literature will generally be required (cf. bibliographies).

A. *The Double in psychology and literature.* Open any volume of contemporary poetry or any poetry quarterly, and chances are that you will find at least one poem about a Double. In literature, study of the Double is little advanced. In psychology, the theory of the Double is well developed, and study could profitably begin with readings in Freud (the *id*) and Jung (the *shadow*). Cases of multiple personality have been well documented (*e.g., The Three Faces of Eve*).

Related topics: the conception of the devil; Antichrist; the external soul (cf. Frazer); chthonic deities; witches' familiars; werewolves.

Bibliography: Guerard, ed., *Stories of the Double;* Jung, *Psyche and Symbol;* Margaret Murray, *The Witch-Cult in Western Europe;* Tymms, *Doubles in Literary Psychology;* Watts, *The Two Hands of God;* Zimmer, *The King and the Corpse.*

B. *Symbolic beasts.* Literature, from epic to fairy tale, is rich in Beast episodes and stories which invite investigation. Emblematic beasts figure in the religions of all ages. Yet, outside of the commentaries upon bestiaries, little has been written on the subject.

Related topics: the unicorn; the chimera; dragons; Leviathan; Tiamat; the bestiary as a literary genre; the serpent (in *Genesis* and elsewhere); the Minotaur; totemism; the use of animal imagery by Dante, Shakespeare, Blake; the friendly beast in fairy tales.

Bibliography: Jung, *Psychology and Alchemy* (for unicorns); Jung and Karényi, *Essays on a Science of Mythology;* Long, *Alpha: The Myths of Creation;* Ovid, *The Metamorphoses;* Zimmer, *The King and the Corpse.*

C. *The Lady in literature, psychology, art, religion.* The Lady is perhaps the most complex and pervasive of all symbolic figures. She has been the subject of many studies in psychology, religion, mythography, and anthropology. Yet the subject is very far from being exhausted.

Related topics: the Eleusinian Mysteries (Demeter and Kore); The Lady in Shakespeare (Juliet; Desdemona; Cleopatra; Hermione and Perdita; Lady Macbeth; Lear's daughters); mythic motifs and metaphors in the poetry and fiction of women (Emily and Charlotte Brontë; Isak Dinesen; Sylvia Plath; Barbara Howes; Julia Randall); Jung's *anima;* the goddess Kali; the Lady as Muse.

Bibliography: Graves, *The White Goddess;* James, *The Cult of the Mother Goddess;* Neumann, *Amor and Psyche* and *The Great Mother;* Otto, *The Homeric Gods;* Wechsler, *Gods and Goddesses in Art and Legend.*

D. *The Father.* Although the Father has been thoroughly studied in psychology, anthropology, and, of course, religion, little has been written about his role in contemporary poetry.

Related topics: the sacred king; Oedipus; Jung's *animus* and Freud's *ego and superego;* the Father in the poetry of William Blake; male deities in Eastern religions.

Bibliography: Bettelheim, *Symbolic Wounds;* Frazer, *The Golden Bough;* Freud, *Totem and Taboo;* James, *Seasonal Feasts and Festivals;* Mullahy, *Oedipus: Myth and Complex;* Otto, *Dionysus: Myth and Cult;* Perry, *Lord of the Four Quarters.*

E. *Polarity in myth and literature.* Howard Nemerov has said that if poetry has a subject, it is the reconciliation of opposites: male and female, time and eternity, life and death. The subject can be studied most conveniently in short poems, either thematically (*e.g.,* metaphors of death and rebirth) or in the work of a poet of the student's choice.

Related topics: Blake's *Songs of Innocence and Experience;* Tiresias (as male and female); the conception of immortality in literature; myths of death and rebirth; Brahma, Vishnu, and Shiva in Hinduism.

Bibliography: Eliade, *Cosmos and History: The Myth of the Eternal Return;* Henderson and Oakes, *The Wisdom of the Serpent: The Myths of Death, Rebirth, and Resurrection;* Watts, *The Two Hands of God: Myths of Polarity.*

F. *Fairy tales* (Other possible genres are fantasy, utopian fiction, allegory, comic strips). An immense literature exists concerning folk tales from all quarters of the world, but the *interpretation* of fairy tales and study of their use in poetry present unlimited possibilities for original research.

Related topics: the tales of the brothers Grimm; The Sleeping Beauty in poetry; tales of the maiden and the hag (*e.g.,* in

Chaucer and Malory); giants, the Wise Old Man, friendly animals, the forbidden room, etc., in fairy tales.

Bibliography: Campbell, *The Hero with a Thousand Faces;* Fromm, *The Forgotten Language;* Jung, *Psyche and Symbol;* Jung and Kerényi, *Essays on a Science of Mythology;* Zimmer, *The King and the Corpse.*

G. *Transformation, change, metamorphosis, in psychology, anthropology, and literature.* The necessity for change (both psychological and physical) is emphasized in accounts of tribal ritual, in the annals of psychoanalysis, and in many works of poetry and fiction.

Related topics: rites of initiation; metamorphosis in the poetry of Randall Jarrell; the threshold of adulthood: the Hero's initiation in "apprenticeship" novels; Blake's *Book of Thel;* the trial of youth in Shakespeare's *A Midsummer Night's Dream, As You Like It, The Tempest;* Jung's concept of individuation.

Bibliography: Eliade, *Rites and Symbols of Initiation: The Mysteries of Birth and Rebirth;* Henderson, *Thresholds of Initiation;* Jung, *Symbols of Transformation* (and the commentary in Jacobi, *The Way of Individuation*); Róheim, *The Eternal Ones of the Dream;* von Gennep, *The Rites of Passage.*

H. *Dreams and their relationship to myth and literature.* The literature of psychoanalysis points up the close parallels between the symbolism of dreams, the characters and action of myths, and metaphor in poetry and fiction.

Related topics: the meaning of dreams; dream-poems (contemporary and traditional); the role of dreams in psychoanalysis; dream symbolism in psychology and literature.

Bibliography: Freud, *The Interpretation of Dreams;* Fromm, *The Forgotten Language;* Herzog, *Psyche and Death: Archaic Myths and Modern Dreams;* Rank, Sachs, *et al., Psychoanalysis As an Art and a Science.*

I. *The psychology of art and creativity.* The experience of the artist, like that of the dreamer, is often comparable to the Hero's on the Road of Trials. Psychology, in analyzing the creative process, sheds considerable light upon the meaning of metaphor.

Related topics: myths of creation; Pygmalion; the unconscious mind and artistic creation; art and neurosis; the artist as Hero; the psychological interpretation of literature.

Bibliography: Bodkin, *Archetypal Patterns in Poetry;* Freud, *On Creativity and the Unconscious;* Ghiselin, ed., *The Creative Process;* Lesser, *Fiction and the Unconscious;* Long, *Alpha: The Myths of Creation;* Lucas, *Literature and Psychology;* Neumann, *Art and the Creative Unconscious.*

J. *Religion in art and literature.* The relationship between ritual, myth, religion, and literature—and of all of these to the psyche— is intimate and functional. It is touched upon in some way in every section of *Hero's Way.*

Related topics: the origins of Greek drama; pagan symbols in Christian religion and literature; the psychology of religion; the Hero as god; apotheosis; symbols of the divine in literature.

Bibliography: Ediade, *Myths, Dreams, and Mysteries* and *The Sacred and the Profane;* Fromm, *The Dogma of Christ;* Harrison, *Ancient Art and Ritual;* Jung, *Psychology and Religion;* Seznec, *The Survival of the Pagan Gods;* Weston, *From Ritual to Romance.*

The prefatory essays in *Hero's Way* have several functions which the editor hopes they fulfill sufficiently at least to raise questions and stimulate discussion. These are: (1) to provide a running general account of the mythic Quest; (2) to relate the episodes of the Quest to the student's experience; (3) to point up the relationship between mythic elements in contemporary poetry and parallel materials in earlier literature, various versions of the most essential myths themselves, and certain psychological concepts—especially in the work of Freud and Jung; (4) to suggest starting points for the interpretation of representative poems in each section, relative to their association with some aspect of the Quest. The teacher will readily understand that to accomplish all of these objectives satisfactorily in a brief space was difficult, not to say impossible. It is to be hoped that both instructors and students will be disposed to challenge, correct, and augment the materials set forth in the prefaces as their reading in *Hero's Way* proceeds.

III

The teacher will notice that the prefaces in *Hero's Way* do not include detailed analyses of poems and that they make no attempt to assess the absolute or relative quality of the poems included in the collection. No doubt the merit and weight of the poems vary considerably. All have been tried out in college classes and have proved useful and interesting in various ways. The editor wishes, however, to dissociate himself from each of the following propositions: (1) that the poems in *Hero's Way* are to be uncritically approved merely because they are in some way associated with myth; (2) that the value of the poems derives exclusively or even primarily from their association with the mythic tradition; (3) that the poems are necessarily superior to many others which have no clear-cut association with myth or, if they have it, are not presented here.

The editor believes that the arrangement of poems in *Hero's Way* will speed the student's recognition of familiar patterns beneath what may at first appear the strange and forbidding idiom of poems by his contemporaries. Surely, if these poems were arranged alphabetically by authors and no mention were made of their relationship to the Quest, they would still constitute a worthy representative selection of contemporary poetry. However, in the editor's opinion, much would be lost. *Hero's Way* is based upon two premises: (1) that much of the best poetry now being written, like that of every age, is mythic in pattern; and (2) that the student can therefore best become acquainted with this poetry in a context which associates it with the myths and mythic works from which it derives. The incidents of the Quest can be perceived in as many ways as there are individuals to supply them with specific materials from their experience and to color them with the quality of their imagination. The richness, complexity, and variety of poetic vision is without limit; yet the objects upon which this vision may be focused are the same today as they were for Dante or Homer, for they are the immutable concerns of humankind. In poetry generally, and in the poems in *Hero's Way* in particular, novelty of viewpoint and expression coexists with the traditional. Everyone who learns to understand poetry does so by an accretion of experience with its recurrent elements, and especially with metaphors which change with the years in their particulars, but not in their essentials. Such metaphors are, of course, the common property of all poetry and, indeed, of all literature. One can study them in poems which are not obviously related to the Quest. However, because the Quest encompasses the destiny and vision of the human spirit in its entirety, it offers a complete vocabulary of perennially recurrent metaphors, set in a framework which suggests the full range of their significance. To learn this vocabulary is to take an essential step toward understanding the language not of the Quest alone, but of all poetry.

Hero's Way, like any other poetry text, presents certain distinct pedagogical advantages and difficulties. One wants to introduce the entire context of the Quest at the outset, as each part of that narrative is relevant to every other part, and each episode is a reflection of the whole. For this reason, Part I of the text (Versions of the Quest) presents poems which deal with the full scope of the Hero's adventure. In reading and discussing these eight poems, the student should become aware, in a general way, of the principal elements of the Quest—what its objective is, the hazards of the road, and some of the ways in which the Hero reaches or falls short of his objective. When this initial study has been completed, it may be advantageous to conduct a fairly rapid survey of the book by assigning a poem or two from each successive section, from Part II (The Call) through Part VI (The End and the Beginning). When this survey has been completed, further poems in each section, taken sequentially or out of order, can be studied with an insight made possible by the broad perspective which has been acquired.

A second matter of concern is that while the poems are being considered in relation to incidents of the Quest, the instructor will also wish to introduce the class to the techniques of literary analysis, looking at individual poems in considerable detail. Actually, of course, the two objectives are not incompatible. A close inspection of any given poem in a section of Hero's Way will have the effect of illuminating all of the other poems in that section, because the poems are linked not only by a common general subject but also, in many instances, by related metaphors and elements contributing to mood, tone, and "characterization" both of the protagonist and of the personae who share the action with him. The remarks with which this preface concludes concern the analysis of the poems in Part I.

They are intended to suggest some of the possibilities for analysis within the context which the thematic structure of *Hero's Way* provides.

IV

Reading Part I: Versions of the Quest

Part I of *Hero's Way* contains eight narrative poems, in which a hero is trying to accomplish something, though he is sometimes doing this involuntarily ("Whirlwind") and sometimes is unsure of exactly what his objective is ("Childe Roland," "Captain Carpenter," "Boundbrook"). The objective may be to reach Atlantis, to gain self-understanding ("The Hero with One Face"), to liberate a captive princess ("Fairy Tale") or nobleman ("Tam Lin"). And what is actually achieved may be, on the negative side, self-destruction ("Childe Roland," "Captain Carpenter"), murder and rape ("Fairy Tale"), or frustration ("The Hero with One Face"); or, on the positive side, a glimpse of Atlantis (salvation) or a renewed sense of community with man and nature ("Boundbrook," "Whirlwind").

In the context of these poems, *irony* is generated in direct proportion to the Hero's impotence. It is interesting to compare the ironic effect of "The Hero with One Face" (quizzical bafflement), "Captain Carpenter" (undaunted futility), "Childe Roland" (resignation to defeat), and "Fairy Tale" (failure to understand defeat—a result of madness). The *tone* of these poems varies with the author's attitude toward the Hero or the Hero's attitude toward himself: Ransom's attitude toward Captain Carpenter is officially respectful and solicitous, but this tone is undercut by the ridiculousness of the Hero, and the resultant effect is *mock-heroic*. John Frederick Nims first presents the hero of "Fairy Tale" with the objectivity of a sociologist but then shifts to the Hero's point of view; "romantic" illusion is thus superimposed upon brutal reality, and the tone which this produces can perhaps best be described as *sardonic*.

The poems in *Hero's Way* are, for the most part, narrative; that is, they usually present one or more characters engaged in a metaphoric action. The reader's first question may therefore always appropriately be, "What happens in the poem?" Fortunately, to answer this question accurately and in detail does not exceed the

capacity of the average reader. Most students are *able* to read ac-
curately, even though they are often unaccustomed to doing so and
will therefore fail to understand a poem simply because they have
not read it with sufficient attention. It is only fair to impress upon
students (1) that a poem must be read not once but several times;
(2) that repeated readings will make clear what happens in the
poem; and (3) that when the reader knows this—and *only* then—he
will be in a position to consider the *meaning* of the poem. Inex-
perienced readers must be discouraged from indulging their charac-
teristic tendency to cast about for the meaning of a poem while
ignoring the details in which that meaning is implicit.

A Sample Question

An instructor can be most useful to students at the outset of
discussion of a poem simply by asking questions about what hap-
pens in the poem. For example, what is the protagonist doing at the
beginning of the action of (1) "Fairy Tale," (2) "Tam Lin," (3)
"Boundbrook," (4) "The Whirlwind"? The answers, which are
quite literal and explicit, might be put thus: (1) cutting the glass
from a window in preparation for entering the house of Duffy the
grocer; (2) listening, with other ladies of the court, while her father
forbids maidens to visit a place called Carterhaugh; (3) deciding to
follow a "fair" man whom she has met in the woods; (4) playing
Monopoly on a porch. It is a fair bet that most readers will not
be able to supply the correct answers after a first reading of the
poems in question. Later, when subsequent readings permit them to
answer these and similar questions, they will begin to have con-
fidence in the poems' making sense and in their ability to grasp the
meaning of the poems.

Indirection and Syntactical Complexity
in Narrative Technique

Students may profitably be advised that the principal diffi-
culties which lie in the way of understanding the "story" of a poem
are (1) complexities of syntax which result from the characteristic
and necessary condensation of expression in verse, and (2) the poet's
use of indirection in conveying certain of the narrative "facts" of
the poem and in making transitions between stages of the action.
Perhaps typical of the first type of difficulty is the fifth stanza of

Auden's "Atlantis." The stanza consists of a single sentence, more complex than an average prose sentence but no less grammatically consistent and complete:

> *Assuming you beach at last*
> *Near Atlantis, and begin*
> *The terrible trek inland*
> *Through squalid woods and frozen*
> *Tundras where all are soon lost;*
> *If, forsaken then, you stand,*
> *Dismissal everywhere,*
> *Stone and snow, silence and air,*
> *Remember the noble dead*
> *And honour the fate you are,*
> *Travelling and tormented,*
> *Dialectic and bizarre.*

Possibly one will need to read this sentence two or three times before the structure emerges clearly: It begins with two subordinate clauses, the gist of which is: assuming that you *beach* near Atlantis and *begin* the terrible trek inland, if you stand forsaken then . . . . The main clause is reached with the imperatives *remember* and *honour*, which are the heart of the sentence. Once the reader understands this, he can confidently fit in such further subordinate elements as the modification of "trek" (Through . . . lost), "stand" (Dismissal . . . air), and "the fate you are" (Travelling . . . bizarre). A reader may hang up temporarily on recognizing "beach" (line 1) as a verb and perceiving the equivalence of "fate" and "you" (line 10). Finally, he may be unfamiliar with certain words: tundras, dialectic, and bizarre. However, it will probably not be essential for him to look up their meaning, as "tundras" is sufficiently defined by "squalid woods . . . Stone and snow," and "Travelling and tormented" will do to suggest the quality of "the fate you are."

The second difficulty—indirection—is a more pervasive and challenging one, for it obliges the reader of a poem to supply missing information by making inferences. The need for such active participation by the reader of poetry is constant, and the ability to participate effectively is an acquired skill which only resolute practice can develop. Though, admittedly, this need imposes a strain upon the reader whenever he approaches a poem for the first time, one should resist the impulse to blame poets for "not being clearer." Their effects can only be achieved by indirection; explicit writing often yields not poetry but prose. Furthermore, the reader's pleasure depends, to a great extent, upon his ability to respond to the poet's indirection, exercising his imagination and becoming a partner in the poetic process. As one begins to master the art of doing this, he finds the experience a far more refreshing and exhilarating one than is provided by the "spectator sport" of passive reading.

Examples of Indirection

The "cinematic" technique of the ballad provides excellent practice in responding to the characteristic indirection of poetry. Consider a few examples of the contributions which the reader must make to the story of "Tam Lin." (1) Who is speaking in stanza one? The answer is to be found in stanza eight, when Janet returns to "her father's ha," for this tells us that the father is a person in authority (a king or lord) and that, as such, he undoubtedly issued the prohibition upon visits by maidens to Carterhaugh. (2) Why does Janet go to Carterhaugh despite her father's prohibition? The answer is to be found in stanzas six and seven, where we learn that Carterhaugh has been given to Janet by her father; it is natural that she should refuse to be denied access to her own territory, or even to ask permission to visit there. Incidentally, this suggests a great deal about Janet's character—inferences which are consonant with the boldness and impetuousness implied by details of her appearance, actions, and speeches throughout the poem. (3) Why is Janet "As green as onie glass" (stanza ten) when she returns from Carterhaugh? The answer is given in the amusing dialogue of stanzas eleven through sixteen: She is with child by Tam Lin. And so on. More difficult, perhaps, are the inferences required for understanding "The Hero with One Face." (1) We know that the protagonist is an Everyman, because he was chosen for the Quest by virtue simply of being born (stanza one). (2) We know that the Hero supersedes the Father as consort of the Lady, because, in stanza twelve, he kisses his crown and is content with Ozma or Beatrice (the Lady in any one of her infinite number of manifestations). (3) We infer that the Hero's winning of the Lady is false or flawed, because the apocalyptic "Glory" which follows that event (stanzas nine and ten) leaves him feeling worse and soon gives way to hostile visitations by "The shadows of the underworld," and his journey, "recoiled" to its starting place, ends in blindness and frustration.

In "Fairy Tale," the critical point for inference arrives in stanzas ten and eleven, where the rape of Duffy the grocer's wife is recounted in terms of the protagonist's illusory rescue of the Lady:

> *He flung back curtains, found the secret door;*
> *Crooned as he swung it with the golden key.*

The wife's murder is affirmed in stanza thirteen, and one knows, of course, that the princess is a figment of the demented imagination of the "prince." The account of the double murder and rape in this poem, being metaphorically conveyed as an heroic exploit, gives us simultaneously a "realistic" narrative and a "psychological" one—*i.e.*, we enter into the protagonist's consciousness and experience the events as he sees and feels them.

Probably the most challenging poem in Versions of the Quest is "Boundbrook," which provides a very slender narrative thread and relies heavily, though not excessively, upon the reader's power of inference. Here, several points of *transition* are crucial to following the action as it unfolds. The protagonist's meeting with "a man" (stanza one) is followed by a second episode introduced only by the word "then" (stanza two). The reader infers that the heroine has followed the man of stanza one into a "great park land," but no details of the journey are given. All we know is that she arrives there. Between stanza three and the first line of stanza four, we infer that touching the "master" has endowed the heroine with magic powers, capable of changing a world; but we immediately proceed to the further inference that his magic power is drastically flawed, inasmuch as its effect is to change the pleasant park land into "Circe's Pen," populated by beasts. The last line of stanza four tells us that the heroine herself has become a beast. The final transition occurs in the opening lines of the last stanza, where the heroine, having "died" as a beast, finds herself home again, her adventures at an end. When one has followed the action thus, one needs only to answer a rather simple question in order to know what, in psychological or human terms, the poem is about: "What does it mean for a woman to be transformed, by a man, into a captive beast and then, when her heart's blood has broken, to escape from this imprisonment?" The answer is, of course, that she has succumbed to infatuation, has suffered from that peculiarly agonizing experience, has at last recovered from it, and has finally reclaimed her ability to possess the world through losing herself in disinterested love of it.

When the point of a poem is expressed clearly in prose, the prose statement is, of course, no substitute for the poem itself. In "Boundbrook," the *quality* of the protagonist's experience is conveyed by the metaphoric action which is its *vehicle* of expression. The dream-like events which the poem recounts, the sudden transformations, suggest more accurately than prose the wonder, the horror, the frustration, and the sense of release and of restoration that are the essence of the heroine's psychological and emotional state as it unfolds. Perhaps the value of metaphor in "Boundbrook" can most clearly be suggested by offering a version of the poem (composed by the editor with the permission of Julia Randall) which adheres faithfully to the original subject, while depriving it of all that makes Miss Randall's work fresh and distinctive:

INFATUATION

I met a man and he was fair.
He set my senses so astir
That I believed his love could give
All I had ever dreamed to have:
A private paradise for me
Of never-ending ecstasy.

It turned out otherwise. In time
My selfish love grew wearisome,
And sensuality at last
Became a famine, not a feast:
I was transformed, in my own sight,
Into a beast of appetite.

My heart rebelled, until despair
Killed that obsessive love affair;
And when I ceased demanding love,

> I loved indeed, because I *gave*,
> And earned anew, to ease my pain,
> Rapport with nature and with man.

With this travesty before him, the student will surely return to "Boundbrook" gratefully. Good poems are necessarily difficult, but their imaginative vigor handsomely rewards one for the effort which it costs him to read them with full emotional as well as intellectual understanding.

If the *vehicle* of the poems in *Hero's Way* is generally derived from some part of the action of the heroic Quest, the reference of the *tenor* is to subjective human experience, at one level localized in an individual consciousness (*e.g.*, that of a madman engaged in committing crimes of violence), and at another level in the consciousness of Everyman, who has, in his own experience, a sufficient sampling of all possible states of mind to provide reference for him to whatever a poem may truly be "about." Thus one can share in the peculiar frustrations of Captain Carpenter and Childe Roland and in the joyful sense of reconciliation and festivity with which "Whirlwind" closes. Students should be firmly advised that poems are not versified nuggets of wisdom and have little to do, directly, with moral sentiments, not to speak of preachments. Poems *are* experience, vicarious to be sure, but authentic to the degree that the poet is skillful and the reader adequate to the rewarding task of making that experience his own.

Foreword

It will be apparent to every reader that the plan of *Hero's Way* and the essays which it contains owe a great deal to scholarly works in several fields. Those which have proven most useful to me are included in the Bibliography. A special word of thanks is due to Professor Joseph Campbell of Sarah Lawrence College, whose book, *The Hero with a Thousand Faces*, is an indispensable introduction to the myths of all ages and cultures and to their significance. Professor Campbell has kindly permitted me to use certain of his headings for the stages of the heroic Quest which are represented in the plan of *Hero's Way*.

My first attempt to associate short poems with the hero's Quest was an unanticipated result of an Independent Study seminar which I conducted a number of years ago at the suggestion of a talented student, Fontaine Belford (1962). As *Hero's Way* was taking shape, students in my writing and literature classes contributed poems to the collection and proposed interpretations for them and for the myths with which they are associated. I am most grateful to all of these students for their enthusiastic collaboration.

In preparing *Hero's Way* for publication, I have been fortunate in having for an assistant Gayle Johnson (1969), who is well versed in mythography, both as scholar and as poet. It has also been my pleasure to work with three excellent secretaries: Mur Sherman (1969), and Louise Lively and Faye Ivanhoe of the

English Department. My wife, Josephine, served as an acute first reader for the introductory essays.

Finally, I am much indebted to the many poets who have made their poems available for reprint, and, in particular, to Louise Bogan, John Ciardi, Daniel Hoffman, A. D. Hope, Howard Nemerov, William Jay Smith, and Richard Wilbur for their distinguished *gentilesse*.

JOHN ALEXANDER ALLEN
Hollins College, Virginia

I

VERSIONS
OF
THE QUEST

Suppose, as W. H. Auden suggests, you are "set on the idea / Of getting to Atlantis." How do you find the way? In part, your chances of success depend upon the strength of your determination. A man who undertakes so difficult and problematic a journey will meet discouragement at every turn. In the eyes of the world, he is sure to appear some kind of fool, and he must be prepared to be taken for an ordinary one, and to pose as merely "one of The Boys." Again and again, the worldly wise will demonstrate to him that "there cannot be / Such a place as Atlantis," but he will notice, under the witty surface of their arguments, "A simple enormous grief." He will be tested every step of the way. In a bar, when some tart "strokes his hair and says, 'This is Atlantis, Dearie,' " he must listen to her and observe her carefully, for,

> *unless*
> *You become acquainted now*
> *With each refuge that tries to*
> *Counterfeit Atlantis, how*
> *Will you recognize the true?*

Not all of the Heroes in the poems which follow reach Atlantis. One loses heart, another seems to have *only* heart to guide him, and several fall into the snare of that notorious tart, whose name is Circe.

The role of Circe, the enchantress, is to distract the Hero by offering him a lesser good, a reasonable facsimile of Atlantis, in order to test the seriousness of his commitment to the greater good inherent in the genuine article. David Wagoner's Hero ("The Hero with One Face") has made a creditable record battling "Gorgons, ghouls with whirligigs, / And dragons," but the critical trial is yet to come. When they bring Her in, "The witch already beautiful," he can only ask himself, "How could I know Her without pain?" The lady is possessed by "the evil King," and the most direct means of obtaining her is to depose that monarch and seize both crown and Queen. But the way that is least painful is not always, finally, the best one, as Macbeth and Hamlet's Uncle Claudius can testify. The "Glory" which follows this Hero's conquest of the Lady seems, at first, to suggest that he has found Atlantis:

> *The deaf-and-dumb rose up and cried,*
> *Cripples came striding, golden fleece*
> *Fell from the holy air like lace . . .*

But these appearances are illusory; after they have passed, he is left, like a wassailer on the morning after, only feeling worse. When he is offered the customary boon, he asks, as every Hero should, to know who he really is. The reply is left to the reader's imagination, but we know that it is anything but flattering. Deposed from lotos-land, the disillusioned Hero is last seen back at his starting point again, mulling over the fact that his second birth has proved to be only a second blindness.

Julia Randall's protagonist ("Boundbrook"), in accordance with her sex, is hoodwinked by a *male* Circe (Merlin) who, with a Christ-like air, bestows largesse. No sooner has the specious boon been given and accepted than "The waters dropped, the meadow furled," and the pseudo-Eden shows its populace of "swine, and goats, and picking cocks," all of which are the unhappy heroine's kin. As a beast, she passes seven years a-dying before she can return to "the poplar fields of home" whose common men and whistling blackbirds are as good as revelation after imprisonment in the land where the "heart's blood broke." As for the unenchanting Prince of Mr. Nims ("Fairy Tale"), one may be inclined to write him off as one who has no relevance to our experience: He is a homicidal maniac and a rapist, suffering from the delusion that a Lady, "Gracious and golden-haired," lies captive in the house of Duffy the grocer, waiting for her Prince to set her free. The Prince arrives, dispatches the ogre (Duffy) with a scout knife, and prepares to deal with the "witch-woman by his side," a Circe whose embrace, he suddenly perceives, is the "secret door" and "the golden key" by means of which he will liberate the Princess. These are the delusions of insanity, and yet,

> *The deacon two streets over under his steeple*
> *Is dreaming this; his grating molars groan;*
> *It runs with many faces through the people . . .*

Shocked, we realize that the demented Prince is actually Everyman, observed when his guard is down and his wish-fulfilling faculties, uninhibited by sober daylight, have free reign.

As Heroes, Browning's Childe Roland and John Crowe Ransom's Captain Carpenter have little in common, except that both have made an irrevocable choice of path, and it is one which cannot lead them to Atlantis. Browning tells us that "Childe Roland to the Dark Tower Came" is an accurate account of his actual dream. If so, we may infer that the sanguine poet harbored, somewhere in his psyche, a thorough knowledge of the Slough of Despond. Childe Roland, when we meet him at the crossroad of his journey, has already been so long engaged in the Quest that the ghost of his hope is no longer "fit to cope / With that obstreperous joy success would bring," and his heart takes a gloomy pleasure, now, in "finding failure in its scope." On the journey to the Dark Tower, he trudges through a dreary waste land, filled with negative inversions of such hopeful signs as sometimes spur more fortunate Heroes on their way: a half-dead horse must do for soaring Pegasus; knights gone bad stand in for members of the Table Round; the "spiteful" river substitutes for the lucid streams of Eden; the skewered water-rat screams like a child; the bird of hell mocks messengers of the spirit; and warring mountains rise in place of Sinai or Olympus. The final blow is the dungeon-like Dark Tower itself and its prisoners of darkness, gloating over the advent of another victim.

If the finale of Childe Roland's Quest is merciful, like putting a wounded animal out of its misery, the last sortie of John Crowe Ransom's Captain Carpenter strikes a note that is more ironic still, and yet is somehow not uncheerful. However sadly comic the defeat of this "honest gentleman" may be, he sticks in our minds as an embodiment of the unconquerable spirit. His Quest had hardly begun when "a pretty lady twined him of his nose for evermore," but we know that he will not capitulate. After years in which his only achievement is the progressive loss of almost his entire anatomy, he suffers an ultimate humiliation at the hands of "the neatest knave that ever was seen / Stepping in perfume from his lady's bower." This rogue at last removes the Captain's "round red heart," thus stilling both that organ and the tongue which voiced defiance to the end. Like Matthew Arnold's Oxford, the bosom of Captain Carpenter is the "home of lost causes, and forsaken beliefs, and unpopular names, and impossible loyalties." Without undue severity, one can say that this Hero's first and fatal error is, as Howard Nemerov puts it in "A Predecessor of Perseus," to confuse "The being called and being chosen." It is a confusion which we recognize with ease in others. But Sancho Panza's common sense is powerless to disillusion Don Quixote.

"Tam Lin" and "Whirlwind" tell of Quests by Heroes who *are* chosen and whose successful missions ultimately are crowned with unequivocal boons. One must admire fair Janet, with her tucked-up skirt and snooded hair, scouring off to Carterhaugh precisely because her father has forbidden her to do so. Janet's recklessness, unlike Captain Carpenter's, has the authentic Hero's mark upon it: She denies the prudent edict of conventional opinion and authority to take her chances with "an elfin grey" who has a reputation as the scourge of maidenhood. Certainly, he has his way with Janet, yet he is no vulgar masher, bent on exploiting women. He is a captive of the Fairy Queen, who has him tabbed for early sacrifice, and we infer that he can only be set free by a woman who bears his child in love; also, it should be added, one for whom a "gloomy, gloomy" night and an "eerie way" will hold no terrors. On all counts, Janet qualifies superbly, and her boon, of course, is the father of her child—not elfin after all, but a Prince as charming as any maid has ever dreamt of.

An entirely different metaphor gives dramatic form to the discovery of Atlantis in John Alexander Allen's "Whirlwind." Here, the protagonist does not volunteer for adventure; nothing is further from his thoughts. They are occupied with measuring out his chances on a Monopoly board when a chill wind stirs in the wisteria, and in an instant everything has changed. Now the Hero is himself the counter in a game beyond his control. The will of the cyclone whirls him into the upper air. His money and his "red / Hotels," his dog and cat—in short, "the ballast of a tidy world," roars up the flue. High in the void, where "Darkness / Glimmered with occulting stars," a second unaccountable event occurs: The Lady is at his side, like a wise sister. She directs his gaze upon the little world below: "look down, look down," she says, "The wind / Has blown your debts away, unmortgaged all / Your properties"—and it is so. Whirling down again toward earth, where the parish church and its attendant cemetery resemble "A planet orbited by graves," the Hero finds himself in a transfigured world:

> *The neighbors came. The moon*
> *Slid into sight and shone. And all night long*
> *The tall and lean, the short and round*

And in between, the halt and blind trod out
The nine man's morris on the village green.

It is a time for music and dancing, one when animosities dissolve, old bonds are reaffirmed, and all seem, as they do at the close of Shakespeare's *The Winter's Tale*, to have "heard of a world ransomed, or one destroyed" (V.ii.16–17).

When the Quest becomes most nearly unendurable, you still should "Stagger on rejoicing," Auden says, remembering "the noble dead," honoring your necessity to be what you are, content to travel on, tormented—an exemplar of the bizarre and enchanting, "Dialectic" race of man. And what if, finally, "you collapse / With all Atlantis gleaming / Below you yet you cannot / Descend"? Even such an ending to the Quest is not to be confused with failure:

> *you should still be proud*
> *Just to peep at Atlantis*
> *In a poetic vision:*
> *Give thanks and lie down in peace,*
> *Having seen your salvation.*

ATLANTIS

Being set on the idea
    Of getting to Atlantis,
You have discovered of course
    Only the Ship of Fools is
Making the voyage this year,
As gales of abnormal force
    Are predicted, and that you
    Must therefore be ready to
Behave absurdly enough
    To pass for one of The Boys,
At least appearing to love
    Hard liquor, horseplay and noise.

Should storms, as may well happen,
   Drive you to anchor a week
In some old harbour-city
   Of Ionia, then speak
With her witty scholars, men
Who have proved there cannot be
   Such a place as Atlantis:
   Learn their logic, but notice
How their subtlety betrays
   A simple enormous grief;
Thus they shall teach you the ways
   To doubt that you may believe.

If, later, you run aground
   Among the headlands of Thrace
Where with torches all night long
   A naked barbaric race
Leaps frenziedly to the sound
Of conch and dissonant gong;
   On that stony savage shore
   Strip off your clothes and dance, for
Unless you are capable
   Of forgetting completely
About Atlantis, you will
   Never finish your journey.

Again, should you come to gay
   Carthage or Corinth, take part
In their endless gaiety;
   And if in some bar a tart,
As she strokes your hair, should say
'This is Atlantis, dearie,'
   Listen with attentiveness
   To her life-story: unless
You become acquainted now
   With each refuge that tries to
Counterfeit Atlantis, how
   Will you recognize the true?

Assuming you beach at last
   Near Atlantis, and begin
The terrible trek inland
   Through squalid woods and frozen
Tundras where all are soon lost;
If, forsaken then, you stand,
   Dismissal everywhere,
   Stone and snow, silence and air,
Remember the noble dead
   And honour the fate you are,
Travelling and tormented,
   Dialectic and bizarre.

Stagger onward rejoicing;
   And even then if, perhaps
Having actually got
   To the last col, you collapse
With all Atlantis gleaming
Below you yet you cannot
   Descend, you should still be proud
Just to peep at Atlantis
   In a poetic vision:
Give thanks and lie down in peace,
   Having seen your salvation.

All the little household gods
   Have started crying, but say
Good-bye now, and put to sea.
   Farewell, dear friend, farewell: may
Hermes, master of the roads
And the four dwarf Kabiri,
   Protect and serve you always;
   And may the Ancient of Days
Provide for all you must do
   His invisible guidance,
Lifting up, friend, upon you
   The light of His countenance.

W. H. AUDEN

THE HERO WITH ONE FACE

They chose me, not that I might learn,
But only because I was born,
And gave me amulets of clay,
Some armor, and a brief goodbye.

And at the threshold of the pool,
The looking-glass, the spoiled well,
The hole beneath the whirling tree,
I waited meekly.　They called me.

I turned a corner, and was there,
Where all the other places are:
The other side of the cupped moon,
Oz, Heaven-Hell, and the Unknown.

I had too many purposes:
Although they hadn't said, "Find keys,
Find maidens, answers, and lost loves,"
I knew they wanted these themselves,

And I was bound to seek them all
Or be transformed, or die, or fall.
All the horned gods soared by and looked,
Hoping to stain my smallest act.

And there were beasts: three-headed dogs,
Gorgons, ghouls with whirligigs,
And dragons both alive and dead
For me to master, and I did.

I did, and O they brought Her in:
My Mother, the Queen upon a throne,
The Circe with a mouth to fill,
The witch already beautiful.

How could I know Her without pain?
I turned: there sat the evil King,

Betrayer, jealous brother, God.
I loved him much more than I should.

Then Glory rattled from a cloud,
The deaf-and-dumb rose up and cried,
Cripples came striding, golden fleece
Fell from the holy air like lace,

And broken curses rained, and time
Gave birth, gave birth, and returned home
Where all of the unmade desires
Are made at last.   And I felt worse,

And I was elected to a boon,
A final wish for every man.
I chose what I was told to choose:
They told me gently who I was.

It scarcely mattered.   I lay down
And ate the lotos, kissed my crown,
And gazed at Ozma, Beatrice,
And sighed, and was content with this.

But no—two-legged horses came,
Ogres, winds, and mothers-in-loam,
Provoked husbands with their wives,
Little people with long knives,

The shadows of the underworld;
And all my journey was recoiled,
Drawn back to the uneasy place
Where each benign beginning is.

Now, like Ulysses, master of
The world under, world above,
The world between—and one beyond
Which was not near enough to find—
I wait, and wonder what to learn:
O here, twice blind at being born.

DAVID WAGONER

"CHILDE ROLAND TO THE DARK TOWER CAME"

(See Edgar's song in "Lear")

I

My first thought was, he lied in every word,
   That hoary cripple, with malicious eye
   Askance to watch the working of his lie
On mine, and mouth scarce able to afford
Suppression of the glee, that pursed and scored
   Its edge, at one more victim gained thereby.

II

What else should he be set for, with his staff?
   What, save to waylay with his lies, ensnare
   All travellers who might find him posted there,
And ask the road?   I guessed what skull-like laugh
Would break, what crutch 'gin write my epitaph
   For pastime in the dusty thoroughfare,

III

If at his counsel I should turn aside
   Into that ominous tract which, all agree,
   Hides the Dark Tower.   Yet acquiescingly
I did turn as he pointed: neither pride
Nor hope rekindling at the end descried,
   So much as gladness that some end might be.

IV

For, what with my whole world-wide wandering,
   What with my search drawn out thro' years, my hope
   Dwindled into a ghost not fit to cope
With that obstreperous joy success would bring,—
I hardly tried now to rebuke the spring
   My heart made, finding failure in its scope.

V

As when a sick man very near to death
  Seems dead indeed, and feels begin and end
  The tears and takes the farewell of each friend,
And hears one bid the other go, draw breath
Freelier outside ("since all is o'er," he saith,
  "And the blow fallen no grieving can amend;")

VI

While some discuss if near the other graves
  Be room enough for this, and when a day
  Suits best for carrying the corpse away,
With care about the banners, scarves and staves:
And still the man hears all, and only craves
  He may not shame such tender love and stay.

VII

Thus, I had so long suffered in this quest,
  Heard failure prophesied so oft, been writ
  So many times among "The Band"—to wit,
The knights who to the Dark Tower's search addressed
Their steps—that just to fail as they, seemed best,
  And all the doubt was now—should I be fit?

VIII

So, quiet as despair, I turned from him,
  That hateful cripple, out of his highway
  Into the path he pointed.   All the day
Had been a dreary one at best, and dim
Was settling to its close, yet shot one grim
  Red leer to see the plain catch its estray.

IX

For mark! no sooner was I fairly found
  Pledged to the plain, after a pace or two,
  Than, pausing to throw backward a last view
O'er the safe road, 't was gone; gray plain all round:
Nothing but plain to the horizon's bound.
  I might go on; nought else remained to do.

X

So, on I went. I think I never saw
   Such starved ignoble nature; nothing throve.
   For flowers—as well expect a cedar grove!
But cockle, spurge, according to their law
Might propagate their kind, with none to awe,
   You'd think; a burr had been a treasure trove.

XI

No! penury, inertness, and grimace,
   In some strange sort, were the land's portion. "See
   Or shut your eyes," said Nature peevishly,
"It nothing skills: I cannot help my case:
" 'T is the Last Judgment's fire must cure this place,
   "Calcine its clods and set my prisoners free."

XII

If there pushed any ragged thistle-stalk
   Above its mates, the head was chopped; the bents
   Were jealous else. What made those holes and rents
In the dock's harsh swarth leaves, bruised as to baulk
All hope of greenness? 't is a brute must walk
   Pashing their life out, with a brute's intents.

XIII

As for the grass, it grew as scant as hair
   In leprosy; thin dry blades pricked the mud
   Which underneath looked kneaded up with blood.
One stiff blind horse, his every bone a-stare,
Stood stupefied, however he came there:
   Thrust out past service from the devil's stud!

XIV

Alive? he might be dead for aught I know,
   With that red gaunt and colloped neck a-strain,
   And shut eyes underneath the rusty mane;
Seldom went such grotesqueness with such woe;
I never saw a brute I hated so;
   He must be wicked to deserve such pain.

XV

I shut my eyes and turned them on my heart.
  As a man calls for wine before he fights,
  I asked one draught of earlier, happier sights,
Ere fitly I could hope to play my part.
Think first, fight afterwards—the soldier's art:
  One taste of the old time sets all to rights.

XVI

Not it! I fancied Cuthbert's reddening face
  Beneath its garniture of curly gold,
  Dear fellow, till I almost felt him fold
An arm in mine to fix me to the place,
That way he used. Alas, one night's disgrace!
  Out went my heart's new fire and left it cold.

XVII

Giles then, the soul of honour—there he stands
  Frank as ten years ago when knighted first.
  What honest man should dare (he said) he durst.
Good—but the scene shifts—faugh! what hangman hands
Pin to his breast a parchment? His own bands
  Read it. Poor traitor, spit upon and curst!

XVIII

Better this present than a past like that;
  Back therefore to my darkening path again!
  No sound, no sight as far as eye could strain.
Will the night send a howlet or a bat?
I asked: when something on the dismal flat
  Came to arrest my thoughts and change their train.

XIX

A sudden little river crossed my path
  As unexpected as a serpent comes.
  No sluggish tide congenial to the glooms;
This, as it frothed by, might have been a bath

For the fiend's glowing hoof—to see the wrath
Of its black eddy bespate with flakes and spumes.

XX

So petty yet so spiteful!   All along,
Low scrubby alders kneeled down over it;
Drenched willows flung them headlong in a fit
Of mute despair, a suicidal throng:
The river which had done them all the wrong,
Whate'er that was, rolled by, deterred no whit.

XXI

Which, while I forded,—good saints, how I feared
To set my foot upon a dead man's cheek,
Each step, or feel the spear I thrust to seek
For hollows, tangled in his hair or beard!
—It may have been a water-rat I speared,
But, ugh! it sounded like a baby's shriek.

XXII

Glad was I when I reached the other bank.
Now for a better country.   Vain presage!
Who were the strugglers, what war did they wage,
Whose savage trample thus could pad the dank
Soil to a plash?   Toads in a poisoned tank,
Or wild cats in a red-hot iron cage—

XXIII

The fight must so have seemed in that fell cirque.
What penned them there, with all the plain to choose?
No foot-print leading to that horrid mews,
None out of it.   Mad brewage set to work
Their brains, no doubt, like galley-slaves the Turk
Pits for his pastime, Christians against Jews.

XXIV

And more than that—a furlong on—why, there!
What bad use was that engine for, that wheel,

Or brake, not wheel—that harrow fit to reel
Men's bodies out like silk? with all the air
Of Tophet's tool, on earth left unaware,
　Or brought to sharpen its rusty teeth of steel.

XXV

Then came a bit of stubbed ground, once a wood,
　Next a marsh, it would seem, and now mere earth
　Desperate and done with (so a fool finds mirth,
Makes a thing and then mars it, till his mood
Changes and off he goes!) within a rood—
　Bog, clay, and rubble, sand and stark black dearth.

XXVI

Now blotches rankling, coloured gay and grim,
　Now patches where some leanness of the soil's
　Broke into moss or substances like boils;
Then came some palsied oak, a cleft in him
Like a distorted mouth that splits its rim
　Gaping at death, and dies while it recoils.

XXVII

And just as far as ever from the end!
　Nought in the distance but the evening, nought
　To point my footstep further! At the thought,
A great black bird, Apollyon's bosom-friend,
Sailed past, nor beat his wide wing dragon-penned
　That brushed my cap—perchance the guide I sought.

XXVIII

For, looking up, aware I somehow grew,
　'Spite of the dusk, the plain had given place
　All round to mountains—with such name to grace
Mere ugly heights and heaps now stolen in view.
How thus they had surprised me,—solve it, you!
　How to get from them was no clearer case.

XXIX

Yet half I seemed to recognize some trick
   Of mischief happened to me, God knows when—
   In a bad dream perhaps. Here ended, then,
Progress this way. When, in the very nick
Of giving up, one time more, came a click
   As when a trap shuts—you're inside the den!

XXX

Burningly it came on me all at once,
   This was the place! those two hills on the right,
   Crouched like two bulls locked horn in horn in fight;
While to the left, a tall scalped mountain . . . Dunce,
Dotard, a-dozing at the very nonce,
   After a life spent training for the sight!

XXXI

What in the midst lay but the Tower itself?
   The round squat turret, blind as the fool's heart,
   Built of brown stone, without a counterpart
In the whole world. The tempest's mocking elf
Points to the shipman thus the unseen shelf
   He strikes on, only when the timbers start.

XXXII

Not see? because of night perhaps?—why, day
   Came back again for that! before it left,
   The dying sunset kindled through a cleft.
The hills, like giants at a hunting, lay,
Chin upon hand, to see the game at bay,—
   "Now stab and end the creature—to the heft!"

XXXIII

Not hear? when noise was everywhere! it tolled
   Increasing like a bell. Names in my ears
   Of all the lost adventurers my peers,—
How such a one was strong, and such was bold,

And such was fortunate, yet each of old
   Lost, lost! one moment knelled the woe of years.

XXXIV

There they stood, ranged along the hill-sides, met
   To view the last of me, a living frame
   For one more picture! in a sheet of flame
I saw them and I knew them all. And yet
Dauntless the slug-horn to my lips I set,
   And blew *"Childe Roland to the Dark Tower came."*

ROBERT BROWNING

CAPTAIN CARPENTER

Captain Carpenter rose up in his prime
Put on his pistols and went riding out
But had got wellnigh nowhere at that time
Till he fell in with ladies in a rout.

It was a pretty lady and all her train
That played with him so sweetly but before
An hour she'd taken a sword with all her main
And twined him of his nose for evermore.

Captain Carpenter mounted up one day
And rode straightway into a stranger rogue
That looked unchristian but be that as may
The Captain did not wait upon prologue.

But drew upon him out of his great heart
The other swung against him with a club
And cracked his two legs at the shinny part
And let him roll and stick like any tub.

Captain Carpenter rode many a time
From male and female took he sundry harms
He met the wife of Satan crying "I'm
The she-wolf bids you shall bear no more arms."

Their strokes and counters whistled in the wind
I wish he had delivered half his blows
But where she should have made off like a hind
The bitch bit off his arms at the elbows.

And Captain Carpenter parted with his ears
To a black devil that used him in this wise
O Jesus ere his threescore and ten years
Another had plucked out his sweet blue eyes.

Captain Carpenter got up on his roan
And sallied from the gate in hell's despite
I heard him asking in the grimmest tone
If any enemy yet there was to fight?

"To any adversary it is fame
If he risk to be wounded by my tongue
Or burnt in two beneath my red heart's flame
Such are the perils he is cast among.

"But if he can he has a pretty choice
From an anatomy with little to lose
Whether he cut my tongue and take my voice
Or whether it be my round red heart he choose."

It was the neatest knave that ever was seen
Stepping in perfume from his lady's bower
Who at this word put in his merry mien
And fell on Captain Carpenter like a tower.

I would not knock old fellows in the dust
But there lay Captain Carpenter on his back
His weapons were the old heart in his bust
And a blade shook between rotten teeth alack.

The rogue in scarlet and grey soon knew his mind
He wished to get his trophy and depart
With gentle apology and touch refined
He pierced him and produced the Captain's heart.

God's mercy rest on Captain Carpenter now
I thought him Sirs an honest gentleman
Citizen husband soldier and scholar enow
Let jangling kites eat of him if they can.

But God's deep curses follow after those
That shore him of his goodly nose and ears
His legs and strong arms at the two elbows
And eyes that had not watered seventy years.

The curse of hell upon the sleek upstart
That got the Captain finally on his back
And took the red red vitals of his heart
And made the kites to whet their beaks clack clack.

JOHN CROWE RANSOM

FAIRY TALE

This is the hero; he is black or white,
Jewish or not-chosen, as you will.
He is villain too; porch-pillared from moonlight
And fondling with stub thumb the window sill.

Night wind laps back his hair; why, you all know him.
Eye a little pale, a yes-sir, no-sir mouth.
Disliked his heavy-hand pa; just to show him
He ran away from high school once down south.

He brings the laundry, brown purse a foot wide;
He rattles garbage cans, taxies you home.
Once when in rain you let him step inside
He looked beyond you to the living room.

Eyes narrowed, he hates *come* and *do* and *carry*.
Prince am I none, he feels, yet princely born.
Some stories read when he was ten and scary
Hard upon Shaftoe and the crumpled horn

Expressed him maybe; he didn't know; he forgot them
Glowering and drew secret maps in class.
Squirrels chuckled at him and by god he shot them.
His dreams have brought him here and cut this glass,

Or not his dreams. The imprisoned lady rather,
Her snow-white forearms bound, gazed and he came.
Gracious and golden-haired, unlike his mother.
Her hands were like his mother's just the same—

Not that he knew. He only knew the window
Tilted and stuck. Impatient, his blood cursed.
But his two secret words cónjured the window.
He thought a moment, swung his left leg first.

Once in, he heard them breathing. Slow, excited,
Clasping her image he made for their den.
A nervous click, the door rushed at him lighted,
All lamps and glass and draperies, the woman

Bolt upright, unbelieving. He came closer.
The ogre snored beside her, red mouth deep;
Disguised (as always) like Duffy the grocer,
He lay enchanted in a beery sleep.

And threshed and gurgled as the good scout-knife
Cut in, cut deeper, and the skin spread wide.
"She is half free," he thought, "this saves my darling."
And now for that witch-woman by his side.

But slow, but soft; this is liturgy. Once more
He saw the lady beckon, one arm free.
He flung back curtains, found the secret door;
Crooned as he swung it with the golden key.

The deacon two streets over under his steeple
Is dreaming this; his grating molars groan;
It runs with many faces through the people;
Dali will paint it with live telephones.

For this prince saw the ogre red and still;
Killed the enchantress (this was not *his* word);
A fountain of plumes, mounted the glass hill
Led by white reindeer and a silver bird.

Later, in alleys crouched, he never winces
As wheels skid shrieking, men shout, sirens wind.
A prince, he turns his back, smiles at the princess,
And both ride off together down his mind.

JOHN FREDERICK NIMS

TAM LIN

O I forbid you, maidens a',
    That wear gowd on your hair,
To come or gae by Carterhaugh,
    For young Tam Lin is there.

There's nane that gaes by Carterhaugh
    But they leave him a wad,
Either their rings, or green mantles,
    Or else their maidenhead.

Janet has kilted her green kirtle,
    A little aboon her knee,
And she has snooded her yellow hair
    A little aboon her bree,
And she's awa to Carterhaugh,
    As fast as she can hie.

When she came to Carterhaugh
    Tam Lin was at the well,
And there she fand his steed standing,
    But away was himsel.

She had na pu'd a double rose,
    A rose but only twa,
Till up then started young Tam Lin,
    Says, Lady, thou's pu nae mae.

Why pu's thou the rose, Janet,
  And why breaks thou the wand?
Or why comes thou to Carterhaugh
  Withoutten my command?

'Carterhaugh, it is my ain,
  My daddie gave it me;
I'll come and gang by Carterhaugh
  And ask nae leave at thee.'

* * *

Janet has kilted her green kirtle
  A little aboon her knee,
And she has snooded her yellow hair
  A little aboon her bree,
And she is to her father's ha,
  As fast as she can hie.

Four and twenty ladies fair
  Were playing at the ba,
And out then cam the fair Janet,
  Ance the flower amang them a'.

Four and twenty ladies fair
  Were playing at the chess,
And out then cam the fair Janet,
  As green as onie glass.

Out then spak an auld grey knight,
  Lay oer the castle wa,
And says, Alas, fair Janet, for thee
  But we'll be blamed a'.

'Haud your tongue, ye auld fac'd knight,
  Some ill death may ye die!
Father my bairn on whom I will,
  I'll father nane on thee.'

Out then spak her father dear,
  And he spak meek and mild;

'And ever alas, sweet Janet,' he says,
  'I think thou gaes wi child.'

'If that I gae wi child, father,
  Mysel maun bear the blame;
There's neer a laird about your ha
  Shall get the bairn's name.

'If my love were an earthly knight,
  And he's an elfin grey,
I wad na gie my ain true-love
  For nae lord that ye hae.

'The steed that my true-love rides on
  Is lighter than the wind;
Wi siller he is shod before,
  Wi burning gowd behind.'

Janet has kilted her green kirtle
  A little aboon her knee,
And she has snooded her yellow hair
  A little aboon her bree,
And she's awa to Carterhaugh,
  As fast as she can hie.

When she cam to Carterhaugh,
  Tam Lin was at the well,
And there she fand his steed standing,
  But away was himsel.

She had na pu'd a double rose,
  A rose but only twa,
Till up then started young Tam Lin,
  Says, Lady, thou pu's nae mae.

Why pu's thou the rose, Janet,
  Amang the groves sae green,
And a' to kill the bonie babe
  That we gat us between?

'O tell me, tell me, Tam Lin,' she says,
   'For's sake that died on tree,
If eer ye was in holy chapel,
   Or christendom did see?'

'Roxbrugh he was my grandfather,
   Took me with him to bide,
And ance it fell upon a day
   That wae did me betide.

'And ance it fell upon a day,
   A cauld day and a snell,
When we were frae the hunting come,
   That frae my horse I fell;
The Queen o Fairies she caught me,
   In yon green hill to dwell.

'And pleasant is the fairy land,
   But, an eerie tale to tell,
Ay at the end of seven years
   We pay a tiend to hell;
I am sae fair and fu o flesh,
   I'm feared it be mysel.

'But the night is Halloween, lady,
   The morn is Hallowday;
Then win me, win me, and ye will,
   For weel I wat ye may.

'Just at the mirk and midnight hour
   The fairy folk will ride,
And they that wad their true-love win,
   At Miles Cross they maun bide.'

'But how shall I thee ken, Tam Lin,
   Or how my true-love know,
Amang sae mony unco knights
   The like I never saw?'

'O first let pass the black, lady,
    And syne let pass the brown,
But quickly run to the milk-white steed,
    Pu ye his rider down.

'For I'll ride on the milk-white steed,
    And ay nearest the town;
Because I was an earthly knight
    They gie me that renown.

'My right hand will be glovd, lady,
    My left hand will be bare,
Cockt up shall my bonnet be,
    And kaimd down shall my hair,
And thae's the takens I gie thee,
    Nae doubt I will be there.

'They'll turn me in your arms, lady,
    Into an esk and adder;
But hold me fast, and fear me not,
    I am your bairn's father.

'They'll turn me to a bear sae grim,
    And then a lion bold;
But hold me fast, and fear me not,
    As ye shall love your child.

'Again they'll turn me in your arms
    To a red het gaud of airn;
But hold me fast, and fear me not
    I'll do to you nae harm.

'And last they'll turn me in your arms
    Into the burning gleed;
Then throw me into well water,
    O throw me in wi speed.

'And then I'll be your ain true-love,
    I'll turn a naked knight;

Then cover me wi your green mantle,
  And cover me out o sight.'

Gloomy, gloomy was the night,
  And eerie was the way,
As fair Jenny in her green mantle
  To Miles Cross she did gae.

About the middle o the night
  She heard the bridles ring;
This lady was as glad at that
  As any earthly thing.

First she let the black pass by,
  And syne she let the brown;
But quickly she ran to the milk-white steed,
  And pu'd the rider down.

Sae weel she minded what he did say,
  And young Tam Lin did win;
Syne covered him wi her green mantle,
  As blythe's a bird in spring.

Out then spak the Queen o Fairies,
  Out of a bush o broom:
'Them that has gotten young Tam Lin
  Has gotten a stately groom.'

Out then spak the Queen o Fairies,
  And an angry woman was she:
'Shame betide her ill-far'd face,
  And an ill death may she die,
For she's taen awa the boniest knight
  In a' my companie.

'But had I kend, Tam Lin,' she says,
  'What now this night I see,
I wad hae taen out thy twa grey een,
  And put in twa een o tree.'

ANONYMOUS

BOUNDBROOK

I met a man and he was fair.
All the birds said Follow.
Every leaf in the wood
Shook gold onto my head
And my heart felt all its blood.

Then it was a great park land
By a willow-trailing brook bound round.
Stag and peacock walked
For pleasure in the corn,
And Merlin wound the horn.

Merlin or his tribe it was
Spun that park and lordly palace
Pearled as Helen's pin.
My master said, Walk in,
And, Touch me.   It is yours.

I had a hand could change a world.
The waters dropped, the meadow furled,
That field was Circe's pen.
The shaggy beasts growled at the shucks,
Great swine, and goats, and picking cocks,
And they were all my kin.

Seven years I sojourned there,
The blacksnake nested in the briar,
Every bird was black.
Insects stained the air like smoke.
I struck and ravined in the thick
Until my heart's blood broke.

And I lay down, a beast, to die
And rose up seven years ago
In the popular fields of home.
There the streams go out and in,
All the men are common men,

The blackbird whistles in the corn.
Touch me. It is mine.

JULIA RANDALL

THE WHIRLWIND

No one noticed how the gloom had gathered.
Hunched on the veranda, taken up in rents
And purchases, we measured out our chances,
Square by square. A chill precursor stirred
In the wisteria; and, sheer as doom, a fury
Fell on things familiar: heaved the rug up,
Flung the potted plant, the table, wicker
Chairs. The board, a flapping pterodactyl,
Made erratic passes; and the flesh—yea, all
Which it inherited, roared up the flue.

Gold, yellow, orange and blue, my bills
Banked in the air like ravaged leaves.
My houses, ranked and windowless, on Boardwalk,
Ventnor, Oriental, vanished with my red
Hotels. The cat extended her electric legs
In limbo. Streamlined by the wind, the dog
Stretched out the frantic pennant of his tail.
My real estate, my revenue, the ballast
Of a tidy world, ascended. Into the dark,
The flotsam of the wind, I whirled.

Above, the rushing wind abated. Darkness
Glimmered with occulting stars. Not far away,
My sister caught my gaze. Where had her grace
Been hidden, while I counted, one by one,
The uncommunicating years? "Take hands,"
She said, "look down, look down. The wind
Has blown your debts away, unmortgaged all
Your properties." Below, the parish church,
A planet orbited with graves, spun like a top
And leapt to meet us, slowing as we neared,

And stopped.   The dizzy green shaped into trees.
A band struck up.   The trumpet and the piccolo,
The glockenspiel, the clarinet and sousaphone
Curled in my ear.   The cat, on terra firma,
Fluffed her tail and stiffened to the lop-eared
Clown's pursuit.   The neighbors came.   The moon
Slid into sight and shone.   And all night long
The tall and lean, the short and round
And in between, the halt and blind trod out
The nine man's morris on the village green.

                                    JOHN ALEXANDER ALLEN

II

THE CALL

The Call is a summons to adventure, physical or mental and spiritual. In the life of Everyman, it signals the recurrent need for casting off familiar modes of thought and action, an accustomed vocation and habitat, and adopting others which are sure to be daunting, simply because they are unknown. In the nature of things, one is always being asked or forced to try something new, as that is the way of all developing organisms; but while the caterpillar, in its remarkable metamorphosis, responds to purely physical stimuli, human creatures may or may not learn in time to grow and spread their wings. We all grow old, but we do not all become adult; and those who do may nevertheless in some degree fall short of their full potentiality for thought, imagination, leadership. Few of us contain the stuff of legendary heroes, but it seems likely that everyone can hope to find some tincture of the heroic hidden away in an unsuspected corner of himself, ready for use when the Call sounds and the need is great. Most of us, from time to time, have found ourselves rising unexpectedly to meet a sudden challenge. On however modest a scale, we know what it is to be a Hero, and therefore it is with inner knowledge that we respond to the heroic enterprise, both in life and literature. However, we have also, on occasion, given way to laziness, inertia, boredom, and mere cowardice; and, to the degree that this has become habitual, we find ourselves sinking into such a slough of wistful timidity as Eliot has typified in the dilemma of J. Alfred Prufrock, a man for whom the mermaids sing in vain.

Like all the essentials of the human condition, the necessity for change is an inexhaustible motif, a perennial ingredient of fairy tale and myth, novel, epic, story, play, and poem. In myth, the Hero, if he is not a god, is at any rate a god-like man and is therefore fully adequate to the task at hand, however difficult and dangerous. Heracles is required by the goddess Hera to perform twelve extraordinary labors, each seemingly more impossible than the last, and he proves equal to them all, whereupon he earns his promised immortality. On the other hand, the biblical Jonah declines to heed the Call, although it is the voice of God himself which speaks to him, saying, "Arise, go to Nineveh, that great city, and cry against it." He imagines that he can escape the will of his creator, but the ship aboard which he would flee and the whale which swallows him only serve to return him to the necessity which he would evade.

The protagonists of heroic poems, for all their human failings, heed the Call and meet the ensuing difficulties with some measure of success. In the Medieval poem, *Sir Gawain and the Green Knight*, Gawain is making merry at Christmastide with his companions at Arthur's court when lo! an immense stranger appears and issues a fantastic challange. Is there a champion among them, the Green Knight asks, who is bold enough to cut the giant's head from his shoulders? And, if so, will he agree to surrender his own head in exchange in one year's time? Not an attractive bargain, but Gawain, being a Hero by profession, will not decline a sporting proposition. Off goes the Green Knight's head, and Gawain is fairly launched upon his most exacting test. In contrast, Dante, as the protagonist of *The Divine Comedy*, is an unsuspecting Everyman who "comes to himself" in a dark and savage wood and finds that the path which he must follow in attaining his salvation leads through the terrifying depths of hell. Other Heroes, while aspiring to adventure, seem strikingly inadequate to their vocation. A bumpkin altogether in-experienced in derring-do appears, in Spenser's *Faerie Queene*, at the court of Queen Gloriana. Oddly enough, he wishes to become a knight. He is an Everyman with a vengeance, one with whom the unheroic reader can readily identify. Yet he is entrusted with no less vital a mission than the liberation of mankind from a dragon "terrible and stern," Satan himself, an antagonist with whom the would-be Christian must do battle, however insufficient for the task he may appear. Perhaps the most reluctant Hero in literature is the one who differs least of all from each of us—Everyman himself, in the play by that name, who is going about his business cheerfully when the voice of death, speaking in a tone which thrills him with horror, bids him prepare at once for "a pilgrimage to his pain." Only because he has no choice, the Hero comes to grips with the last great change which mortal circumstance demands, making such provision for his journey as he can.

The poets of our own time, no less than those of former ages, deal with moments of decision and of indecision, when the Hero faces, but is not always equal to, the demand of his spirit for invigo-rating change. The tense of poetry, says John Crowe Ransom, is the past. Certainly, many poems deal with a sense of loss (Section One) which is symptomatic of vanished graces and opportunities unrealized. The ironic mode, which seems especially congenial to contemporary writers, depicts the Hero (the anti-Hero, really!) as the more or less conscious victim of Stagnancy (Section Two) as thick as glue, which will not set him free to seek renewal. Nevertheless, the Call continues to ring out clearly in modern verse, even to the ears of the deaf and the hard of hearing. Certain Intimations (Section Three) filter through to them and hint of a hell which must be reckoned with if it is to be conquered, or of a promised land which the jaded spirit might yet seek, if only it had sufficient courage, if only it could find the way.

ONE

Loss

Our common talk is full of sayings that spring from a sense of Loss: "Things aren't what they used to be," "in the good old days," "when I was a boy." Happiness seems to lie in the past, and the present broods upon a giant absence. Like Villon, we ask, "Where are the snows of yesteryear?"

One reads in the paper of men who suddenly throw up their jobs, abandon their families, and disappear. Life as they know it has become intolerably constricting, and they have kicked over the traces, heeding the Call or what, at any rate, they took to be the Call. Cults of the simple life—back to the farm movements, the revival of home arts and crafts, nudist colonies—attract adherents. Unconsciously following a venerable mythic and poetic tradition, we castigate the giddy complexity of the present and contrast it with an imagined easier, more spontaneous and natural order of things.

Thus, Everyman. And the poet, in particular, tends to idealize a real or fancied golden past. Here, the pristine myth of our tradition is, of course, that of Adam and Eve in the garden, before the Fall. There, as we learn from *Genesis*, our first parents, sovereign over every beast and creeping thing, enjoyed the bounty of the Lord. In *Paradise Lost*, elaborating upon the tradition, Milton adds details: man and animals were vegetarians, no fruit or flower decayed, there was no death. Free from destructive passions—wrath, despair, lust, terror—Adam and Eve knew instinctively all they needed to know and enjoyed a perfect oneness with their creator.

But all this they foolishly cast away, and we are heirs to their original sin: to death, disease, war, and a pervasive sense of Loss.

The myth of the happy garden is not exclusively a Judeo-Christian one. The Greeks, and after them the Romans, looked back to a Golden Age under Cronus (Saturn) when all men lived in peace, enjoying material abundance, innocent and uncorrupt. The notion of a blissful epoch in the past is apparently rooted in the very nature of man, a universal cue for his nostalgia; hence the traditional poetic formula, *Ubi sunt?*

The desire to recapture childhood, Eden, the Golden Age— even the realization that these are lost—is, for Everyman, a form of the Call. Though it cannot bring back youth or an age of heroic simplicity, it can and does serve to dramatize the deficiencies, especially those of the imagination, which are commonly the product of a humdrum life. However, the sense of Loss which poets labor to arouse is not truly an invitation to return to an epoch of the past, but a cue to go forward to a new maturity, the "higher innocence" of Blake's philosophy.

To lapse into sentimental regret for a lost past is easy, and poets properly regard that attitude with irony; but to transmute the sense of Loss into a Call for difficult changes requires fortitude and is, in fact, the Hero's way. To cite a venerable example, the speaker of the Old English poem, "The Seafarer," is perpetually dissatisfied with the self-indulgent life of the "wine-flushed" land-lubber and is restless, even in spring when nature renews itself, to put out to sea once again. He remembers, to be sure, a time when the lords of earth were god-like in power and generosity, while now only the weak remain to inherit a decadent world. However, knowing that the past cannot be reclaimed, the Seafarer refuses to despair but strengthens his mind and spirit upon the stormy "whale's way" in preparation for the final judgment and, as he hopes, his acceptance into the kingdom of heaven.

As one might expect, poems about Loss are likely to derive their metaphoric material from the myth of Adam and Eve or from evocations of idealized childhood. Hyam Plutzik, in "The Begetting of Cain," refers directly to events in the Garden of Eden; and Winfield Townley Scott's poem, "Merrill's Brook," evokes the reader's sense of aboriginal innocence, intruded upon by "the hairy Adam," although his immediate concern is with remembered details from a childhood swimming hole. In their various ways, the seventeenth-century Welshman, Henry Vaughan; the nineteenth-century Englishman, Thomas Hood; and the contemporary Americans, Randall Jarrell and Robert Penn Warren, deal with a poignant sense of the irrevocable retreat from childhood.

Jarrell's "Jack" is interesting and instructive in that it employs a variation of the familiar fairy tale, "Jack and the Beanstalk," to convey the boundless possibilities of youth, unrealized even when they were at hand and now recalled in age with deepening frustration. At a time when his famous adventure has become a distant memory and he is reduced to sitting as though "bound in some terrible wooden charm," Jack muses on the beanstalk that once gave him access to the world of the sky, the goose that laid the golden eggs, the singing harp; above all, the wife of the giant who, in protecting him from that ogre by hiding him in her oven, precluded forever the possibility that he would pursue his heroic vocation to its destined goal and win "the strait princess" for his own. Timidity and greed were his undoing. In his haste to escape from danger and return safely home with his treasures, Jack lost his opportunity to produce for himself and for others a coherent and illuminated world. He is left with the pieces of "the world's puzzle" which can only rust as he turns them over idly in his hands. He has long since acknowledged his failure and, sitting by an oven like that in which he hid from the adversary long ago, he remembers, but can never regain, "The land that the harp sang so loudly."

Still more bleakly ironic is the restless spirit of the grandmother in Robert Penn Warren's "Keepsakes." In this poem, the appearance of the old woman's ghost provokes a dialogue between two speakers (one of whom is the subject's grandchild) who have observed her, night by night, fussing about with a bureau in a house which she once inhabited. Still following dutifully the habits of a lifetime, she polishes the bureau and then, as though searching for something which she has mislaid, looks into its top drawer. There, she does not find what she is seeking, but only a prayer book (which she cannot read without her glasses), a bundle of contraceptives (which she, as an unquestioning bearer of children, cannot understand), and odds and ends which, because they belonged to strangers, only aggravate to tears her own remembered grief.

We learn that the object which the grandmother's spirit is seeking lies in the bottom drawer of the bureau: an old-fashioned doll, "naked and violated." This doll, disturbingly enough, now shows signs of coming to life, for its eyes move, it whispers "I died for love," and the hole in its body, from which its sawdust stuffing once leaked, now bleeds treacle from its heart. Whining "like a dog in the dark and shade," the grandmother's ghost is

> *hunting somebody to give*
> *Her the life they had promised her she would live.*

The doll that was hers as a child is now identified with "that poor self she'd mislaid." She has not found it as yet, but when she does so on "some summer night," the bonds of death will scarcely be strong enough to withstand the passionate "stink and stir" of the old lady mourning her Loss, striving fiercely to reclaim the life which, before, she had somehow failed to live.

In pushing the sense of Loss beyond the grave, endowing sockets of bone with eyes and with bitter tears, Warren evokes the restless urgency of the Call. It sounds with an insistence all the more powerful because it has gone unheeded until it is too late, and life has broken its promise to a woman who did not know what it was to be alive until she was dead.

THE RETREAT

Happy those early days, when I
Shined in my Angel-infancy!
Before I understood this place
Appointed for my second race,
Or taught my soul to fancy aught
But a white, celestial thought;
When yet I had not walk'd above
A mile or two from my first Love,

And looking back—at that short space—
Could see a glimpse of His bright face:
When on some gilded cloud or flower,
My gazing soul would dwell an hour,
And in those weaker glories spy

Some shadows of eternity;
Before I taught my tongue to wound
My Conscience with a sinful sound,
Or had the black art to dispense
A several sin to every sense,
But felt through all this fleshly dress
Bright shoots of everlastingness.

O how I long to travel back,
And tread again that ancient track!
That I might once more reach that plain
Where first I left my glorious train;
From whence th' enlighten'd spirit sees
That shady City of Palm trees!
But ah! my soul with too much stay
Is drunk, and staggers in the way!
Some men a forward motion love,
But I by backward steps would move;
And when this dust falls to the urn,
In that state I came, return.

HENRY VAUGHAN

ANIMULA

'Issues from the hand of God, the simple soul'
To a flat world of changing lights and noise,
To light, dark, dry or damp, chilly or warm;
Moving between the legs of tables and of chairs,
Rising or falling, grasping at kisses and toys,
Advancing boldly, sudden to take alarm,
Retreating to the corner of arm and knee,
Eager to be reassured, taking pleasure
In the fragrant brilliance of the Christmas tree,
Pleasure in the wind, the sunlight and the sea;
Studies the sunlit pattern on the floor
And running stags around a silver tray;
Confounds the actual and the fanciful,
Content with playing-cards and kings and queens,

What the fairies do and what the servants say.
The heavy burden of the growing soul
Perplexes and offends more, day by day;
Week by week, offends and perplexes more
With the imperatives of 'is and seems'
And may and may not, desire and control.
The pain of living and the drug of dreams
Curl up the small soul in the window seat
Behind the *Encyclopædia Britannica*.
Issues from the hand of time the simple soul
Irresolute and selfish, misshapen, lame,
Unable to fare forward or retreat,
Fearing the warm reality, the offered good,
Denying the importunity of the blood,
Shadow of its own shadows, spectre in its own gloom,
Leaving disordered papers in a dusty room;
Living first in the silence after the viaticum.

Pray for Guiterriez, avid of speed and power,
For Boudin, blown to pieces,
For this one who made a great fortune,
And that one who went his own way.
Pray for Floret, by the boarhound slain between the yew trees,
Pray for us now and at the hour of our birth.

                              T. S. ELIOT

PAST AND PRESENT

I remember, I remember
  The house where I was born,
The little window where the sun
  Came peeping in at morn;
He never came a wink too soon
  Nor brought too long a day;
But now, I often wish the night
  Had borne my breath away.

I remember, I remember
  The roses, red and white,

The violets, and the lily-cups—
　　Those flowers made of light!
The lilacs where the robin built,
　　And where my brother set
The laburnum on his birth-day,—
　　The tree is living yet!

I remember, I remember
　　Where I was used to swing,
And thought the air must rush as fresh
　　To swallows on the wing;
My spirit flew in feathers then
　　That is so heavy now,
And summer pools could hardly cool
　　The fever on my brow.

I remember, I remember
　　The fir trees dark and high;
I used to think their slender tops
　　Were close against the sky:
It was a childish ignorance,
　　But now 'tis little joy
To know I'm farther off from Heaven
　　Than when I was a boy.

THOMAS HOOD

JACK

The sky darkened watching you
And the year sinking in its journey
Seem to you the slit beanstalk
And the goose crumpled in its pen.

The river, the spilt boats,
And the giant like a cloud falling
Are all pieces in your mind
Of a puzzle that, once joined,

Might green again the rotting stack.
Now, the oven's stiff creaking
Vexes you, but lifelessly,
Shameless as someone else's dream;

The harp crying out as you ran
Seems, rustling, your daughters' yellow hair . . .
As, bound in some terrible wooden charm,
You sit here rigid and aghast,

Sometimes, in your good memory,
The strait princess, the giant's simpler wife
Come torn and gazing, begging
The names you could never comprehend,

And in the narrowing circle, sitting
With the world's puzzle rusting in your hands,
You know then you can never regain
The land that the harp sang so loudly.

RANDALL JARRELL

THE BEGETTING OF CAIN

Longing at twilight the lovesick Adam saw
The belly of Eve upon the golden straw
Of Paradise, under the limb of the Tree.
He thought that none was near, but there were three
Who were upon the mortal grass that dusk,
Under the wispy cloud, breathing the musk
Of the young world. Creature of pointed ear,
Of the cleft hoof and the tight-mouthed sneer,
The other passed, wound round within his thought.
And Adam in his mounting passion caught
The white shoulders of that woman there. . . .
All were engulfed—these two, the birds of the air,
The burrowers of the earth, by the quenchless mind
Roaming insatiate on that lowland, blind
In its lonely hunger, lusting to make all things
One with itself. Brief as the flutter of wings

Was his mastery, though ranging through world and void
To the dusk-star shining. But all, all were destroyed:
The two on the odorous earth in the garden there;
The beasts, the birds in the nest, the fireflies in the air.

HYAM PLUTZIK

MERRILL'S BROOK

Sun over all and air over all and clover
Ripens with bees the summer afternoon
Where pasture right angles at the slanted oak
And swirls the narrow brook to a round brown pool.

The banks are skin-shiny with twenty boys
That flicker warm light into the shade and out,
Running. They leap to a hang of rope and swing
Above the water, let go with a shouting plunge.

The larger and skillful revolve their bald behinds
On a wheel of headover diving, and here jounce
Beginners flouncing, one foot careful in shallows,
Dog-paddlers, and ankle deep a little brother

Who stands blondly glistening, unspoken-to.
One anxious mongrel circles among the bathers
Who jump back and forth, amphibious of June:
The air's white-knived with knees and shoulder-blades.

Or loll in grass; and now and then pair off
To hide in alder thickets with hot hands,
Emerging red to dive—the hurried thud
Of racing bare-soled on bluet-bevelled earth.

So on so on a hundred summer days
Till the stranger, the stout and hairy Adam, came
With soap and a pleading smile and called to us
While we scrambled to clothes and ran and ran away.

WINFIELD TOWNLEY SCOTT

HORSES

Those lumbering horses in the steady plough,
On the bare field—I wonder why, just now,
They seemed terrible, so wild and strange,
Like magic power on the stony grange.

Perhaps some childish hour has come again,
When I watched fearful, through the blackening rain,
Their hooves like pistons in an ancient mill
Move up and down, yet seem as standing still.

Their conquering hooves which trod the stubble down
Were ritual that turned the field to brown,
And their great hulks were seraphim of gold,
Or mute ecstatic monsters on the mould.

And oh the rapture, when, one furrow done,
They marched broad-breasted to the sinking sun!
The light flowed off their bossy sides in flakes;
The furrows rolled behind like struggling snakes.

But when at dusk with streaming nostrils home
They came, they seemed gigantic in the gloam,
And warm and glowing with mysterious fire
That lit their smouldering bodies in the mire.

Their eyes as brilliant and as wide as night
Gleamed with a cruel apocalyptic light.
Their manes the leaping ire of the wind
Lifted with rage invisible and blind.

Ah, now it fades! it fades! and I must pine
Again for that dread country crystalline,
Where the blank field and the still-standing tree
Were bright and fearful presences to me.

EDWIN MUIR

TARTAR HORSEMEN
for George Garrett

The upraised spears
And wild hairy shouts.
The river was muddy
And the chieftain's pony
Stumbled once, then made
The shore.

The way had been long,
The armor of the enemy,
Their swords, and our women
Writhing in the tents.

There were pine forests
And needled ground
That the snow seldom touched,
And sharp blue water
That the sun sailed
For hours before it slept.

The pony and our chief,
Father of our blood,
Looked back but once.
We wept and waited,
Even then, his return.

The wind turns the edges
Of our tents. The dogs
Howl and the small girls
Stir in their sleep,
Dream of the north
And our chief, the mover
Of our blood.

We stand in the wind.
We await his return.

R. H. W. DILLARD

THE CAGE

Take, then, this image for what it is worth:
the eagle that I saw once, loved where he stood,
a sad brown thing roosting like a hen on a pole.
He was, of course, a captive. It was the zoo.
The cage was round and domed and let in light
and some of the jigsawed blue of the sky.
(I was a boy then. Love was fiercely caged.)

Outside there were peacocks on the grass.
They strutted on the clipped lawn like
elegant ancestors, folding and unfolding
intricate fans adorned with magic eyes.
He was alone with scattered winks of sky
and broken weather. Bald as a monk,
he seldom moved from his perch, never flew,

though there was room enough. He waited.
Sometimes he would stir, open his huge wings.
Then, I thought, seeing the beak and the cruel talons,
and the shadows of his wings like twin sails,
that nothing made of iron could keep him.
But that was only a whim, a ghostly gesture.
He wouldn't eat and so he died.

Afterwards there were still the peacocks to look at,
and all the small birds in their delicate cages,
and the rare ones with beaks and coloring to prove
God has a sense of humor in some climates.
But chiefly there was the cage like a great wound.
Like an eye put out, like space where a tree has been.
Wind howled in that empty place and I wanted to pray.

                              GEORGE GARRETT

HUNTER, IMMOBILE

In another land (or hour) how fierce and cunning
he would be for his celestial rights:

hacking the creepers, swimming cheek by jowl
with crocodiles, staring the tiger down;

crouched under the thin moon, at his trip's end,
till the signal: there-or there. For a hutful of glory,

for a chalice on a suitcase in a loft. For four words
at night, or the least-brave hour before dawn.

But smugness never looked like a wicked river; and the boor,
the lout, the bigot, showed not fangs nor fur.

Scenting small hunger in communion-breakfasts,
he ignored news of any final supper.

And hid his hunter's heart, without a quarry—
forgetful how tigers are sometimes masks and masks are tigers.

JOSEPHINE JACOBSEN

IN THOSE DAYS

In those days—they were long ago—
The snow was cold, the night was black.
I licked from my cracked lips
A snowflake, as I looked back

Through branches, the last uneasy snow.
Your shadow, there in the light, was still.
In a little the light went out.
I went on, stumbling—till at last the hill

Hid the house. And, yawning,
In bed in my room, alone,
I would look out: over the quilted
Rooftops, the clear stars shone.

How poor and miserable we were,
How seldom together!

And yet after so long one thinks:
In those days everything was better.

RANDALL JARRELL

THE LOSS

If I much concern myself with this,
You do too, and all who do not seem
Stone faces dreaming stone's dream
Of nothing, nothing, like the images
On Easter Island. All the animals
Follow us with their eyes as we go by
Wondering what we look for. In the sky
Red fades out to black and the night falls,
Night and the ignorance of eyes; but we
Light matches, matches; on our hands and knees
Ransacking every hummock, every tree's
Droppings for any nickel, dime, or cent
Of the incredible emolument
We never lost until we looked to see.

E. L. MAYO

THE RETURN

I see myself sometimes, an old old man
Who has walked so long with time as time's true servant,
That he's grown strange to me—who was once myself—
Almost as strange as time, and yet familiar
With old man's staff and legendary cloak,
For see, it is I, it is I. And I return
So altered, so adopted, to the house
Of my own life. There all the doors stand open
Perpetually, and the rooms ring with sweet voices,
And there my long life's seasons sound their changes,
Childhood and youth and manhood all together,
And welcome waits, and not a room but is

My own, beloved and longed for. And the voices,
Sweeter than any sound dreamt of or known,
Call me, recall me. I draw near at last,
An old old man, and scan the ancient walls
Rounded and softened by the compassionate years,
The old and heavy and long-leaved trees that watch
This my inheritance in friendly darkness.
And yet I cannot enter, for all within
Rises before me there, rises against me,
A sweet and terrible labyrinth of longing,
So that I turn aside and take the road
That always, early or late, runs on before.

EDWIN MUIR

HEARD IN OLD AGE
   (*for Robert Frost*)

That sweet fire in the veins, while everywhere
The Furies' filth keeps raining down, the young
Make love, make war, make music: the common tongue
Of private wounds, of the outrage that they share,
Or sing in desperate mockery of despair.

Is there a song left, then, for aged voices?
They are worse than cracked: half throttled by the thumbs
Of hard self-knowledge. To the old, dawn comes
With ache of loss, with cold absence of choices.
What heart, waking to this, drumming assent, rejoices?

Traffic rousing, gulls' cries, or cock crow, score
The body's ignominy, the mind's delays;
Till the Enigma, in a wandering phrase,
Offers a strain never audible before:
Immense music beyond a closing door.

BABETTE DEUTSCH

PROVIDE, PROVIDE

The witch that came (the withered hag)
To wash the steps with pail and rag
Was once the beauty Abishag,

The picture pride of Hollywood.
Too many fall from great and good
For you to doubt the likelihood.

Die early and avoid the fate.
Or if predestined to die late,
Make up your mind to die in state.

Make the whole stock exchange your own!
If need be occupy a throne,
Where nobody can call *you* crone.

Some have relied on what they knew,
Others on being simply true.
What worked for them might work for you.

No memory of having starred
Atones for later disregard
Or keeps the end from being hard.

Better to go down dignified
With boughten friendship at your side
Than none at all.   Provide, provide!

ROBERT FROST

THE CUPOLA

A mirror hangs on the wall of the draughty cupola.
Within the depths of glass mix the oak and the beech leaf,
Once held to the boughs' shape, but now to the shape of the
    wind.

Someone has hung the mirror here for no reason,
In the shuttered room, an eye for the drifted leaves,
For the oak leaf, the beech, a handsbreadth of darkest reflection.

Someone has thought alike of the bough and the wind
And struck their shape to the wall.   Each in its season
Spills negligent death throughout the abandoned chamber.

LOUISE BOGAN

THE WITCH OF COOS
   (*Two Witches: I*)

I stayed the night for shelter at a farm
Behind the mountain, with a mother and son,
Two old-believers.   They did all the talking.

MOTHER.   Folks think a witch who has familiar spirits
She could call up to pass a winter evening,
But won't, should be burned at the stake or something.
Summoning spirits isn't "Button, button,
Who's got the button," I would have them know.

SON.   Mother can make a common table rear
And kick with two legs like an army mule.

MOTHER.   And when I've done it, what good have I done?
Rather than tip a table for you, let me
Tell you what Ralle the Sioux Control once told me.
He said the dead had souls, but when I asked him
How could that be—I thought the dead were souls—
He broke my trance.   Don't that make you suspicious
That there's something the dead are keeping back?
Yes, there's something the dead are keeping back.

SON.   You wouldn't want to tell him what we have
Up attic, mother?

MOTHER. Bones—a skeleton.

SON. But the headboard of mother's bed is pushed
Against the attic door: the door is nailed.
It's harmless. Mother hears it in the night,
Halting perplexed behind the barrier
Of door and headboard. Where it wants to get
Is back into the cellar where it came from.

MOTHER. We'll never let them, will we, son? We'll never!

SON. It left the cellar forty years ago
And carried itself like a pile of dishes
Up one flight from the cellar to the kitchen,
Another from the kitchen to the bedroom,
Another from the bedroom to the attic,
Right past both father and mother, and neither stopped it.
Father had gone upstairs; mother was downstairs.
I was a baby: I don't know where I was.

MOTHER. The only fault my husband found with me—
I went to sleep before I went to bed,
Especially in winter when the bed
Might just as well be ice and the clothes snow.
The night the bones came up the cellar stairs
Toffile had gone to bed alone and left me,
But left an open door to cool the room off
So as to sort of turn me out of it.
I was just coming to myself enough
To wonder where the cold was coming from,
When I heard Toffile upstairs in the bedroom
And thought I heard him downstairs in the cellar.
The board we had laid down to walk dry-shod on
When there was water in the cellar in spring
Struck the hard cellar bottom. And then someone
Began the stairs, two footsteps for each step,
The way a man with one leg and a crutch,
Or a little child, comes up. It wasn't Toffile:
It wasn't anyone who could be there.
The bulkhead double doors were double-locked

And swollen tight and buried under snow.
The cellar windows were banked up with sawdust
And swollen tight and buried under snow.
It was the bones. I knew them—and good reason.
My first impulse was to get to the knob
And hold the door. But the bones didn't try
The door; they halted helpless on the landing,
Waiting for things to happen in their favor.
The faintest restless rustling ran all through them.
I never could have done the thing I did
If the wish hadn't been too strong in me
To see how they were mounted for this walk.
I had a vision of them put together
Not like a man, but like a chandelier.
So suddenly I flung the door wide on him.
A moment he stood balancing with emotion,
And all but lost himself. (A tongue of fire
Flashed out and licked along his upper teeth.
Smoke rolled inside the sockets of his eyes.)
Then he came at me with one hand outstretched,
The way he did in life once; but this time
I struck the hand off brittle on the floor,
And fell back from him on the floor myself.
The finger-pieces slid in all directions.
(Where did I see one of those pieces lately?
Hand me my button-box—it must be there.)
I sat up on the floor and shouted, "Toffile,
It's coming up to you." It had its choice
Of the door to the cellar or the hall.
It took the hall door for the novelty,
And set off briskly for so slow a thing,
Still going every which way in the joints, though,
So that it looked like lightning or a scribble,
From the slap I had just now given its hand.
I listened till it almost climbed the stairs
From the hall to the only finished bedroom,
Before I got up to do anything;
Then ran and shouted, "Shut the bedroom door,
Toffile, for my sake!" "Company?" he said,
"Don't make me get up; I'm too warm in bed."

So lying forward weakly on the handrail
I pushed myself upstairs, and in the light
(The kitchen had been dark) I had to own
I could see nothing. "Toffile, I don't see it.
It's with us in the room, though. It's the bones."
"What bones?" "The cellar bones—out of the grave."
That made him throw his bare legs out of bed
And sit up by me and take hold of me.
I wanted to put out the light and see
If I could see it, or else mow the room,
With our arms at the level of our knees,
And bring the chalk-pile down. "I'll tell you what—
It's looking for another door to try.
The uncommonly deep snow has made him think
Of his old song, 'The Wild Colonial Boy,'
He always used to sing along the tote road.
He's after an open door to get outdoors.
Let's trap him with an open door up attic."
Toffile agreed to that, and sure enough,
Almost the moment he was given an opening,
The steps began to climb the attic stairs.
I heard them. Toffile didn't seem to hear them.
"Quick!" I slammed to the door and held the knob.
"Toffile, get nails." I made him nail the door shut
And push the headboard of the bed against it.
Then we asked was there anything
Up attic that we'd never want again.
The attic was less to us than the cellar.
If the bones liked the attic, let them have it.
Let them stay in the attic. When they sometimes
Come down the stairs at night and stand perplexed
Behind the door and headboard of the bed,
Brushing their chalky skull with chalky fingers,
With sounds like the dry rattling of a shutter,
That's what I sit up in the dark to say—
To no one any more since Toffile died.
Let them stay in the attic since they went there.
I promised Toffile to be cruel to them
For helping them be cruel once to him.

SON. We think they had a grave down in the cellar.

MOTHER. We know they had a grave down in the cellar.

SON. We never could find out whose bones they were.

MOTHER. Yes, we could too, son. Tell the truth for once.
They were a man's his father killed for me.
I mean a man he killed instead of me.
The least I could do was to help dig their grave.
We were about it one night in the cellar.
Son knows the story: but 'twas not for him
To tell the truth, suppose the time had come.
Son looks surprised to see me end a lie
We'd kept all these years between ourselves
So as to have it ready for outsiders.
But tonight I don't care enough to lie—
I don't remember why I ever cared.
Toffile, if he were here, I don't believe
Could tell you why he ever cared himself. . . .

She hadn't found the finger-bone she wanted
Among the buttons poured out in her lap.
I verified the name next morning: Toffile.
The rural letter box said Toffile Lajway.

ROBERT FROST

KEEPSAKES

(Ballad of a Sweet Dream of Peace: 2)

Oh, what brings her out in the dark and night?
She has mislaid something, just what she can't say,
But something to do with the bureau, all right.
Then why, in God's name, does she polish so much, and not look
in a drawer right away?
Every night, in God's name, she does look there,
But finds only a Book of Common Prayer,

A ribbon-tied lock of gold hair,
A bundle of letters, some contraceptives, and an orris-root
sachet.
Well, what is the old fool hunting for?
Oh, nothing, oh, nothing that's in the top drawer,
For that's left by late owners who had their own grief to
withstand,
And she tries to squinch and frown
As she peers at the Prayer Book upside down,
And the contraceptives are something she can't understand,
And oh, how bitter the tears she sheds, with some stranger's old
letters in hand!

You're lying, you're lying, she can't shed a tear!
Not with eyeballs gone, and the tear ducts, too.
You are trapped in a vulgar error, I fear,
For asleep in the bottom drawer is a thing that may prove
instructive to you:
Just an old-fashioned doll with a china head,
And a cloth body naked and violated
By a hole through which sawdust once bled,
But drop now by drop, on a summer night, from her heart it is
treacle bleeds through.
In God's name, what!—Do I see her eyes move?
Of course, and she whispers, "I died for love,"
And your grandmother whines like a dog in the dark and
shade,
For she's hunting somebody to give
Her the life they had promised her she would live,
And I shudder to think what a stink and stir will be made
When some summer night she opens the drawer and finds that
poor self she'd mislaid.

ROBERT PENN WARREN

TWO

Stagnation

At least from the time when Eliot's "The Love Song of J. Alfred Prufrock" first appeared, Stagnation, the refusal or inability to heed the Call (the mermaids' singing) has been dwelt upon insistently in modern literature. It is natural that this should be so, because the prevailing attitude in writers of our day is one which shies away from the direct affirmation of values that one finds dramatized in Spenser, Milton, or Wordsworth and prefers to make its comment in ironic fashion by setting before the reader versions of the anti-Hero as exemplar of unrealized ideals and thwarted purpose. The protagonist of poetry, drama, and fiction in which the ironic mode predominates is likely to be an Everyman conspicuously unsuited for heroic enterprise: timid, irresolute, and self-deceived. He is a far cry from such stout champions as Heracles, Odysseus, or Aeneas, heroes whose modern counterparts—superman, the western sheriff, Tarzan—are, for the most part, subliterary. The irresolution of J. Alfred Prufrock or the frustration of Arthur Miller's salesman, Willie Loman, do not inspire the reader's emulation. Their portrayal does, however, generate a telling pathos, short of tragedy; and their equivalents in comedy—for instance, Thurber's henpecked Walter Mitty and Shulz's cartoon character, Charlie Brown—can make us laugh while at the same time calling forth our sympathy. Further than this, many characters in the so-called theater of the absurd, like some protagonists in modern poetry, are so nearly reduced to impotence as to evoke a baffled ridicule which verges on

contempt. Yet, if the achievements of the modern Everyman fall
woefully short of his aspirations, he nevertheless continues to aspire.
The Hero is with us still, although we perhaps are most familiar
with his shadow side or negative inversion.

Like all phenomena of permanent significance to mankind,
Stagnation of the spirit (known in older times as *accidie* or spiritual
dryness) lends itself readily to a rich variety of metaphoric expres-
sion. The flesh and bones of poems which deal with this affliction
of the spirit are likely to be derived from the tangible constricting
and debilitating properties of common ills: *e.g.*, from miserliness
("Callers"), imprisonment ("The Known World"), disease ("The
Uninfected"), and, above all, the abortive journey.

In Robert Watson's "Callers," we find an old woman, Miss
Burckhardt, resisting certain unwanted visitors with a fearful stub-
bornness which is a measure of her unwillingness truly to assess her
miser's heart. After ninety years of piling up bills, like refuse, under
her sink, she can only believe that the persons at her door plan to
rob her of her hoarded savings. Terrified of thieves and bill-
collectors, she has long ignored all signals from the world outside her
cell-like house—the ringing of the telephone and doorbell—and has
spent her time adding up the taxes which she owes, cursing those
who seem to "grasp and grasp" at her security. But the inevitable
intruders whose knock she has long imagined in every tap of the
tree at her window, in the sound of the wind and rain, even in the
dust settling, are not interested in her money. They have come, at
last, for *her*. Like Everyman, she cannot escape the final reckoning.
Though, by material criteria, she is rich, she is in spirit bankrupt; or,
to push the matter one step further, though she is physically alive,
she is in every other sense already dead—a truth which her im-
portunate visitors will no longer permit her to evade.

No immediate danger threatens the security of Brewster
Ghiselin's tiger in "The Known World." Yet he is perhaps even
closer to nonentity than the unfortunate Miss Burckhardt, because
he has managed to forget altogether that the world goes on outside
the bars of his cage, the "too-little place" in which he is imprisoned.
So far from desiring to escape from his confinement, he denies that
a "green city" exists outside of it or that there is such a thing as a
"snake-green jungle" to which he might return. His rage is blinded,
his claws wrapped by "things as they are." In his acquiescence, he
becomes not only pathetic but contemptible, the antihero in a tiger's
skin, self-defeated by timidity.

Still more deeply ironic is the complacency of E. L. Mayo's protagonist in "The Uninfected." Finding himself surrounded on every hand by persons palpably suffering from leprosy, he is seized, briefly, by the suspicion that he may himself be infected with the disease. But the "shop window mirror-glass" into which he looks shows him only what he wants to see: "Still no infection, not a single spot." In the end, he is taken away to a sanitorium—not one for lepers, to be sure, but, although he does not know it, one for the insane. There, in the oblivion of madness, he continues to think of himself as the only healthy person in an infected world, eating what he likes, sound as a bell.

The traveler in poems concerning Stagnancy may, like the speaker of Louis MacNeice's "Perdita," never get started on his trip at all, but merely meditate upon traveling companions who have long since disappeared, while his trunks molder in the attic, and the train that would carry him away to the "green country" where "the broom is gold" is always about to leave the station but never actually does. A variant upon the journey that never was, is one that is in progress but never arrives at its destination. Clifford Dyment's traveler in "The Snow" has long been slogging through a huge and trackless waste land, as though he were going somewhere, but he realizes in despair that

all the walking I had done
Was on a journey not begun.

Snow covers the ground, fills the air, and soon obliterates his shallow footsteps. He does not know where he has been or where he is going. He is on the wrong journey altogether. Yet he has no choice but to pursue it pointlessly into the future, just as he has done in the past.

The Everyman of Stagnation appears in all his regimented hopelessness in "The Line" by Daniel Hoffman, the central metaphor of which reminds one of Franz Kafka's unfathomable bureaucratic hell in *The Trial* and *The Castle*. Accustomed to waiting patiently for his turn in some unidentified ritual of routine, the protagonist whiles away his time in line by observing his companions while they variously react to an intolerable tedium with glum resignation, fidgeting, and attempts to strike up a lively conversation. When at last his turn comes, he finds, around the corner at the head of the line, only "An empty desk / A vacant chair." Then he is once more

at the tail of the "long serpentine / Assemblage," waiting, waiting
all over again in what is clearly part of an unending cycle. In lan-
guage appropriately suggestive of bureaucratic jargon, the victim of
this meaningless exercise says that "It was of first essentiality / To
wait on line." For him, the Call is only the bleak imperative of
routine, habit, conformity. The contemplation of his idiotic round
is enough to make one wish to shake the sleep-walker in the poem
and force the truth upon him, crying out, "You've gone through it
all before! It won't get you anywhere! Break out of line!" And
doubtless the poet, who, like all his tribe, is the sworn enemy of
Stagnation, intended that we should react in exactly that way.

CALLERS

   "May we visit you, Miss Burckhardt, my dear?
Come from behind the blinds you peer through.
Telephone and doorbell ring and ring,
You have spent your lifetime in not answering.
Now callers you should not ignore are here."

   "I will go on unanswering all each day.
Silence!   While I add infernal taxes up—
Federal, state, city grasp and grasp
What I have spent my lifetime saving.
Wolves at my door, callers, away, away!"

   "We have come for you, Miss Burckhardt, my dear,
Not money hidden as refuse, breeding,
You have spent ninety years concealing
Under your sink, bill upon bill upon bill.
Now callers you cannot ignore are here."

   "Will telephone, doorbell, voices never cease?
All night the beech tree knocks at my window,
Wind at door, rain at roof, dust at floor;
I can scarcely total numbers anymore.
When will you give, O Lord, this servant peace?"

"We must have you, Miss Burckhardt, my dear.
Take from your dresser that old brown sock,
Where you keep your house and strong box keys,
Limp on your cane, unbolt the triple lock.
A thief? Behold, I stand at the door and knock."

The knocking and ringing and calling at last
Shook up her head like a dynamite blast.
She limped to her dresser, to her sock for her keys.
She unbolted her door, but saw nothing there,
Not caller, not thief, not tree, dust, nor air.

ROBERT WATSON

GERONTION

>   *Thou hast nor youth nor age*
>   *But as it were an after dinner sleep*
>   *Dreaming of both.*

Here I am, an old man in a dry month,
Being read to by a boy, waiting for rain.
I was neither at the hot gates
Nor fought in the warm rain
Nor knee deep in the salt marsh, heaving a cutlass,
Bitten by flies, fought.
My house is a decayed house,
And the jew squats on the window sill, the owner,
Spawned in some estaminet of Antwerp,
Blistered in Brussels, patched and peeled in London.
The goat coughs at night in the field overhead;
Rocks, moss, stonecrop, iron, merds.
The woman keeps the kitchen, makes tea,
Sneezes at evening, poking the peevish gutter.
                                I an old man,
A dull head among windy spaces.

Signs are taken for wonders. "We would see a sign!"
The word within a word, unable to speak a word,

Swaddled with darkness. In the juvescence of the year
Came Christ the tiger

In depraved May, dogwood and chestnut, flowering judas,
To be eaten, to be divided, to be drunk
Among whispers; by Mr. Silvero
With caressing hands, at Limoges
Who walked all night in the next room;

By Hakagawa, bowing among the Titians;
By Madame de Tornquist, in the dark room
Shifting the candles; Fräulein von Kulp
Who turned in the hall, one hand on the door.
      Vacant shuttles
Weave the wind. I have no ghosts,
An old man in a draughty house
Under a windy knob.

After such knowledge, what forgiveness? Think now
History has many cunning passages, contrived corridors
And issues, deceives with whispering ambitions,
Guides us by vanities. Think now
She gives when our attention is distracted
And what she gives, gives with such supple confusions
That the giving famishes the craving. Gives too late
What's not believed in, or if still believed,
In memory only, reconsidered passion. Gives too soon
Into weak hands, what's thought can be dispensed with
Till the refusal propagates a fear. Think
Neither fear nor courage saves us. Unnatural vices
Are fathered by our heroism. Virtues
Are forced upon us by our impudent crimes.
These tears are shaken from the wrath-bearing tree.

The tiger springs in the new year. Us he devours. Think at
      last
We have not reached conclusion, when I
Stiffen in a rented house. Think at last
I have not made this show purposelessly
And it is not by any concitation

Of the backward devils.
I would meet you upon this honestly.
I that was near your heart was removed therefrom
To lose beauty in terror, terror in inquisition.
I have lost my passion: why should I need to keep it
Since what is kept must be adulterated?
I have lost my sight, smell, hearing, taste and touch:
How should I use them for your closer contact?

These with a thousand small deliberations
Protract the profit of their chilled delirium,
Excite the membrane, when the sense has cooled,
With pungent sauces, multiply variety
In a wilderness of mirrors. What will the spider do,
Suspend its operations, will the weevil
Delay? De Bailhache, Fresca, Mrs. Cammel, whirled
Beyond the circuit of the shuddering Bear
In fractured atoms. Gull against the wind, in the windy straits
Of Belle Isle, or running on the Horn,
White feathers in the snow, the Gulf claims,
And an old man driven by the Trades
To a sleepy corner.

Tenants of the house,
Thoughts of a dry brain in a dry season.

T. S. ELIOT

CUPIDON

"To love is to give," said the crooked old man.
    "To love is to be poor."
And he led me up his accordion stair,
    And closed his iron door.

"To love is to give." His words like wire
    Dragged the ocean floor.
"Throw ten of your blankets on the fire,
    Then throw ten thousand more."

His room was the prayer on the head of a pin.
     As clean as a diamond cut
Was the iron door which opened in
     And would not open out.

"To love is to give, to give, to give.
     Give more and more and more."
And the wind crept up his accordion stair,
     And under his iron door.

                              WILLIAM JAY SMITH

THE MAN WHO LOST HIS VISION

"What sight is that?" the rich astronomer cried,
And wiped again the cold expensive glass.
When unpredicted shapes appeared, he sighed,
And turned away his head. The shapes would pass.

And yet he wondered, were they really there,
Or just the workings of a tired mind
That fills the boredom of the empty air
With images that it alone can find?

He tried to isolate the world. Pursued
By shapes, he could not set himself apart.
"They steal into my inward eye," he rued,
"And cause an awful beating in my heart."

That night, while dreaming in his haunted bed,
The shapes stole off, and left the poor man dead.

                              ROBERT PACK

THE DEATH OF UNCLE DAN

Has anyone bothered his head about Uncle Dan
Today? Not Sonny. On the roof, he's sending

Messages, by wig-wag, to the scout
Across the way. Nor Mamma. She has flung
The bedroom window up and, shaking a mop,
Appears to be purging winter out. For a moment,
She communes with blue, and then with green—
The lawn, where Sister spends a penny's
Worth of thought on anyone, a man,
In the way of conversation, pleasant enough
To come and carry her off. The twins,
Who chattered daylight in, are at it still.

I ought to be sad about Uncle Dan. He hasn't
Taken a whiff all day of this delicious
Air. I can't remember his step on the floor,
Or even a tap on any or all of the four
Walls of the room he's bound to call his own—
A spot he seems to treasure, dim as it is,
That seems to be cut exactly to his measure.
On the table in the hall, his mail
Piles up, neglected. I wonder whether his ship,
Whatever its cargo was, should it appear
In port at last, just when he least
Expected it, could rouse his spirit yet.

Oh, Uncle Dan's at home, but not receiving;
Done with hatching plans to no avail,
With dying to make a living in a calling
Still unknown. No one drags him into
The conversation now. Cat's got his tongue.
Isn't a man entitled to be alone?
It's not an accident, after all, that he hasn't
A TV in his room, or even a phone
Or radio. In fact, he lacks a proper
Knob on the door. And what's to be done
Is now to be done with Uncle Dan, whose room
Is the only one in the house without a window.

JOHN ALEXANDER ALLEN

HENRY GRIFFITH

A shaft of dark in lightness,
Henry Griffith casts a crooked shadow;
And the sun can't tell him
From a crow caught on a rotting limb.

Like him, his buckled shack,
Rasping, nearly touches foreheads
With the fronting hill
That holds the highway's halting grind.

He tends a stoneless steel bone-yard,
And gaunt steps take him restless round
Air-eaten bodies
Where he finds the vital parts to sell.

Awed cadavers in the yellow of the sun
Stare after him with eyeless pits of chrome;
And in their cushioned laps hide snakes,
Biding, till the silver sliver of the night

Shall set them free
From bodies of weed-ravished ribs.
Henry Griffith too releases
Final gasps from poisoned sacks.

The night can't tell him
From the bringer of the long black box.
A shaft of dark in darkness,
Henry Griffith lies down, straight at last.

JANE GENTRY

ORIGINAL SIN: A SHORT STORY

Nodding, its great head rattling like a gourd,
And locks like seaweed strung on the stinking stone,
The nightmare stumbles past, and you have heard

It fumble your door before it whimpers and is gone:
It acts like the old hound that used to snuffle your door and
  moan.

You thought you had lost it when you left Omaha,
For it seemed connected then with your grandpa, who
Had a wen on his forehead and sat on the veranda
To finger the precious protuberance, as was his habit to do,
Which glinted in sun like rough garnet or the rich old brain
  bulging through.

But you met it in Harvard Yard as the historic steeple
Was confirming the midnight with its hideous racket,
And you wondered how it had come, for it stood so imbecile,
With empty hands, humble, and surely nothing in pocket:
Riding the rods, perhaps—or Grandpa's will paid the ticket.

You were almost kindly then, in your first homesickness,
As it tortured its stiff face to speak, but scarcely mewed.
Since then you have outlived all your homesickness,
But have met it in many another distempered latitude:
Oh, nothing is lost, ever lost! at last you understood.

It never came in the quantum glare of sun
To shame you before your friends, and had nothing to do
With your public experience or private reformation:
But it thought no bed too narrow—it stood with lips askew
And shook its great head sadly like the abstract Jew.

Never met you in the lyric arsenical meadows
When children call and your heart goes stone in the bosom—
At the orchard anguish never, nor ovoid horror,
Which is furred like a peach or avid like the delicious plum.
It takes no part in your classic prudence or fondled axiom.

Not there when you exclaimed: "Hope is betrayed by
Disastrous glory of sea-capes, sun-torment of whitecaps
—There must be a new innocence for us to be stayed by."
But there it stood, after all the timetables, all the maps,
In the crepuscular clutter of *always, always,* or *perhaps.*

You have moved often and rarely left an address,
And hear of the deaths of friends with a sly pleasure,
A sense of cleansing and hope which blooms from distress;
But it has not died, it comes, its hand childish, unsure,
Clutching the bribe of chocolate or a toy you used to treasure.

It tries the lock. You hear, but simply drowse:
There is nothing remarkable in that sound at the door.
Later you may hear it wander the dark house
Like a mother who rises at night to seek a childhood picture;
Or it goes to the backyard and stands like an old horse cold in
    the pasture.

ROBERT PENN WARREN

THE SNOW

In no way that I chose to go
Could I escape the falling snow.

I shut my eyes, wet with my fears:
The snow still whispered at my ears.

I stopped my ears in deaf disguise:
The snow still fell before my eyes.

Snow was my comrade, snow my fate,
In a country huge and desolate.

My footsteps made a shallow space,
And then the snow filled up the place,

And all the walking I had done
Was on a journey not begun.

I did not know the distance gone,
But resolutely travelled on

While silently on every hand
Fell the sorrow of the land,

And no way that I chose to go
Could lead me from the grief of snow.

CLIFFORD DYMENT

POLAR EXPLORATION

Our single purpose was to walk through snow
With faces swung to their prodigious North
Like compass needles. As clerks in whited banks
Leave bird-claw pen-prints columned on white paper,
On snow we added footprints.
Extensive whiteness drowned
All sense of space. We tramped through
Static, glaring days, Time's suspended blank.
That was in Spring and Autumn. Summer struck
Water over rocks, and half the world
Became a ship with a deep keel, the booming floes
And icebergs with their little birds:
Twittering Snow Bunting, Greenland Wheatear,
Red-throated Divers; imagine butterflies,
Sulphurous cloudy yellow; burnish of bees
That suck from saxifrage; crowberry,
Bilberry, cranberry, *Pyrola Uniflora.*
There followed winter in a frozen hut
Warm enough at the kernel, but dare to sleep
With head against the wall—ice gummed my hair!
Hate Culver's loud breathing, despise Freeman's
Fidget for washing: love only the dogs
That whine for scraps, and scratch. Notice
How they run better (on short journeys) with a bitch.
In that, different from us.
Return, return, you warn! We do. There is
Your city, with railways, money, words, words, words.
Meals, papers, exchanges, debates,
Cinema, wireless: then there is Marriage.
I cannot sleep. At night I watch
A clear voice speak with words, like drawing.
Its questions are white rifts:—Was

Ice, our rage transformed? The raw, the motionless
Skies, were these the Spirit's hunger?
The continual hypnotized march through snow,
The dropping nights of precious extinction, were these
Only the wide circuits of the will,
The frozen heart's evasions? If such thoughts seem
A kind of madness here, a coldness
Of snow like sheets in summer—is the North
Over there, a palpable, true madness,
A solid simplicity, absolute, without towns,
Only with bears and fish, a raging eye,
A new and singular sex?

                           STEPHEN SPENDER

MEDUSA

I had come to the house, in a cave of trees,
Facing a sheer sky.
Everything moved,—a bell hung ready to strike,
Sun and reflection wheeled by.

When the bare eyes were before me
And the hissing hair,
Held up at a window, seen through a door.
The stiff bald eyes, the serpents on the forehead
Formed in the air.

This is a dead scene forever now.
Nothing will ever stir.
The end will never brighten it more than this,
Nor the rain blur.

The water will always fall, and will not fall,
And the tipped bell make no sound.
The grass will always be growing for hay
Deep on the ground.

And I shall stand here like a shadow
Under the great balanced day,
My eyes on the yellow dust, that was lifting in the wind,
And does not drift away.

LOUISE BOGAN

NEARING AGAIN THE LEGENDARY ISLE

(*The Magnetic Mountain: 6*)

Nearing again the legendary isle
Where sirens sang and mariners were skinned,
We wonder now what was there to beguile
That such stout fellows left their bones behind.

Those chorus-girls are surely past their prime,
Voices grow shrill and paint is wearing thin,
Lips that sealed up the sense from gnawing time
Now beg the favour with a graveyard grin.

We have no flesh to spare and they can't bite,
Hunger and sweat have stripped us to the bone;
A skeleton crew we toil upon the tide
And mock the theme-song meant to lure us on:

No need to stop the ears, avert the eyes
From purple rhetoric of evening skies.

C. DAY LEWIS

NEITHER OUT FAR NOR IN DEEP

The people along the sand
All turn and look one way.
They turn their back on the land.
They look at the sea all day.

As long as it takes to pass
A ship keeps raising its hull;
The wetter ground like glass
Reflects a standing gull.

The land may vary more;
But wherever the truth may be—
The water comes ashore,
And the people look at the sea.

They cannot look out far.
They cannot look in deep.
But when was that ever a bar
To any watch they keep?

ROBERT FROST

THE END OF A JOURNEY

There at the last, his arms embracing her,
She found herself, faith wasted, valour lost,
Raped by a stranger in her sullen bed;
And he, for all the bloody passion it cost
To have heard the sirens sing and yet have fled,
Thought the night tedious, coughed and shook his head,
An old man sleeping with his housekeeper.

But with the dawn he rose and stepped outside.
A farm-cart by the doorway dripped and stank,
Piled with the victims of his mighty bow.
Each with her broken neck, each with a blank,
Small, strangled face, the dead girls in a row
Swung as the cold airs moved them to and fro,
Full-breasted, delicate-waisted, heavy-thighed.

Setting his jaw, he turned and clambered down
A goat-track to the beach; the tide was full.
He stood and brooded on the breaking wave
Revolving many memories in his skull:
Calypso singing in her haunted cave,

The bed of Circe, Hector in his grave
And Priam butchered in his burning town.

Grimly he watched his enemy the sea
Rage round the petty kingdom he called home;
But now no trident threatened from the spray.
He prayed but knew Athene would not come.
The gods at last had left him, and the day
Darkened about him. Then from far away
And long ago, he seemed once more to be

Roped to a mast and through the breakers' roar
Sweet voices mocked him on his reeling deck:
"Son of Laertes, what delusive song
Turned your swift keel and brought you to this wreck,
In age and disenchantment to prolong
Stale years and chew the cud of ancient wrong,
A castaway upon so cruel a shore?"

A. D. HOPE

POETRY OF DEPARTURES

Sometimes you hear, fifth-hand,
As epitaph:
He chucked up everything
And just cleared off,
And always the voice will sound
Certain you approve
This audacious, purifying,
Elemental move.

And they are right, I think.
We all hate home
And having to be there:
I detest my room,
Its specially-chosen junk,
The good books, the good bed,
And my life, in perfect order:
So to hear it said

He walked out on the whole crowd
Leaves me flushed and stirred,
Like *Then she undid her dress*
Or *Take that you bastard;*
Surely I can, if he did?
And that helps me stay
Sober and industrious.
But I'd go today,

Yes, swagger the nut-strewn roads,
Crouch in the fo'c'sle
Stubbly with goodness, if
It weren't so artificial,
Such a deliberate step backwards
To create an object:
Books; china; a life
Reprehensibly perfect.

PHILIP LARKIN

TANJONG MALIM: 1934

Rain on the roof, bamboo,
His hand, the glass, splintered
Fingernails and wrinkled suit,
Dirty white, his face, the suit,
And chuk, chuk, chuk, the wooden
Paddles of the turning fan.

Malays, empty faces, rubber pots,
The rows and rows of draining trees,

And now the rain, the heat, his face
Is dry, his eyes are blank, but not

Within

    a dancer, small child, girl,
Her hands are sinuous as her eyes,

Thin thighs, small feet, the ching,
And ching, ching, ching, musicians
Drunk with god and wine, it sways,
Her head, the hollow clong and ching,
Ching.

Mildewed piano, broken keys, old songs,
Moons, loves that last, broken hearts,

(Outside in the rain, sleek with rain,
Eyes slit toward the light, the sound,
The curve of his knife easy on his finger's
Tip, he crouches, watches, waits, waits.)

Pasteboard lovers, counterfeit love, and baby
Wait for me, for me, old tinkle, clatter
And the negro's hands, his teeth gone,
Sings with tight lips, old songs,

                            the clong,
And clatter, so small, in his hands so small,
A child,
                    our love,
A moon, Miami in the spring, Paree, Dubuque,

    she moved like silk, was dirty,
Small, ching, ching, no sobs, just silk,
The clong, clatter, cries, and ching.
His hand lies easy on the drink, he doesn't
Drink, his face is dirty white and gray,
And listens to the rain, the rap and tattle
Of the rain, no songs, just rain, and whispers
In the bar, (The dark is wet and waits.) his
Eyes are open, teeth yellow in his smile,
Eyes open, chuk, chuk and chuk, the rain,
The rain upon the bamboo shutters and the roof.

A hollow clong, cluk, ching and ching.

                        R. H. W. DILLARD

THE KNOWN WORLD

With tiger pace and swinging head,
With gentle tread and turning grace
The walking stripes, the walking stripes
Of the mind stride in their too-little place.

But what if it escaped and walked
    In the green city?
There is no city, said the tiger mind.

There is the cage, the absolute bar,
Things as they are, that bind my rage
And wrap my claws, said the turning jaws
And prisoner eyes in their too-little place.

But what if it burst its world and ran
    To the snake-green jungle?
There is no jungle, sighed the striped mind.

                              BREWSTER GHISELIN

THE UNINFECTED

I saw a man whose face was white as snow
Come slowly down the mall,
And he was followed by another one
Till there were seven in all.

Now this is very strange that lepers be
Allowed to walk abroad in broad daylight.
I shook myself, and quickly turned to call
A bluecoat, and as suddenly caught sight

Of one in blue ruling the thoroughfare
Who made me passage through that brawling sea
With one raised hand.   I spoke, and he inclined
To hear my word, the face of leprosy.

I turned and went straight on to search my own
Face in the next shop window mirror-glass—
Still no infection, not a single spot,
So I stood there and watched the lepers pass

Till four drove up to take me to a place
Where I live now, attended very well
By several strong male lepers dressed in white,
Eating what I like, sound as a bell.

E. L. MAYO

THE LINE

It was of first essentiality
To stand on line,
To take one's place
At the tail of the long serpentine
Assemblage among strangers
And see, behind one, strangers coming
To take their places at the tail
Of the serpentine assemblage
That slowly shrivelled toward its head
Around the corner.
Some stood in line with stoical
Glum resignation,
Some fidgeted, some wagged
In lively conversation;
Intimacies sprang up
But time would not be killed
And the line was long.
When my time came I turned
The corner we had inched up on.
There was no one behind me.
I turned again: No corner.
I stood, a stalk of flesh
Midway between the ringed horizons
An empty desk
A vacant chair.

It was of first essentiality
To wait on line,
To take one's place among the strangers
In serpentine assemblage
That shrinks toward its own head.

DANIEL HOFFMAN

PERDITA

The glamour of the end attic, the smell of old
Leather trunks—Perdita, where have you been
Hiding all these years?   Somewhere or other a green
Flag is waving under an iron vault
And a brass bell is the herald of green country
And the wind is in the wires and the broom is gold.

Perdita, what became of all the things
We said that we should do?   The cobwebs cover
The labels of Tyrol.   The time is over-
Due and in some metropolitan station
Among the clank of cans and the roistering files
Of steam the caterpillars wait for wings.

LOUIS MAC NEICE

THREE

Intimations

The day is oppressively hot. You are slumped nervelessly in a chair, your mind circling wearily around the great heap of tasks which demand your attention but for which you have neither appetite nor energy. You are bored, vaguely worried, and depressed. Then, suddenly, you are aware of a breath of cool air stirring about your arms and neck, pleasantly fanning your cheek. It is unlikely that you respond to this refreshing impulse by reciting, "Let us, then, be up and doing, / With a heart for any fate," but something does rouse within you: an impulse to get on with the job at hand, stray thoughts of someone you would like to see, an image of cool shadows under a tree, a sailboat driving gaily through the waves, the long prospect from a mountaintop. It is a moment suggestive of renewal, a wordless Intimation of new life. Without thinking about it, you have experienced the meaning of a traditional symbol for re-birth of the spirit. In the words of Jesus, given by St. John,

> *Marvel not that I said unto thee, Ye*
> *must be born again.*
>
> *The wind bloweth where it listeth,*
> *and thou hearest the sound thereof,*
> *but canst not tell whence it cometh,*
> *and whither it goeth; so is every one*
> *that is born of the Spirit.*

Mysteriously, unpredictably, the freshening wind, actual or symbolic, comes to stir the flagging spirit.

R. P. Blackmur's "Mirage" describes exactly such a moment of Intimation, remembered from the past but, like Wordsworth's "emotion recollected in tranquillity," capable of arousing the imagination in the present. There is no wind upon the great expanse of the sea,

> *The day had gathered to its heart of noon*
> *The sum of silence, heat, and stricken time.*

The speaker of the poem and his companions feel threatened by oblivion, "seeing nothing," and, punningly, must walk about to keep their hearts "from stopping / at nothing." Then from the horizon rises the green and golden mountain; and the surf which breaks against its base, the spray and spume that fly into the sky, are evidence that *there* a vigorous wind is blowing. We are familiar with that shining mountain. Like the wind, it is a part of the vocabulary of metaphor which every poem employs and which everyone, when his imagination and emotions are in good working order, finds as readily comprehensible as common speech. Its numerous analogues are mythic: Helicon, home of the Muses, and Olympus, home of the gods; biblical: Mt. Sinai, which Moses climbed in order to converse with the Lord, the "high mountain" on whose summit the transfiguration of Jesus came to pass; and epic: the Garden of Eden, high above the surrounding plain in *Paradise Lost* and atop the mountain of Purgatory in *The Divine Comedy*. The culminating vision of Wordsworth's *Prelude* occurs on a mountain-top, and Ernest Hemingway makes good metaphoric use of an actual African mountain in his short story, "The Snows of Kilimanjaro." We know what is meant when the speaker of "Mirage," even though he recognizes his vision as an illusion, tells us that "there I have been living ever since." *Levavi Oculos:* I have lifted up mine eyes unto the hills, from whence cometh my help.

It is, of course, not accidental that the mountain in Blackmur's poem lifts itself up out of the sea. Biologically, the sea is in fact the source from which all life originally sprang; mythologically, it is the birthplace of Aphrodite (Venus), goddess of love and of the fruits of love. Thus does the truth of myth anticipate the findings of science. Psychologically, the sea is a symbol for the unconscious mind, the region of the self into which one descends in sleep and from which, when we least expect it, mysterious Intimations arise, from time to time, to change our lives.

Both the course of human history, from its unrecorded beginnings to our own well-documented time, and the relationship of the unconscious to the conscious mind of man can be represented metaphorically as movement from the depths to the heights, from *down under* to *up on top*. Many of the poems in the section that follows employ variations of this basic metaphor: Old Triton rises from the deep in Wordsworth's "The World Is Too Much with Us," as does the fabulous creature glimpsed by the mariners in W. S. Merwin's "Sea Monster." Sylvia Plath, in "Lorelei," envisions the Sirens rising from "the nadir," "their limbs ponderous / With richness, hair heavier / Than sculpted marble"; and the speaker of James Dickey's "Orpheus before Hades" asks that the hillside before which he waits in every season "be opened in heartbreak" to return Eurydice to the upper world "From the place where she changes, each season, / *Her death.*"

Reading Barbara Howes' "City Afternoon" for a second or third time, one realizes that the poem gives us more than an ironic version of the secure garden on the mountaintop, here an apartment in which the inhabitants "sit invisible . . . / Behind glass." It also hints at the entire scope of geological time: from the days when dinosaurs roamed the earth, through successive epochs of archaic man, typified by layers of discarded artifacts, to the finest flower of civilization—the high-rise living-machine reaching into the smog-dimmed sky. But even in the cozy "cupboard" of his urban habitat, the city dweller is found out, in "a scalping / Silence," by an unwanted reminder of the past, of the down-under. He hears the growl of the beast far below, the whisper of the Iron Maiden, suggesting all that is buried and repressed by the conscious mind, all of the savagery and inhumanity which history records. The implication is, of course, that no one can be secure in the present until he has reckoned with his buried past and with his buried self. The poem is not so much a Call to adventure as a warning that adventure comes uncalled-for to one who leads, in the phrase of Socrates, an "unexamined life."

To Muriel Rukeyser, in "Crayon House," a child's drawing recalls the free movement and sustenance which typify a vigorous imaginative life, and with the recollection comes "A suddenness of doors, windows, bread and rolls." Unlike the outcast sun which "serves its lean meat of light" in Miss Howes' poem, the sun in the child's picture is "surrounded by his crown, continually given." But that cheerful vision of the world, "where grass sparkles and shines," is not, for the speaker of this poem, lost with the child who originally perceived it. Then, to be sure, "joy began"; but it has never ceased to be a possibility for one "seeking through the green world, wild and no longer wild, / always beginning again." What the child saw and captured in a crayon house is real. Paradoxically, art may be more real than what we think of commonly as actuality. The writing of a poem, the drawing of a picture are adventures; and one who contrives to see with the artist's eye of innocence has power to bring the dead to life. "Roads are in all I know," says the protagonist. With luck, one may travel all that open up before one, and never want for "steady giving and green decision."

WHEN I HEARD THE LEARN'D ASTRONOMER

When I heard the learn'd astronomer,
When the proofs, the figures, were ranged in columns before
    me,
When I was shown the charts and diagrams, to add, divide, and
    measure them,
When I sitting heard the astronomer where he lectured with
    much applause in the lecture-room,
How soon unaccountable I became tired and sick,
Till rising and gliding out I wander'd off by myself,
In the mystical moist night-air, and from time to time,
Look'd up in perfect silence at the stars.

WALT WHITMAN

THE SEA AND THE SKYLARK

On ear and ear two noises too old to end
    Trench—right, the tide that ramps against the shore;

With a flood or a fall, low lull-off or all roar,
Frequenting there while moon shall wear and wend.

Left hand, off land, I hear the lark ascend,
   His rash-fresh re-winded new-skeinèd score
   In crisps of curl off wild winch whirl, and pour
And pelt music, till none's to spill nor spend.

How these two shame this shallow and frail town!
   How ring right out our sordid turbid time,
Being pure! We, life's pride and cared-for crown,

   Have lost that cheer and charm of earth's past prime:
Our make and making break, are breaking, down
   To man's last dust, drain fast towards man's first slime.

                    GERARD MANLEY HOPKINS

THE SOUND OF TREES

I wonder about the trees.
Why do we wish to bear
Forever the noise of these
More than another noise
So close to our dwelling place?
We suffer them by the day
Till we lose all measure of pace,
And fixity in our joys,
And acquire a listening air.
They are that that talks of going
But never gets away;
And that talks no less for knowing,
As it grows wiser and older,
That now it means to stay.
My feet tug at the floor
And my head sways to my shoulder
Sometimes when I watch trees sway,
From the window or the door.
I shall set forth for somewhere,

I shall make the reckless choice
Some day when they are in voice
And tossing so as to scare
The white clouds over them on.
I shall have less to say,
But I shall be gone.

ROBERT FROST

LYING AWAKE

This moth caught in the room tonight
Squirmed up, sniper-style, between
The rusty edges of the screen;
Then, long as the room stayed light,

Lay here, content, in some cornerhole.
Now that we've settled into bed
Though, he can't sleep.   Overhead,
He hurls himself at the blank wall.

Each night hordes of these flutterers haunt
And climb my study windowpane;
Fired by reflection, their insane
Eyes gleam; they know what they want.

How do the petulant things survive?
Out in the fields they have a place
And proper work, furthering the race;
Why this blind fanatical drive

Indoors?   Why rush at every spark,
Cigar, headlamp or railway warning
To knock off your wings and starve by morning?
And what could a moth fear in the dark

Compared with what you meet inside?
Still, he rams the fluorescent face
Of the clock, thinks that's another place
Of light and families, where he'll hide.

We'd ought to trap him in a jar,
Or come, like the white-coats, with a net
And turn him out toward living. Yet
We don't; we take things as they are.

W. D. SNODGRASS

THE RING

I will try to be exact.
I was lying down last night with my eyes shut,
but this was not a dream. I was awake in my room.
A dog turned; the truck tires sounded
like an intense wind off the Interstate.
Then they were silent.

I cannot say by what light I saw it,
both saw it and was in it, like all our sight
and all we claim to create:
something of me is in this word, and yet
the word is separate.

My body, lying down, was surrounded
by what I will call a ring, but without extent.
It was not made of any element
that we know, not light, not air,
not water; but earthiness was entirely absent
from it. I will call it power,
for it lived, but not with our atomic life.
It had presence, but no shape. It did not speak.
To say so would be a projection of our categories
(and I have heard, in other circumstance, that other voice
with my skin ear, my echo ear, that needed then
to be Job's child, commanded to rejoice
when all excuse for love was lost).

No. It was as if the spirit breathed,
without a lung, its peace; or the forked tongue
followed its other way, not that of speech,
but gesture. There is language in a stone,

as every poet knows; as every lover
spells, in his ecstasy, illiterate bone.

It promised nothing, not being made of words
or of blood, that can invent. It did not imply
our only heart's desire: you have been sent.

It was power, power that stood by
for all our needs, and seemed to say
(for I must phrase it): here am I. Take me.

I have done nothing all day but stare
at the dishes, and read Wordsworth
on hiding-places, him who knew so well
what we see clear, but clumsily half-tell.

I walked by the stream. The hay was loud
with bugs escaping; they know
what danger is. I too
feared once the many-bladed mower.
Once, but not now.

                              JULIA RANDALL

A VISITATION

Now why would a visitation from the Isles
Of the Blessèd come to Swarthmore,
Pa. 19081, a borough zoned
For single-family occupancy? No
Rocks of Renunciation on our
Assessors' rolls. Somewhere,
A consecrated shore
Ringed by dolmens where the wind speaks.
I listen to the hunger of the owl
Enclose the chipmunk in the quavering night,
I hear the plantain stretch its leaves to smother
Grass-shoots reaching toward the light.
The thick obituary of a lost day

Lies still on our writhing lawn.
And now the sky, black widow, pales
At the arrival of her new lover.
Between the thighs of trees old graves of sorrows
Open, and a fresh wind stirs.

DANIEL HOFFMAN

MIRAGE

(*Sea Island Miscellany: IX*)

The wind was in another country, and
the day had gathered to its heart of noon
the sum of silence, heat, and stricken time.
Not a ripple spread. The sea mirrored
perfectly all the nothing in the sky.
We had to walk about to keep our eyes
from seeing nothing, and our hearts from stopping
at nothing. Then most suddenly we saw
horizon on horizon lifting up
out of the sea's edge a shining mountain
sun-yellow and sea-green; against it surf
flung spray and spume into the miles of sky.
Somebody said mirage, and it was gone,
but there I have been living ever since.

R. P. BLACKMUR

ON THE LEAN DIVIDER

Not a child, nor a woman either,
Caught with the day on the edge of noon,
Amphibian of the pond and sun,
She takes her ease in sand, by water;
Keys her breath to the sibilant stir
That weaves in the grass along the shore,
Lifts, in passing, a strand of her hair,
And ravels a path to who knows where.

No further visitant, no sound
Disturbs that drowsiness, no ripple
Flaws the unwrinkled face of the pond;
But the mottled cove extends a supple
Hand to the hills, and there, dark-pined,
Draws down a cottage by a weedy stair
And touches a tentative finger-end
To a boat half floating, half on the sand.

JOHN ALEXANDER ALLEN

CRAYON HOUSE

Two or three lines across;   the black ones, down,
into the ground where grass sparkles and shines;
but the foundation is the green and the shine.
Windows are drawn in.   Overhead the sun
surrounded by his crown, continually given.
It is a real place, door, floor, and windows.

I float past it.   I look in at the little children.
I climb up the straight and planted path, alone.
In the city today grown, walking on stone,
a suddenness of doors, windows, bread and rolls.

Roads are in all I know :   weapon and refugee,
color of thunder calling   Leave this room,
Get out of this house.   Even then, joy began,
went seeking through the green world, wild and no longer wild,
always beginning again.   Steady giving and green decision,
and the beginning was real.   The drawing of a child.

MURIEL RUKEYSER

IN THE MUSEUM

Like that, I put the next thing in your hand—
this piece of rock the farthest climbers found,
or this, a broken urn volcano-finished.

Later you'll walk out and say, "Where's home?"
There will be something lacking in each room,
a part you held and casually laid down.

You never can get back, but there'll be other
talismans. You have learned to falter
in this good way: stand still, walk on, remember—

Let one by one things come alive like fish
and swim away into their future waves.

WILLIAM STAFFORD

THE WORLD IS TOO MUCH WITH US

The world is too much with us; late and soon,
Getting and spending, we lay waste our powers:
Little we see in Nature that is ours;
We have given our hearts away, a sordid boon!
This Sea that bares her bosom to the moon;
The winds that will be howling at all hours,
And are up-gathered now like sleeping flowers;
For this, for everything, we are out of tune;
It moves us not.—Great God! I'd rather be
A Pagan suckled in a creed outworn;
So might I, standing on this pleasant lea,
Have glimpses that would make me less forlorn;
Have sight of Proteus rising from the sea;
Or hear old Triton blow his wreathèd horn.

WILLIAM WORDSWORTH

FOR ONCE, THEN, SOMETHING

Others taunt me with having knelt at well-curbs
Always wrong to the light, so never seeing
Deeper down in the well than where the water
Gives me back in a shining surface picture

Me myself in the summer heaven, godlike,
Looking out of a wreath of fern and cloud puffs.
Once, when trying with chin against a well-curb,
I discerned, as I thought, beyond the picture,
Through the picture, a something white, uncertain,
Something more of the depths—and then I lost it.
Water came to rebuke the too clear water.
One drop fell from a fern, and lo, a ripple
Shook whatever it was lay there at bottom,
Blurred it, blotted it out. What was that whiteness?
Truth? A pebble of quartz? For once, then, something.

ROBERT FROST

SEA MONSTER

We were not even out of sight of land
That afternoon when we saw it. A good day
With the sea making but still light. Not
One of us would have hesitated
As to where we were, or mistaken the brown
Cliffs or the town on top. Just after
The noon watch, it was, that it slid
Into our sight: a darkness under
The surface, between us and the land, twisting
Like a snake swimming or a line of birds
In the air. Then breached, big as a church,
Right there beside us. None of us will
Agree what it was we saw then, but
None of us showed the least surprise, and truly
I felt none. I would say its eyes
Were like the sea when the thick snow falls
Onto it with a whisper and slides heaving
On the gray water. And looked at us
For a long time, as though it knew us, but
Did not harm us that time, sinking at last,
The waters closing like a rush of breath. Then
We were all ashamed at what we had seen,
Said it was only a sea-trick or
A dream we had all had together. As it

May have been, for since then we have forgotten
How it was that, on sea or land, once
We proved to ourselves that we were awake.

W. S. MERWIN

DREAM

One day in a dream as I lay at the edge of a cliff,
The black water rose, and the children bobbed in the street.
Death with her bonfires signaled the planes to land
Where glass-beaked birds had pecked at my bound feet.

The water's bare hands reached round the base of the cliff,
And my heart cried, "Hope!" and my brain, "There is nothing
   unknown."
I looked at my charts, and my kingdoms lay buried in sand,
My desiccate body picked clean as a bird's breastbone.

The ships for the west weighed anchor; I watched them depart.
And on what impossible port were their prows then set,
That they moved with a grace defying the mind and the heart,
With tackle of cloud, with decks encumbered and wet?

The air was like chalk; I was nothing. I thought I had
Reached the end of my dream; and I might have if
The waves had not risen and roared, the winds gone mad—
And when I awoke I lay at the edge of a cliff.

WILLIAM JAY SMITH

CITY AFTERNOON

Far, far down
The earth rumbles in sleep;
Up through its iron grille,
The subway, black as a chimney-
Sweep, growls. An escalator rides
On dinosaur spines
Toward day. And on beyond,

Old bones, bottles,
A dismantled piano, sets
Of Mrs. Humphrey Ward all whirl
In the new disposal-unit; above
Its din, apartments are tenanted
Tight as hen-houses, people roosting
In every cupboard.   Eighty storeys
Up, pigeons nest on the noise
Or strut above it; higher,
The outcast sun serves its lean meat
Of light.

The whinnying
Of Venetian blinds has ceased: we sit
Invisible in this room,
Behind glass.   In a lull,
A chance abatement of sound, a scalping
Silence, far
Down we hear the Iron
Maiden whisper,
Closing upon her spikes.

                              BARBARA HOWES

LORELEI

It is no night to drown in:
A full moon, river lapsing
Back beneath bland mirror-sheen,

The blue water-mists dropping
Scrim after like fishnets
Though fishermen are sleeping,

The massive castle turrets
Doubling themselves in a glass
All stillness.   Yet these shapes float

Up toward me, troubling the face
Of quiet.   From the nadir
They rise, their limbs ponderous

With richness, hair heavier
Than sculpted marble. They sing
Of a world more full and clear

Than can be. Sisters, your song
Bears a burden too weighty
For the whorled ear's listening

Here, in a well-steered country,
Under a balanced ruler.
Deranging by harmony

Beyond the mundane order,
Your voices lay siege. You lodge
On the pitched reefs of nightmare,

Promising sure harborage;
By day, descant from borders
Of hebetude, from the ledge

Also of high windows. Worse
Even than your maddening
Song, your silence. · At the source

Of your ice-hearted calling—
Drunkenness of the great depths.
O river, I see drifting

Deep in your flux of silver
Those great goddesses of peace.
Stone, stone, ferry me down there.

SYLVIA PLATH

LA FIGLIA CHE PIANGE

   O quam te memorem virgo . . .

Stand on the highest pavement of the stair—
Lean on a garden urn—
Weave, weave the sunlight in your hair—

Clasp your flowers to you with a pained surprise—
Flying them to the ground and turn
With a fugitive resentment in your eyes:
But weave, weave the sunlight in your hair.

So I would have had him leave,
So I would have had her stand and grieve,
So he would have left
As the soul leaves the body torn and bruised,
As the mind deserts the body it has used.
I should find
Some way incomparably light and deft,
Some way we both should understand,
Simple and faithless as a smile and shake of the hand.

She turned away, but with the autumn weather
Compelled my imagination many days,
Many days and many hours:
Her hair over her arms and her arms full of flowers.
And I wonder how they should have been together!
I should have lost a gesture and a pose.
Sometimes these cogitations still amaze
The troubled midnight and the noon's repose.

T. S. ELIOT

THE VOICE

Woman much missed, how you call to me, call to me,
Saying that now you are not as you were
When you had changed from the one who was all to me,
But as at first, when our day was fair.

Can it be you that I hear?   Let me view you, then,
Standing as when I drew near to the town
Where you would wait for me: yes, as I knew you then,
Even to the original air-blue gown!

Or is it only the breeze, in its listlessness
Traveling across the wet mead to me here,
You being ever dissolved to wan wistlessness,
Heard no more again far or near?

    This I; faltering forward,
    Leaves around me falling,
Wind oozing thin through the thorn from norward,
    And the woman calling.

THOMAS HARDY

IN PRAISE OF HER

We shall be led to praise her, hard by the hand,
If we don't move before.
She shall grow restless in her changes
If we stand
Sun-struck and stable as we were and are.
She shall walk with her sickle through trees
And tall cities.
Full, she shall push far inland
The soft shore,
To your window,
To your door.
She shall come withered with her white demand.
Worn and shrivelled, she is quicker to rage
Than in her slender or rounded age.
We shall be hard led to praise, if we don't move before.
The river rises, and all the steeples fall.
Father and even his mortal son
Crack from their own abstraction.

JON SWAN

ORPHEUS BEFORE HADES

The leaf down from the branch,
Swirling, unfastened, falls;

Halfway from there to the ground
Is hypnotized, and stays.
No leaf is as still as that.
The earth-colored forest sways
Whose leaf is the center of waiting.

A great gray cloud lets fall
Its leaves, like the eyelids of fossils,
To a great stone skin on the ground.
I stand in the frozen field
In tow-sacks and burlap arrayed.
My breath disappears overhead
And white is the center of waiting.

The Spring comes out of the ground.
A wood shades into the air.
Each bough is as light as a fern;
All of life comes in on a breath.
My eyes turn green with the silence
Of the thing that shall move from the hillside
Where love is the center of waiting.

My tongue is of cloth, and I sing
As she would be singing, like water,
In a land where the cricket is flaking,
Yet chirrs, on the copper grassblade.
The sunlight is thinking of woman,
And black is the world, in its body,
When flesh is the center of waiting.

God add one string to my lyre
That the snow-flake and leaf-bud shall mingle
As the sun within moonlight is shining:
That the hillside be opened in heartbreak
And the woman walk down, and be risen
From the place where she changes, each season,
Her death, at the center of waiting.

JAMES DICKEY

III

THE JOURNEY

All poems, said Robert Frost, possess duplicity, a doubleness which is in their very nature. For the language of poetry is metaphor, and the poet's use of this language endows him, like the prophets of old, with the gift of tongues. Frost's own poem, "Stopping by Woods on a Snowy Evening," is a distinguished instance of duplicity. Going home at dusk, a man pauses for a moment to watch the woods fill up with snow. He is deeply attracted by their repose: they are "lovely, dark and deep." But he cannot afford to dawdle, he has "promises to keep" and, rousing himself, gets on with his journey. Can this pellucid poem, so coherent and comprehensible in everyday terms, be metaphoric? Indeed, it can be—and it is. The incident that it recounts suggests, without stating, the juxtaposition in everyone's life of the routine and familiar and the mysterious and inscrutable. In one sense, the speaker's commonplace journey has merely been interrupted by a brief interlude of daydreaming: the important matter is that he has miles to go before bedtime. But, in another sense, it is the commonplace journey that is the interruption, the illusion, that will lead at last, by however circuitous a route, to the reality of the dark woods—timeless and inescapable.

In dreams and daydreams and in moments of crisis, the journey into the unknown, the quest, cuts across one's ordinary progress through the expanse of time that leads from infancy to old age. It is these exceptional journeys, swift and singular as a moment's insight or as prolonged and various with incident as a ten-years' odyssey, which are of peculiar interest to the poet. The crossing of the threshold, the first step on the hero's itinerary, is a familiar motif in fiction as well as poetry. It occurs in *Heart of Darkness* when Marlow leaves the advanced trading post behind him and heads up the Congo to the remote interior and the savage world of Kurtz; in *Huckleberry Finn* when Huck escapes from his guardian and launches forth upon the Mississippi; in *Moby Dick* when Ishmael, giving up his vocation as a schoolteacher, signs on as a member of the Pequod's crew. In each instance, the hero's setting forth is recounted in a fashion so convincingly realistic that we may fail, at first, to notice its duplicity. But the shadow of Prometheus soon appears behind the figure of mad Ahab; the white whale evolves from an elusive albino mammal into a devil and a god. Poetry is, in a sense, a less deceptive form than fiction, for its metaphoric nature is, more often than not, impossible to miss. No one mistakes *The Rime of the Ancient Mariner* for an account of an actual journey, although, to be sure, it begins matter-of-factly enough. The Mariner, heading for an unspecified destination, watches the familiar shore recede behind his ship: in turn, the church, the hill, and the lighthouse drop out of sight beneath the horizon. Then, for a time, the direction and progress of the vessel can be determined by observation of the sun. But a sudden violent storm strikes the ship as it reaches the equator, and when we arrive with the swiftness of a dream in the remote and terrifying land of the fog and mist, we know that we are in the world of metaphor.

The Road of Trials, which lies beyond the threshold of the symbolic journey, differs essentially from that of the real-life adventurer: Admiral Byrd or Sir Edmund Hilary. Such doughty explorers rely for their success upon their wits and experience, their specially designed equipment, their physical prowess. And we, whose travels are less spectacular, are also equipped for the exigencies of the road. To serve us, we have common sense, an accepted code of morality, the advice of lawyer, doctor, plumber. We look to parents, king or president, the army, and the police to protect us. All civilization exists to serve us in our need. But it can do little to assist us when we are a prey to isolation, fear, or violent impulse. In such crises, we do not act but are acted upon. We discover that we harbor within ourselves beasts and angels, strangers malevolent and benign, and we realize that these ambivalent creatures are more powerful by far than either our reason or our will.

When his usual resources fail, the individual, either in life or in literature, becomes the agent of forces beyond his control. Consider again the history of the Ancient Mariner. In the land of the fog and mist, his vessel is about to be crushed between towering cliffs of ice, ice which roars and howls like a titanic beast. He is entirely helpless. But now, as though by magic, appears the bird of good omen, the albatross. It is hospitably received and, as though in gratitude, provides a favorable wind that saves the ship from destruction. Then, just as mysteriously, the Mariner is seized by an impulse to murder and betray: with his crossbow he kills the gracious bird, his benefactor. There is no reason for his vicious act; it is as much beyond his control, in a diabolical way, as the kindly agency of the albatross was in a heavenly one. But the Mariner has nevertheless determined his fate. He must suffer an excruciating isolation in a silent sea, divorced from man, from nature, and from God.

The events which befall the traveler on the Road of Trials are as incalculable as divinity or as the unknown self. He seems to be a pawn in a game whose rules he does not know, and only his suffering is his own. The vessel of the Mariner is becalmed in the vast sea. The sun burns down upon him cruelly. His shipmates, dying, curse him with their eyes. The sea itself seems to rot, while loathesome creatures crawl upon its decaying surface. The Mariner is the captive of Life-in-Death, deprived of all that holds promise of new life: wind, rain, and wholesome growing things. But when he has endured a seeming eternity of this torment, the nature of things has another surprise in store for him. Suddenly, incredibly, he is visited by grace, a welling up of love; and the universe which had imprisoned and tortured him now offers signs that promise his re-birth—wind, rain, and the pleasant sounds of spring. The redemptive process has begun.

The penance of the Mariner, like that of Cain and Ahasuerus, is never final and complete. At intervals, he must relive his experience by recounting it to a listener whom he transfixes with his hypnotic gaze. In this role, the Mariner is, like the poet, custodian and purveyor of the mythic journey of mankind. The details of this journey he may recount, in any one of a thousand forms, to one wedding guest in three. But the wedding guests who avoid his glittering eye and go their way to the festivities are not immune from the Quest, nor are the bride and groom. It is, of course, not accidental that the recital of the Mariner's tale is set in the context of a wedding. Ritual, like myth, and poetry in the mythic tradition, signalizes the passage from one stage of life to another. The bride and groom stand on the threshold, ready to put childhood behind them and embrace adult responsibility. In so doing, they affirm the sanctity of the domestic bond which assures the security and continuity of civilization. The price they pay is their surrender of individual sovereignty; the boon they gain is the formation of a more perfect self, compounded of male and female, thou and I. Further, their wedding is analogous to the mystic union of Christ and the Church and suggests, in symbolic terms, the reconciliation of opposites—the human and the divine, the spirit and the flesh— those clashing rocks which, like the Mariner's cliffs of ice, surround mankind and threaten to destroy him. In marriage, bride and groom combine their "mortal forces" to "slay mortality." And, at the same time they set the seal upon their own destruction; for the production of offspring is the older generation's acknowledgement, both actual and symbolic, of its capitulation to those who will, in due season, supersede them. Bride and groom are Everyman and Everywoman protected, for the moment, from the Road of Trials, the agony of the silent sea. As the Mariner and the poet know, they are simultaneously more and less than they believe themselves to be. Unconsciously, they tread a path over the abyss, and at any moment their eyes may be opened to their peril and their helplessness. But they are agents of a force which transcends and dignifies the merely mortal; through them, in terrible and wondrous wise, flows the indestructible energy which links the temporal world with the immortal source.

ONE

The Setting Forth

The Heroes of myth and poetry are commonly blessed or af-
flicted with wanderlust, the heady urge to be on the move which
Walt Whitman so powerfully evoked in "The Song of the Open
Road." To be sure, the conception of sedentary contentment as a
way of life, and of humility as a guiding virtue, have had their
advocates in poetry, from Horace onward. Shakespeare's Henry
VI, seated upon a molehill while Queen Margaret leads his troops
into battle, reflects that

> *the shepherd's homely curds,*
> *His cold thin drink out of his leather bottle,*
> *His wonted sleep under a fresh tree's shade,*
> *All which secure and sweetly he enjoys,*
> *Is far beyond a prince's delicates . . .*

(*King Henry the Sixth:* II.v.47–51)

But Henry is a dismal failure as a king. The pastoral mood may
form an interlude in the Hero's career, but its prolongation would
be enervating, even ridiculous. The enjoyment of capital gains, in
a visionary Eden which contains no serpent adversary, too easily
becomes a fool's paradise, a slothful lotos-land, the death-like trance
of Sleeping Beauty. Myth and mythopoeic poetry cannot be ac-
cused of serving as opiates to the reader; and poets who would have

us believe, with Pope, that everything that is, is right, are not, finally, persuasive.

Despite, or perhaps because of, the Victorian era's reputation for complacent conservatism, Tennyson and Browning were consistent foes of the Establishment. Tennyson's "Ulysses," in glorifying the restless aspiration of the Hero, reaches us, as we may presume it reached his contemporaries, even in the comfortable familiarity of our peculiar ruts. The Ulysses who speaks in the poem has finally achieved, after twenty years of arduous adventuring, reunion with his faithful wife, Penelope, and peaceful sovereignty over the peoples of his native Ithaca. Why should he be praised for wishing, as he does, to abandon wife and subjects? One can only say, why should he not? Like a good father, Ulysses has taught the art of government to his son, Telemachus, whose "slow prudence" can be relied upon. He has done his duty and now yields, as a father not only may but must, to the younger generation. But for Ulysses the Quest is never-ending. Despite the traditional valediction of the fairy tale, no Hero ever lives happily ever after. For Ulysses, his aged wife and his subjects "That hoard, and sleep, and feed" have become a prison, not a safe retreat. Instinctively, he turns in revulsion from the miserliness of spirit which would persuade him, "For some three suns," to "store and hoard" himself, when inwardly he is "yearning in desire"

> *To follow knowledge like a sinking star*
> *Beyond the utmost bound of human thought.*

We are reminded of Carl Sandburg's sergeant at Belleau Woods, who called to his men, "Come on, you . . . Do you want to live forever?"

Each of us, like Ulysses, is not one person but two. In psychological terms, we live for the most part with our everyday identity, what Carl Jung calls the *persona*, which is the subject of our conscious thought, the character that we present to society; but often we are aware that this persona is only a small part of our total being. Finding ourselves by night involuntarily threading the labyrinths of dreams and often behaving by the light of day in unaccountable ways, we realize that the unconscious mind exists and is a territory largely unexplored. At certain moments in their lives, persons behave as though they were possessed. Shakespeare's Macbeth, a loyal and honorable henchman of the good King Duncan, prompted by the Witches and his Lady, murders the king and steals the throne; and the worldly Gloucester, in *King Lear*, whose rule has been expediency, finds himself sacrificing both his eyes in protest at the savage persecution of the aged Lear.

He who would come to terms with his unknown self must crash the barrier at the frontier, explore the depths of the sea, rise up and walk when the rock rolls from his tomb. In the nature of things, he will find that he is not prepared for what is to come; but if one waits for that, the Journey never begins. The young couple in A. D. Hope's "Crossing the Frontier" are face to face with a crucial question: Will they become captives of the elders who have shaped their lives, or boldly, ruthlessly cut off their outworn ties and set forth truly on their own? Finding his way blocked at the frontier by parent, priest, bank manager, and even faithful Fido, the bridegroom is about to capitulate: "We must turn back"; but the Lady is more courageous, telling her wavering mate, "Get out! / Change seats! Be quick!"; and, to the strains of "the wedding march from *Lohengrin*," she drives the car through all such barriers as will not rise to let them pass, and they are off,

> *with Dad's moustache*
> *Beside her twitching still round waxen lips*
> *And Mother's tears still streaming down the glass.*

So far so good, but this, of course, is only the beginning. Crossing the threshold sets in motion an irreversible change, and on the farther side of it, for better or for worse, one sees things differently. The title figure in "The Diver" (E. L. Mayo), plunging into alien depths, perhaps believes that his mission is routine. He will seek out treasure which "May yet be lifted up by creaking crane, / Splashing out of the green"; but the essence of the experience is his brush with "inhuman life," with "what lies under," and this can be communicated by "no human gesture and no word." The Florida frogmen who are the "heroes of the common mind" in Howard Nemerov's "Limits," if they are indeed to "Find New World," as the headline in the *Times* announces, will not do so with "the dividing eye" of ordinary humankind. Nemerov imagines these apostles of light, "Air gone, and battery burned out," being drawn, like the frog prince of the fairy tale, toward a metamorphosis undreamed-of by their "science." The Hero who sets forth with missionary zeal, equipped with song, the power to heal, "seed for new land" (Julia Randall, "Journey") may be excused for thinking his provisions adequate; but, before he returns, experience will "grow / Nerves in the traveller / Where no nerves were." Rightly understood, the questing hero's "nightwork" is no task for children; it is not departure only but transfiguration, violent as murder and miraculous as rising from the dead.

The note of violence is appropriate to the sudden break with accustomed things which the Setting Forth entails. According to James Seay, one who grabbles in Yokna Bottom, not for the surfacing fish and eels but for "a cleaner meat,"

> *Must cram his arm and hand beneath the scum*
> *And go by touch where eye cannot reach . . .*
> *. . . . .*
> *Grab up what wraps itself cold-blooded*
> *Around flesh or flails the water to froth . . .*

He must be prepared to feel the jaws of the loggerhead turtle clamp down on his hand or the fangs of the cottonmouth "burn like heated needles." To grabble in Yokna Bottom, one needs the courage and the recklessness that spring only from sharp hunger. One's attitude, finally, can only be "to hell with it. If we burn, we burn" (William Dickey, "Exploration over the Rim"). By the time "the darkness sur- / rounds us," and we set out like a rocket in our "goddamn big car" (Robert Creeley, "I Know a Man"), it may or may not be of service if a friend yells after us a bit of normally sound advice: "for / christ's sake, look / out where yr going."

The Hero, being a man with an urgent mission, generally may be excused if he neglects some of the rules that govern conventional behavior and polite society. The biblical Jacob wins our admiration by the unscrupulous tactics which he employs to receive his father Isaac's blessing, seize the birthright that belonged, if seniority were observed, to Esau; trick Laban out of a quantity of spotted and ring-straked sheep; then, in a wrestling match with an angel of the Lord, win reconciliation with the offended Esau. A narrow line divides the scoundrel and the man of destiny. In *The Legend of Good Women*, Chaucer collects examples of the Hero's betrayal of ladies whose only fault was their ingenuous willingness to give their love.

The unhappy Ariadne, standing on the shore of Naxos, vainly waves a handkerchief after the departing vessel of Theseus. Virgil's Aeneas is obliged, by Jupiter, to abandon the gracious Dido who has befriended him; were his Quest not to continue to the end, a mighty empire would remain unborn. No one can predict the destiny of the Hero in Peter Levi's "The Fox-Coloured Pheasant Enjoyed His Peace," but we know that he wins an exhausting contest with an adversary who stands between himself and the ocean, where his Quest is to begin. When the sky is "crimson and bright" with dawn, he says,

> *I ran past as quick as I could*
> *and the wet stones rang loudly*
> *along the wharf where the ships stood*
> *and the sea lifting proudly.*

The Hero has proved equal to the challange at the threshold, and his destination awaits him somewhere in the perilous and infinitely promising reaches of the sea.

DAREST THOU NOW O SOUL

Darest thou now O soul,
Walk out with me toward the unknown region,
Where neither ground is for the feet nor any path to follow?

No map there, nor guide,
Nor voice sounding, nor touch of human hand,
Nor face with blooming flesh, nor lips, nor eyes, are in that
    land.

I know it not O soul,
Nor dost thou, all is a blank before us,
All waits undream'd of in that region, that inaccessible land.

Till when the ties loosen,
All but the ties eternal, Time and Space,
Nor darkness, gravitation, sense, nor any bounds bounding us.

Then we burst forth, we float,
In Time and Space O soul, prepared for them,
Equal, equipt at last, (O joy! O fruit of all!) them to fulfill O
  soul.

WALT WHITMAN

EXPLORATION OVER THE RIM

Beyond that sandbar is the river's turning.
There a new country opens up to sight,
Safe from the fond researches of our learning.
Here it is day; there it is always night.

Around this corner is a certain danger.
The streets are streets of hell from here on in.
The Anthropophagi and beings stranger
Roast in the fire and meditate on sin.

After this kiss will I know who I'm kissing?
Will I have reached the point of no return?
What happened to those others who are missing?
Oh, well, to hell with it. If we burn, we burn.

WILLIAM DICKEY

I KNOW A MAN

As I sd to my
friend, because I am
always talking,—John, I

sd, which was not his
name, the darkness sur-
rounds us, what

can we do against
it, or else, shall we &
why not, buy a goddamn big car,

drive, he sd, for
christ's sake, look
out where yr going.

ROBERT CREELEY

ULYSSES

It little profits that an idle king,
By this still hearth, among these barren crags,
Match'd with an aged wife, I mete and dole
Unequal laws unto a savage race,
That hoard, and sleep, and feed, and know not me.
I cannot rest from travel; I will drink
Life to the lees. All times I have enjoy'd
Greatly, have suffer'd greatly, both with those
That loved me, and alone; on shore, and when
Thro' scudding drifts the rainy Hyades
Vext the dim sea. I am become a name;
For always roaming with a hungry heart
Much have I seen and known,—cities of men
And manners, climates, councils, governments,
Myself not least, but honor'd of them all,—
And drunk delight of battle with my peers,
Far on the ringing plains of windy Troy.
I am a part of all that I have met;
Yet all experience is an arch wherethro'
Gleams that untravell'd world whose margin fades
For ever and for ever when I move.
How dull it is to pause, to make an end,
To rust unburnish'd, not to shine in use!
As tho' to breathe were life! Life piled on life
Were all too little, and of one to me
Little remains; but every hour is saved
From that eternal silence, something more,
A bringer of new things; and vile it were
For some three suns to store and hoard myself,
And this gray spirit yearning in desire
To follow knowledge like a sinking star,
Beyond the utmost bound of human thought.
This is my son, mine own Telemachus,

To whom I leave the scepter and the isle,—
Well-loved of me, discerning to fulfil
This labor, by slow prudence to make mild
A rugged people, and thro' soft degrees
Subdue them to the useful and the good.
Most blameless is he, centered in the sphere
Of common duties, decent not to fail
In offices of tenderness, and pay
Meet adoration to my household gods,
When I am gone.   He works his work, I mine.
— There lies the port; the vessel puffs her sail;
There gloom the dark, broad seas.   My mariners,
Souls that have toil'd, and wrought, and thought with me,—
That ever with a frolic welcome took
The thunder and the sunshine, and opposed
Free hearts, free foreheads,—you and I are old;
Old age hath yet his honor and his toil.
Death closes all; but something ere the end,
Some work of noble note, may yet be done,
Not unbecoming men that strove with Gods.
The lights begin to twinkle from the rocks;
The long day wanes; the slow moon climbs; the deep
Moans round with many voices.   Come, friends,
'T is not too late to seek a newer world.
Push off, and sitting well in order smite
The sounding furrows; for my purpose holds
To sail beyond the sunset, and the baths
Of all the western stars, until I die.
It may be that the gulfs will wash us down;
It may be we shall touch the Happy Isles,
And see the great Achilles, whom we knew.
Tho' much is taken, much abides; and tho'
We are not now that strength which in old days
Moved earth and heaven, that which we are, we are,—
One equal temper of heroic hearts,
Made weak by time and fate, but strong in will
To strive, to seek, to find, and not to yield.

                                    ALFRED, LORD TENNYSON

ODYSSEUS

for George Kirstein

Always the setting forth was the same,
Same sea, same dangers waiting for him
As though he had got nowhere but older.
Behind him on the receding shore
The identical reproaches, and somewhere
Out before him, the unravelling patience
He was wedded to. There were the islands
Each with its woman and twining welcome
To be navigated, and one to call "home."
The knowledge of all that he betrayed
Grew till it was the same whether he stayed
Or went. Therefore he went. And what wonder
If sometimes he could not remember
Which was the one who wished on his departure
Perils that he could never sail through,
And which, improbable, remote, and true,
Was the one he kept sailing home to?

W. S. MERWIN

OUT OF SIGHT, OUT OF MIND

for John and Elizabeth Rodenbeck

The hawser parts, snap,
Stands erect. The ship,
The quay, the water and the dock
Are packed as the deck
Begins to tilt with the sea.

Was the banner green, or
Was it red? The queen, she
Wept, but the king had
A stiff upper lip. Mad

Cristobal or was it Christoforo
Strode the crowd, with a shout
Cried out and the ship stood
Still.

A caravan, the camel fought
The driver's clothes, brought
The East to court, egged
The wild Italian forth:

The sail was crossed;
The sea was red.

And in her silken bed,
Spread like a cross herself,
In a pout, she lay, still
Warm from Columbo's breath

At sea. To sea. The West
And spices of a golden
Land. Mad Cristobal
Forgets to wave good-bye.

                              R. H. W. DILLARD

THE TRAVELLER

Into the forest again
whence all roads depend
this way and that
to lead him back.

Upon his shoulders
he places boulders,
upon his eye
the high wide sky.

                         ROBERT CREELEY

THE STARRY NIGHT

> *That does not keep me from having a terrible need of—*
> *shall I say the word—religion.   Then I go out at night*
> *to paint the stars.*
>
> VINCENT VAN GOGH in a letter to his brother

The town does not exist
except where one black-haired tree slips
up like a drowned woman into the hot sky.
The town is silent.   The night boils with eleven stars.
Oh starry starry night!   This is how
I want to die.

It moves.   They are all alive.
Even the moon bulges in its orange irons
to push children, like a god, from its eye.
The old unseen serpent swallows up the stars.
Oh starry starry night!   This is how
I want to die:

into that rushing beast of the night,
sucked up by that great dragon, to split
from my life with no flag,
no belly,
no cry.

ANNE SEXTON

IN THE NIGHT FIELDS

I heard the sparrows shouting "Eat, eat,"
And then the day dragged its carcass in back of the hill.
Slowly the tracks darkened.

The smoke rose steadily from no fires.
The old hunger, left in the old darkness,
Turned like a hanged knife.

I would have preferred a quiet life.
The bugs of regret began their services
Using my spine as a rosary. I left the maps
For the spiders.
Let's go, I said.

                          Light of the heart,
The wheat had started lighting its lanterns,
And in every house in heaven there were lights waving
Hello good-bye. But that's
Another life.
Snug on the crumbling earth
The old bottles lay dreaming of new wine.
I picked up my breast, which had gone out.
By other lights I go looking for yours

Through the standing harvest of my lost arrows.
Under the moon the shadow
Practices mowing. Not for me, I say,
Please not for my
Benefit. A man cannot live by bread
Alone.

                       W. S. MERWIN

A JOURNEY

You are always walking away
With the light, bright journeyman.
I wander under the leaves
Of the old town.
The signal hours fall;
Shop, office, hall
Attend, as if the sun
Could never say farewell.
I must make the sun my own.

For the traveller travels well,
Carrying songs to spend,

Branches whose touch can heal,
Seed for new land.
Yet travels heavier
Returning, from the freight
Of foreign syllables,
Beasts crying at night,
Pulses of wind, and hot
Odors that grow
Nerves in the traveller
Where no nerves were.

Now in Virginia
The orange lilies patch
June's raggedy green dress.
Some apples have red rust.
It has all happened before.
What should we be but poor?

The hours answer.
In the central dark
Where we are not loved enough,
Something heavy as gold
Glints by the mineshaft:
The sun in a vein of rock,
Beating mysteriously!
Children at nightwork
Lament the murdered day,
Tremble at what is not
Departure, but a way
Of rising up to walk
When the rock rolls away.

JULIA RANDALL

THE IMPROVEMENT OF PRAYER

I prayed the little words like children's games
Safe and secret from terminals and streets.
I played the shiny imaginary names

Like toys, hiding delight from solemn speeds
And powers, from the tall buildings and adult noise.

I spoke a star, a baby God, a stable.
I whispered haloes in oxen-eye and straw.
Repentant, I indulged my vice of fable
With crucifix and beads, I counted the row
Of saints and martyrs in parables of creeds.

Then as if a child picked up a seed
And found that he'd uprooted a universe,
I heard my secret splitting with public speed
Through husks of noise, I saw my words swing doors
And leave the grown-up streets little with toys.

ERNEST SANDEEN

"THE FOX-COLOURED PHEASANT ENJOYED HIS
PEACE . . ."

The fox-coloured pheasant enjoyed his peace,
there were no labourers in the wheat,
dogs were stretched out at ease,
the empty road echoed my feet.

It was the time for owls' voices,
trees were dripping dark like rain,
and sheep made night-time noises
as I went down the hill lane.

In the streets of the still town
I met a man in the lamplight,
he stood in the alley that led down
to the harbour and the sea out of sight.

Who do you want? he asked me,
Who are you looking for in this place?
The houses echoed us emptily
and the lamp shone on his face.

Does your girl live here?
(There were no girls or sailors about.)
I have no girl anywhere,
I want a ship putting out.

He stood under the lamplight
and I stepped up close to him,
his eyes burned like fires at night
and the lamp seemed dim.

He came closer up and pressed
his crooked knee to my knee,
and his chest to my chest,
and held my shoulders and wrestled with me.

It was the middle time of night
with five hours to run till day,
but the sky was crimson and bright
before he stood out of my way.

I ran past as quick as I could
and the wet stones rang loudly
along the wharf where the ships stood
and the sea lifting proudly.

PETER LEVI, S.J.

CROSSING THE FRONTIER

Crossing the frontier they were stopped in time,
Told, quite politely, they would have to wait:
Passports in order, nothing to declare,
And surely holding hands was not a crime;
Until they saw how, ranged across the gate,
All their most formidable friends were there.

Wearing his conscience like a crucifix,
Her father, rampant, nursed the Family Shame;
And, armed with their old-fashioned dinner-gong,

His aunt, who even when they both were six,
Had just to glance towards a childish game
To make them feel that they were doing wrong.

And both their mothers, simply weeping floods,
Her head-mistress, his boss, the parish priest,
And the bank manager who cashed their cheques;
The man who sold him his first rubber-goods;
Dog Fido, from whose love-life, shameless beast,
She first observed the basic facts of sex.

They looked as though they had stood there for hours;
For years; perhaps for ever. In the trees
Two furtive birds stopped courting and flew off;
While in the grass beside the road the flowers
Kept up their guilty traffic with the bees.
Nobody stirred. Nobody risked a cough.

Nobody spoke. The minutes ticked away;
The dog scratched idly. Then, as parson bent
And whispered to a guard who hurried in,
The customs-house loudspeakers with a bray
Of raucous and triumphant argument
Broke out the wedding march from *Lohengrin.*

He switched the engine off: "We must turn back."
She heard his voice break, though he had to shout
Against a din that made their senses reel,
And felt his hand, so tense in hers, go slack.
But suddenly she laughed and said: "Get out!
Change seats! Be quick!" and slid behind the wheel.

And drove the car straight at them with a harsh,
Dry crunch that showered both with scraps and chips,
Drove through them; barriers rising let them pass;
Drove through and on and on, with Dad's moustache
Beside her twitching still round waxen lips
And Mother's tears still streaming down the glass.

A. D. HOPE

PRODIGAL SON

Poor grimy pit of a closing town,
It cradles its citizens
Like so many sacks of gold
Tossed hurriedly down.
Daylight slips from the inner buildings,
Dodders briefly by rain in gutters
And, at the end of a vanishing street,
Shows for a moment as no muddled hag
But the faultless blue pause of heaven
Arrayed behind windy green flags.

At dusk, alone, with winter coming on,
The young man feels nerve enough
In seignorial flesh
To stir the sockets of his bones.
Roaming dumb as an ox with great round eyes
Or a giant fish deep in the swerving
Wind of a hostile city,
He drifts easily past the guard
Of a last few strangers, stilted in twilight,
Who inwardly feed their eyes
On the cast off flesh of the solid world
Like crabs in the cold ebb tide.

Eastward he sights the harbor,
Black with the hulls and whipping flags
Of his long forgotten native land,
The emerald avaricious sea.

JEAN FARLEY

GRABBLING IN YOKNA BOTTOM

The hungry come in a dry time
To muddy the water of this swamp river
And take in nets what fish or eel
Break surface to suck at this world's air.

But colder blood backs into the water's wood—
Gills the silt rather than rise to light—
And who would eat a cleaner meat
Must grabble in the hollows of underwater stumps and roots,

Must cram his arm and hand beneath the scum
And go by touch where eye cannot reach,
Must seize and bring to light
What scale or slime is touched—

Must in that instant—on touch—
Without question or reckoning
Grab up what wraps itself cold-blooded
Around flesh or flails the water to froth,

Or else feel the fish slip by,
Or learn that the loggerhead's jaw is thunder-deaf,
Or that the cottonmouth's fangs burn like heated needles
Even under water.

The well-fed do not wade this low river.

JAMES SEAY

LIMITS

FLORIDA FROGMEN FIND NEW WORLD—*The New York Times*

Within the limestone mantle of the shelf
　　Beneath the swamp, the cypress root,
　　　　The great resort hotels
　　　　Of Florida, other hells
　　Are trespassed by the webbèd foot
Beating to print the water's self with self.

　　　Leaching the whole of truth,
　　　Ruined heroes of the daily mind,
　　Those undergoing scholars climb upstream

Into a darkness prior to their dream,
  Where the dividing eye is blind.
    Therein they spend their youth.

  Inside the pouched, hard hide of the riddled earth
    They flutter, determined frogmen, ready
      To carry air and light
      Into the condemned, tight
    Tenements of the old landlady
  Till she have rent them more than bed and birth.

      Under the rib, inside,
    Air gone, and battery burned out,
  Is there a second, till the lungs have burst,
  Of a second freedom, greater than the first,
    When the young frog prince, born of doubt,
      Swims down upon his bride?

  She drags him to her as a mirror would.
    Now shrieking Oedipus is blind
      And fair Narcissus cold,
      The dragon-guarded gold,
    All that was lost, they fall to find,
  Losing their science, which is understood.

                    HOWARD NEMEROV

THE DIVER

Dressed in his clumsy, stiff, aquatic clothes,
His helmet screwed fast on so that he can
Do, say, see nothing in the world of man,
The diver shambles to the boatside, goes
Down the ladder, and the waters close
Over the steel that seals his sacred brain.
Over the boatside lean, his shadow scan
As it descends, shapeless and wavering.
It is no devilfish, is still a man—
But now it's gone.
                    Creatures beyond our ken

He will describe in words on his return—
Pale words for objects seen—
The inhuman life that swirled before his sight,
Or fled, or fought. The treasure he seeks out
May yet be lifted up by creaking crane,
Splashing, out of the green, but in his brain
The jungles of the sea must flower still,
Whose hook has drawn the pale blood of the shark,
And when his streaming bulk climbs back aboard,
We'll mutter, say some contract has been signed
With what lies under, and that that occurred
Which has no human gesture and no word.

E. L. MAYO

❧ TWO ❧

The Road of Trials

The unexamined life, said Socrates, is not worth living. It is an uncomfortable saying which we, like the Athenians who prescribed the hemlock for its author, are prone to regard with scepticism or hostility. Why stir up trouble? Admittedly, we have our faults, but we take some pride in being well-intentioned persons, sane for the most part, reasonably honest, public-spirited, industrious. We see no need for plunging off into the fearful trials that are said to await the Hero on the perilous sea, in the dark woods, or in the labyrinth far under the surface of the earth. Few, in fact, have ever volunteered for such a mission. Some, perhaps, are born great, but many of our best known heroes had their greatness thrust upon them: Dante came to himself in a dark wood, the tasks of Heracles were imposed upon him by the jealous Hera, Jonah was thrown overboard, and Dorothy was whirled away by a tornado to the land of Oz. When ordinary persons cross the threshold and set off upon the Road of Trials, they do so only because the harsh necessity is upon them.

Everyman, in the play which bears his name, is quite content with the life he leads. He is equipped with adequate Beauty, Discretion, Strength, and enjoys the daily presence and support of Kindred, Fellowship, and Goods. Then, when he least expects it, he is rudely summoned by the voice of Death. His world is suddenly a quagmire; no one will stand by him, though he desperately needs companionship and advice on the involuntary pilgrimage to his pain, for he finds that he must make a reckoning, and his accounts are somehow badly in the red. His Goods inform him plainly that they do not belong to him at all, but were only lent to him; so far from being his ally, they have plotted against him, lulling him with comfort when he should have been preparing for his journey. It is an appalling revelation, one which opens the whited sepulchre of everyone's complacency. If we are inclined to dismiss accounts of peril to the soul, including *The Divine Comedy* and *Pilgrim's Progress*, pleading the privilege of a secular age, then T. S. Eliot is at our elbow, offering, in *The Waste Land*, a contemporary version of the life and times of Everyman besieged by death; and K., in Kafka's *The Castle*, resembles Bunyan's Mr. Christian in all respects but one: He has no sure guide to assist him on his way.

The contemporary poet, like the poet in every age, is professionally committed to reality. His stock in trade are the awkward facts which we succeed in forgetting most of the time: that we begin to die at the moment of our birth; that we are a prey to fears which spring alive at unguarded moments during the day and assume spontaneous dramatic form in dreams; and that the office manager, the social worker, and the housewife often fight an urge to beat their heads against the wall. If they have questions, who will answer them? When the traditional hero needs an answer, it is supplied, says Robert Creeley ("The Hero"):

> *Each voice which was asked*
> *spoke its words, and heard*
> *more than that, the fair question,*
> *the onerous burden of the asking.*

Faced with a riddle, Joseph dreams the answer; Medea taught Jason how to handle the fire-breathing bulls, the armed warriors, the old dragon. The rest seems easy enough, and the hero "stepped that gracefully / into his redemption." Where, asks Creeley, are the Lady and the Father now? His "mind is dark like the night"; but when he turns for help to the familiar figures of the Quest, he finds that the forms are there, but the fire has gone out of them; the oracles are silent, biding their time. In fearful ignorance, he seeks out the pit into which so many Heroes have descended, and he asks of them, "the tears upon your hands, / how can you stand it?" As he plunges into the dark, the cry of "hero! hero!" comes to him, filtered through the accumulated fears of many ages and, with that small comfort, he is on his way. The Road of Trials begins just on the other side of desperation, and the terrain through which it leads is as uncharted for the Hero of this moment as it was for the first who passed that way. Yet when one is living the experience, the old forms will arise from their graves to terrify, waylay, and maul the aspirant; later, they may exhort, importune, and begin to drop the necessary clues; and, from time to time, where "the way lies dark and fierce" (Kenneth Pitchford, "Journey"), they will permit a vision of "a river flowing, / green through the trees and swift in the sun," toward which the hero's "dark ways run."

The Road of Trials leads through a land of nightmare toward an awakening to self-transcendence which, like the Phoenix, rises from the ashes of the shattered purblind will. This is the "ripeness" which Hamlet seeks and which is finally attained by Lear. Whitman wrote that "to die is different from what any one supposed, and luckier." The Hero who presents the same face to the world on his return that he showed it when he crossed the threshold may congratulate himself on saving his skin, but he will bring with him no dram nor scruple of the water of life. If the old husk of the self could serve our purposes, we shouldn't need to trouble "Stravaging through the Dark Wood" (Howard Nemerov, "A Predecessor of Perseus"). Howard Nemerov's Everyman as Hero, confusing "The being called and being chosen," wonders when he will meet the wolf, the leopard, or the lion, "not to mention Virgil." As he persists in traveling his road, "Passing the skinless elder skeletons," sooner or later he may stumble on Medusa's lair; but, having no mirror, he will meet the eyes of "the grey unbearable she of the world" and anticlimactically be "stricken in the likeness of himself." It is as though the magician says "Presto, Change-o" and nothing happens. The rule for heroes is metamorphosis, not ossification. The Redcrosse Knight in Spenser begins his Quest as a bumbling country fellow, becomes a Christian champion, and finally emerges as St. George and a type of Christ; the Frog Prince progresses from despised amphibian to royal mammal; Heracles dies in agony and becomes a god. It is not thus for Robert Graves' feckless traveler in "The Witches' Cauldron." With rumors of metamorphosis all around him—the elixir of the cauldron itself, the phallic monolith, the dead snake, the sound of the roaring bull—he follows an illusory "broad green road," and all that he sees is "Coloured with day-dreams"; when a finger-post points in his face, the message clearly is that he has gotten nowhere, being impervious to transmutation, and his anger overcomes him.

For the "best of knights," the consummate Hero, or even for the ordinary one who attracts the incalculable gifts of the gods, the Road of Trials provides a shattering experience, the necessary prologue to new life, new understanding. The objective of the journey always is the source of energy which courses through the veins of everything that lives. Edwin Muir's protagonist in "The Bridge of Dread" gives warning of the stony causeway which no one crosses without being shaken violently out of himself—a kind of titanic shock therapy. Here, the Source is "a burning wire" that shoots from the ground, a weed or flower of fire, like the burning bush from the midst of which God called unto Moses, saying "Here am I" (Exod.: 3.4). The burning bush that is unconsumed; the Lady of leprous brow and "rowan-berry lips," who is Life-in-Death (Robert Graves, "The White Goddess"); the "something dreadful and another" which "Look quietly upon each other" (Louise Bogan, "A Tale")—all are metaphoric embodiments of those pairs of opposites which lie at the heart of mortal quandaries. How can death be reconciled with life, time with eternity, the ego with the universal will? The Argonauts are nearly crushed between the stony sides of the Symplegades, and Odysseus between Scylla and Charybdis. They will prove fatal to one who believes that his life is his own to have and to hoard. But the Hero yields to death and is reborn. The Flower of Fire, charged with the incalculable voltage of the force of life, springs up at the midpoint of the Bridge of Dread, where opposites are joined. Muir's traveler is transfixed for "an endless moment" by his vision of the "burning beam." Then he is past; but the experience is fixed forever in his "dreaming head."

When the Hero has crossed the Bridge of Dread, what then? He has been revivified by energy from the primal source, and thus has put the waste land far behind him. "The country that seemed / Malevolence itself / Has gone back from the heart" (David Wagoner, "Words above a Narrow Entrance"), and with it "The warlock in disguise" and the giant who "overlooked / nothing living in the land" (George Garrett, "The Quest"). Now, George Garrett's traveler has reached

> *the point*
> *Where the enchanted may be free,*
> *all charms be neutralized and everything*
> *be what it, shining, seems to be.*

For David Wagoner's Hero also, everything is what it seems to be, but is not so much "shining" as alive with energy and potentiality: "water on fire," "noise from a rock," "a poisonous expanse / Where light knocks down the trees." For both poets, this is "The land of the different mind," what one experiences when the ego prison opens and the ugly spawn of fear have lost their power to oppress. One poet envisions a transfigured world, the other a confused mélange of building materials from which an infinite number of new creations might arise. Yet, in the brawling chaos of the latter country, the Hero is not by any means uncompensated. The words above the narrow entrance to this land assured him that, while he travels here,

> *Nothing will be at ease,*
> *Nothing at peace, but you.*

THE HERO

Each voice which was asked
spoke its words, and heard
more than that, the fair question,
the onerous burden of the asking.

And so the hero, the
hero! stepped that gracefully
into his redemption, losing
or gaining life thereby.

Now we, now I
ask also, and burdened,
tied down, return
and seek the forest also.

Go forth, go forth,
saith the grandmother, the fire
of that old form, and turns
away from the form.

And the forest is dark,
mist hides it, trees
are dim, but I turn
to my father in the dark.

A spark, that spark of hope
which was burned out long ago,
the tedious echo
of the father image

—which only women bear,
also wear, old men, old cares,
and turn, and again find
the disorder in the mind.

Night is dark like the mind,
my mind is dark like the night.
O light the light! Old
foibles of the right.

Into that pit, now pit of
anywhere, the tears upon your hands,
how can you stand
it, I also turn.

I wear the face, I face
the right, the night, the way,
I go along the path
into the last and only dark,

hearing *hero! hero!*
a voice faint enough, a spark,
a glimmer grown dimmer through years
of old, old fears.

ROBERT CREELEY

THE OLD MAN'S ROAD

Across the Great Schism, through our whole landscape,
Ignoring God's Vicar and God's Ape,

Under their noses, unsuspected,
The Old Man's Road runs as it did

When a light subsoil, a simple ore
Were still in vogue: true to His wherefore,

By stiles, gates, hedge-gaps it goes
Over ploughland, woodland, cow meadows,

Past shrines to a cosmological myth
No heretic to-day would be caught dead with,

Near hill-top rings that were so safe then,
Now stormed easily by small children

(Shepherds use bits in the high mountains,
Hamlets take stretches for Lovers' Lanes),

Then through cities threads its odd way,
Now without gutters, a Thieves' Alley,

Now with green lamp-posts and white curb,
The smart Crescent of a high-toned suburb,

Giving wide berth to an old Cathedral,
Running smack through a new Town Hall,

Unlookable for, by logic, by guess;
Yet some strike it, and are struck fearless.

No life can know it, but no life
That sticks to this course can be made captive,

And who wander with it are not stopped at
Borders by guards of some Theocrat,

Crossing the pass so almost where
His searchlight squints but no closer

(And no further where it might by chance):
So in summer sometimes, without hindrance,

Apotropaically scowling, a tinker
Shuffles past, in the waning year

Potters a coleopterist, poking
Through yellow leaves, and a youth in spring

Trots by after a new excitement,
His true self, hot on the scent.

The Old Man leaves his Road to those
Who love it no less since it lost purpose,

Who never ask what History is up to,
So cannot act as if they knew:

Assuming a freedom its Powers deny,
Denying its Powers, they pass freely.

W. H. AUDEN

SONG OF A JOURNEY

Halfway to heartbreak,
The rutted road gave out
Onto a darkening field,
And a wood loomed dark about.
Halfway to heartbreak,
I followed my lonely way.

I plodded through the torn field,
And breathless finally stood
At the ragged brambly
Edge of the fearsome wood.

Halfway to heartbreak,
I kept the darkening way.

I lost the path in the wood;
And the darkness closed around,
With only the flutter
Of nightbirds for sound.
Halfway to heartbreak,
In the wood I lost my way.

I stumbled on, cobwebs
Brushing wet on my face,
In the black and pathless wood,
One of the lonely race.
Halfway to heartbreak,
I wandered without a way.

I longed despairing to turn
In my night-fallen track;
I stumbled restless on,
Thinking of turning back.
Halfway to heartbreak,
I longed to give up the way.

Halfway to heartbreak,
My silly will was bent;
But the only way for love
Was on, and on I went.
Halfway to heartbreak,
I went on my lonely way.

ROBERT WALLACE

JOURNEY

Dark are the ways of my enduring,
black is my hand against the sun.
Dark lies the heart in the live breast burning;
    then it is done.

Gulled by the winds of my first faring,
into calmed latitudes I steer,
all from my skull's round cabin staring
        at the smooth face of fear.

Deep I must go to find my country,
deeper than eye or kiss can pierce;
deep as the heart, past all returning,
        the way lies dark and fierce.

There I will find a river flowing,
green through the trees and swift in the sun:
to that bright cove of my enduring
        all my dark ways run.

                        KENNETH PITCHFORD

A PREDECESSOR OF PERSEUS

Since he is older than Hamlet or Stavrogin,
Older than Leopold Bloom; since he has been
Stravaging through the Dark Wood several years
Beyond the appointed time, meeting no wolf,
Leopold, or lion, not to mention Virgil;
And long since seen the span of Keats conclude,
And the span of Alexander,—he begins
At last to wonder.

                    Had his sacred books
Misled him?   Or had he deceived himself?
Like some he knew, who'd foolishly confused
The being called and being chosen; they
Ran down the crazy pavement of their path
On primrose all the way.

                    An old friend said,
"The first thing to learn about wisdom is
This, that you can't do anything with it."
Wisdom. If that was what he had, he might,

Like a retired witch, keep it locked up
In the broom closet. But he rides his road,
Passing the skinless elder skeletons
Who smile, and maybe he will keep on going
Until the grey unbearable she of the world
Shall raise her eyes, and recognize, and grin
At her eternal amateur's approach,
All guts no glass, to meet her gaze head on
And be stricken in the likeness of himself
At least, if not of Keats or Alexander.

HOWARD NEMEROV

THE WITCHES' CAULDRON

In sudden cloud, that blotting distance out,
Confused the compass of the traveller's mind,
Biased his course: three times from the hill's crest
Trying to descend but with no track to follow,
Nor visible landmark—three times he had struck
The same sedged pool of steaming desolation,
The same black monolith rearing up before it.
This third time then he stood and recognized
The Witches' Cauldron, only known before
By hearsay, fly-like on whose rim he had crawled
Three times and three times dipped to climb again
Its uncouth sides, so to go crawling on.

By falls of scree, moss-mantled slippery rock,
Wet bracken, drunken gurgling watercourses
He escaped, limping, at last, and broke the circuit—
Travelling down and down; but smooth descent
Interrupted by new lakes and ridges,
Sprawling unmortared walls of boulder granite,
Marshes; one arm hung bruised where he had fallen;
Blood in a sticky trickle smeared his cheek;
Sweat, gathering at his eyebrows, ran full beads
Into his eyes, which made them smart and blur.

At last he blundered on some shepherd's hut—
He thought, the hut took pity and appeared—
With mounds of peat and welcome track of wheels
Which he now followed to a broad green road
That ran from right to left; but still at fault,
The mist being still on all, with little pause
He chose the easier way, the downward way.
Legs were dog-tired already, but this road,
Gentle descent with some relief of guidance,
Maintained his shambling five miles to the hour
Coloured with day-dreams. Then a finger-post
Moved through the mist, pointing into his face,
Yet when he stopped to read gave him no comfort.

Seventeen miles to—somewhere, God knows where—
The paint was weathered to a puzzle
Which cold-unfocused eyes could not attempt—
And jerking a derisive thumb behind it
Up a rough stream-wet path: "The Witches' Cauldron,
One mile." Only a mile
For two good hours of stumbling steeplechase!
There was a dead snake by some humorous hand
Twined on the pointing finger; far away
A bull roared hoarsely, but all else was mist.

Then anger overcame him . . . .

ROBERT GRAVES

NUKUHIVA

Nukuhiva, the scene of Melville's Typee, *is one of the
Marquesas Islands. The islanders whom Melville de-
scribes are now almost extinct.*

FOR STEPHEN SPENDER

I

It was in time of war, and yet no war,
No sound of war, and scarce the memory of one
So terrible that none forget, troubled
Our passage, the ship's dark keel breaking
The phosphorescent water, foam riding the halyards.
Far, far, far from home, the sailor busy with the day's routine,
We came one morning where the mountains rose
Upon a semicircular and emerald bay,
And a few birds circled like a flaw,
To the beautiful island of Nukuhiva.

Here Melville came, pursuing and pursued,
An angry spirit in a lasting rage,
Came tracked by time and all its skeletal
Transactions, the decay of empires, tracked
By life and death, and worlds of lies,
To Nukuhiva, and the whaleback bay,
An animal that listens with its eyes.

Seaweed trailed from scupper-hole, and folded sail,
The whaler rode the water, and the sailor's gaze
Went out to greet the islanders, the great
Canoes tilting with stalwart oarsmen, and the girls
As gold as morning diving from the surf,
The scent of oil and flowers.

II

                          The ship's boat swung
From the davits, then the wildcat purr of motors broke
The circling silence, and the jumbled rocks ashore
Came nearer, steady, up, the whip and lash of waves.

This was a place that memory corrupts,
A tumbling house half-seen through green and mottled
Foliage. The Frenchman talked of Paris and of youth,
Of Suez and Arabia and the East,

While the furious sunlight beat upon the rocks,
And words crept out like lizards on the leaves—
Bird-song, wind-song, sun.

The horses waited, cropping the dry brown grass
By the open gate, the crumbling wall; we swung
Into the saddle, sunlight flecking the hooves.

What was the island then?   And who will say,
The wind, the sun, the moon?   So much is buried there
In what was scarce a century ago
The center of a commerce and a colony,
Amalgam of Soho and a Yukon town,
Where drunken planter strode, and trader dipped,
And the bishop like a fat persimmon sat
Under the green palmetto in the afternoon.

III

Up, up, up, we rode through trees and tangled vines,
Struggling as one struggles in a dream
Across a moving mass of melting snow,
Words fail, the trail is lost among the trees.
Up the temple steps, the chipped, black stone
Breaking the clumsy branches, horses' froth
Smelling of papaya and mango.

Winding and unwinding like a leash,
We came to the burial platforms, the plateau,
And heard the water crashing through the vines,
And heard behind us, upward from the bay:
Revenez, revenez!   On avait des copains!
Always in a language that was never mine.

Nukuhiva, Hivaoa, Raiatea,
The islands and the names are poetry,
And they are spoken by the voices of the drowning,
By the voices of the men who are remembered
By the cold, white, lonely presence of the sea.

IV

Whatever we had come for lay behind,
And what we sought lay still ahead.
As we approached the beach, the west was red;
The pompoms of the sailors danced upon the waves
Like poppies on the distant fields of Brittany
Across the semi-circular and horseshoe bay,
And all the wailing places of the dead.

WILLIAM JAY SMITH

THE CITY OF SATISFACTIONS

As I was travelling toward the city of satisfactions
On my employment, seeking the treasure of pleasure,
Laved in the superdome observation car by Muzak
Soothed by the cool conditioned and reconditioned air,
Sealed in from the smell of the heat and the spines
Of the sere mesquite and the seared windblast of the sand,
It was conjunction of a want of juicy fruit
And the train's slowdown and stopping at a depot
Not listed on the schedule, unnamed by platform sign,
That made me step down on the siding
With some change in hand. The newsstand, on inspection,
Proved a shed of greyed boards shading
A litter of stale rags.
Turning back, I blanched at the Silent Streak: a wink
Of the sun's reflection caught its rear-view window
Far down the desert track. I grabbed the crossbar
And the handcar clattered. Up and down
It pumped so fast I hardly could grab hold it,
His regal head held proud despite the bending
Knees, back-knees, back-knees, back-knees propelling.
His eyes bulged beadier than a desert toad's eyes.
His huge hands shrank upon the handlebar,
His mighty shoulders shrivelled and his skin grew
Wrinkled while I watched the while we reeled
Over the mesquite till the train grew larger

And pumping knees, back-knees, we stood still and
Down on us the train bore,
The furious tipping of the levers unabated
Wrenched my sweating eyes and aching armpits,
He leapt on long webbed feet into the drainage
Dryditch and the car swung longside on a siding
Slowing down beside the Pullman diner
Where the napkined waiter held a tray of glasses.
The gamehen steamed crisp-crust behind the glass.
I let go of the tricycle and pulled my askew necktie,
Pushed through the diner door, a disused streetcar,
A Danish half devoured by flies beneath specked glass,
Dirty cups on the counter,
A menu, torn, too coffeestained for choices, told
In a map of rings my cryptic eyes unspelled
Of something worth the digging for right near by
Here just out beyond the two-door shed.
The tracks were gone now but I found a shovel,
Made one, that is, from a rusting oildrum cover,
A scrap of baling wire, a broken crutch,
And down I heaved on the giving earth and rockshards
And a frog drygasped once from a distant gulley
And up I spewed the debris in a range
Of peaks I sank beneath and sweated under till
One lunge sounded the clunk of iron on brass
And furious scratch and pawing of the dryrock
Uncovered the graven chest and the pile of earth downslid
While under a lowering sky, sweatwet, I grasped and wrestled
The huge chest, lunged and jerked and fought it upward
Till it toppled sideways on the sand. I smashed it
Open, and it held a barred box. My nails broke
On the bars that wouldn't open. I smashed it
Open and it held a locked box. I ripped my knuckles
But couldn't wrest that lock off till I smashed it
Open and it held a small box worked
In delicate filigree of silver with
A cunning keyhole. But there was no key.
I pried it, ripped my fingers underneath it
But couldn't get it open till I smashed it
Open and it held a little casket

Sealed tight with twisted wires or vines of shining
Thread. I bit and tugged and twisted, cracked my teeth
But couldn't loose the knot. I smashed it
Open and the top came off, revealing
A tiny casket made of jade. It had
No top, no seam, no turnkey. Thimblesmall
It winked unmoving near the skinbreak
Where steakjuice pulsed and oozed. I thought aroma
Sifted, thinning till the dark horizon
Seemed, and then no longer seemed, a trifle
Sweetened. I knelt before
A piece of desert stone. When I have fitted
That stone into its casket, and replaced
The lid and set that casket in its box,
Fitted the broken top and set that box within
The box it came in and bent back the bars
And put it in the chest, the chest back in the hole,
The peaks around the pit-edge piled back in the pit,
Replaced the baling wire and crutch and oildrum cover
And pushed back through the diner, will the train
Sealed in from the smell of heat and mesquite
Envelop me in Muzak while it swooshes
Past bleak sidings such as I wait on
Nonstop toward the city of satisfactions roaring?
If I could only make this broken top
Fit snug back on this casket

DANIEL HOFFMAN

WHY WERE THE BANDIT'S EYES
HIDDEN BEHIND A GREEN MASK?

The stuttering bishop,
The midwife,
And there were the children
Strung across the highway
Like Christmas festoons.

The carriage was of gold
And gleamed,

And the peasants bore rakes
To ravish the ladies.
(That year was a time.)
The leaves fell early.

The dust lay low.

The horse's ears were back,
His beribboned tail,
The pinwheels of his eyes,
The foam,
His teeth were flat and wide,
And the bridge we never reached.

R. H. W. DILLARD

THE BRIDGE OF DREAD

But when you reach the Bridge of Dread
Your flesh will huddle into its nest
For refuge and your naked head
Creep in the casement of your breast,

And your great bulk grow thin and small
And cower within its cage of bone,
While dazed you watch your footsteps crawl
Toadlike across the leagues of stone.

If they come, you will not feel
About your feet the adders slide,
For still your head's demented wheel
Whirls on your neck from side to side

Searching for danger. Nothing there.
And yet your breath will whistle and beat
As on you push the stagnant air
That breaks in rings about your feet

Like dirty suds. If there should come
Some bodily terror to that place,

Great knotted serpents dread and dumb,
You would accept it as a grace.

Until you see a burning wire
Shoot from the ground. As in a dream
You'll wonder at that flower of fire,
That weed caught in a burning beam.

And you are past. Remember then,
Fix deep within your dreaming head
Year, hour or endless moment when
You reached and crossed the Bridge of Dread.

EDWIN MUIR

A TALE

This youth too long has heard the break
Of waters in a land of change.
He goes to see what suns can make
From soil more indurate and strange.

He cuts what holds his days together
And shuts him in, as lock on lock:
The arrowed vane announcing weather,
The tripping racket of a clock;

Seeking, I think, a light that waits
Still as a lamp upon a shelf,—
A land with hills like rocky gates
Where no sea leaps upon itself.

But he will find that nothing dares
To be enduring, save where, south
Of hidden deserts, torn fire glares
On beauty with a rusted mouth,—

Where something dreadful and another
Look quietly upon each other.

LOUISE BOGAN

THE QUEST

The road was menaced by a dwarf,
sharp-tongued with a mind like a trap
for tigers. Later a dragon loomed,
snorted fire and made his wings flap

like starchy washing in brisk wind.
Farther still, the obsolete castle and
the improbable giant overlooked
nothing living in the land.

One is a long time coming to the point
where the enchanted may be free,
all charms be neutralized and everything
be what it, shining, seems to be.

GEORGE GARRETT

WORDS ABOVE A NARROW ENTRANCE

The land behind your back
Ends here: never forget
Signpost and weathercock
That turned always to point
Directly at your eyes;
Remember slackening air
At the top of the night,
Your feet treading on space.
The stream, like an embrace,
That swamped you to the throat
Has altered now; the briar
Rattling against your knees,
The warlock in disguise,
The giant at the root—
The country that seemed
Malevolence itself
Has gone back from the heart.

Beyond this gate, there lies
The land of the different mind,
Not honey in the brook,
None of the grass you dreamed.
Foresee water on fire,
And notches in a cloud;
Expect noise from a rock,
And faces falling apart.
The pathway underfoot,
Heaving its dust, will cross
A poisonous expanse
Where light knocks down the trees,
And whatever spells you took
Before, you will take anew
From the clack in the high wind.
Nothing will be at ease,
Nothing at peace, but you.

DAVID WAGONER

CAPE DREAD

For those who come after, that is how we named it;
You may find that some other suits it better. Only
We pray you, for no saint christen it. The toll of us
That it took, we do not yet know the unhallowed
End of it, any more than we can assess
Our own ends beforehand. All summer
We had coursed a strange ocean, the winds driving
From quarters that seemed unnatural, and the set
Of the currents sorted not with our learning.
But in autumn sometimes all waters seem familiar,
With leaves, quite far out, littering the ground swell
On smooth days when the wind is light. And in
The haze then you can believe you are anywhere:
Standing off a home shore, and can even smell
The sweet dankness of smoke from known hearths. So we

Bore on, feeling courage more fresh in us
Than on the day of our sailing, musing
How far we might fetch before winter. Then
Through the mist we raised it, the abrupt cape
Looming dark and too near to leeward;
And recognized, like a home-thought too, in that landfall
The other side of autumn: that the year
Would bear us no farther, that we would not
Get beyond this. Perhaps it was named
At that moment in our minds, when we sighted
The shape of what we knew we would not pass.
You cannot mistake it: the dun headland
Like a dreaming Dutchman, dough-faced, staring
Seaward to the side we did not penetrate.
You almost think he will turn as you
Grope your way in with the lead-line. Hope suddenly
Was as far behind us as home, and maybe
That made us clumsy, dull of heart going in.
But the waters are treacherous off that point,
With a fierce knot of currents twisting, even
At slack-tide, snatching you from your seaway,
Sucking over a jagged shelving, and there is
Rough shoal beyond that. Three ships we lost
And many of their men there, and only we
Because we were driven far to port, almost
To the drag at the cliff's foot, and made in
Through the very spray, found the channel. There is
Nine fathoms all the way in there, to the broad pool
Of quiet water behind the tide-race;
You can anchor in five fathoms at
The lowest tide, with good holding, and sheltered.
You will use the harbor; in other years you will
Set out from there, in the spring, and think
Of that headland as home, calling it Cape
Delight, or Dutchman's Point. But what we found
You will find for yourselves, somewhere, for
Yourselves. We have not gone there again,
Nor ventured ever so far again. In
The south corner of the cove there is
An inlet flowing with sweet water,

And there are fruits in abundance, small
But delectable, at least at that season.

W. S. MERWIN

A DREAM OF THE CONSUMER

Charging up an escalator labeled "Down"
Would have been simple. No, it wasn't that.
The willing treadmills swept me off my feet,
But lost themselves in cloverleafs between
Departments. Flanked by lamps and silverware,
"What did you have in mind?" the clerk
In Gifts inquired. I had forgotten, if I ever
Knew, the word to satisfy that frozen smile.

The high-speed elevators leapt to my unspoken
Wish, but hurtled past my floor like meteors.
Old men, solicitous in braided livery,
Dispatched me swiftly past, around,
Just short of, or beside my destination.
In Accounts, the dry factotum moved
In triplicate through sheaves of rustling
Vouchers, breathing, "Can I help you?"

Help me! Customer, floor-walker, store
Detective dinned directions. Four-armed clerks,
Backdropped by stacks of lingerie in drawers
And pigeonholes, slipped chits in vacuum tubes,
All asking, "Can I show you something?"
Lost again in Gifts, I exited, perplexed,
Amid a thick array of crystal knickknacks,
Muttering. I ranged the hydra-headed aisles.

Beguiled by courtesy, I might have hurried
Nowhere yet, but stumbled on the unmarked
Entrance, narrow stair. The angled flights
Required defiance of three gravities at least,
But eased before the final landing, where a wave

Of satisfaction stranded me. My shadow sped
Across the floor and up a wall, flipped
Overhead, and took possession of a dusty garret.

"Testing! Testing!" droned the intercom.
"Cash, budget plan, or lay-away?" The question
Caromed from the four bare walls and ceiling
Serpented with pipes. Sales chits whizzed by,
Hot for the promised land. Five talents gripped
My arm and twisted. In the pit, an elevator
Whined. A list! A list! Look out below!
I took my graven charge-a-plate in hand.

JOHN ALEXANDER ALLEN

THE WHITE GODDESS

All saints revile her, and all sober men
Ruled by the God Apollo's golden mean—
In scorn of which we sailed to find her
In distant regions likeliest to hold her
Whom we desired above all things to know,
Sister of the mirage and echo.

It was a virtue not to stay,
To go our headstrong and heroic way
Seeking her out at the volcano's head,
Among pack ice, or where the track had faded
Beyond the cavern of the seven sleepers:
Whose broad high brow was white as any leper's,
Whose eyes were blue, with rowan-berry lips,
With hair curled honey-coloured to white hips.

Green sap of Spring in the young wood a-stir
Will celebrate the Mountain Mother,
And every song-bird shout awhile for her;
But we are gifted, even in November
Rawest of seasons, with so huge a sense
Of her nakedly worn magnificence

We forget cruelty and past betrayal,
Heedless of where the next bright bolt may fall.

ROBERT GRAVES

PURSUIT

The hunchback on the corner, with gum and shoelaces,
Has his own wisdom and pleasures, and may not be lured
To divulge them to you, for he has merely endured
Your appeal for his sympathy and your kind purchases;
And wears infirmity but as the general who turns
Apart, in his famous old greatcoat there on the hill
At dusk when the rapture and cannonade are still,
To muse withdrawn from the dead, from his gorgeous subal-
terns;
Or stares from the thicket of his familiar pain, like a fawn
That meets you a moment, wheels, in imperious innocence is
gone.

Go to the clinic. Wait in the outer room
Where like an old possum the snag-nailed hand will hump
On its knee in murderous patience, and the pomp
Of pain swells like the Indies, or a plum.
And there you will stand, as on the Roman hill,
Stunned by each withdrawn gaze and severe shape,
The first barbarian victor stood to gape
At the sacrificial fathers, white-robed, still;
And even the feverish old Jew stares stern with authority
Till you feel like one who has come too late, or improperly
clothed, to a party.

The doctor will take you now. He is burly and clean;
Listening, like lover or worshipper, bends at your heart.
He cannot make out just what it tries to impart,
So smiles; says you simply need a change of scene.
Of scene, of solace: therefore Florida,
Where Ponce de Leon clanked among the lilies,
Where white sails skit on blue and cavort like fillies,

And the shoulder gleams white in the moonlit corridor.
A change of love: if love is a groping Godward, though blind,
No matter what crevice, cranny, chink, bright in dark, the pale
                     tentacle find.

In Florida consider the flamingo
Its color passion but its neck a question.
Consider even that girl the other guests shun
On beach, at bar, in bed, for she may know
The secret you are seeking, after all;
Or the child you humbly sit by, excited and curly,
That screams on the shore at the sea's sunlit hurlyburly,
Till the mother calls its name, toward nightfall.
Till you sit alone: in the dire meridians, off Ireland, in fury
Of spume-tooth and dawnless sea-heave, salt rimes the lookout's
                     devout eye.

Till you sit alone—which is the beginning of error—
Behind you the music and lights of the great hotel:
Solution, perhaps, is public, despair personal,
But history held to your breath clouds like a mirror.
There are many states, and towns in them, and faces,
But meanwhile, the little old lady in black, by the wall,
Admires all the dancers, and tells you how just last fall
Her husband died in Ohio, and damp mists her glasses;
She blinds and croaks, like a toad or a Norn, in the horrible
                     light,
And rattles her crutch, which may put forth a small bloom,
                     perhaps white.

ROBERT PENN WARREN

THREE

The Beast

Man, as Sir Thomas Browne was fond of pointing out, is an amphibian. His total personality, known and unknown—what Carl Jung calls the *self*—is split in a multitude of ways, each of which is frequently a cause of civil war within the being of any man and Everyman. Flesh and spirit, reason and passion look disdainfully on one another; ego tries to ignore the id, which proves rebellious; heart complains of chilly intellect, and intellect condescends to the blundering heart; the conscious mind receives disquieting rumors of an unknown life at work in the unconscious, and the unconscious seems to amuse itself by surfacing and playing hob with well-laid plans and carefully groomed assumptions. In view of all this, one can see that the Beast is an indispensable metaphor whose function, generally, is to convey the shame, distaste, hostility, and terror with which any given faction, from its parochial viewpoint, looks upon another. The Hero's task is to effect a reconciliation or Atonement of the warring parties and, in particular, to disarm the composite Beast of the fear which it inspires. When it is repressed and sullen, the Beast is mischievous at best and often murderous; and, even when it is not hostile, it is likely to inspire in us a superstitious dread of the unknown (*vide*, Winfield Townley Scott, "The Difference"; Robert Penn Warren, "Eidolon").

The more optimistic accounts of Beast-taming seem to suggest that what the Hero has to fear from Gorgon, Giant, or Minotaur is mostly fear itself. This belief underlies the urgent musings of the desert traveler in James Stephens' "In Waste Places." He is aware that the lion that lurks behind every cactus, making ready to spring at him, would soon dispatch him if it knew that he is "frightened as a maid"; but when the speaker can find the strength to dare his fear, he will not only "call / The lion out to lick [his] hand," but will also be enabled to escape the "desert land" in which he is the restless captive of his fear. Courage is an admirable virtue, but it avails the Hero little if he must depend on his own resources to sustain and implement it. Perseus has generous assistance from the gods in conquering the Gorgon, Medusa: a helmet which renders its wearer invisible, winged sandals, a curved sword belonging to Hermes, and a brass shield that will permit him to look at the Gorgon's reflected image rather than directly into her deadly eyes. Assistance from the gods expresses metaphorically that inexplicable access of power and knowledge which, if one is fortunate, flows like multipurpose adrenalin into the sinew and brain of the hero when his need is critical. Relative to Everyman's threading of the labyrinth which leads to the Minotaur, Isabella Gardner says, "Each man must journey naked there / nor arm himself with wing or stone" ("The Minotaur"); that is, no Hero can really know in advance that he has the power to slay the Beast. But this is not to say that he goes to meet it unequipped. Somewhere in the dark, he has learned to "walk with all that once he fled," and that, for him, is wings and sword and shield enough. Louise Bogan's dreamer ("The Dream") is about to be crushed by a ramping horse, and has nearly swooned with fear, when "Another woman . . . Leapt in the air, and clutched at the leather and chain." The secret, this Lady says, is to give the fierce creature "some poor thing you alone claim," whereupon the "terrible beast" will "put down his head in love." In Muriel Rukeyser's "The Minotaur," the Beast is the speaker's own heart, lonely and betrayed. Its suffering, fear, and pride have made it fiercely invulnerable to the love which seeks to set it free. The necessary miracle does not always come to pass.

The Beast is often associated with the elemental power of whatever is wholly or partially beyond the control of reason and the will: the passions, the id, and the unconscious mind. To persons seated comfortably around the fireplace in May Swenson's "Hypnotist," the fire suggests "our unused daring," "the red locks of the sun / brought home to a cage"; and the cozy teatime atmosphere is disturbed by a perverse wish to "loosen in ourselves the terrible." On the other hand, "the terrible" is depicted on a rampage in Sylvia Plath's "The Bull of Bendylaw," and the people of that kingdom are assuredly the worse for it. When the black bull of the sea "Hove up against Bendylaw," the king and queen were quietly passing the time of day in the palace garden—she staring stiffly from the mulberry arbor, he gravely fingering his beard. As "The great bronze gate" begins to crack under the bull's assault, an unseemly panic seizes the dignified courtiers and ladies-in-waiting:

> *Along box-lined walks in the florid sun*
> *Toward the rowdy bellow and back again*
> *The lords and ladies ran.*

No "daisy chain" of propriety, and no words of wisdom from any "learned man" can have the slightest restraining effect upon the Beast, who has the elemental power of a cyclone or a volcanic eruption. The Kingdom of Bendylaw, the seat of civilized virtues, succumbs without a struggle to the primitive force which it had maddened by restraint. The orgy and ecstasy of Dionysus, the noble bull, is the nemesis of the rule of prudence and dogmatic morality and the polar opposite of the "God Apollo's golden mean" (Robert Graves, "The White Goddess"). When King Pentheus of Thebes refused to acknowledge the divinity of Dionysus, he was torn to shreds by the frenzied female votaries of the god, led by his own mother, Agave. Psychologically, such rebellion is the thwarted id's revenge—a phenomenon which is often dramatized in literature and in world politics. Defeated Germany breeds a Hitler. The unfortunate missionary in Somerset Maugham's "Rain" and Angelo in Shakespeare's *Measure for Measure* are moral perfectionists who yield so suddenly and involuntarily to sexual attraction that they become not lovers but criminal rapists. Under ideal circumstances, however, the raw energy of the id is the fuel of creativity—the propagation of offspring and of works of art. Benedick, the reluctant lover of Shakespeare's *Much Ado about Nothing*, justifies his friends' prediction that "In time the savage bull doth bear the yoke"; and the music of Orpheus, before the intoxicated votaries of Dionysus silenced it, possessed not only charms to soothe the savage breast but power to make "trees, stones, and floods" draw near and listen (*The Merchant of Venice:* V.i.80).

Attempts to exalt one human faculty at the expense of another always result in disaster of some kind. When George Garrett's hunter ("Narcissus") succeeds in severing "reality and the fierce dream," he recognizes as his own the "frozen features" of the Beast which he has slain. Although the werewolf is hardly an attractive creature (*vide* Richard Wilbur's "Beasts"), his ferocity has a certain rapport with natural phenomena such as the cries of "The ripped mouse, safe in the owl's talon," while "suitors of excellence," enamoured of "the painful / Beauty of heaven," make such dreams for men "As told will break their hearts always, bringing / Monsters into the city." For the intellect, impatient with human emotion and the notion of nature as kind and solicitous, the created order may be conceived of as a "geometrical necessity" that has the beautiful certainty of mathematics but is "brute" because it is, by definition, indifferent to man. The perverse allure and potential deadliness of such a conception is embodied by Randall Jarrell in the title Beast of "The Snow-Leopard," which watches "incuriously" as a human caravan winds the intense cold and thinning atmosphere of a mountain pass, headed for extinction in "the heart of heartlessness."

If we think of the Beast as the embodiment of all that is frightening to children and to childish adults, then the Hero who rids the world of this scourge may actually be doing man a disservice, as Richard Wilbur shows in "Beowulf." Not to reckon with the Beast is to remain forever a child, but to destroy him altogether is to cut off the hidden springs of vitality which only the propitiated Beast can make available. The only Beast that can stop our hearts, says John Ciardi, is that most equivocal of deities, Success ("Song for an Allegorical Play"). "When best we love / we have no reason but to fail," and what we learn from love is that "we cannot fail what we forgive." The "church mouse" of the spirit and the "wart hog" of the flesh can be atoned, if "mercy be our sign"; under that sign, neither Beast will destroy the other, but they "shall rise, grown admirable, and be . . . each by each set free." Mythically expressed, the admirable composite Beast appears as the "noble animal" of the dream in "Chimera" (Barbara Howes). This creature has two heads—that of a lion and a goat—and a dragon's body, which it manages so well that it becomes the image of Atonement between its several parts: "each reckless / Nature in balance,

flying apart in one." Whether this Beast is "phantom or real," says
the dreamer, is irrelevant. Looking upon it as it "ramped and ran,"
she says, "My heart took heart."

THE DIFFERENCE

The buffalo loomed at the far loop of the field:
Though mildly grazing in twilight, a thunderhead tethered.
Spectators—man and two children—some others—
Clutched tickets and kept their distance, regarding the rare
beast.

We were—after all—suddenly there—there in the same grass
At the edge of our town: the familiar vacant lot
Usurped by the savage shape which grazed inattentive:
We grew—embarrassed, frightened—into shy invaders.

Staring and silent, we stood back. Though the crickets rang
And the evening star opened low over the western fence
The shadowy field was bisontine; the ground shook—
Once—with the thud of an absent-minded forefoot.

The little girl said to her father "I want to go see him";
But the boy dared not; he watched them hand in hand
Go slowly within the dusk to confront—quite close—
While he stayed alone among strangers—that hunching dark-
ness.

Silhouette now: the buffalo: horned ghost
Of an ancient philosopher, bearded and ominous,
Transmigrated, neither free nor dead. Nothing occurred
To the father and sister. They returned safe. The three went
home.

WINFIELD TOWNLEY SCOTT

THE MOST OF IT

He thought he kept the universe alone;
For all the voice in answer he could wake
Was but the mocking echo of his own
From some tree-hidden cliff across the lake.
Some morning from the boulder-broken beach
He would cry out on life, that what it wants
Is not its own love back in copy speech,
But counter-love, original response.
And nothing ever came of what he cried
Unless it was the embodiment that crashed
In the cliff's talus on the other side,
And then in the far-distant water splashed,
But after a time allowed for it to swim,
Instead of proving human when it neared
And someone else additional to him,
As a great buck it powerfully appeared,
Pushing the crumpled water up ahead,
And landed pouring like a waterfall,
And stumbled through the rocks with horny tread,
And forced the underbrush—and that was all.

ROBERT FROST

EIDOLON

All night, in May, dogs barked in the hollow woods;
Hoarse, from secret huddles of no light,
By moonlit bole, hoarse, the dogs gave tongue.
In May, by moon, no moon, thus: I remember
Of their far clamor the throaty, infatuate timbre.

The boy, all night, lay in the black room,
Tick-straw, all night, harsh to the bare side.
Staring, he heard; the clotted dark swam slow.
Far off, by wind, no wind, unappeasable riot
Provoked, resurgent, the bosom's nocturnal disquiet.

What hungers kept the house? under the rooftree
The boy; the man, clod-heavy, hard hand uncurled;
The old man, eyes wide, spittle on his beard.
In dark was crushed the may-apple: plunging, the rangers
Of dark remotelier belled their unhoused angers.

Dogs quartered the black woods: blood black on
May-apple at dawn, old beech-husk. And trails are lost
By rock, in ferns lost, by pools unlit.
I heard the hunt. Who saw, in darkness, how fled
The white eidolon from the fanged commotion rude?

ROBERT PENN WARREN

THE IMAGE

A spider in the bath. The image noted:
Significant maybe but surely cryptic.
A creature motionless and rather bloated,
The barriers shining, vertical and white:
Passing concern, and pity with spite.

Next day with some surprise one finds it there.
It seems to have moved an inch or two, perhaps.
It starts to take on that familiar air
Of prisoners for whom time is erratic:
The filthy aunt forgotten in the attic.

Quite obviously it came up through the waste,
Rejects through ignorance or apathy
That passage back. The problem must be faced;
And life go on though strange intruders stir
Among its ordinary furniture.

One jibs at murder, so a sheet of paper
Is slipped beneath the accommodating legs.
The bathroom window shows for the escaper
The lighted lanterns of laburnum hung
In copper beeches—on which scene it's flung.

We certainly would like thus easily
To cast out of the house all suffering things.
But sadness and responsibility
For our own kind lives in the image noted:
A half-loved creature, motionless and bloated.

ROY FULLER

IN WASTE PLACES

As a naked man I go
    Through the desert sore afraid;
Holding high my head, although
    I'm as frightened as a maid.

The lion crouches there!   I saw
    In barren rocks his amber eye!
He parts the cactus with his paw!
    He stares at me, as I go by!

He would pad upon my trace
    If he thought I was afraid!
If he knew my hardy face
    Veils the terrors of a maid.

He rises in the night-time, and
    He stretches forth!   He snuffs the air!
He roars!   He leaps along the sand!
    He creeps!   He watches everywhere!

His burning eyes, his eyes of bale
    Through the darkness I can see!
He lashes fiercely with his tail!
    He makes again to spring at me!

I am the lion, and his lair!
    I am the fear that frightens me!
I am the desert of despair!
    And the night of agony!

Night or day, whate'er befall,
    I must walk that desert land,
Until I dare my fear, and call
    The lion out to lick my hand!

                              JAMES STEPHENS

DESERT PLACES

Snow falling and night falling fast, oh, fast
In a field I looked into going past,
And the ground almost covered smooth in snow,
But a few weeds and stubble showing last.

The woods around it have it—it is theirs.
All animals are smothered in their lairs.
I am too absent-spirited to count;
The loneliness includes me unawares.

And lonely as it is, that loneliness
Will be more lonely ere it will be less—
A blanker whiteness of benighted snow
With no expression, nothing to express.

They cannot scare me with their empty spaces
Between stars—on stars where no human race is.
I have it in me so much nearer home
To scare myself with my own desert places.

                              ROBERT FROST

THE MINOTAUR

The labyrinthine forest's spoor
lead to the patient Minotaur
Deep in the dark and structured core
the bull-man waits inside the maze
and he who dares explore will raze
the beast of fear behind the door.

No Ariadne and no crone
will point the way. Each man alone
must thread his path, unreel his own
life spool and fumble to the lair.
Each man must journey naked there
nor arm himself with wing nor stone.

For he who goes his armor shed
and walks with all that once he fled
that man will face the hornèd head
the unimaginable eyes
and find there where the monster dies
the ichor that the terror bled.

ISABELLA GARDNER

THE DREAM

O God, in the dream the terrible horse began
To paw at the air, and make for me with his blows.
Fear kept for thirty-five years poured through his mane,
And retribution equally old, or nearly, breathed through his
    nose.

Coward complete, I lay and wept on the ground
When some strong creature appeared, and leapt for the rein.
Another woman, as I lay half in a swound,
Leapt in the air, and clutched at the leather and chain.

Give him, she said, something of yours as a charm.
Throw him, she said, some poor thing you alone claim.
No, no, I cried, he hates me; he's out for harm,
And whether I yield or not, it is all the same.

But, like a lion in a legend, when I flung the glove
Pulled from my sweating, my cold right hand,
The terrible beast, that no one may understand,
Came to my side, and put down his head in love.

LOUISE BOGAN

THE MINOTAUR

Trapped, blinded, led; and in the end betrayed
Daily by new betrayals as he stays
Deep in his labyrinth, shaking and going mad.
Betrayed. Betrayed. Raving, the beaten head
Heavy with madness, he stands, half-dead and proud.
No one again will ever see his pride.
No one will find him by walking to him straight
But must be led circuitously about,
Calling to him and close and, losing the subtle thread,
Lose him again; while he waits, brutalized
By loneliness. Later, afraid
Of his own suffering. At last, savage and made
Ravenous, ready to prey upon the race
If it so much as learn the clews of blood
Into his pride his fear his glistening heart.
Now is the patient deserted in his fright
And love carrying salvage round the world
Lost in a crooked city; roundabout,
By the sea, the precipice, all the fantastic ways
Betrayal weaves its trap; loneliness knows the thread,
And the heart is lost, lost, trapped, blinded and led,
Deserted in the middle of the maze.

MURIEL RUKEYSER

THE THING THAT EATS THE HEART

The thing that eats the heart comes wild with years.
It died last night, or was it wounds before,
But somehow crawls around, inflamed with need,
Jingling its medals at the fang-scratched door.

We were not unprepared: with lamp and book
We sought the wisdom of another age
Until we heard the action of the bolt.
A little wind investigates the page.

No use pretending to the pitch of sleep;
By turnings we are known, our times and dates
Examined in the courts of either / or
While armless griefs mount lewd and headless doubts.

It pounces in the dark, all pity-ripe,
An enemy as soft as tears or cancer,
In whose embrace we fall, as to a sickness
Whose toxins in our cells cry sin and danger.

Hero of crossroads, how shall we defend
This creature-lump whose charity is art
When its own self turns Christian-cannibal?
The thing that eats the heart is mostly heart.

STANLEY KUNITZ

BEASTS

Beasts in their major freedom
Slumber in peace tonight. The gull on his ledge
Dreams in the guts of himself the moon-plucked waves below,
And the sunfish leans on a stone, slept
By the lyric water,

In which the spotless feet
Of deer make dulcet splashes, and to which
The ripped mouse, safe in the owl's talon, cries
Concordance. Here there is no such harm
And no such darkness

As the selfsame moon observes
Where, warped in window-glass, it sponsors now
The werewolf's painful charge. Turning his head away
On the sweaty bolster, he tries to remember
The mood of manhood,

But lies at last, as always,
Letting it happen, the fierce fur soft to his face,
Hearing with sharper ears the wind's exciting minors,

The leaves' panic, and the degradation
Of the heavy streams.

Meantime, at high windows
Far from thicket and pad-fall, suitors of excellence
Sigh and turn from their work to construe again the painful
Beauty of heaven, the lucid moon
And the risen hunter,

Making such dreams for men
As told will break their hearts as always, bringing
Monsters into the city, crows on the public statues,
Navies fed to the fish in the dark
Unbridled waters.

RICHARD WILBUR

NARCISSUS

Hunter in the lonely field,
figure of our primal grace,
all that seems, all that's real,
united, lead you in the chase.

The arrow of the heart is keen;
if your hand is steady, true,
reality and the fierce dream,
stricken, will be cut in two.

And triumphantly you pose
beside the victim of your aim
whose frozen features now disclose
the beast you hunted had your name.

GEORGE GARRETT

HYPNOTIST

His hair framed beneath the clock
a red-haired beast hypnotic in the room

glazes our eyes and draws us close
with delicious snarls and flickers of his claws
We stir our teacups and our wishes feast
on his cruelty

Throw the Christian chairs to him
A wild child in us cries
Or let us be Daniel bared
to that seething maze his mane
Loops of his fur graze the sill
where the clock's face looks scared

Comfort-ensnared and languorous
our unused daring roused resembles him
fettered on the hearth's stage
behind the iron dogs
He's the red locks of the sun
brought home to a cage

Hunched before his flaring shape
we stir our teacups
We wish he would escape
and loosen in ourselves the terrible
But only his reflection pounces
on the parquet and the stair

                              MAY SWENSON

THE BULL OF BENDYLAW

The black bull bellowed before the sea.
The sea, till that day orderly,
Hove up against Bendylaw.

The queen in the mulberry arbor stared
Stiff as a queen on a playing card.
The king fingered his beard.

A blue sea, four horny bull-feet,
A bull-snouted sea that wouldn't stay put,
Bucked at the garden gate.

Along box-lined walks in the florid sun
Toward the rowdy bellow and back again
The lords and ladies ran.

The great bronze gate began to crack,
The sea broke in at every crack,
Pellmell, blueblack.

The bull surged up, the bull surged down,
Not to be stayed by a daisy chain
Nor by any learned man.

O the king's tidy acre is under the sea,
And the royal rose in the bull's belly,
And the bull on the king's highway.

SYLVIA PLATH

THE SNOW-LEOPARD

His pads furring the scarp's rime,
Weightless in greys and ecru, gliding
Invisibly, incuriously
As the crystals of the cirri wandering
A mile below his absent eyes,
The leopard gazes at the caravan.
The yaks groaning with tea, the burlaps
Lapping and lapping each stunned universe
That gasps like a kettle for its thinning life
Are pools in the interminable abyss
That ranges up through ice, through air, to night.
Raiders of the unminding element,
The last cold capillaries of their kind,
They move so slowly they are motionless
To any eye less stubborn than a man's . . . .

From the implacable jumble of the blocks
The grains dance icily, a scouring plume,
Into the breath, sustaining, unsustainable,
They trade to that last stillness for their death.
They sense with misunderstanding horror, with desire,
Behind the world their blood sets up in mist
The brute and geometrical necessity:
The leopard waving with a grating purr
His six-foot tail; the leopard, who looks sleepily—
Cold, fugitive, secure—at all that he knows,
At all that he is: the heart of heartlessness.

RANDALL JARRELL

BEOWULF

The land was overmuch like scenery,
The flowers attentive, the grass too garrulous green;
In the lake like a dropped kerchief could be seen
The lark's reflection after the lark was gone;
The Roman road lay paved too shiningly
For a road so many men had traveled on.

Also the people were strange, were strangely warm.
The king recalled the father of his guest,
The queen brought mead in a studded cup, the rest
Were kind, but in all was a vagueness and a strain,
Because they lived in a land of daily harm.
And they said the same things again and again.

It was a childish country; and a child,
Grown monstrous, so besieged them in the night
That all their daytimes were a dream of fright
That it would come and own them to the bone.
The hero, to his battle reconciled,
Promised to meet that monster all alone.

So then the people wandered to their sleep
And left him standing in the echoed hall.
They heard the rafters rattle fit to fall,

The child departing with a broken groan,
And found their champion in a rest so deep
His head lay harder sealed than any stone.

The land was overmuch like scenery,
The lake gave up the lark, but now its song
Fell to no ear, the flowers too were wrong,
The day was fresh and pale and swiftly old,
The night put out no smiles upon the sea;
And the people were strange, the people strangely cold.

They gave him horse and harness, helmet and mail,
A jeweled shield, an ancient battle-sword,
Such gifts as are the hero's hard reward
And bid him do again what he has done.
These things he stowed beneath his parting sail,
And wept that he could share them with no son.

He died in his own country a kinless king,
A name heavy with deeds, and mourned as one
Will mourn for the frozen year when it is done.
They buried him next the sea on a thrust of land:
Twelve men rode round his barrow all in a ring,
Singing of him what they could understand.

RICHARD WILBUR

LOVE AMONG THE MANICHEES

The blond cowl terse as a blunt threat to injure,
The claws instinctive to a triggering nerve,
I am a shut spring in my fanged disguises,
Aping the beast I serve.

I would be for you an offering of clear spirit,
Like water glistening over your spread hands,
Like the pattern described in air when the bird has left it,
Like not yet peopled lands.

Tick-laden fur ruffling for winds of danger,
I gorge on honey in the fallen tree,

Snarl at approachers to these laden acres
That bind their fruit to me.

I would be for you like a length of fallow
From the earliest world, like open mountainside
Too high for spurred seed to beat and follow,
For the edged wing to glide.

Puzzled, the shared beast lurks under my eyelids,
Dumb, menacing, not able to let go,
Or to conceive that who comes unconstrainèd
Stays the most easily so.

I would be for you as a willing mirror,
Plain crystal, undefined, of itself dumb,
That shapes its voice when you first look into it,
Smiling, "Now you have come."

WILLIAM DICKEY

SONG FOR AN ALLEGORICAL PLAY

Ah could we wake in mercy's name—
the church mouse in each other's eyes
forgiven, the wart hog washed in flame
confessed—when paunch from paunch we rise,
false and unmartyred, to pretend
we dress for Heaven in the end.

To look and not to look away
from what we see, but, kindly known,
admit our scraping small decay
and the gross jowls of flesh on bone—
think what a sweetness tears might be
in mercy, each by each set free.

Only Success is beast enough
to stop our hearts. Oh twist his tail
and let him howl. When best we love

we have no reason but to fail,
in reason learning as we live
we cannot fail what we forgive.

That mouse is in your eyes and mine.
That wart hog wallows in our blood.
But, ah, let mercy be our sign,
and all our queer beasts, understood,
shall rise, grown admirable, and be,
in mercy, each by each set free.

JOHN CIARDI

CHIMERA

After a fearful maze where doubt
Crept at my side down the terrible lightless channel,
I came in my dream to a sandspit parting
Wind-tossed fields of ocean. There,
Lightstepping, appeared
A trio of moose or mules,
Ugly as peat,
Their trotters slim as a queen's.
"Hippocampi!" cried a voice as they sped
Over black water, their salty course,
And away. From the heaving sea
Then sprang a fabulous beast
For its evening gallop.
Head of a lion, goat's head rearing
Back, derisive, wild—the dragon
Body scaling the waves; each reckless
Nature in balance, flying apart
In one. How it sported
Across the water, how it ramped and ran!
My heart took heart. Awaking, I thought:
What was disclosed in this vision
Was good; phantom or real,
I have looked on a noble animal.

BARBARA HOWES

❧ FOUR ✆

The Double

"A man goes far to find out what he is." So says Theodore Roethke ("In a Dark Time"), and the experience of the Hero amply bears him out. The Double is the unknown self personified, an individual sometimes sinister, sometimes radiant with promise, but always charged with the fascination of being at the same time known and unknown, intimate as one's bones and blood, yet also deeply alien. The Double sometimes is an image of wholeness, Christ-like in his generosity of spirit: "He is loved and he is happy with his endless loving" (Winfield Townley Scott, "The Far-off Man"). To know him would be to cast off fear, loneliness, and the insatiable struggle of the will to assert its sovereignty; but to find him seems too difficult: "I should have to go so deep and open so far." More familiar is the conception of the Double as the *shadow*, the term used by Carl Jung to signify the sum of those impulses and character traits which we would like to disown and for this reason shove down out of the conscious mind, as we might fail to acknowledge a relative whose lack of cultivation embarrasses us in front of our friends. In any case, the Double must be reckoned with if a man is to solve the riddle of his own identity, "Which I is *I*?"

Coming to terms with the Double is necessarily painful, for the process, in the end, demolishes the flattering self-image that we devise to show the world. It is as though unconsciously we all are playwrights, fashioning a role for ourselves to play and to half believe in. In keeping with the theatrical analogy, Jung uses the term *persona* for ourselves as the character whom we create. It would seem that the persona is a necessary fiction and may serve us well enough until, as often happens without apparent cause, the footsteps of the Double begin to dog our trail. The persona cannot ignore that threatening presence, try though it will; sometimes gradually, sometimes with dramatic suddenness, it begins to crack like an outworn chrysalis, and a process no less dangerous than rich in promise has begun. The Hero has no choice but to seek the Double out, somewhere in darkness, and to bring him into the light, where he may become a friend; or to remain in darkness as the prisoner of an enemy impossible to reconcile.

Few novels equal in imaginative appeal *The Portrait of Dorian Gray* and *The Strange Case of Dr. Jekyll and Mr. Hyde*—a fact which testifies to the Double's vital role in Everyman's experience. In Wilde's novel, the title figure retains the handsome, clean-cut visage of his youth, although he falls ever more deeply into corruption; but his portrait, stowed away out of sight but never quite forgotten, prepares for the destruction of Gray's suave persona by recording in detail the aging ugliness that corresponds to the inner degradation of the man. Quaffing a potion, Stevenson's highly respectable Dr. Jekyll becomes the beastly Mr. Hyde. An interesting experiment! But it is more than that, for the ruthless inhumanity of Hyde has a perverse attraction for the frail civility of Dr. Jekyll's much-esteemed persona. An antidote, which serves at first to restore the doctor to himself, loses its efficacy with continued use; and the despairing Jekyll, clinging ever more tenuously to human nature, finally changes, like a werewolf, into his repellent counterpart, whether he will or no. One must suppose that if Dr. Jekyll had acknowledged his relationship with Mr. Hyde, sharing his guilt, the latter's power over him might have been broken; but he is at pains to conceal his latent depravity, while taking pleasure in yielding to it secretly. As a result, for Dr. Jekyll, the path that leads to the Inferno has no exit. A contrasting case is dramatized by Conrad in *The Secret Sharer*. Here, a sympathetic understanding develops between the protagonist, a ship's captain, and Leggatt, a murderer who takes refuge on his ship. The captain's function is to permit the Double to escape punishment for a crime of passion which he finds possible to excuse and forgive; and, as Leggatt swims away to freedom, the self-doubt of the captain yields to a new self-mastery and authority which save his ship and assure him of success in his command.

The process of redemption, as it is acted out between persona and shadow, has little hope of success unless it is mutual and voluntary. Josephine Miles, in "The Savages," brings cogent sarcasm to bear upon the settlers of America whose cruelty to their "brazen images," the Indians, hypocritically gave way to the persuasion that "It was an act of love to seek their salvation." This brand of missionary zeal, and the civilization that attends it, merely "Brings Dionysus to the mesa and the cottonwood grove," while Apollo continues, for the benefit of civic groups, "to harp on hope." Nothing, of course, can come of evading the issue; attempts to suppress "our images" or to "buy them off" must always fail. If redemption is to occur, our negotiations with the individual and collective shadow must be tuned for a positive response to the always possible generosity of the oppressed: "*We cannibals must help these Christians.*" The redemptive act is always sacrificial. The plight of the protagonist in "To a Face in a Crowd" (Robert Penn Warren) stems from the failure of his courage in some dim ancestral past. He has had civilization imposed upon him but he has not earned his place in it by joining those who, in the face of primal darkness, "Wrestled with the ocean"; hence he suffers from an unappeasable dread of darkness, of the sea, and of the "black and turbulent blood." Now, shrinking from the Quest which he himself lacked courage to pursue, he seeks a twin, a brother who will not "Renounce the night" as he has done but boldly settle the score on his behalf. If his chosen substitute should prove no stronger than he, the two of them will meet, he says, "As weary nomads in this desert at last, / Borne in the lost procession of these feet." It is a valid warning, certainly, and, just as certainly, will prove to be a self-fulfilling prophecy.

One of the poet's functions is to serve as spokesman for the desperate need of the other self, the shadow stretching out a hand in the dark (Archibald MacLeish, "The Revenant"), the outwardly resolved persona which cannot conceal the desolation of an inward loneliness. Failure of love lies at the heart of the voyeur's problem in "The Corridor" (Thom Gunn). He cannot accept commitment to another, for he does not wish to be a mere "inhabitant / Of someone else's world." Therefore he takes his simple pleasure by observing lovers through a keyhole, and he can only imagine, for a friend, another parasite who lives vicariously by watching *him*. On the other hand, the "most chaste" speaker of "Strumpet Song" (Sylvia Plath) stumbles on warmth of sympathy by discovering that her Double's anguish is her own. She herself is that despised "foul slut" whose mouth is "Made to do violence on" and who cries out in pain,

> *Walks there not some such one man*
> *As can spare breath*
> *To patch with brand of love this rank grimace.*

The plight of prisoners in our "made world" confronts the eye at every turn. Finding something of ourselves in the "great consenting gaze" of dummies in the window of a department store, we can imagine that we see "a world's bones" emerging from those lifeless bodies (Randall Jarrell, "Dummies"). Pygmalion proved the quality of his art when he conceived and executed a statue of Galatea so beautiful that he fell in love with it. Then, to his joy, Venus granted his prayer that the statue should become a living woman. The Hero as Pygmalion champions the living dead who are, after all, his counterparts.

On the whole, the concept of the Double is a heartening one, implying as it does an existence that is "a steady storm of correspondences" ("In a Dark Time") and of mutual dependencies. In the dualistic view of myth, the world is held together by a tension of apparent opposites which interchange and yield a positive image at one time, a negative at another. Always there is a hint of final and essential oneness. In Milton and Dante, heaven corresponds to hell; Milton's Messiah goes forth to make a universe, and Satan to destroy one; Kore is the spring for earth and spirit, also the Queen of the Land of the Dead; and the World Tree can reach no farther into the heavens than its roots descend into darkness. In the human sphere, as Shakespeare's Theseus observes, poet, madman, and lover correspond; our dreams draw from our waking lives, and we act out our dreams by daylight. The "purpose of playing," says Hamlet, "is to hold, as 'twere, the mirror up to nature." Daniel Hoffman's "wiser brother" ('When my wiser brother') is a native of "that republic of pure possibility" which the poet figures forth in words. The Hero, finding his difficult way through a maze of dark rooms, may find a clew to light in a "crazy tune" that sings inside his head (David Ferry, "In the Dark"); and, at the end of the last long hall,

approaching light as though it were "a friend / Long since of-
fended," he may discover that the windows which he sought are,
after all, none other than his eyes: "Outside myself what a beautiful
landscape lies!"

A BLIND MAN LOCKING HIS HOUSE

The tall clock in the hallway strikes
The half-hour chime:
Twelve-thirty. Now the hour has come
For footsteps in the dark, that like
To wander through this house from room to room.

My wife and I live here alone,
So my wife thinks;
But in the dark my dark eye blinks,
Down passageways of pure unknown
The hunter starts to stalk, and my heart sinks.

I rise and gird myself to face
This sounding house,
One hand stretched out against the blows
From chairs that will not stay in place,
From anarchy that sightlessness allows,

The other rummaging for keys
In my coat pocket.
At each door, as I pause to lock it,
Relentless blood assails my eyes
And drives them crazy: useless in their sockets,

They still roll upward in my head.
By force of will
I aim them downward: through this chill,
Pretending to look straight ahead,
I make the footsteps think I see, until

Between me and this heavy tread
At least one door
Is safely locked. From door to door
I pass, and learn I am misled:
There is no safe place for me any more.

To such thoughts does this presence tempt me
As floorboards creak
That I might drive myself to break
My heart at last, and find it empty,
Because some thing stalks me and will not speak.

The hallway clock clangs like my heart,
In time with feet
That flee, and press behind, and meet
At last, and all of this is part
Of all this house. My pitiful conceit

Breaks down, and I shall not escape.
Older than air
Or the stairway, he is somewhere
In dust and stone that saps all hope;
When I lie down that sound will still be there.

Time and again my wife has said
No one is there;
But in the weather of despair
As I climb up through dark to bed
I hear his step behind me on the stair.

HENRY TAYLOR

THE BURGLAR

I lock all the doors each night, I lock
Off separate rooms, I seal the house
As tight as glue about me, force
Myself to try and sleep—still in the dark
The whole thing isn't mine; I think,

I hear the clock, next to that a chink
Of noise below from one who's in, who knows
His way like I do, stands and stops and goes
Like I do, link by link
Dismantling treasure till each shelf is bare

Then straight back to the night, where the black air
Shuts like a gate behind him into place.
I think of day, the sun's beat on my face.
I toss and turn till morning. Don't ask me where
He's from or why I've never loved the things
He steals, or why I don't compare
Him with myself. I know one thing:
At night he comes, I hear him working there.

J. P. WARD

NOBODY

Nobody, ancient mischief, nobody,
Harasses always with an absent body.

Nobody coming up the road, nobody,
Like a tall man in a dark cloak, nobody.

Nobody about the house, nobody,
Like children creeping up the stairs, nobody.

Nobody anywhere in the garden, nobody,
Like a young girl quiet with needlework, nobody.

Nobody coming, nobody, not yet here,
Incessantly welcomed by the wakeful ear.

Until this nobody shall consent to die
Under his curse must everyone lie—

The curse of his envy, of his grief and fright,
Of sudden rape and murder screamed in the night.

ROBERT GRAVES

FUNERAL

Now he is gone where worms can feed
Upon him, a discarded rind,
God's image, and a thinking reed,
 In blindness blind

As any taxidermist's owl.
He who was tall and fleet and fair
Is now no more; the winds howl,
 The stones stare.

Your double who went dressed in black
And beat the lions to their cage
Lies in blood; the whips crack,
 The beasts rage.

Don your somber herringbone
And clap your top hat to your head.
The carriage waits; the axles groan;
 While prayers are said,

Rest your hot forehead on the plush;
And hear, beyond the measured, sad
Funeral drums, above the hush,
 The lions pad

Intently through some sunless glade,
The body's blood-fed beasts in all
Their fury, while the lifted spade
 Lets earth fall.

    WILLIAM JAY SMITH

THE SAVAGES

As we rowed from our ships and set foot on the shore
In the still coves,
We met our images.

Our brazen images emerged from the mirrors of the wood
Like yelling shadows,
So we searched our souls,

And in that hell and pit of everyman
Placed the location of their ruddy shapes.
We must be cruel to ourselves.

Then through the underbrush we cut our hopes
Forest after forest to within
The inner hush where Mississippi flows

And were in ambush at the very source,
Scalped to the cortex. Yet bought them off.
It was an act of love to seek their salvation.

President Jackson asked,
What good man would prefer a forester country ranged
    with savages
To our extensive republic studded with cities
With all the improvements art can devise or industry
    execute?

Pastor Smiley inquired,
What good man would allow his sins or his neighbors'
To put on human dress and run in the wilds
To leap out on innocent occasions?

Miss Benedict proposed,
The partial era of enlightenment in which we live
Brings Dionysus to the mesa and the cottonwood grove,
And floats Apollo to the barrows of the civic group
To ratify entreaties and to harp on hope.

Professor Roy Harvey Pearce quoted,
These savages are outlandish Tartars and Cain's children,
Though someone reported once, "They do not withhold
    assent
From the truth set forth in a credible manner."
Is it possible?

Henry David Thoreau,
The most popular highbrow overseas reading-material
For the armed forces, because while they work and wait
They see before them in the green shade
His ruddy image, said, as his last word when he died,
  Indians.

Reading today this manual of wisdom,
In the still coves
We meet our images

And, in ambush at the very source,
Would buy them off.   It is an act of love
To seek their salvation.

One party to the purchase
Receipts the purchase price and hands us back
His token of negotiation which redeems:
We cannibals must help these Christians.

                              JOSEPHINE MILES

TO A FACE IN A CROWD

Brother, my brother, whither do you pass?
Unto what hill at dawn, unto what glen,
Where among the rocks the faint lascivious grass
Fingers in lust the arrogant bones of men?

Beside what bitter waters will you go
Where the lean gulls of your heart along the shore
Rehearse to the cliffs the rhetoric of their woe?
In dream, perhaps, I have seen your face before.

A certain night has borne you and me;
We are the children of an ancient band
Broken between the mountains and the sea.
A cromlech marks for you that utmost strand

And you must find the dolorous place they stood.
Of old I know that shore, that dim terrain,
And know how black and turbulent the blood
Will beat through iron chambers of the brain

When at your back the taciturn tall stone,
Which is your fathers' monument and mark,
Repeats the waves' implacable monotone,
Ascends the night and propagates the dark.

Men there have lived who wrestled with the ocean;
I was afraid—the polyp was their shroud.
I was afraid.   That shore of your decision
Awaits beyond this street where in the crowd

Your face is blown, an apparition, past.
Renounce the night as I, and we must meet
As weary nomads in this desert at last,
Borne in the lost procession of these feet.

ROBERT PENN WARREN

MEDUSA

There is a tale of brow and clotted hair
Thrust in the window of a banquet room
Which froze eternally the revellers there,
The lights full on them in their postured doom:
The queen still held the carmine to her lips,
The king's mouth stood wide open for its laugh,
The jester's rigid leer launched silent quips;
Only a blind man moved and tapped his staff.
I cannot guess that physiognomy
The sight of which could curdle into stone
The gazer, though pities, horrors, terrors I
Have made encounter of and sometimes known.
But I knew one who turned to stone with terror
Of facing quietly a flawless mirror.

WILLIAM ALEXANDER PERCY

THE CORRIDOR

A separate place between the thought and felt
The empty hotel corridor was dark.
But here the keyhole shone, a meaning spark.
What fires were latent in it!   So he knelt.

Now, at the corridor's much lighter end,
A pierglass hung upon the wall and showed,
As by an easily deciphered code,
Dark, door, and man, hooped by a single band.

He squinted through the keyhole, and within
Surveyed an act of love that frank as air
He was too ugly for, or could not dare,
Or at a crucial moment thought a sin.

Pleasure was simple thus: he mastered it.
If once he acted as participant
He would be mastered, the inhabitant
Of someone else's world, mere shred to fit.

He moved himself to get a better look
And then it was he noticed in the glass
Two strange eyes in a fascinated face
That watched him like a picture in a book.

The instant drove simplicity away—
The scene was altered, it depended on
His kneeling, when he rose they were clean gone
The couple in the keyhole; this would stay.

For if the watcher of the watcher shown
There in the distant glass, should be watched too,
Who can be master, free of others; who
Can look around and say he is alone?

Moreover, who can know that what he sees
Is not distorted, that he is not seen

Distorted by a pierglass, curved and lean?
Those curious eyes, through him, were linked to these—

These lovers altered in the cornea's bend.
What could he do but leave the keyhole, rise,
Holding those eyes as equal in his eyes,
And go, one hand held out, to meet a friend?

THOM GUNN

IN A DARK TIME

In a dark time, the eye begins to see,
I meet my shadow in the deepening shade;
I hear my echo in the echoing wood—
A lord of nature weeping to a tree.
I lived between the heron and the wren,
Beasts of the hill and serpents of the den.

What's madness but nobility of soul
At odds with circumstance?   The day's on fire!
I know the purity of pure despair,
My shadow pinned against a sweating wall.
That place among the rocks—is it a cave,
Or winding path?   The edge is what I have.

A steady storm of correspondences!
A night flowing with birds, a ragged moon,
And in broad day the midnight come again!
A man goes far to find out what he is—
Death of the self in a long, tearless night,
All natural shapes blazing unnatural light.

Dark, dark my light, and darker my desire.
My soul, like some heat-maddened summer fly,
Keeps buzzing at the sill.   Which I is *I*?
A fallen man, I climb out of my fear.
The mind enters itself, and God the mind,
And one is One, free in the tearing wind.

Was nature kind?   The heart's core tractable?
All waters waver, and all fires fail.
Leaves, leaves, lean forth and tell me what I am;
This single tree turns into purest flame.
I am a man, a man at intervals
Pacing a room, a room with dead-white walls;
I feel the autumn fail—all that slow fire
Denied in me, who has denied desire.

                              THEODORE ROETHKE

LADY WEEPING AT THE CROSSROADS

Lady, weeping at the crossroads,
Would you meet your love
In the twilight with his greyhounds,
And the hawk on his glove?

Bribe the birds then on the branches,
Bribe them to be dumb,
Stare the hot sun out of heaven
That the night may come.

Starless are the nights of travel,
Bleak the winter wind;
Run with terror all before you
And regret behind.

Run until you hear the ocean's
Everlasting cry;
Deep though it may be and bitter
You must drink it dry,

Wear out patience in the lowest
Dungeons of the sea,
Searching through the stranded shipwrecks
For the golden key,

Push on to the world's end, pay the
Dread guard with a kiss,
Cross the rotten bridge that totters
Over the abyss.

There stands the deserted castle
Ready to explore;
Enter, climb the marble staircase
Open the locked door.

Cross the silent empty ballroom,
Doubt and danger past;
Blow the cobwebs from the mirror
See yourself at last.

Put your hand behind the wainscot,
You have done your part;
Find the penknife there and plunge it
Into your false heart.

W. H. AUDEN

STRUMPET SONG

With white frost gone
And all green dreams not worth much,
After a lean day's work
Time comes round for that foul slut:
Mere bruit of her takes our street
Until every man,
Red, pale or dark,
Veers to her slouch.

Mark, I cry, that mouth
Made to do violence on,
That seamed face
Askew with blotch, dint, scar
Struck by each dour year.

Walks there not some such one man
As can spare breath
To patch with brand of love this rank grimace
Which out from black tarn, ditch and cup
Into my most chaste own eyes
Looks up.

SYLVIA PLATH

DUMMIES

O the dummies in the windows!
Their big round arms are fair as milk,
They look through lashes, comb back locks
Of glittering embroidery silk.

How can the weak designer bear
The strength of that constructed face?
Resist when his own eyes give back
Their great consenting gaze?

Yet through that wax dream at last
Press a new world's different bones,
Eyes look, with their silk lashes gone,
At love and terror all their own.
Love laughs, when through our made world breaks
A stranger's real and difficult face.

RANDALL JARRELL

IN THE DARK

I wandered in my mind as in the dark.
I stumbled over a chair, ran into a wall,
Or another wall, I wandered down a hall,
And into another room, the same as before.
I stumbled against a wall, I felt the floor
Carefully with each foot, I found a door,
And into another room, the same as before.

I wandered in my mind, I was in the dark.
I sidled up against another wall,
I shouldered along it, searching for a door,
And found one, opening out into a hall
That led to another room, the same as before.
In fear I turned my voice to a little tune,
A crazy tune that sang inside my head,
And followed the tune as one would follow a thread
That leads one to or from a minotaur.
And that tune led me back or forward mazily,
That sang inside my head so crazily!

I followed or fled at last into a hall
That had a little light. Down at the end
Of the hall, a long way off, two windows were,
And into the windows came a little light.
I followed down the hall as to a friend
Long since offended. Timidly I wore
An anxious smile, eager to please. The light
Grew brighter still, till at last to the end
Of the hall I came. What a wonderful sight!
I found that I was looking through my eyes!
Outside of myself what a beautiful landscape lies!

DAVID FERRY

THE REVENANT

O too dull brain, O unperceiving nerves
That cannot sense what so torments my soul,
But like torn trees, when deep Novembers roll
Tragic with mighty winds and vaulting curves
Of sorrowful vast sound and light that swerves
In blown and tossing eddies, branch and bole
Shudder and gesture with a grotesque dole,
A grief that misconceives the grief it serves.

O too dull brain—with some more subtle sense
I know him here within the lightless room

Reaching his hand to me, and my faint eyes
See only darkness and the night's expanse,
And horribly, within the listening gloom,
My voice comes back, still eager with surprise.

ARCHIBALD MAC LEISH

"WHEN MY WISER BROTHER"

When my wiser brother
Who speaks so rarely
And only in my voice

(He is too busy matching souls
To the trees they will resemble, lovers
With one another,
The seahorse and the sun,
Sweet labor,
There's little time for speech)—when he

Finds words
Acceptable I will declare him,
For I am ready:
My phonemes, signs, parentheses
Await his spell.

All will be well
Disposed to consecrate the map
Of new peninsulas he will bequeath me.
But just when I've stepped out to choose the wine
For the banquet of our fond reunion
He will be gone,
Off to that republic
Of pure possibility
Where he plots a *coup d' état* against my exile.
Sometime, he may reveal it,

Though I am left meanwhile
Unbrothered,

My words all fled from split cicada skins
Into a busy fraction of the day.

DANIEL HOFFMAN

THE FAR-OFF MAN

That man in the far-off room who looks like me—
I think of him, I imagine him in the morning.
He works at his work, he goes among many people,
He is loved and he is happy with his endless loving.
He is young yet he waits, he watches with the long
Patience of the born wise; and I think of him,
I imagine him there, but I shall not know him.
I should have to go so deep and open so far.

WINFIELD TOWNLEY SCOTT

IV

THE LADY

The role of the Lady in the Hero's Quest is that of intermediary between the Hero and the Father. It is with her that he must deal along the way, and until he has worked out an accord with her, it is quite impossible for him to achieve atonement with the Father and receive from him that share in immortality which only the Father can bestow. When this is accomplished, he is ready to return to the starting point of his journey, bearing with him the Boon of his enlightenment and offering to share it with mankind.

To the sceptical modern mind, the Lady frequently appears in negative inversion—that is, as Nature in her ruthless and destructive aspect, or as the spirit shorn of its power to alleviate or transcend the fear and ignorance of her mortal incarnation. Such a conception figures strongly in Conrad's *Heart of Darkness*. In the office of the company for whom he is to pilot a boat up the Congo river into the heart of Africa, Marlow, the protagonist, is struck by a waking vision of two women whose resemblance to the Fates he reflects upon uneasily:

> *I thought of those two, guarding the door of Darkness, knitting black wool as for a warm pall, one introducing, introducing continuously to the unknown, the other scrutinizing the cheery and foolish faces with unconcerned old eyes.*

During his journey up the Congo, the jungle is, for Marlow, "an implacable force brooding over an inscrutable intention"; and the latent violence of this force is typified for him by the "black and incomprehensible frenzy" of the natives' dancing. When he reaches the Inner Station, he finds that the native consort of Kurtz, the Station's Chief, is the epitome of the vital and corrupting savagery to which the once-idealistic Kurtz has utterly succumbed:

> *She was savage and superb, wild-eyed and magnificent . . . the colossal body of the fecund and mysterious life seemed to look at her, pensive, as though it had been looking at the image of its own tenebrous and passionate soul.*

To balance this portrayal of the dark qualities of the Lady, we have only a description of a painting by Kurtz, "representing a woman, draped and blindfolded, carrying a lighted torch. . . . The move-

ment of the woman was stately, and the effect of the torchlight on
the face was sinister"—a far cry from such torchbearers as Liberty
and Knowledge! Nevertheless, the painting seems to be a symbolic
portrait of Kurtz's fiancée, whom we meet after the death of Kurtz,
when Marlow visits her on his return to Europe. On that occasion,
Marlow sees at once that this woman "had a mature capacity for
fidelity, for belief, for suffering"; yet, as he talks to her, the room
grows darker, and before their conversation ends, "only her fore-
head, smooth and white, remained illumined by the unextinguishable
light of belief and love." Marlow cannot bring himself to tell her
of the ultimate degradation of the Kurtz in whom she still believes,
and so she remains blindfolded, in effect, her faith untested by the
brutal fact, and the brutal fact unmitigated by the powers of trans-
figuration which the Lady, in other contexts, often has displayed.

The venerable folk tale of the loathly lady (*e.g.*, as told in the
fifteenth-century poem, "The Weddynge of Sir Gawen and Dame
Ragnell") metaphorically conveys the accord which the consum-
mate Hero, "the best of all Knights," can reach with the Lady in her
role as Nature. The essence of the tale is this: To save his life, a
young knight is obliged to answer the question, "What do women
most desire?" The answer is known only to an old Hag, whose
person is in all respects repulsive; and she will not reveal it unless
the knight will promise to marry her. Preferring misery to death,
he gives his promise and is told that women most desire to have
sovereignty over men. It is, of course, the correct answer, and it
signifies that Nature, the physical embodiment of the feminine
principle, demands that men should bend their will to hers. Soon,
the unhappy husband finds himself in bed with a creature whose
demand for love is a challenge all but impossible for him to meet.
However, he summons every ounce of courage and magnanimity at
his command and, with triumphant generosity, gives his loathly wife
a hearty kiss. Immediately, she is transformed into as fair a girl as
his heart could wish! But the test is not yet at an end. The lady
tells the knight that her beauty will not last. She will be either fair
by night and foul by day, or the other way around. Which does
he prefer? The baffled husband does not know the meaning of the
dilemma thus imposed on him, which is simply this: So long as man
conceives of his greatest good as the satisfaction of his own desires,
Nature appears to him in the guise of fickle Fortune, who freely
offers gifts at one time and at another snatches them away. After

painful deliberation, the knight decides that he is unable to make the choice, and he tells her to decide the matter in whichever way best pleases her. Thereupon, he is at once rewarded by a second miracle: The Lady, having attained sovereignty over her husband, freely gives her promise to be fair and faithful at all times, both night and day.

In her rôle as spirit (psyche, anima), the Lady, when the hero first encounters her, is often stern and unrelenting—a circumstance which is the harder for him to bear when she appears in the form of his own daughter (as in the anonymous medieval poem, *The Pearl*) or in that of a mortal girl whom he has loved. In *The Divine Comedy*, having completed his ascent of the purgatorial mountain, Dante stands in Eden on the banks of the river Lethe. When he has tasted of the river's waters, his spirit will be cleansed of the memory of evil, but before this can happen he has a test to meet. He is approached by Beatrice, a lady whom he had loved when she was mortal and who is now, in her immortal aspect, the embodiment of Revelation. Turning to the angelic presences that witness the interview, Beatrice speaks of her old relationship with Dante and justly accuses him of having forsaken her:

> *When I was risen from flesh to spirit, and beauty and virtue were increased within me, I was less precious and pleasing to him.*

> (*Purg:* XXX.127–29)

For this reason, she explains, she had no choice but to prepare him for the present meeting by directing his path through the land of "the lost people"—the Inferno. Hearing this, Dante is so overcome with shame that he loses consciousness, and when he comes to himself, he is neck-deep in the stream, and he plunges in his head and drinks. Then, just before the power of the water obliterates all "sad memories" in him, he weeps and whispers his confession: "Present things with their false pleasure turned away my steps as soon as your face was hidden" (*Purg:* XXXI.34–36). Accepting his contrition, Beatrice then rewards her "faithful one" with a smile whose beauty, like "heaven in its harmony," words cannot describe. He is ready to resume his journey toward Paradise and, ultimately, the vision of God.

Perhaps the Lady is best known for the physical attractiveness which has always distinguished her, from Eve to the newly crowned Miss Universe. Often it is her role to assume a seductive form and test the hero's seriousness of purpose by offering him what the repentant Dante calls "Present things with their false pleasure." Circe, among others, has this function in *The Odyssey*, as does Acrasia, the nymphet whose Bower of Bliss is almost fatal to Sir Guyon, the Knight of Temperance, in Spenser's *The Faerie Queene* (Book II). However, it would be a grave mistake to imagine that the Lady is an enemy of the pleasures of the flesh. The companions of Aphrodite are the Graces: Beauty, Brightness, and Joy; and these qualities are the gifts of the love goddess to all who come upon the Lady in an amorous mood. Chastity and marriage, as Spenser and Milton were careful to point out, are by no means incompatible. Although Spenser's Charissa (Charity) hates "Cupid's wanton snare," she is herself the image of serene and bountiful motherhood:

> *A multitude of babes about her hung,*
> *Playing their sports that joyed her to behold.*
> . . . . . .
> *Her neck and breasts were ever open bare,*
> *That aye thereof her babes might suck their fill.*
>
> (*Faerie Queene:* Bk. I: X.31.1–2; 30.7–8)

In Charissa, maternal and spiritual love exist in harmony, just as they do in Aphrodite, by whose law all living species are replenished and bonds of amity are established and endure, not between lovers only, but between man and man, king and subject, nation and nation. She could be called the Goddess of Relationship, as Chaucer's Wife of Bath might testify, who proclaims that she is "al Venerien / In feelynge." It is not only appropriate but inevitable that love's healing impulse should visit the despairing Ancient Mariner under the aegis of "the moving Moon." Coleridge's prose gloss of the passage in which this event occurs is a fine tribute to the Triple Goddess who, as Artemis, Aphrodite, and Persephone, governs the changing world of man and gives it a mysterious constancy:

> *In his loneliness and fixedness he yearneth towards the journey-*
> *ing Moon, and the stars that still sojourn, yet still move on-*

ward; and everywhere the blue sky belongs to them, and is their appointed rest, and their native country and their own natural homes, which they enter unannounced, as lords that are certainly expected and yet there is a silent joy at their arrival.

ONE

Her Nature

The Lady, who is both the companion and the goal of the Hero's Quest, is known to Everyman in her bewildering variety, as mother, sister, sweetheart, wife, mother-in-law, and daughter; as Dame Nature, Mother Earth, with all her progeny; as Psyche, Liberty, Justice, Mercy, Love, and Peace. Further, if we are to believe Carl Jung, her influence is even more pervasive as the *anima*, the archetypal feminine being who arises from and represents the unconscious mind of man. She appears to him personified in visions, dreams, and fantasies; and her projected image finds embodiment in every female individual whom he meets. The Lady is incarnate in every woman. When a poet writes a sonnet to the girl he loves, she ceases to be Stella, Laura, Beatrice, or Delia and becomes a goddess—the universal object of man's love affair with the created universe and with the unseen loveliness that leads him on the tortuous way to the source of light. She stands beside him as he writes, she grasps his pen "And lets the ink run slowly down [the] page" (William Jay Smith, "The Ten"), for she is the Muse and dictates her own praise.

In her pristine form, the Lady is not, for most of us, Athene, Demeter, Artemis, Aphrodite, Persephone, or their equivalents in the Roman pantheon, but Adam's consort in the Garden of Eden, the "Daughter of God and Man, accomplish'd Eve." The story in *Genesis* and in *Paradise Lost* of her temptation by Satan, her eating of the Forbidden Fruit, and her success in persuading Adam to follow her into Original Sin has fixed her in our minds as the temptress who is mother of all our woes, but she is also Mother of Mankind, the First Mary, in whose line the Second Mary and the Redeemer stand. If, as the archangel Michael promises Adam at the end of *Paradise Lost*, he may hope to find "A paradise within [him], happier far" than the one which he must leave, then there can be no doubt that Eve will be his consort there.

In the context of the Lady's archetypal role, one may think of the Quest as the perennial search, on the part of Adam's sons, to find the original Eve. In Spenser's *The Faerie Queene* (Book I), the companion of the Redcrosse Knight (potential holiness) is a maiden named Una (truth or true religion). Throughout their travels together, she wears a black veil in mourning for the misfortune of her parents (Adam and Eve), who are besieged and imprisoned by a ferocious dragon (Satan). Una may not remove her veil until her Knight has killed this monster and set her parents free. When this happy event at last occurs, the lady appears, as bright as the morning star which tells "That dawning day is drawing near,"

> *So fair and fresh as freshest flower in May;*
> *For she had laid her mournful stole aside,*
> *And widow-like sad wimple thrown away,*
> *Wherewith her heavenly beauty she did hide.*

> (XII. 22.1–4)

Her garment is "All lily white withouten spot or pride," and words cannot express "The blazing brightness of her beauty's beam, / And glorious light of her sunshiny face." This epiphany recalls the incident which is its ironic counterpart—the unmasking of Una's double or alter ego, Duessa (duplicity, false religion), who for a time had worked her seductive wiles to alienate the affections of the Redcrosse Knight. Stripped of her "royal robes and purple pall," she proves to be "A loathly, wrinkled hag." Her ugliness had been concealed from him by the blindness of his willful pride, a peril which, as Spenser remarks, enfolds "The righteous man to make him daily fall" (VIII.46.2,8;1.2).

In "She," Richard Wilbur imagines Eve as the lady with a thousand faces. Adam, when his "will was whole," gazed upon the beauty of her "naked face"; but when Eve descended from the Garden and dwelt "amid / The flocks of Abel and the fields of Cain," she was "Clothed in their wish, her Eden graces hid"; and, since that time, the wish of men has clothed her in successive guises: that of the Corn Maiden, Greek and Roman goddesses of many different attributes, the captive princess of romance, the sovereign lady of the knight of chivalry, and the Church. Now, having led the quest for freedom to the "virgin country" of the West, she is revealed ("truest in eclipse") as the "subject goddess of the dreams of men." Looking ahead to "the latter age," Wilbur says that Eve will become visible again, as she was in Eden, when the crumbling of blind willfulness at last will permit man to behold the epiphany of her original loveliness.

From the feminine point of view, the Lady's role is, as one might expect, significantly different. She is preoccupied, sometimes to an oppressive degree, with biological processes, the reproduction of the species (*vide*, Jean Farley, "Korê to Coed"); she is said to have invented agriculture and maintains a devoted interest in the practical arts of civilization: "God's best gift is the human hand" (George Garrett, "Figure Study"). As exemplar of these concerns, Athene gave mankind the art of spinning and weaving, the plow, the ship, the wagon, and the olive tree; she counseled and encouraged Odysseus on his long journey home to the faithful Penelope; and she was responsible (with Apollo) for persuading the fierce Erinyes to abandon the old law of vengeance and accept the law of mercy (*vide*, Aeschylus, *The Eumenides*). All of this being true, it is not surprising that women do not commonly share man's yearning for the garden of Eden. Julia Randall imagines, in "A Ballad of Eve," that "The blessed worm of Eden" sang to Eve of an eternity of "Love unbought," dependence on "One god, of all the gods that be"; in short, of a peace that would prove the enemy of "hand and heart and tongue." Now, having "walked the years from paradise," with more than enough of "Danger and pride and pain" to occupy her, the descendant of Eve can "fashion true" the song which was sung to her, not by Satan but by the Lord, "Where God beside me lay."

As the life of everything that lives, the Lady is Aphrodite, who sprang from the foam where the severed genitals of Uranus fell into the sea; she stepped ashore on the island of Cythera, and flowers sprang up wherever she set her foot. She is the goddess of reproduction, and she tricks, cajoles, seduces, and impels both men and women into the fruitful act of love. She fired Zeus with desire for mortal women, with the result that the divine is mingled with the mortal nature of mankind. As Chaucer says in praise of Venus, her benignity appeases the fierce wrath of Mars. She is the cause of friendship and the bond that unifies the household and the kingdom (*Troilus and Criseyde:* III.Prol.). Human relationships, and in particular love in all of its aspects, holds first importance for her, and she is the fount of what Chaucer calls the Gifts of Grace: patience in adversity, compassion, and forgiveness. Yet, in her sexual role, she is often in violent conflict with the morality of the Establishment. Geoffrey Hill, in "Venus Reborn," envisions Venus as a shark, driven "to estuary-water" by the tempestuous wrath of the Lord of Righteousness, warring upon iniquity. There, un-flurried, but the more dangerous for being at bay, she lies in wait for "all / Strayers, and searchers of the fanged pool."

The Lady is the death of all that dies and is thus, in a sense, in conflict with herself. Demeter and Persephone (Kore) are doubles of one another: when the daughter is ravished away to the Land of the Dead, the mother grieves, and earth is gripped by famine and death; but when she returns in spring, the mother her-self is restored, together with the fertility of the fields and the con-tinuity of the race of man. The Hindu goddess Kali bestows boons with one hand and holds in the other the sword of destruction. It is as executioner that John Ciardi pictures the Lady in "Damn Her." She is a cat at its mousehole, poised to pounce upon its victim. But her ruthlessness is commensurate with the "flaps and bellies" of a mortal grossness which complacently believes the world to be its oyster. Circe, the Lady as sorceress, turns men into beasts, not be-cause she is wicked and misanthropic but because the greed of men, which she cannot control, is itself the trap she springs, "the hideous spell." Grieving, she longs to be delivered from the "charge of alien blood"; but "barks and howls, the scream of birds" are the only answer to "Her uncontrollable, aching cry of love" (A. D. Hope, "Circe").

SHE

What was her beauty in our first estate
When Adam's will was whole, and the least thing

Appeared the gift and creature of his king,
How should we guess?   Resemblance had to wait

For separation, and in such a place
She so partook of water, light, and trees
As not to look like any one of these.
He woke and gazed into her naked face.

But then she changed, and coming down amid
The flocks of Abel and the fields of Cain,
Clothed in their wish, her Eden graces hid,
A shape of plenty with a mop of grain,

She broke upon the world, in time took on
The look of every labor and its fruits.
Columnar in a robe of pleated lawn
She cupped her patient hand for attributes,

Was radiant captive of the farthest tower,
And shed her honor on the fields of war,
Walked in her garden at the evening hour,
Her shadow like a dark ogival door,

Breasted the seas for all the westward ships
And, come to virgin country, changed again—
A moonlike being truest in eclipse,
And subject goddess of the dreams of men.

Tree, temple, valley, prow, gazelle, machine,
More named and nameless than the morning star,
Lovely in every shape, in all unseen,
We dare not wish to find you as you are,

Whose apparition, biding time until
Desire decay and bring the latter age,
Shall flourish in the ruins of our will
And deck the broken stones like saxifrage.

RICHARD WILBUR

ANOTHER SEPTEMBER

Dreams fled away, this country bedroom, raw
With the touch of the dawn, wrapped in a minor peace,
Hears through an open window the garden draw
Long pitch black breaths, lay bare its apple trees,
Ripe pear trees, brambles, windfall-sweetened soil,
Exhale rough sweetness against the starry slates.
Nearer the river sleeps St. John's, all toil
Locked fast inside a dream with iron gates.

Domestic Autumn, like an animal
Long used to handling by those countrymen,
Rubs her kind hide against the bedroom wall
Sensing a fragrant child come back again
—Not this half-tolerated consciousness
That plants its grammar in her yielding weather
But that unspeaking daughter, growing less
Familiar where we fell asleep together.

Wakeful moth-wings blunder near a chair,
Toss their light shell at the glass, and go
To inhabit the living starlight.   Stranded hair
Stirs in the still linen.   It is as though
The black breathing that billows her sleep, her name,
Drugged under judgment, waned and—bearing daggers
And balances—down the lampless darkness they came,
Moving like women: Justice, Truth, such figures.

THOMAS KINSELLA

A BALLAD OF EVE

The blessed worm of Eden sang
At my immortal ear:
The rose will riot on the vine
Year after year;

Night after night in love unbought
The man beside you lie,
And children run on painless feet
Around you day by day;

One god, of all the gods that be,
His table will suffice,
And hand and heart and tongue will know
No enemy but peace.

I walked alone into the dark,
Looking for my deed.
I struck my hand upon a rock
And could not make it bleed.

I lay across the lion's path
Who skirted softly on.
That whole wood was passionless
Up to the edge of dawn.

And there upon the bough it lay,
That made my first heart break.
With human hands I plucked the sky,
With human hunger ate.

And then such plenty was to do,
Danger and pride and pain,
It took me years to fashion true
God's dreaming song again,

The voice that doubled in my ear
Then, in my first of days,
And seasoned love with pity so
I had no tongue for praise,

That now sing back, daylong, the dark
And nightlong sing the day
I walked the years from paradise
Where god beside me lay.

                              JULIA RANDALL

THE DARK AND THE FAIR

A roaring company that festive night;
The beast of dialectic dragged his chains,
Prowling from chair to chair in the smoking light,
While the snow hissed against the windowpanes.

Our politics, our science, and our faith
Were whiskey on the tongue; I, being rent
By the fierce divisions of our time, cried death
And death again, and my own dying meant.

Out of her secret life, that griffin-land
Where ivory empires build their stage, she came,
Putting in mine her small impulsive hand,
Five-fingered gift, and the palm not tame.

The moment clanged: beauty and terror danced
To the wild vibration of a sister-bell,
Whose unremitting stroke discountenanced
The marvel that the mirrors blazed to tell.

A darker image took this fairer form
Who once, in the purgatory of my pride,
When innocence betrayed me in a room
Of mocking elders, swept handsome to my side,

Until we rose together, arm in arm,
And fled together back into the world.
What brought her now, in the semblance of the warm,
Out of cold spaces, damned by colder blood?

That furied woman did me grievous wrong,
But does it matter much, given our years?
We learn, as the thread plays out, that we belong
Less to what flatters us than to what scars;

So, freshly turning, as the turn condones,
For her I killed the propitiatory bird,
Kissing her down. Peace to her bitter bones,
Who taught me the serpent's word, but yet the word.

STANLEY KUNITZ

FIGURE STUDY

I *The Photographer to the Nude*

They say the Zulus or some such tribe
(I forget which. Let them simply be
dark, our shadows, our consciences.)

believe in no such thing as a straight
line. Believe? They can't conceive
of it. Their houses are all round,

and their implements are curved,
and if you try and civilize them—
put them to ploughing fields, building

fences or just going from here to there—
they achieve it all in gracious circles.
There's truth in that. Nothing I know of

is perfectly straight unless a hand
touched and twisted and tormented it.
The wheel's the noblest act of man.

Be still, be natural, my moon.
Be all the snow of the world's dome.
Be the high sea dreaming in its bed of stars.

And I, ducking behind a dark cloth,
I'll disappear like magic and become
a Zulu with an uncorrupted eye.

II *The Nude to the Photographer*

There's a wilderness in women
You haven't dreamed of. We are
dark continents, not sea, not snow.

The panther moving like a swimming thing,
the tiger like a creature all on fire,
we know by heart and fear.

The world's a heavy weight, the moon's
a lonely journey in a vacant sky.
Flesh stumbles for a crooked mile.

What is beautiful? An arrow finding
target's shiny eye, a keen plane
smoothing rough wood to a level,

and clay rejoicing in the kiln.
Choirs of stone sing from a well-made wall.
And God's best gift is the human hand.

For God's sake don khaki and pith helmet!
Bring axes, ploughs, bulldozers, and
conquer, colonize, convert!

Bring light to cast some shadow.
Bless me with angles and I'll be
yours in two dimensions for forever.

GEORGE GARRETT

HER KIND

I have gone out, a possessed witch,
haunting the black air, braver at night;
dreaming evil, I have done my hitch
over the plain houses, light by light:
lonely thing, twelve-fingered, out of mind.

A woman like that is not a woman, quite.
I have been her kind.

I have found the warm caves in the woods,
filled them with skillets, carvings, shelves,
closets, silks, innumerable goods;
fixed the suppers for the worms and the elves:
whining, rearranging the disaligned.
A woman like that is misunderstood.
I have been her kind.

I have ridden in your cart, driver,
waved my nude arms at villages going by,
learning the last bright routes, survivor
where your flames still bite my thigh
and my ribs crack where your wheels wind.
A woman like that is not ashamed to die.
I have been her kind.

ANNE SEXTON

THE TEN

> "... *one of the best-dressed ten women.*"
> —A newspaper reference to Mme. Henri Bonnet

Mme. Bonnet is one of the best-dressed ten;
But what of the slovenly six, the hungry five,
The solemn three who plague all men alive,
The twittering two who appear every now and again?

What of the sexual seven who want only to please,
Advancing in unison down the hospital hall,
Conversing obscenely, wearing no clothing at all,
While under your sterile sheet you flame and freeze?

What will you say of the weird, monotonous one
Who stands beside the table when you write,

Her long hair coiling in the angry light,
Her wild eyes dancing brighter than the sun?

What will you say of her who grasps your pen
And lets the ink run slowly down your page,
Throws back her head and laughs as from a cage:
"Mme. Bonnet is one, you say?   . . . And then?"

WILLIAM JAY SMITH

BEWARE, MADAM

Beware, madam, of the witty devil,
The arch intriguer who walks disguised
In a poet's cloak, his gay tongue oozing evil.

Would you be a Muse?   He will so declare you,
Pledging his blind allegiance,
Yet remain secret and uncommitted.

Poets are men: are single-hearted lovers
Who adore and trust beyond all reason,
Who die honourably at the gates of hell.

The Muse alone is licensed to do murder
And to betray: weeping with honest tears
She thrones each victim in her paradise.

But from this Muse the devil borrows an art
That ill becomes a man.   Beware, madam:
He plots to strip you bare of woman-pride.

He is capable of seducing your twin-sister
On the same pillow, and neither she nor you
Will suspect the act, so close a glamour he sheds.

Alas, being honourably single-hearted,
You adore and trust beyond all reason,
Being no more a Muse than he a poet.

ROBERT GRAVES

I KNEW A WOMAN

I knew a woman, lovely in her bones,
When small birds sighed, she would sigh back at them;
Ah, when she moved, she moved more ways than one:
The shapes a bright container can contain!
Of her choice virtues only gods should speak,
Or English poets who grew up on Greek
(I'd have them sing in chorus, cheek to cheek).

How well her wishes went! She stroked my chin,
She taught me Turn, and Counter-turn, and Stand;
She taught me Touch, that undulant white skin;
I nibbled meekly from her proffered hand;
She was the sickle; I, poor I, the rake,
Coming behind her for her pretty sake
(But what prodigious mowing we did make).

Love likes a gander, and adores a goose:
Her full lips pursed, the errant note to seize,
She played it quick, she played it light and loose;
My eyes, they dazzled at her flowing knees,
Her several parts could keep a pure repose,
Or one hip quiver with a mobile nose
(She moved in circles, and those circles moved).

Let seed be grass, and grass turn into hay:
I'm martyr to a motion not my own;
What's freedom for? To know eternity.
I swear she cast a shadow white as stone.
But who would count eternity in days?
These old bones live to learn her wanton ways:
(I measure time by how a body sways).

THEODORE ROETHKE

LORE

Man walks, I learn, in fear of woman,
Possession of the constant moon;

Because the moon has strength to summon
Her blood to the full and ebb again,
And gives her strength beyond her own.

A girl then, Graves writes in his book,
Can fade the purple out of cloth
And tarnish mirrors with her look,
And by the power of her thought
Make one branch grow and another rot.

And if she should, at such a time,
Go further, lifting up her dress
She can find out the hidden crime,
Flatten a storm on the high seas,
Cure either boils or barrenness.

So great the power of her moon
That, as the Talmud said,
If she should walk between two men
And no appropriate prayer is read,
The one of them will drop down dead.

                    HOWARD NEMEROV

DAMN HER

Of all her appalling virtues, none
leaves more crumbs in my bed, nor
more gravel in my tub
than the hunch of her patience
    at its mouseholes.

She would, I swear, outwait
the Sphinx in its homemade quandaries
once any scratching in the walls
has given her to suspect
    an emergence.

It's all in the mind, we say. With her
it's all in the crouch, the waiting

and the doing indistinguishable. Once
she hunches to execution, time is merely
  the handle of the switch:

she grasps it and stands by for whatever
will come, certainly, to her sizzling
justice. Then, inevitably always daintily
she closes her total gesture
  swiftly disdainfully as

a glutton tosses off a third dozen
oysters—making light of them—as if
his gluttony were a joke that all
may share. (The flaps and bellies
  of his grossness

are waiting, after all, for something
much more substantial than
appetizers.) —"Bring on the lamb!" her look
says over my empty shells. "Bring on
  the body and the blood!"

JOHN CIARDI

THE REBIRTH OF VENUS

And now the sea-scoured temptress, having failed
To scoop out of horizons what birds herald—
Tufts of fresh soil—shakes off an entire sea,
Though not as the dove, harried. Rather, she,

A shark hurricaned to estuary-water
(The lesser hunter almost by a greater
Devoured) but unflurried, lies, approaches all
Stayers, and searchers of the fanged pool.

GEOFFREY HILL

THE GULLET OF THE CROCODILE

The ballet of the clown,
A clumsy dance at best
Before the jury box of bishops,
Bulging bishops in their vests

Ding, dong, the bonging bells
Across the villages and wheat,
That body on the ground, the bonging
Of the bells, and geysers,
Bloody geysers from the body,
Rocky freshets on the ground

No sound in these plush chambers
Save the bishops' belly growls,
The clown, son of the carpenter,
Sets a lantern on the ground,
He dances round and round,
Splits his side with silent laughter,
As the bishops grump and frown

The sluggish wallow of the Nile,
The golden scaly fishes and childish
Virgin's smile, for Alice, bulging
Alice knows the grinning crocodile.

                                        R. H. W. DILLARD

KORÊ TO COED

Archaic Smile

A proper fledgling blown awry,
You wear the foolish look, my dear, not I.
Burly and cross on a windy branch
That somehow found your feet,
My sister, my sparrow, be chipper.

Get you a fitting smile to your cheek
While breezes nibble and the year is weak.
A venerable wind is shifting afar
To uphold your fitful wings
And gull you forever of a timid heart.
Midway in the migration of your life,
With substance of flesh grown secretly thin
In a most fruitful year,
You must bear in the steady wind
My beakèd smile from ear to ear.

JEAN FARLEY

CIRCE

after the painting by Dosso Dossi

Behind her not the quivering of a leaf
Flutters the deep enchantment of the wood;
No ripple at her feet disturbs the well;
She sits among her lovers dazed with grief,
Bewildered by the charge of alien blood.
Herself transfigured by the hideous spell

She sits among her creatures motionless,
Sees the last human shadow of despair
Fade from the sad, inquisitive, animal eyes,
The naked body of the sorceress
Mocked by the light, sleek shapes of feather and hair.
And as on snout and beak and muzzle dies

The melancholy trace of human speech,
For the first time her heart is rich with words
And with her voice she disenchants the grove.
The lonely island and the sounding beach
Answer with barks and howls, the scream of birds,
Her uncontrollable, aching cry of love.

A. D. HOPE

MAIDEN WITH ORB AND PLANETS

She stands now, shy among the destinies,
Daughter and mother of the silent crossings.
That is what beauty is, the petaled time
In a child's tomb, the besalt time that waits
In the Valley of the Kings, the swaying time
That smoothes the rivers through the summer nights
And polishes the stone and dulls the eye.
A china dynasty, the May fly's day,
Tremble to balance at her either hand,
And her blood moves as the dark rivers move,
While all the sailing stars pass and return.
Her stillness makes the moment of the world
Strike once, and that is what beauty is,
To stand as Agamemnon's daughter stood
Amid great armies waiting on the wind.

                         HOWARD NEMEROV

TWO

The Meeting

The meeting between the Hero and the Lady lies at the dramatic center of the Quest. Its essentials are daily acted out for us in episodes from the perennial battle of the sexes. The amorous female offers a cornucopia of selfless bounty; but, when her love is scorned or abused, she displays a deadly cold ferocity. On the other hand, the idealizing male adores, protects, and rules benignly, but becomes a brutal despot when his will is challenged or defied. In myth and mythopoeic literature, and perhaps in life as well, he who yields too readily to the Lady's seductive charm becomes imprisoned: Heracles is demeaned and effeminate as the domestic captive of Omphale; when Antony's passion for Cleopatra undermines his military power, he sinks to petulant impotence. On the other hand, the stubborn chastity of Hippolytus so infuriates Aphrodite that she plots and executes his destruction (*vide,* Euripides, *Hippolytus*), and the obstinate resistance of Shakespeare's Adonis to the blandishments of Venus establishes the certainty that he will be gored to death by the wild boar which he hunts.

The Lady can give her love to a mortal man without stint or reservation, but she will, in the end, be obliged to forsake him nonetheless, because her nature demands his sacrifice in the mutable world of time. When she seeks to violate this principle, she falls into the predicament of Selene, whose Endymion can never die but also cannot be awakened from his perpetual slumber; of Aurora, who asked the gods to grant her husband Tithonus immortality, but neglected to request that he retain his youth (*vide,* Tennyson, "Tithonus"); or, in the world of comedy, of Shakespeare's Titania, who dotes on Bottom and fondly believes she speaks the truth when she tells him, "I will purge thy mortal grossness so / That thou shalt like an airy spirit go" (*A Midsummer Night's Dream:* III.i.145–46).

Plato's myth of the sexes in *The Symposium* is instructive: It seems that man at one time was man-and-woman, a composite or complete being who was so powerful that the gods, fearing lest this being should displace them, carved it in half; and, since that time, the separate sexes restlessly have sought one another in order to re-establish the union which they once possessed. This union can be accomplished fleetingly in the act of propagation, but this is only the first step in the ladder which leads upward, through ever-broadening circles of apprehended beauty, until it reaches Beauty itself, which is the goal of all existence. That much-misunderstood conception, Platonic Love, is represented by such encounters between Hero and Lady as that of Boethius with Dame Philosophy, who points out to him in his imprisonment the path to spiritual freedom (*The Consolation of Philosophy*); of Dante with Beatrice, who guides him around the torturous circles of the purgatorial mountain to the Garden of Eden at its summit; and of Shakespeare's Lear with Cordelia, the embodiment of Grace or Nature, in the sense of the sum total of physical and spiritual bonds which tie mankind together and permit an evolution toward a fully civilized society—the City of God on earth.

The idea of the Hero's faithful and potentially sacrificial devotion to the Lady is an extremely ancient one whose history includes the matriarchal conception of the Sacred King as the incarnation of a god whose rule and marriage to the Queen is terminated, in due course, by his ritual execution (*vide,* Frazer's *The Golden Bough*). The observation that men are doomed to quick extinction at the hands of a deceptively compliant and seductive womankind clings, in some degree, to the bulk of literature in which the Lady figures, particularly in modern poetry. The helplessness of the male before an omniverous Lady informs the variously comic, ironic, and rueful tone of several of the poems in the following pages, from the wolf-swallowing of the insouciant Little Red Riding Hood to the sourly effective misanthropy of Cinderella and her God's Mother in Randall Jarrell's "Cinderella." Male poets characteristically cele-

brate with a certain relish the obliteration of male pretension, ideal-
ism, bemusement, and timidity when these qualities are put to the
test by that attribute of the Lady which Howard Nemerov calls
"the power of her moon." Sex, as everyone knows, is a titanic
force; a tiny quantity of seemingly innocuous matter holds energy
sufficient to demolish the earth; and such well-disciplined and
public-spirited citizens as Othello and Macbeth (like the protagonist
of W. S. Merwin's "December: Of Aphrodite") run mad and wreak
destruction at the real or fancied provocation of a woman.

Undoubtedly, the female of the species, as the old saw has it,
is deadlier than the male, but poets do not wish it otherwise. The
moon that "has found a soft new bed, / Ice and snow on a field of
red" (George Garrett, "A Modern Fiction") has a merely bathetic
effect upon the ramping lion of the sun to whom she would teach
good manners. Vigorous sexuality can electrify "the half-times of
our lives" (James Seay, "The Girl on the Self-Rising Flour Sign"),
and can be the avenue to the Hero's recognition that in the Lady "his
soul manifests / Itself as tangible" (Daniel Hoffman, "In Cytherea").

Whether for good or ill, for his ennoblement or his destruc-
tion, the Hero cannot choose but serve the Lady. True Thomas,
the hero of the venerable ballad, is instinctively courteous to the
Queen of the Fairies who takes him into her service. One imagines
that he will meet the rigorous tests that she imposes on him during
his seven years in a fairyland which is reached not by the roads that
lead to heaven or hell but by the road along whose course one wades
"thro red blude to the knee." As the story is interpreted for us by
Daniel Hoffman ("The True Testament of Thomas the Rhymer"),
True Thomas took from the Fairy Queen "the fruit of darkness /
That binds [his] bones to her will," and this freed him from his
"lack-love" wandering "from moonless to moonless / Crossroad."
He has lost his will and his soul in exchange for seven years as "king
of the bone and the blood." It may seem a losing bargain, but True
Thomas is a rhymer, and what more can a poet ask than to be one
"True to the end remaining / To the one love, ineluctable"? Donald
Finkel's Ulysses also discovers that he is true to the one love,
whether he will or no. After laboriously resisting the sirens' song,
he finds himself mowing grain in the fields like Lityerses, while "In
his ridiculous, lovely mouth" the strains of the sirens' song takes
shape. He knows the answer to their question, "Do you think /
Wax could have stopped us, or chains?"

Only Samuel Daniel's "worthy Greek" ("Ulysses and the Sirens") displays sufficient strength and rhetorical skill to win a contest with a Siren, his "Delicious Nymph." As he explains to this Lady who would win him to a life of rest and pleasure, such a prospect has no attraction for "natures of the noblest frame." Natures of that rare variety know that wars and dangers, "motions of unrest," are far to be preferred to "a wicked peace," and are, in fact, the only avenues to such epiphanies as mortal life affords. Though she has argued with all her ingenuity to corrupt her adversary, the nymph is overjoyed at last to be defeated. As Ulysses will not come to her, she will go to him, for "beauty hath created bin / To undo or be undone." Her loss is her victory. For the triumphant Hero, the restless strife of time, and the peace that passeth understanding are finally seen to be in accord with one another, opposite sides of the same coin; and to be fully alive in the temporal world is all that he knows or needs to know of immortality.

THE NIGHT DREAM
   to R. L.

Neither her voice, her name,
Eyes, quietness neither,
That moved through the light, that came
Cold stalk in her teeth
Bitten of some blue flower
Knew I before nor saw.
This was a dream. Ah,
This was a dream. There was sun
Laid on the cloths of a table.
We drank together. Her mouth
Was a lion's mouth out of jade
Cold with a fable of water.
Faces I could not see
Watched me with gentleness. Grace
Folded my body with wings.
I cannot love you she said.

My head she laid on her breast.
As stillness with ringing of bees
I was filled with a singing of praise.
Knowledge filled me and peace.
We were silent and not ashamed.
Ah we were glad that day.
They asked me but it was one
Dead they meant and not I.
She was beside me she said.
We rode in a desert place.
We were always happy.   Her sleeves
Jangled with jingling of gold.
They told me the wind from the south
Was the cold wind to be feared.
We were galloping under the leaves—

This was a dream, Ah
This was a dream.
                    And her mouth
Was not your mouth nor her eyes,
But the rivers were four and I knew
As a secret between us, the way
Hands touch, it was you.

ARCHIBALD MAC LEISH

THOMAS RHYMER

True Thomas lay oer yond grassy bank,
  And he beheld a ladie gay,
A ladie that was brisk and bold,
  Come riding oer the fernie brae.

Her skirt was of the grass-green silk,
  Her mantel of the velvet fine,
At ilka tett of her horse's mane
  Hung fifty silver bells and nine.

True Thomas he took off his hat,
   And bowed him low down till his knee:
'All hail, thou mighty Queen of Heaven!
   For your peer on earth I never did see.'

'O no, O no, True Thomas,' she says,
   'That name does not belong to me;
I am but the queen of fair Elfland,
   And I'm come here for to visit thee.

     . . .

'But ye maun go wi me now, Thomas,
   True Thomas, ye maun go wi me,
For ye maun serve me seven years,
   Thro weel or wae as may chance to be.'

She turned about her milk-white steed,
   And took True Thomas up behind,
And aye wheneer her bridle rang,
   The steed flew swifter than the wind.

For forty days and forty nights
   He wade thro red blude to the knee,
And he saw neither sun nor moon,
   But heard the roaring of the sea.

O they rade on, and further on,
   Until they came to a garden green:
'Light down, light down, ye ladie free,
   Some of that fruit let me pull to thee.'

'O no, O no, True Thomas,' she says,
   'That fruit maun not be touched by thee,
For a' the plagues that are in hell
   Light on the fruit of this countrie.

'But I have a loaf here in my lap,
   Likewise a bottle of claret wine,
And now ere we go farther on,
   We'll rest a while, and ye may dine.'

When he had eaten and drunk his fill,
   'Lay down your head upon my knee,'
The lady sayd, 'ere we climb yon hill,
   And I will show you fairlies three.

'O see not ye yon narrow road,
   So thick beset wi thorns and briers?
That is the path of righteousness,
   Tho after it but few enquires.

'And see not ye that braid braid road,
   That lies across yon lillie leven?
That is the path of wickedness,
   Tho some call it the road to heaven.

'And see not ye that bonny road,
   Which winds about the fernie brae?
That is the road to fair Elfland,
   Whe[re] you and I this night maun gae.

'But Thomas, ye maun hold your tongue,
   Whatever you may hear or see,
For gin ae word you should chance to speak,
   You will neer get back to your ain countrie.'

He has gotten a coat of the even cloth,
   And a pair of shoes of velvet green,
And till seven years were past and gone
   True Thomas on earth was never seen.

ANONYMOUS

THE TRUE TESTAMENT OF THOMAS THE RHYMER

I heard her singing,
Voice like a fire in a wineflask,

I stepped into the circle where
She sang in the dark of the dolmens,

I remembered the admonitions
That chilled chimney corners and churches,

I remembered the slender curve of her
Waist and her hips' sudden burgeon,

I lay down between the dolmens
Dark as tombs in the moon's lack,

I held her in my arms close,
I took from her the fruit of the darkness

That binds my bones to her will.
Now I cannot remember

What I did when I had a will,
I cannot remember any longer

What I did when I had a soul
But wander from moonless to moonless

Crossroad, a lack-love driven
To stumble through rockpit and furze

In an aching shadow imprisoned
Till all my fivewits serve her;

I have eaten the fruit of the darkness
And am freed thereof

To lie seven years in green bower,
To be king of the bone and the blood,

To be priest in the tabernacle
Of the turf and holy seed,

To defy the coming of rooks' covens
That will whirl winters round my rimed head

Who lay seven years of her kingdom
Emperor and in thrall,

Despite all to be struck down from faithless
Time's tower in the end,

True to the end remaining
To the one love, ineluctable.

DANIEL HOFFMAN

THE SIRENS

The news lapped at us out of all
Horizons: the ticking night full
Of gods; sensed, heard the tactile

Sea turn in his bed, prickling
Among derelicts. When the song
Was clear enough, we spread our hair,

Caught it. Under the comb the strands
Whipped into fresh harmonies, untangled
Again. The wind took it, and he heard.

The droll ship swung leeward;
Caught sight of him (rather, could
Have seen, busy with the fugue)

Yanking his bonds, the strings of his wide
Neck drawn like shrouds, his scream
Caught in the sails.
                        Now in a sea

Of wheat he rows, reconstructing.
In his ridiculous, lovely mouth the strains
Tumble into place. Do you think
Wax could have stopped us, or chains?

DONALD FINKEL

LA BELLE DAME SANS MERCI

O, what can ail thee, knight-at-arms,
   Alone and palely loitering?
The sedge has wither'd from the lake,
   And no birds sing.

O, what can ail thee, knight-at-arms,
   So haggard and so woe-begone?
The squirrel's granary is full,
   And the harvest's done.

I see a lilly on thy brow,
   With anguish moist and fever dew;
And on thy cheeks a fading rose
   Fast withereth too.

I met a lady in the meads,
   Full beautiful—a faery's child,
Her hair was long, her foot was light,
   And her eyes were wild.

I made a garland for her head,
   And bracelets too, and fragrant zone;
She look'd at me as she did love,
   And made sweet moan.

I set her on my pacing steed,
   And nothing else saw all day long;
For sidelong would she bend, and sing
   A faery's song.

She found me roots of relish sweet,
   And honey wild, and manna dew,
And sure in language strange she said—
   'I love thee true'.

She took me to her elfin grot,
   And there she wept and sigh'd full sore,

And there I shut her wild wild eyes
  With kisses four.

And there she lulled me asleep
  And there I dream'd—Ah! woe betide!
The latest dream I ever dream'd
  On the cold hill side.

I saw pale kings and princes too,
  Pale warriors, death-pale were they all;
They cried—'La Belle Dame sans Merci
  Hath thee in thrall!'

I saw their starved lips in the gloam,
  With horrid warning gaped wide,
And I awoke and found me here,
  On the cold hill's side.

And this is why I sojourn here
  Alone and palely loitering,
Though the sedge has wither'd from the lake,
  And no birds sing.

JOHN KEATS

DIANA AND ACTAEON

When he burst flushed and sweating from the woods
Into the glade, and saw her at her bath
She did not really care: cool liberal gods
Had long outgrown the furious routine
Of outraged majesty and vengeance. Death
Seemed an old barbarous penance for small sin.

How could her still immortal beauty change
Or the least trickle of her power be lost
To human eye-beam: why should she disarrange
A marble pose for his symbolic lance?
The nymphs ran screaming; but she only cast
From a pure shoulder's curve a backward glance.

And he, who never thought of goddesses,
Or anything but hounds and boar-spears, read
Nothing at all in lightning of her eyes—
Except the shadow of some blunt mistake;
The hot Boeotian athlete simply stared
After the stag fast vanished in the brake.

She knew it well enough, lust of the chase,
Momently felt the hunter's sympathy.
Divinity can in a flash embrace
A mortal passion; but immortal fire
Burns with a ray whose mere proximity
Blasts, tears, or turns to stone, without desire.

An old dumb logic harsher than the god's will
Decrees whoever trips upon their power
Must fall its prey.   Fate hangs about them still.
From hunter he must be the quarry; see,
Horns spring from his brow; she must forbear
To halt the doom she would have had him flee.

She could forgive, and maybe time would too,
That this great innocent had chanced to spy
Her loneliness.   And then the old taboo
Stirred in the grove, swelled through the sacred bounds,
And through her white throat in a shivering sigh
Its voice cried havoc to the yelping hounds.

                              GRAHAM HOUGH

COUP DE GRÂCE

Just at the moment the Wolf,
Shag jaws and slavering grin,
Steps from the property wood,
O, what a gorge, what a gulf
Opens to gobble her in,
Little Red Riding Hood!

O, what a face full of fangs!
Eyes like saucers at least
Roll to seduce and beguile.
Miss, with her dimples and bangs,
Thinks him a handsome beast;
Flashes the Riding Hood Smile;

Stands her ground like a queen,
Velvet red of the rose
Framing each little milk-tooth,
Pink tongue peeping between.
Then, wider than anyone knows,
Opens her minikin mouth

Swallows up Wolf in a trice;
Tail going down gives a flick,
Caught as she closes her jaws.
Bows, all sugar and spice.
O, what a lady-like trick!
O, what a round of applause!

A. D. HOPE

TO A YOUNG WOMAN,
ENTERING A FORMAL GARDEN

Comes on with butterflies, whose stray
Parabolas become her presence, cool
As convoluted labyrinths of box
And borders where the passing compliment
She pays, by sleight of hand on flowers,
Here and there delays the royal progress.

The obliging fool, her gentleman, observing
In despair the mere accomplishment
Of that repose, and lacking heart to hint
At rank and foxy promptings of the will,
Takes no account of wantonness,
Like scent, attendant on her every pulse.

Oh, round archaic mouth no butter
Dares to melt in, you will come to terms,
On your terms only, with the earth.
The youth awaits you, edgily attentive
On an ironwork bench, as twisted
As the curious aisles between the box.

He twists in anguish, dreading to commit
The breath he greets her with; but she,
Whose spirits quicken on the trace
Of palpitating commonplace, may yet
Appear at path's turning, bare as Eve,
Only to feed upon his stricken face.

JOHN ALEXANDER ALLEN

CLIMATE

The web shakes under the wind's hand.
Spider moves into the curled grass core.
The wasp that buries a beetle in the sand
Shovels dirt against that beetle's door.
Ants pull wings into their darkened town.
Beneath their work, the hungry worm
Eats at the earth, and feels the storm
As moisture, weight, pressing his soft walls down.

Lady steps across the shadowed grass.
Between trees the man follows without laughter.
His body feels new pain approach and pass
From body into brain, and moves to touch her.
Takes her in his arms like danger.
Lifts her lightly over the garden wall.
Mother watches their return with anger.
Meets them, smiling, in the darkened hall.

JON SWAN

CONQUISTADOR

I sing of the decline of Henry Clay
Who loved a white girl of uncommon size.
Although a small man in a little way,
He had in him some seed of enterprise.

Each day he caught the seven-thirty train
To work, watered his garden after tea,
Took an umbrella if it looked like rain
And was remarkably like you or me.

He had his hair cut once a fortnight, tried
Not to forget the birthday of his wife,
And might have lived unnoticed till he died
Had not ambition entered Henry's life.

He met her in the lounge of an hotel
—A most unusual place for him to go—
But there he was and there she was as well,
Sitting alone. He ordered beers for two.

She was so large a girl that when they came
He gave the waiter twice the usual tip.
She smiled without surprise, told him her name,
And as the name trembled on Henry's lip,

His parched soul, swelling like a desert root,
Broke out its delicate dream upon the air;
The mountains shook with earthquake under foot;
An angel seized him suddenly by the hair;

The sky was shrill with peril as he passed;
A hurricane crushed his senses with its din;
The wildlife crackled up his reeling mast;
The trumpet of a maelstrom sucked him in;

The desert shrivelled and burnt off his feet;
His bones and buttons an enormous snake

Vomited up; still in the shimmering heat
The pygmies showed him their forbidden lake

And then transfixed him with their poison darts;
He married six black virgins in a bunch,
Who, when they had drawn out his manly parts,
Stewed him and ate him lovingly for lunch.

Adventure opened wide its grisly jaws;
Henry looked in and knew the Hero's doom.
The huge white girl drank on without a pause
And, just at closing time, she asked him home.

The tram they took was full of Roaring Boys
Announcing the world's ruin and Judgment Day;
The sky blared with its grand orchestral voice
The Götterdämmerung of Henry Clay.

But in her quiet room they were alone.
There, towering over Henry by a head,
She stood and took her clothes off one by one,
And then she stretched herself upon the bed.

Her bulk of beauty, her stupendous grace
Challenged the lion heart in his puny dust.
Proudly his Moment looked him in the face:
He rose to meet it as a hero must;

Climbed the white mountain of unravished snow,
Planted his tiny flag upon the peak.
The smooth drifts, scarcely breathing, lay below.
She did not take the trouble to smile or speak.

And afterwards, it may have been in play,
The enormous girl rolled over and squashed him flat;
And, as she could not send him home that way,
Used him thereafter as a bedside mat.

Speaking at large, I will say this of her:
She did not spare expense to make him nice.

Tanned on both sides and neatly edged with fur,
The job would have been cheap at any price.

And when, in winter, getting out of bed,
Her large soft feet pressed warmly on the skin,
The two glass eyes would sparkle in his head,
The jaws extend their papier-mâché grin.

Good people, for the soul of Henry Clay
Offer your prayers, and view his destiny!
He was the Hero of our Time. He may
With any luck, one day, be you or me.

A. D. HOPE

CINDERELLA

Her imaginary playmate was a grown-up
In sea-coal satin. The flame-blue glances,
The wings gauzy as the membrane that the ashes
Draw over an old ember—as the mother
In a jug of cider—were a comfort to her.
They sat by the fire and told each other stories.

"What men want . . ." said the godmother softly—
How she went on it is hard for a man to say.
Their eyes, on their Father, were monumental marble.
Then they smiled like two old women, bussed each other,
Said, "Gossip, gossip"; and, lapped in each other's looks,
Mirror for mirror, drank a cup of tea.

Of cambric tea. But there is a reality
Under the good silk of the good sisters'
Good ball gowns. *She* knew. . . . Hard-breasted, naked-eyed,
She pushed her silk feet into glass, and rose within
A gown of imaginary gauze. The shy prince drank
A toast to her in champagne from her slipper

And breathed, "Bewitching!"   Breathed, "I am bewitched!"
—She said to her godmother, "Men!"
And, later, looking down to see her flesh
Look back up from under lace, the ashy gauze
And pulsing marble of a bridal veil,
She wished it all a widow's coal-black weeds.

A sullen wife and a reluctant mother,
She sat all day in silence by the fire.
Better, later, to stare past her sons' sons,
Her daughters' daughters, and tell stories to the fire.
But best, dead, damned, to rock forever
Beside Hell's fireside—to see within the flames

The Heaven to whose gold-gauzed door there comes
A little dark old woman, the God's Mother,
And cries, "Come in, come in!   My son's out now,
Out now, will be back soon, may be back never,
Who knows, eh?   *We* know what they are—men, men!
But come, come in till then!   Come in till then!"

RANDALL JARRELL

THE TROLL'S NOSEGAY

A simple nosegay! was that much to ask?
(Winter still nagged, with scarce a bud yet showing).
He loved her ill, if he resigned the task.
'Somewhere,' she cried, 'there must be blossom blowing.'
It seems my lady wept and the troll swore
By Heaven he hated tears: he'd cure her spleen—
Where she had begged one flower he'd shower fourscore,
A bunch fit to amaze a China Queen.

Cold fog-drawn Lily, pale mist-magic Rose
He conjured, and in a glassy cauldron set
With elvish unsubstantial Mignonette

And such vague bloom as wandering dreams enclosed.
But she?
      Awed,
            Charmed to tears,
                      Distracted,
                              Yet—
Even yet, perhaps, a trifle piqued—who knows?

ROBERT GRAVES

THE CAP AND BELLS

The jester walked in the garden:
The garden had fallen still;
He bade his soul rise upward
And stand on her window-sill.

It rose in a straight blue garment,
When owls began to call:
It had grown wise-tongued by thinking
Of a quiet and light footfall;

But the young queen would not listen;
She rose in her pale night-gown;
She drew in the heavy casement
And pushed the latches down.

He bade his heart go to her,
When the owls called out no more;
In a red and quivering garment
It sang to her through the door.

It had grown sweet-tongued by dreaming
Of a flutter of flower-like hair;
But she took up her fan from the table
And waved it off on the air.

'I have cap and bells,' he pondered,
'I will send them to her and die';

And when the morning whitened
He left them where she went by.

She laid them upon her bosom,
Under a cloud of her hair,
And her red lips sang them a love-song
Till stars grew out of the air.

She opened her door and her window,
And the heart and the soul came through,
To her right hand came the red one,
To her left hand came the blue.

They set up a noise like crickets,
A chattering wise and sweet,
And her hair was a folded flower
And the quiet of love in her feet.

W. B. YEATS

A VISION OF THE GODDESS KALI
AS A CHILDHOOD SWEETHEART

You've led me up the garden path, Lucille.
I say that, though it isn't really true.
The maze I tread began in grammar school,
Thanks to your eyes, and it will end with you.

Commencement day, when Mrs. Grady stood
To ply her trade in the assembly hall,
I felt the virtue of your maidenhood
Go forth and name me to the principal.

High on the stage, in one propitious hand
She held my prize, a ribboned *Little Men;*
And bid me, with the other, understand
The hungry love a mother lends her children.

Like a bride, she drew me down the aisle,
Gesturing, "Fear not my patronage";

And, dying then of her triumphant smile,
I met you in the garden of my age.

"Fear not, beloved!" says your hand, Lucille.
Decked as a bride, beside the pleasant fountain
You attend me; and again my will
Winds home upon the silken clew you spun.

The rising moon, above the garden wall,
Renews her countenance. Breath of my breath,
With either hand you grant my boon, Lucille,
And lead me, smiling, up the garden path.

JOHN ALEXANDER ALLEN

ULYSSES AND THE SIREN

Siren

Come, worthy Greek! Ulysses, come,
    Possess these shores with me:
The winds and seas are troublesome,
    And here we may be free.
Here we may sit and view their toil
    That travail in the deep,
And joy the day in mirth the while,
    And spend the night in sleep.

Ulysses

Fair Nymph, if fame or honour were
    To be attained with ease,
Then would I come and rest with thee,
    And leave such toils as these.
But here it dwells, and here must I
    With danger seek it forth:
To spend the time luxuriously
    Becomes not men of worth.

Siren

Ulysses, oh, be not deceived
    With that unreal name!
This honour is a thing conceived,
    And rests on others' fame;
Begotten only to molest
    Our peace, and to beguile
The best thing of our life—our rest,
    And give us up to toil.

Ulysses

Delicious Nymph, suppose there were
    Nor honour nor report,
Yet manliness would scorn to wear
    The time in idle sport:
For toil doth give a better touch
    To make us feel our joy,
And ease finds tediousness as much
    As labour yields annoy.

Siren

Then pleasure likewise seems the shore,
    Whereto tends all your toil,
Which you forego, to make it more,
    And perish oft the while.
Who may disport them diversely
    Find never tedious day,
And ease may have variety
    As well as action may.

Ulysses

But natures of the noblest frame
    These toils and dangers please;
And they take comfort in the same
    As much as you in ease;
And with the thought of actions past
    Are recreated still;
When pleasure leaves a touch, at last,
    To show that it was ill.

Siren

That doth opinion only cause
  That's out of custom bred,
Which makes us many other laws
  Than ever nature did,
No widows wail for our delights,
  Our sports are without blood;
The world, we see, by warlike wights
  Receives more hurt than good.

Ulysses

But yet the state of things require
  These motions of unrest;
And these great spirits of high desire
  Seem born to turn them best;
To purge the mischiefs that increase
  And all good order mar;
For oft we see a wicked peace,
  To be well changed for war.

Siren

Well, well, Ulysses, then I see
  I shall not have thee here;
And therefore I will come to thee,
  And make my fortune there.
I must be won, that cannot win,
  Yet lost were I not won;
For beauty hath created bin
  To undo, or be undone.

SAMUEL DANIEL

DECEMBER: OF APHRODITE

Whatever the books may say, or the plausible
Chroniclers intimate; that I was mad,
That an unsettling wind that season

Fretted my sign and fetched up violence
From the vagaries of dream, or even that pride
Is a broad road with few turnings, do not
Believe them.   In her name I acted.

(Vidal once, the extravagant of heart,
For the love of a woman went mad, mad as a dog,
And the wolves ate him; Hercules, crazed
By that jealous goddess, murdered his children;
Samson, from a woman's lap, woke blinded,
Turning a mill in Gaza; Adam, our father,
Eating from his wife's hand, fell from the garden.)

Not that from heaven she twisted my tenderness
Into a hand of rage, nor because she delighted
In burnt offering, I in my five senses
Cut throats of friends, burned the white harvest, waged
Seven months' havoc even among
Her temples; but because she waited always
There in the elegant shell, asking for sweetness.

And though it was in her name the land was ravaged,
Spilled and dishonored, let it not be said
That by her wiles it was done, nor that she gave
That carnage her blessing.   All arrogant demons
Pretending changelessness, who came first when she called,
Have faded and are spent, till out of the strong,
Without death, she conjured the honeycomb.

She sits at evening under a gray arch
Where many marvels fell, where all has fallen:
The blue over her dolphins, the popular leaves,
The cold rain, all but the grave myrtle
And the rings of her ringdoves.   The doge of one calendar
Would give her a name of winter, but where I stand
In the hazed gold of her eyes, the world is green.

W. S. MERWIN

A MODERN FICTION

A lion with a fiery mane,
    roaring and raging came,
came to a field where roses grow,
where roses in perfect stillness grow.

The lady was pale as the snow.
    The lion leaped in her eyes
like brightness stolen from the sky,
like the fire from the heart of the sky.

She held white lilies in her hand,
    wore violets in her hair,
hair as yellow as a full moon and
robed like the lilies in her hand.

—He has come from the burning sky.
    He's wild, she said, but I
will put out the flame and learn his name
and teach him manners when he's tame.

—The pale moon has tumbled down,
    grumbled incredulous lion.
The moon has found a soft new bed,
ice and snow on a field of red.

It was the lion who fled,
    fearing that walking cold.
—How marvelous to see, the lady said,
the sun go running, red and gold!

GEORGE GARRETT

THE MAJORETTE ON THE SELF-RISING FLOUR SIGN

We came each day to where
You had been laid

In tall grass behind the football field,
Twice again as large as any half-time majorette.
Where you once stood and smiled beside our practice field
Some more comely figure had reared herself
To suggest we try her snowy white self-rising flour.
But she stood beyond our ready grasp;
You waited in easy weeds,
Offering the self-same flour.
Although your soldier-girl suit was out of style
We rose to the red, white, and blue of your flower,
Imagined ourselves clasped
Between your flaking white thighs,
And peeled the red away to see
What secrets lay beneath your uniform—
We found the galvanized lie,
Slowly peeled you all away,
And went to other flower fields.

From where we sit tonight
We do not see your skeleton in the weeds.
New floodlights now blaze above us
And players from another generation
Prepare their kick-off on this worried ground.
Dutifully we rise for The Star-Spangled Banner
And over the loudspeaker a prayer comes
For good clean sports.
Behind the top-row bleachers on less familiar signs
Are this age's superwomen,
Their painted smiles saying merely someone has the ball.

And now as half-time majorettes cover the grid
We go to the cables for a closer look.
A new routine is announced.
But when the floodlights go off
Nothing new comes; our bloodshot eyes
Reject the dark, begin to probe beyond the field,
Catch on something, snatch and seize a form that parts the
    grass—
In our flaming hands on these retaining wires
We feel an old charge now current our night,

For you arise from those self-same weeds
And under goal posts take flesh
And come to where we hang on cables,
Breathless.

You pitch and toss across the field
And at the end throw your fire batons
Into the night—
We watch with galvanized eyes
As you come again full-fleshed
In these half-times of our lives.

JAMES SEAY

IN CYTHEREA

She looses, then shakes free her hair.
    Wrists, slim as seabirds' throats,
Waft across the plangent air
    Certain amicable notes.

Her fingers, rippling on the lute
    Like minnows, plunge among the strings;
Her shoulders' curve, the curve of fruit,
    Distracts his mind from what she sings.

He peers through slitted branches bent
    In windows for the shaded spy;
The sun, possessive, insolent,
    Covers her with naked eye.

Coral and alabaster breasts,
    Twin moons, refine that arrant gaze.
O, there his own soul manifests
    Its self as tangible: What praise

Of tongue, of hand what gift or touch
    Could serve as seal of sacrament

To this epiphany, nor smutch
  With smart of earth what's heaven-sent?

Within their hutch of skin, five wits
  Sniff her measure, pace, and twitch.
Who would deny them benefits
  That pleasure soul?   They'll have their flitch—

Let soul's ambrosial trencher sate
  Co-tenants in that bower of bone;
Were not all justice insensate
  Should soul, they fasting, feast alone?

The intellect, third triumvir,
  From his cloistral tower comes down,
Adjudicates their sharing her
  To each according to his own.

Joint force confers, resolves, deploys,
  Encircling her from base in bush.
Her song sweetens the wind . . . A noise!
  She starts; the air hums with her hush.

A swoop of knuckles binds lithe wrists,
  His harsh beard briars her breath-stopt throat,
His dizzied senses sweat, she twists,
  They famish, lunge, with glee they gloat

And root for nectar—she rends free,
  Half leaps, half slithers down pell-mell,
Plunges, spuming, in the sea.
  Her long hair streams on the combers' swell.

He lollops across the beaten sands:
  Waves that wreathe impassive rocks
Curl and uncurl in his hands.
  Cold undertows swirl round his hocks.

                          DANIEL HOFFMAN

THREE

The Rescue

Lovers rescue each other from their self-imprisonment—if they are lucky. It happens just as Josephine Miles tells it ("Meeting"), sparing the details so that the most commonplace of events (boy meets girl) is revealed in its simplicity as a mythic pattern: A thousand years of desire, a thousand miles of travel, no certainty of final satisfaction, but the meeting finally does take place: "Miraculous life!" It always has our vote. We have only to be shown a girl standing at her window, and a boy, a stranger, standing in the cold outside and looking in, and, as Howard Nemerov says ("De Anima"), we want them together:

> These pure divisions hurt us in some realm
> Of parable beyond belief, beyond
> The temporal mind.

The dominant metaphor of The Rescue is, of course, imprisonment, followed in propitious circumstances by a prison break. The girl in the poem sees only her own image in the window pane; the boy "sees clearly, and hopelessly desires, / A life that is not his." It is intolerable! The list of prisons in the poems that follow is extensive; for a sample: the cave of Don Juan's skull, where the old exploiter of women relives his past with a girl whom he once took prisoner (George Garrett, "Don Juan, Old"); Lie Castle in Denise Levertov's "The Goddess"; an insane asylum in Dylan Thomas' "Love in the

Asylum"; a violin that has waited long for the right musician to play
upon it (Winfield Townley Scott, "William Primrose Gets His
Guarnerius"). One is reminded by all this of Stagnation, and this
indeed is exactly where we are and will remain, unless the rescue
squad and the prisoner keep trying, as though their life depended on
it—which it does.

Howard Nemerov ("De Anima") would seem to have mixed
feelings about the decision, in a given instance, of Cupid, "the blind
embryo," to turn away from lovers, pitying the unborn child which
union would bring into the world of death. Can we call this kind-
ness? To be sure, the death-wish, given leave, would solve all prob-
lems of existence by eliminating life from earth. But neither the
Lady nor the women in whom she is incarnate are likely to approve
that nihilistic formula. The protagonist of Madeline Gleason's "Once
and Upon" watches her mother go about her household business,
doing dishes and the weekly wash. While the mother cans the
"peach and plum in season," the daughter, eating a plum, thinks of
that other Lady, the spinning earth, who is "holy Mother to /
the plentiful fruit." She feels within herself the

> Sisters of grace,
> comely, sea-washed,
> with blond shell hair and skin . . .

and she thinks of the boys who shout and run and swagger and long
for "the sisters' charms." It is a touching evocation of the classical
Graces who personify the festive attributes of their mistress, Aphro-
dite: beauty, brightness, and joy—in nature and humanity. But they
are entirely alien to the domestic web, where father "walks in a web
of work," and mother spins "and plans / for our lives ten thousand
weeks" of Monday washes. The daughter longs to cross the river
Gone and find "the place called New," but "no trees bent down /
to whisper their wisdom / for her becoming." On the other hand,
the female speaker in "The Goddess" (Denise Levertov) is rescued
in no uncertain terms by the Lady herself, who comes upon her,
moping in Lie Castle, seizes her violently by the hair, and throws
her out of doors. Like the girl in Miss Gleason's poem, she tastes—
not a plum, but the mud that splattered her lips when she landed on
the ground: "the seeds of a forest were in it / asleep and growing!
I tasted her power!" Stagnancy, which "returns lie for lie," is not

and can never be a match for the angry Lady, who demands of her votaries not mere lip service, but "flowers, fruits."

Like the flowers and fruits of earth awaiting spring, the Sleeping Beauty lies dormant in the timeless world of her cobwebby castle, awaiting the kiss that will awaken her. Rescue by the Hero is presumably what every woman hopes for. In "Andromeda," however, Graham Hough has imagined the title figure as a plodding domestic creature who has grown so accustomed to the monster, her reputed persecutor, that she no longer understands her need to be liberated from him. Her acceptance of the ugly creature who frets "at unsuccessful business deals" is not to be construed as generosity, like that which won for Beauty, in the fairy tale, a Prince whose qualities she had intuited though they were concealed within the Beast. No disenchantment could transform the beast of this Andromeda or the Andromeda of this beast. She suffers from a dreary lethargy, and all that remains of her capacity for emotion is "A thin dry shudder where her heart had been." A contrast is provided by the speaker of "Her Triumph" (William Butler Yeats), a girl who tells her Perseus (or Saint George) that she "did the dragon's will" before he came, simply because she did not know the meaning of love. The dragon, in this instance, is not a jaded husband like the monster in Graham Hough's poem, but a composite of the suitors who had helped her pass the time away by going through the motions of flirtation. Here, what the Hero had to master was the Lady's mockery, and he was equal to the task. She is freed, and love proves more astonishing than either Hero or Lady had anticipated: Together, they stare at the sea, "And a miraculous strange bird shrieks at [them]." One thinks of Portia, in *The Merchant of Venice*, tempering her boredom by deriding the vanity, stupidity, and affectation of her various suitors—until Bassanio arrives to liberate her picture from the leaden casket. Shakespeare parallels Bassanio's Quest with that of Jason for the Golden Fleece. Like Jason, Bassanio is more than willing to "give and hazard" all he has to gain the treasure, and this, as always, is the winning formula. Portia springs to life at Bassanio's kiss, and from that moment not only her wealth and beauty are his, but a wisdom which can redeem the generous Antonio, and a mercy which is foiled only by the stubborn vengefulness of Shylock.

Often the Hero is rescued by the Lady, and this event is simply the Hero's feat seen from a different point of view. When Shakespeare's Othello, at the end of the play, sees Desdemona once again as she really is—pure, innocent, and faithful—it is as though she rises free from the distorted image of herself which jealousy had bred in his imagination; and, simultaneously, the rediscovery of Desdemona frees Othello from the disillusionment and despair which loss of her true image had occasioned in his mind and spirit. A pair of poems by Thomas Merton illustrates the interdependence of the Hero and the Lady. In "Ariadne," the arrival of the vital force that Theseus represents (his very ship skips, paws, and whinnies!) arouses Ariadne from her slough of boredom, and "Arrows of Light / Resound within her like the strings of a guitar." Then, in "Ariadne at the Labyrinth," the Lady holds the thread at the other end of which the Hero winds his way to find the Minotaur and conquer him. He will return to her in the "white morning," because, in "her wild and gentle wisdom, she forknows / And solves the maze's cruel algebra." Thanks to her, Theseus completes the exploit and emerges from the labyrinth, "The Bravest Soldier, the Wisest Judge, / The Mightiest King!"

The successful Hero, like Odysseus or the husband in Don Geiger's poem ("Love Song by Husband after Being Buried with Wife One Night"), is well supplied with "poise and guile"; but it is the Lady—Athene or the Wife—whose timely intuition keeps his heart "sticking to the bone." Moreover, as the Muse, she is the wellspring of man's imaginative power. Like the Maenads, drunk with praise of Dionysus, her power takes the form of apparent madness. But a world or consciousness reputed to be rational may be, as Dylan Thomas sees it ("Love in the Asylum"), actually a "house not right in the head." Though the girl in Thomas' poem admits the clouds and the light to "the heaven-proof house" and ministers to the patients in "the nightmarish room," her presence and the liberation which it promises seem to the madhouse inmate merely delusive. But they are not. When he is "taken by light in her arms at long and dear last," he can recognize at least the possibility of epiphany. It will be painful to him at first, just as the light of Paradise was painful to Dante and that of the Good to those who escaped from the cave in Plato's allegory, but that is an acceptable price for one to pay, who

may without fail
Suffer the first vision that set fire to the stars.

DE ANIMA

Now it is night, now in the brilliant room
A girl stands at the window looking out,
But sees, in the darkness of the frame,
Only her own image.

And there is a young man across the street
Who looks at the girl and into the brilliant room.
They might be in love, might be about to meet,
If this were a romance.

In looking at herself, she tries to look
Beyond herself, and half become another,
Admiring and resenting, maybe dreaming
Her lover might see her so.

The other, the stranger standing in cold and dark,
Looks at the young girl in her crystalline room.
He sees clearly, and hopelessly desires,
A life that is not his.

Given the blindness of her self-possession,
The luminous vision revealed to his despair,
We look to both sides of the glass at once
And see no future in it.

These pure divisions hurt us in some realm
Of parable beyond belief, beyond
The temporal mind.   Why is it sorrowful?
Why do we want them together?

Is it the spirit, ransacking through the earth
After its image, its being, its begetting?
The spirit sorrows, for what lovers bring
Into the world is death,

The most exclusive romance, after all,
The sort that lords and ladies listen to

With selfish tears, when she draws down the shade,
When he has turned away,

When the blind embryo with his bow of bees,
His candied arrows tipped with flower heads,
Turns from them too, for mercy or for grief
Refusing to be, refusing to die.

                        HOWARD NEMEROV

DON JUAN, OLD

All day this woman dances barefoot on my brain,
Toes crushing spongy stuff, heels bruising,
Until my hollow skull howls like a cave,
like a tunnel when you sound a horn in it
and it screams back at you from wall to wall.

Did I say on? I meant in.
I've captured her. She moves to my whim
and whip, a furtive flickering past
like a package of filthy pictures,
Thumbed through, already smudged by prints.

Seized her off the street. She swept past,
sweater and skirt, flash of scissoring legs
(skirt didn't fit, stocking seams crooked),
a gust of cheap perfume and powder,
lips smeared with hurried, hopeful red.

She ran for a bus. Heels a snare drum
on the pavement. Gray, rainy, city day.
I seized her and stripped her and burned her.
I warmed myself by a white fire.
Trussed lamb, forgive me.

In dreams I can be kind.
Far from gray cities, far from the smell
of powder and sweat and sad perfume,

far from the stockings drying in the bathroom
and the saxophone's moan from your radio

I carry you. To country of palm and patio,
balcony and fountain, sun and shade.
You rest in opulent, unlikely curves,
and I sing for you sweetly although
you pluck out my beard by the roots.

GEORGE GARRETT

ONCE AND UPON

Cross at the morning
and at waking,
with a mourning for summer,
she crossed the bridge Now
over the river Gone
toward the place called New
to begin her Once Upon.

Once and Upon
my daddy long legs
walked in a web of work
for my sisters and me,
as Mother spun round
with silver knives and forks
in a shining of pans,
a wash of Mondays
and plans
for our lives ten thousand weeks.

To cross the bridge Now
over the river Gone
toward the place called New
to begin her Once Upon,
in a mourning for summer, she moved
to write her right becoming
and find her true beloved.

Snippets and tags of Gone,
criss-crossed as retold,
beggared the strumming
of fresh rhythms
that should have stirred her becoming.

Once and Upon
she ate the plum
and from a full mouth
disgorged the pit
into her hand
while Mother spun as she canned
peach and plum in season—
the land, holy Mother to
the plentiful fruit.

To cross.
But where should her steps lead
away from the river?

Through a desert she hurried,
thirsting she ran
to reach becoming,
passed three water holes
but never saw them,
so eager was she to reach
outward evidence
of her inward drawing.

Sisters of grace,
comely, sea-washed,
with blond shell hair and skin,
whirling with intermittent passion
amidst daddy long legs
and Mother awash
among the underthings,
boys shouting and running,
swaggering and dying
for the sisters' charms.
AMEN!

Tops a-spin in a dying dance.
Yoo Hoo, Fatty!   Buck!
Hi, Pete!   Hello, old Gene!

Cross at the morning,
summer crossed with the beginning
of gold,
a sea of brown leaves swirling.

And no trees bent down
to whisper their wisdom
for her becoming.
Ah! Now! Ah! Gone! Ah! New
Ah! Once Upon!

MADELINE GLEASON

THE GODDESS

She in whose lipservice
I passed my time,
whose name I knew, but not her face,
came upon me where I lay in Lie Castle!

Flung me across the room, and
room after room (hitting the walls, re-
bounding—to the last
sticky wall—wrenching away from it
pulled hair out!)
till I lay
outside the outer walls!

There in cold air
lying still where her hand had thrown me,
I tasted the mud that splattered my lips:
the seeds of a forest were in it,
asleep and growing!   I tasted
her power!

The silence was answering my silence,
a forest was pushing itself
out of sleep between my submerged fingers.

I bit on a seed and it spoke on my tongue
of day that shone already among stars
in the water-mirror of low ground,

and a wind rising ruffled the lights:
she passed near me returning from the encounter,
she who plucked me from the close rooms,

without whom nothing
flowers, fruits, sleeps in season,
without whom nothing
speaks in its own tongue, but returns
lie for lie!

DENISE LEVERTOV

THE DOOR

for Robert Duncan

It is hard going to the door
cut so small in the wall where
the vision which echoes loneliness
brings a scent of wild flowers in a wood.

What I understood, I understand.
My mind is sometime torment,
sometimes good and filled with livelihood,
and feels the ground.

But I see the door,
and knew the wall, and wanted the wood,
and would get there if I could
with my feet and hands and mind.

Lady, do not banish me
for digressions. My nature
is a quagmire of unresolved
confessions. Lady, I follow.

I walked away from myself,
I left the room, I found the garden,
I knew the woman
in it, together we lay down.

Dead, night remembers. In December
we change, not multiplied but dispersed,
sneaked out of childhood,
the ritual of dismemberment.

Mighty magic is a mother,
in her there is another issue
of fixture, repeated form, the race renewal,
the charge of the command.

The garden echoes across the room.
It is fixed in the wall like a mirror
that faces a window behind you
and reflects the shadows.

May I go now?
Am I allowed to bow myself down
in the ridiculous posture of renewal,
of the insistence of which I am the virtue?

Nothing for You is untoward.
Inside You would also be tall,
More tall, more beautiful.
Come toward me for the wall, I want to be with You.

So I screamed to You,
who hears as the wind, and changes
multiply, invariably,
changes in the mind.

Running to the door, I ran down
as a clock runs down. Walked backwards,
stumbled, sat down
hard on the floor near the wall.

Where were You.
How absurd, how vicious.
There is nothing to do but get up.
My knees were iron, I rusted in worship, of You.

For that one sings, one
writes the spring poem, one goes on walking.
The Lady has always moved to the next town
and you stumble on after Her.

The door in the wall leads to the garden
where in the sunlight sit
the Graces in long Victorian dresses,
of which my grandmother had spoken.

History sings in their faces.
They are young, they are obtainable,
and you follow after them also
in the service of God and Truth.

But the Lady is indefinable,
she will be the door in the wall
to the garden in sunlight.
I will go on talking forever.

I will never get there.
Oh Lady, remember me
who in Your service grows older
not wiser, no more than before.

How can I die alone.
Where will I be then who am now alone,
what groans so pathetically
in this room where I am alone?

I will go to the garden.
I will be a romantic.   I will sell
myself in hell,
in heaven also I will be.

In my mind I see the door,
I see the sunlight before me across the floor
Beckon to me, as the Lady's skirt
moves small beyond it.

ROBERT CREELEY

MEETING

One there lived on the east side of the city
One who wished to meet
One who lived on the west side of the city,
A thousand miles away.

A thousand years went by.

Then the one who lived on the east side of the city
Set out on the main street
And met the one who lived on the west side of the city
Coming that way.

A thousand years.

Miraculous life! that in its brief and mortal
Progress achieved this union of intents,
Inevitability sprung from the improbable,
Volition moving in the paths of chance.

JOSEPHINE MILES

ARIADNE

All through the blazing afternoon
The hand drums talk together like locusts;
The flute pours out its endless, thin stream,
Threading it in and out the clatter of sticks upon wood-blocks.
Drums and bells exchange handfuls of bright coins,
Drums and bells scatter their music, like pennies, all over the
    air,
And see, the lutanist's thin hand
Rapidly picks the spangling notes off from his wires
And throws them about like drops of water.

Behind the bamboo blinds,
Behind the palms,
In the green, sundappled apartments of her palace
Redslippered Ariadne, with a tiny yawn,
Tosses a ball upon her roulette wheel.

Suddenly, dead north,
A Greek ship leaps over the horizon, skips like a colt, paws the
    foam.
The ship courses through the pasture of bright amethysts
And whinnies at the jetty.
The whole city runs to see:
Quick as closing your hand
The racing sail's down.
Then the drums are stunned, and the crowd, exalted, cries:
O Theseus!   O Grecian hero!

Like a thought through the mind
Ariadne moves to the window.
Arrows of light, in every direction,
Leap from the armor of the black-eyed captain.
Arrows of light
Resound within her like the strings of a guitar.

THOMAS MERTON

ARIADNE AT THE LABYRINTH

Patient, in the fire of noon,
Hands, that hold the thread, crossed,
Ariadne's a Barbadian flower,
And grows by the Labyrinth door.

Under the blue, airy-waters of evening,
Hands folded like white petals,
Watching for the bold adventurer,
Ariadne waits as calm as coral,
Silent as some plant of undersea.

Drums ring at the city's edge:
The speechless hills put on crowns of dark flame;
Dancing citizens fly like little flags
Amid the glad volcano of their congas.
But Ariadne's eyes are lakes
Beside the maze's starwhite wall:
For in the Caribbean midnight
Of her wild and gentle wisdom, she foreknows
And solves the maze's cruel algebra.

But when white morning
Runs with a shout along the jagged mountains
Strength of a cotton thread draws out to Ariadne
The Bravest Soldier, the Wisest Judge,
The Mightiest King!

THOMAS MERTON

AN AMORETTI FOR ANNIE

A golden princess, no lady
Waits, alone, she pushed
That witch into the oven,

Closed the door, and heard
The popple and snap of her roasting.

Down the swinging bridge,
Cataracts, the alligators
(Or crocodiles), afraid,
She runs the labyrinth
Of backyard fences, and
The bellowing of the bull,
Always behind, and then before.

"I have failed to accept
The wine and cheese offered
Me. There was dancing,
But I danced alone. My eyes
Are blue. I have no secrets."

And the bull, a slovenly beast,
All horns and tail, a belching
Rumble right before her. Her
Eyes, her hands, her golden eyes
And gentle hands. The bull,
Half man, still bull, and she,
Who wears no armor, no Britomart,
Looks in his eyes, red eyes,
The bull, that lazy minotaur,
Lowers the curls of his head,
Rests his great horns in her hands,
And as she sings, he casts about,
Leads her from his labyrinth,
And moos farewell.

She leads him home.

They pick flowers.

Small birds sing.

R. H. W. DILLARD

KEMP OWYNE

Her mother died when she was young,
   Which gave her cause to make great moan;
Her father married the warst woman
   That ever lived in Christendom.

She served her with foot and hand,
   In every thing that she could dee,
Till once, in an unlucky time,
   She threw her in ower Craigy's sea.

Says, 'Lie you there, dove Isabel,
   And all my sorrows lie with thee;
Till Kemp Owyne come ower the sea,
   And borrow you with kisses three,
Let all the warld do what they will,
   Oh borrowed shall you never be!'

Her breath grew strang, her hair grew lang,
   And twisted thrice about the tree,
And all the people, far and near,
   Thought that a savage beast was she.

These news did come to Kemp Owyne,
   Where he lived, far beyond the sea;
He hasted him to Craigy's sea,
   And on the savage beast lookd he.

Her breath was strang, her hair was lang,
   And twisted was about the tree,
And with a swing she came about:
   'Come to Craigy's sea, and kiss with me.

'Here is a royal belt,' she cried,
   'That I have found in the green sea;
And while your body it is on,
   Drawn shall your blood never be;

But if you touch me, tail or fin,
   I vow my belt your death shall be.'

He stepped in, gave her a kiss,
   The royal belt he brought him wi;
Her breath was strang, her hair was lang,
   And twisted twice about the tree,
And with a swing she came about:
   'Come to Craigy's sea, and kiss with me.

'Here is a royal ring,' she said,
   'That I have found in the green sea;
And while your finger it is on,
   Drawn shall your blood never be;
But if you touch me, tail or fin,
   I swear my ring your death shall be.

He stepped in, gave her a kiss,
   The royal ring he brought him wi;
Her breath was strang, her hair was lang,
   And twisted ance about the tree,
And with a swing she came about:
   'Come to Craigy's sea, and kiss with me.

'Here is a royal brand,' she said,
   'That I have found in the green sea;
And while your body it is on,
   Drawn shall your blood never be;
But if you touch me, tail or fin,
   I swear my brand your death shall be.'

He stepped in, gave her a kiss,
   The royal brand he brought him wi;
Her breath was sweet, her hair grew short,
   And twisted nane about the tree,
And smilingly she came about,
   As fair a woman as fair could be.

ANONYMOUS

ANDROMEDA

One can get used to anything; the cave
Was dark, smelt bad, and twice a day the wave
Slopped on the floor; however much she swept
Sand, bladder-wrack and dead sea-urchins crept
Over the stones. The monster did not care,
But crouched preoccupied before the door,
Fretted at unsuccessful business deals,
Went out to fish and came back late for meals.

And when at last the heaven-sprung hero came,
Wing-heeled and gorgon-shielded, thirsty for fame,
Red-hot with bravery, he found her sitting
Upon a damp stone, busy with her knitting.
The monster lay asleep, and dinner stood
To simmer by a fire of smouldering wood.
The sword seemed pointless, something was amiss.
She stirred the pot. He had not come for this.

He was too late. The voyage had been too long.
The gorgon shield turned no ill thing to stone.
The gold helm hardly dazzled her at all.
She hung the iron ladle on the wall,
Stood up and faced him. Was the moment come?
But when the monster shivered in the gloom
She bent and spread a cloth over its coiled
Green limbs. The hero's attitude was spoiled.

Had he looked close enough he might have seen
A thin dry shudder where her heart had been,
But saw no thundering wrong to fight about,
Clattered his golden armour and went out;
Finding her patient unrebellious shape
No pretext for a plain heroic rape.
The tide was rising, and she turned once more
To sweep away the dark sea from the door.

GRAHAM HOUGH

HER TRIUMPH

I did the dragon's will until you came
Because I had fancied love a casual
Improvisation, or a settled game
That followed if I let the kerchief fall:
Those deeds were best that gave the minute wings
And heavenly music if they gave it wit;
And then you stood among the dragon-rings.
I mocked, being crazy, but you mastered it
And broke the chain and set my ankles free,
Saint George or else a pagan Perseus;
And now we stare astonished at the sea,
And a miraculous strange bird shrieks at us.

                              WILLIAM BUTLER YEATS

ORPHEUS

Stone lips to the unspoken cave;
Fingering the nervous strings, alone,
I crossed that gray sill, raised my head
To lift my song into the grave
Meanders of unfolding stone,
Following where the echo led
Down blind alleys of our dead.

Down the forbidden, backward street
To the lower town, condemned, asleep
In blank remembering mazes where
Smoke rose, the ashes hid my feet
And slow walls crumpled, settling deep
In rubble of the central square.
All ruin I could sound was there.

At the charred rail and windowsill,
Widows hunched in fusty shawls,
This only once the Furies wept;

The watchdog turned to hear me till
Head by head forgot its howls,
Loosed the torn images it kept,
Let sag its sore jaws and slept.

Then to my singing's radius
Seethed faces like a pauper's crowd
Or flies of an old injury.
The piteous dead who lived on us
Whined in my air, anarchic, loud
Till my soft voice that set them free,
Lost in this grievous enemy,

Rose up and laid them in low slumbers;
I meant to see in them what dark
Powers be, what eminent plotters.
Midmost those hushed, downcast numbers
Starved Tantalus stood upright, stark,
Waistdeep where the declining waters
Swelled their tides, where Danaus' daughters

Dropped in full surf their unfilled tub;
Now leaned against his rolling stone
Slept Sisyphus beneath the hill;
That screaming half-beast, strapped at the hub,
Whom Juno's animal mist had known,
Ixion's wheel creaked and was still.
I held all hell to hear my will.

"Powers of the Underworld, who rule
All higher powers by graft or debt,
Within whose mortgage all men live:
No spy, no shining power's fool,
I think in the unthought worlds to get
The light you only freely give
Who are all bright worlds' negative.

You gave wink in an undue crime
To love—strong even here, they say.
I sing, as the blind beggars sing,

To ask of you this little time
—All lives foreclose in their due day—
That flowered bride cut down in Spring,
Struck by the snake, your underling."

In one long avenue she was
Wandering toward me, vague, uncertain,
Limping a little still, the hair
And garments tenuous as gauze
And drifting loose like a white curtain
Vacillating in black night air
That holds white lilacs, God knows where.

"Close your eyes," said the inner ear;
"As night lookouts learn not to see
Ahead but only off one side,
As the eye's sight is never clear
But blind, dead center, you must be
Content; look not upon your bride
Till day's light lifts her eyelids wide."

I turned my back to her, set out
My own way back and let her follow
Like some curious albino beast
That prowls in areas of drought,
Lured past the town's slack doors, the hollow
Walls, the stream-bed lost in midst,
That breathless long climb, with no least

Doubt she must track me close behind;
As the actual scent of flesh, she must
Trail my voice unquestioning where.
Yet where the dawn first edged my mind
In one white flashing of mistrust
I turned and she, she was not there.
My hands closed on the high, thin air.

It was the nature of the thing:
No moon outlives its leaving night,
No sun its day.   And I went on

Rich in the loss of all I sing
To the threshold of waking light,
To larksong and the live, gray dawn,
So night by night, my life has gone.

W. D. SNODGRASS

LOVE SONG BY HUSBAND AFTER BEING BURIED WITH HIS WIFE ONE NIGHT

Last night I dreamed a Presence
Who said that I had died.
I had my doubts because
I felt her at my side.

That Presence, with an easy,
Ingratiating moan,
Said that we were buried,
Together, bone to bone.

I checked a heap of bones,
And saw that it was true:
The bones were she and I,
Together, if askew.

The Presence said to come
With It a little pace.
I liked it where I was.
I didn't trust Its face.

I thought it odd that she
Said nothing of her will,
But let me do our talking,
And that was odder still.

I let It think It had us,
To catch It by surprise:
"I grant the bones are right;
We see them with my eyes."

I paused, dramatically:
The Thing began to reach;
I winked, that she should know
I'd saved the winning speech.

"If we live," I argued,
"We're not within Your reach.
Please touch these bones. You'll note
Our hearts beat, each to each!"

The Presence, gliding off,
Sighed a plaintive moan:
"I've never seen such hearts
For sticking to the bone."

With pride I turned to hear
Her praise my poise and guile,
But she said nothing, smiling
An irritating smile;

And then I realized
That she had saved her breath
To keep both hearts at work,
While I outwitted Death.

Dismayed, I thought, "She saved
Us, as no woman should,"
And would have called Death back,
But woke before I could.

Outraged, I watched her sleep
Affect indifference,
And found it hard to trust
That showy innocence.

"Yet surely even she
Can't wake me at her will."
But as I drowsed, I thought,
The *dream* was possible.

                         DON GEIGER

EX-SURREALIST

Once
very long upon a time ago
he moved among
dunghills of distress where tragic-eyed
a boy with splintered shinbone
talked to crows.
In other worlds, those
locked behind the groin and eyeball; fetid, tense,
erotic melonbreast and severed vein,
reek, rot and silver stench of lust.
A private pit, his pleasure kingdom
whose monuments wore scarabs of decay.

Doctors do not speak
who know that flowers bloom on blood
in rankroot tangle, crenelated leafshape.
Like waterweeds adrift in coral
death flirts among the branching ribs.

See him in sun
a transient worshipper
conjuring the clean and kind,
content with trees and
dreaming childripe women, placid, loved.
This winter he will find
madonna faces in the bluest snow.

JOANNE DE LONGCHAMPS

THE SLEEPING BEAUTY

In a place where hunchbacks and old women
Quarrelled in their thin voices all the day
This temporizing grew intolerable:
I knew that here the Sleeping Beauty lay.

(Had they known it all the time and been
Sly servitors where I could only seize
Bad temper and distorted images?)
Sight ended the old argument. I saw

Her tower clear against the star-picked blue
Over their hovels. It was no affair
Of a cloud and the moon's subtle conjunction; thorns
Hatched me all criss-cross as I hacked my way through

And stumbled bloody still and breathing still
Into a country where no footsteps fall
And where from moat, to keep, to citadel
Spider-webs lie like water.

I silvered as I entered through the door
Where time cannot prevail
But howls outside forever where I found her
Asleep, beautiful, the cobwebs round her.

                    E. L. MAYO

WILLIAM PRIMROSE GETS HIS GUARNERIUS

No fiddle of morning:
All the light in it
Is traveled.

Guarnerius Viola
Shaped of a woman's body,
Three centuries,
Burnished maple;
The night tone shining.

Her silence and sleep so long
Webbed beneath strung starlight.

But William,
Barefooted in kilts to school,

Kind-fathered past jungles of billboards,
Believing in the resurrection,
Traveled humbly toward her,
Grew into the dark forest, the night tone,
Wordless with music.

Now his face bends upon her,
His bow and fingers move:
From interference of learned mortal love
Across far-traveled light
All hymns arise and sing
Human and deathless.

To awaken this
Required
No ordinary prince.

WINFIELD TOWNLEY SCOTT

LOVE IN THE ASYLUM

A stranger has come
To share my room in the house not right in the head,
A girl mad as birds

Bolting the night of the door with her arm her plume.
Strait in the mazed bed
She deludes the heaven-proof house with entering clouds

Yet she deludes with walking the nightmarish room,
At large as the dead,
Or rides the imagined oceans of the male wards.

She has come possessed
Who admits the delusive light through the bouncing wall,
Possessed by the skies

She sleeps in the narrow trough yet she walks the dust
Yet raves at her will

On the madhouse boards worn thin by my walking tears.

And taken by light in her arms at long and dear last
                    I may without fail
Suffer the first vision that set fire to the stars.

DYLAN THOMAS

V

THE FATHER

Conceptions of the Father in our literature inevitably are conditioned by the association of that mythic figure with the God whose Word, revealed in scripture, is canonical. Homer's playful treatment of the gods of Olympus has not proved incompatible with a reverence both for those deities and for *The Iliad* and *The Odyssey* as sacred works. But God the Father, Son, and Holy Spirit have for us an aura of sanctity which can be daunting to the imagination. Pope, as critic, complained that Milton's God the Father, whose pronouncements are, for the most part, paraphrased from scripture, sounds uncomfortably like "a school divine"; and Samuel Johnson firmly held the opinion that the high truths of religion should be reverently passed over by the poet. However, the role of the Father must remain for us, as it has always been, an essential element of the Quest. If, in the broadest terms, the Lady is all that lives and all that can be known in the created universe, the Father who possesses her is, by definition, both omniscient and omnipotent. It is therefore only from the Father that the Hero can obtain the knowledge and the power which he seeks.

The absolute righteousness of Jehovah and the mild perfection of Jesus have a tendancy to polarize conceptions of the Father in our literature. Such supernal attributes are likely either to inspire the fervor of unquestioning faith or the apostasy of fervent questioning. The problem of the origin of evil, in particular, rises again and again, like an indignant ghost, to point an accusing finger at the untarnished image of the Godhead. In the East, the case is entirely different. Shiva, the Hindu god of destruction, graphically encompasses the brawling opposites of the temporal world: creation and destruction, male and female, joy and sorrow. In the context of this complex amorality, evil is subsumed into the universal scheme of things and thus becomes, for the initiate, no more than an illusion bred of imperfect understanding. Needless to say, a solution of this kind was unavailable to Milton, and it is therefore not surprising that his elaborate attempt, in *Paradise Lost*, to justify the ways of God to man has won, at best, a qualified assent. One can always ask why Satan, who was created without flaw, chose to rebel against the benevolent dominion of a perfect God; and many poets, among them Shelley and Blake, have been moved to champion Satan against what they regard as the cruel persecution of his creator.

Poems about the Father, as he is envisioned in the Judeo-Christian tradition, frequently emphasize the difficulty of communion between the creator and the created, and recount the violent rebellions on the part of the latter. The Atonement that follows is the more moving because it must bridge a vast gap between the realm of high perfection and that of a suffering humanity whose prayers persist but threaten to become mere feckless whining. The strongly authoritarian nature of the Father is reflected in the prominence of hierarchal patterns in the literature which deals with him: God is to the created universe as the sun is to the earth, the king to his subjects, the father to his wife and children. This scheme of Chinese boxes, of macrocosm and microcosm, lies near the heart of the metaphoric structure of many of Shakespeare's plays. For example, in *Macbeth*, the growing alienation of Macbeth and Lady Macbeth from each other corresponds to that of the king from his rebellious subjects; and the murder of King Duncan is paralleled by unnatural events in the physical world. *Paradise Lost*, the scheme of which is radically hierarchal, commands new interest in our schools today, because the vacillation of mankind, assailed on one side by the rule of heaven and on the other by the rebelliousness of hell, has obvious relevance to the social upheavals which are so conspicuous in every segment and at every level of our society.

Thanks to the work of Freud, Jung, and their followers, we are accustomed to conceiving of the human psyche in a way which is most pertinent to our religious and literary traditions. Here, the superego, where the moral sense resides, possesses God-like righteousness; the persona (what we ask the world to think of us) is at loggerheads with the shadow (aspects of ourselves which we repress); and the ego labors to ally itself with reason against the unruly promptings of the id. Just as the Hero in our poetry and fiction seeks to meet the Father face to face, we find in our experience crises of identity; if God is depicted as a fiend or ogre, we recognize in the figure a projection of our oppressive superego or of our thwarted id. In short, it has never been more apparent that Atonement with the Father is a vital concern for Everyman in the commonwealth of the individual psyche, in the social sphere, and in religion. Though religion is believed by some to have lost its relevance to the modern world, the Judeo-Christian myth is vigorously alive; and the concerns of the church, so far from becoming insular, are daily dramatized in every segment of private and public life.

It is significant that three works of fiction which have, in recent years, enjoyed immense popularity among college and high school students all are strongly mythic in pattern, and all deal with aspects of the Father. Salinger's *The Catcher in the Rye* closely resembles and parallels *Hamlet* in probing the pretensions of the Establishment, the phoniness of accepted codes and figures of authority. *Lord of the Flies*, by William Golding, deals with the violent emergence of a hidden savagery in a band of ex-choirboys exiled on an island during a catastrophic war; and the pig-head Lord himself is the ogre-father with a vengeance. Finally, evil and its relationship to the sovereign will is chronicled in what is surely the classic of modern mythopoeic writing: Tolkien's *Lord of the Rings*.

The struggle between the sovereign will and the self-transcendence which is essential to Atonement is, of course, a staple of western literature from Homer to the present day. The crowning incident of that most war-like of epics, *The Iliad*, has little directly to do with battle on the plains of Troy. It is the moving episode in which the venerable Priam, grieving for the loss of Hector, risks his life to beg the body of the slaughtered Hero from an Achilles whose ferocity has been displayed in all of its ruthless strength. When Achilles yields to pity, an atonement follows which, in a qualitative sense, outweighs all of the nightmare pride and vengefulness of many dreary years of war. Our greatest drama of Conflict and Atonement is *King Lear*, a compendium of almost every aspect of the Father that concerns us deeply: the struggle between the proud and vengeful king and his rebellious offspring; the cynicism of the politician seeking power; and the reconciliation of the old man with a daughter whose abounding grace is compensation for his long travail.

Blind and stricken with grief almost beyond endurance, Shakespeare's Earl of Gloucester can find no comfort in the rulers of the universe:

> *As flies to wanton boys are we to th'gods;*
> *They kill us for their sport.*
>
> (*King Lear:* IV.i.36–37)

But his despair proves not to be past cure. Coleridge's Ancient Mariner, at the nadir of his strange eventful history, is the victim of a spiritual isolation that is powerfully conveyed by every detail of his circumstance: His only companions are the dead who have cursed him with their eyes; he parches under a merciless sun on the deck of a dead ship becalmed in a vast ocean, the very waters of which appear to rot. The Father, for him, is the burning copper sun, nailed like a parody of Christ to the mast of the ship, his prison. But the order of grace is also abroad in the Mariner's universe. In his despair, he is given power to love, and at that moment, he obtains release. The rain, the fresh breeze, the homeward course, and the vision of leaves and flowers which accompanies his swift journey home—all of these are the gifts of the Father; and the Mariner, like the poet, accepts his obligation to tell and tell again the story of a voyage and a loss, of solitary suffering, and of the Atonement which, in the end, proceeds from all of these.

The Search

In order to understand well the meaning of the search for the Father, one has only to think of Job, whose dilemma belongs in some degree to every man. He is stricken with every imaginable ill and is informed by his "comforters" that he must have done evil in the sight of the Lord in order to deserve such punishment. Yet Job knows that he has lived a blameless life. In the opinion of his wife, Job should curse God and die, but Job is made of heroic stuff and he endures his agony and bafflement until he is at last enlightened, not by an assurance of God's justice but by a vision of the power and wonder of God, which passeth understanding. Like Job, every man longs to understand the mystery of the eternal Father who creates and conditions our existences in the time-bound world.

The craving for knowledge of the Father is well expressed by W. S. Merwin in "Proteus":

> *The nothing into which a man leans forward*
> *Is mother of all restiveness, drawing*
> *The body prone to falling into no*
> *Repose at last but the repose of falling.*

But the Hero's blunt tactics in attempting to force the "wind of prophecy" from Proteus do not produce an antidote to restiveness. He only learns what everyone in some bleak hour suspects, that he "battles the foolish shapes / of his own death by the insatiate sea."

The Father yields no satisfaction on compulsion. If he reveals himself, it will be in his own time, when the time is ripe, and in his own fashion.

"Eternity," wrote Blake, "is in love with the works of time." The Father sees himself in his creation, for it is the work of his own hand, and, in the beginning, he looked upon it and saw that it was good. The restless human ego, on the other hand, desiring to be sovereign, finds itself thwarted at every turn by ignorance, impotence, and all the ills that flesh is heir to. The mood of the Hero searching for the Father is likely to be that of the lonely, hurt, and rebellious child. He longs for love and understanding but has vengeance in his heart. "The kingdom of God," said Jesus to the Pharisees, "cometh not with observation: Neither shall they say, Lo here! or, lo there! for, behold, the kingdom of God is within you" (Luke: 17.20–21). But many an aspiring Hero looks within, can find no Father at all, and suffers from a sense of alienation; or, like Satan, he perceives the Father as the Great Tormentor, relishing his pain.

Modern poetry about the Father, for the most part, hardly could be called devotional. Written in the ironic vein, it often dramatizes doubt ("The muddy rumors / Of your burial move me / To half-believe"—Sylvia Plath, "Full Fathom Five") or imagines, in the place of a benevolent creator, monsters which are the product of disillusionment, frustration, or despair. John Heath-Stubbs finds in the Sphinx "the implacable image / of male power that smoothly worships itself"; and Yeats, looking upon the twenty centuries that have elapsed since the birth of Christ as so much "stony sleep," envisions the "rough beast" of the second coming, slouching toward Bethlehem to be born. The inhuman slaughter of the Jews at Auschwitz prompts Peter Viereck to imagine a Father who can say

All sights bore Me now but blood.
The main thing is to kill. And kill. And kill.

Sarcasm can hardly go further in the castigation of a Father who is speaking, as the headnote tells us, at a time "shortly after peace and love return to earth."

The path that leads to the Father well deserves to be called a Road of Trials; and the Father is the designer and custodian of the tortuous way. In myth, the purpose of this strenuous testing is sometimes nominally to destroy the Hero: Poseidon angrily does everything in his power to put danger in the path of Odysseus; yet the Hero will at last win through to set things straight again in his native Ithaca. Zeus allows Hera to impose twelve labors upon Heracles in order to prove him worthy of the gift of immortality; Jupiter reminds Aeneas, from time to time, that he is to be the founder of a city and an empire. Apparently both adversity and the power to overcome it prove in the end to be the gifts of the gods. Should fear of Medusa sap the courage of the Hero, he will be turned to stone; but for Perseus, whom the gods have chosen, the encounter with that bogey is only an incident on the path that leads to the throne of Argos.

Greek Heroes can confidently attribute hazards of the Quest to the politics of the gods; and if one god is hostile to their purposes, another, duly supplicated, proves a very present help in trouble. Dante, as protagonist of *The Divine Comedy*, turns in all humility to Virgil, Beatrice, or St. Bernard for counsel as he makes his way through hell, ascends the purgatorial mountain, and progresses through the spheres of heaven toward the immortal source of light. More often than not, however, the modern literary Hero either troubles deaf heaven with his bootless cries or turns his own deaf ear to the promptings of the spirit. Kafka's Hero in *The Castle*, threading an endless labyrinth, learns only that no guide may be relied upon to lead him into the presence of the power whose defenses he can never penetrate unaided; and Melville's Captain Ahab, in his lucid moments, recognizes that his vengeful Quest for God incarnate in the whale is suicidal, but he plunges on to his destruction.

The Father whom the modern Hero meets is characteristically "archaic," "atavistic," "oblivious"; he is a statue made of stone or bronze. As Carl Sandburg's protagonist in "Streets Too Old" wanders about in the old city of this world, the statues of the kings complain, "Is there no loosening? Is this for always?" And one of them cries, "throw the bronze of me to a fierce fire and / make me into neckchains for dancing children." Mankind creates the Father in its own image. When the Hero suffers from the "mind-forg'd manacles" of his constricting ego, he projects an image of the Father as a tyrant god whose death means liberation. Thus the offspring of the dollar-loving Daddy in William Jay Smith's "American Primitive," having found the old man hanging by his black cravat, declares his love for the departed parent in a tone which rings with ghoulish jubilation. The pervasive "anger and ache" of the gods who inhabit "Cellar and choking cave" in Edwin Muir's "The Fathers" will never "leave the living alone" until "they topple and fall, / And fallen let in day." As Emerson wrote, "When half-gods go, / The gods arrive," but the former yield their places most reluctantly. When Jesus told the disciples that he must enter Jerusalem and be put to death, he assured the protesting Peter that

> *whosoever will save his life shall lose it:*
> *and whosoever shall lose his life for my sake shall*
> *find it.*
> *For what is a man profited, if he shall gain the*
> *whole world, and lose his own soul?*

> (Matthew: 16.25–26)

The ogres of our nightmares are the progeny of the sovereign will, which does not wish to be deposed. When they are put to flight, one world is lost and another springs to life which, being ogre-free, gives love its breathing room.

Love, says Daniel Hoffman ('Ignorant of source'), "does not know / Its cause, its end." But the secret is revealed in the brief moment of delight which attends the begetting of progeny, an act which results for man, as did God's creation of the world for him, in "New loves, new / Ways of loving, being loved." The process of creation, which is known by parents, by artists, and by all who observe the beauty, infinite variety, and inexhaustible energy of the physical world, has the power to pull down "the heartless temple" (Hyam Plutzik, "Exhortation to Artists") where the false god tyrannously rules. For Hyam Plutzik, regarding the perennial renewal of the world in the cycle of the seasons, the red osier dogwood "Is the winter lightning, / The retention of the prime fire / In the naked and forlorn season"; and it is knowledge of the prime fire that permits the Hero to disbelieve "the horror at the door" and place his faith in the undying recurrence of "the families / Whom the sun fathers, in the cauldron of his mercy."

⑤

JOY OF MY LIFE! WHILE LEFT ME HERE

Joy of my life! while left me here,
    And still my Love!
How in thy absence thou dost steere
    Me from above!
    A life well lead
    This truth commends,
    With quick, or dead
    It never ends.

2

Stars are of mighty use: The night
    Is dark, and long;
The Rode foul, and where one goes right,
    Six may go wrong.
    One twinkling ray
    Shot o'er some cloud,
    May clear much way
    And guide a croud.

3

Gods Saints are shining lights: who stays
    Here long must passe
O're dark hills, swift streames, and steep ways
    As smooth as glasse;
    But these all night
    Like Candles, shed
    Their beams, and light
    Us into Bed.

4

They are (indeed,) our Pillar-fires
    Seen as we go,
They are that Cities shining spires
    We travell too;
    A swordlike gleame

> Kept man for sin
> First *Out;* This beame
> Will guide him *In.*

HENRY VAUGHAN

PROTEUS

By the splashed cave I found him. Not
(As I had expected) patently delusive
In a shape sea-monstrous, terrible though sleeping,
To scare all comers, nor as that bronze-thewed
Old king of Pharos with staring locks,
But under a gray rock, resting his eyes
From futurity, from the blinding crystal
Of that morning sea, his face flicked with a wisp
Of senile beard, a frail somnolent old man.

Who would harness the sea-beast
To the extravagant burden of his question
Must find him thus dreaming of his daughters,
Of porpoises and horses; then pitiless
Of an old man's complaints, unawed
At what fierce beasts are roused under his grasp,
Between the brutal ignorance of his hands
Must seize and hold him till the beast stands again
Manlike but docile, the neck bowed to answer.

I had heard in seven wise cities
Of the last shape of his wisdom: when he,
Giver of winds, father as some said
Of the triple nightmare, from the mouth of a man
Would loose the much-whistled wind of prophecy.
The nothing into which a man leans forward
Is mother of all restiveness, drawing
The body prone to falling into no
Repose at last but the repose of falling.

Wherefore I had brought foot to his island
In the dead of dawn, had picked my way

Among the creaking cypresses, the anonymous
Granite sepulchres; wherefore, beyond these,
I seized him now by sleeping throat and heel.
What were my life, unless I might be stone
To grasp him like the grave, though wisdom change
From supposition to savage supposition;
Unless the rigor of mortal hands seemed deathly?

I was a sepulchre to his pleadings,
Stone to his arguments, to his threats;
When he leapt in a bull's rage
By horn and tail I held him; I became
A mad bull's shadow, and would not leave him;
As a battling ram he rose in my hands;
My arms were locked horns that would not leave his horns;
I was the cleft stick and the claws of birds
When he was a serpent between my fingers.

Wild as heaven erupting into a child
He burst under my fists into a lion;
By mane and foot I grappled him;
Closer to him than his own strength I strained
And held him longer. The sun had fought
Almost to noon when I felt the beast's sinews
Fail, the beast's bristles fall smooth
Again to the skin of a man. I loosed him then.
The head he turned toward me wore a face of mine.

Here was no wisdom but my own silence
Echoed as from a mirror; no marine
Oracular stare but my own eyes
Blinded and drowned in their reflections;
No voice came but a voice we shared, saying,
"You prevail always, but, deathly, I am with you
Always." I am he, by grace of no wisdom,
Who to no end battles the foolish shapes
Of his own death by the insatiate sea.

W. S. MERWIN

FULL FATHOM FIVE

Old man, you surface seldom.
Then you come in with the tide's coming
When seas wash cold, foam-

Capped: white hair, white beard, far-flung,
A dragnet, rising, falling, as waves
Crest and trough. Miles long

Extend the radial sheaves
Of your spread hair, in which wrinkling skeins
Knotted, caught, survives

The old myth of origins
Unimaginable. You float near
As keeled ice-mountains

Of the north, to be steered clear
Of, not fathomed. All obscurity
Starts with a danger:

Your dangers are many. I
Cannot look much but your form suffers
Some strange injury

And seems to die: so vapors
Ravel to clearness on the dawn sea.
The muddy rumors

Of your burial move me
To half-believe: your reappearance
Proves rumors shallow,

For the archaic trenched lines
Of your grained face shed time in runnels:
Ages beat like rains

On the unbeaten channels
Of the ocean. Such sage humor and
Durance are whirlpools

To make away with the ground-
Work of the earth and the sky's ridgepole.
Waist down, you may wind

One labyrinthine tangle
To root deep among knuckles, shinbones,
Skulls. Inscrutable,

Below shoulders not once
Seen by any man who kept his head,
You defy questions;

You defy other godhood.
I walk dry on your kingdom's border
Exiled to no good.

Your shelled bed I remember.
Father, this thick air is murderous.
I would breathe water.

SYLVIA PLATH

THE SPHINX

It is not feminine: this crouching cat-beast
Kneading a vacant temple between its claws—
Napoleon and the rest
Can fire their guns in its face. In the vicinity
Of the pyramidical Pyramids, where the lanner
Nested, and boys can easily scale,
For a few piastres, an old cove's tombstone,
It will stay, it will gaze
At the rising, rising sun, until the sun

Forgets to rise, and Time ruins, and it, too,
Crumbles—the implacable image
Of male power that smoothly worships itself.

JOHN HEATH-STUBBS

A TUNE FOR THE TELETYPE

O Teletype, tell us of time clocks and trouble,
Wheels within wheels, rings within rings;
In each little ring a pretty wire basket,
In each pretty basket any number of things—

Things to be stamped and despatched in good order:
O tell us of code clerks and typists who toil
So the world may receive the good news in the morning,
And H-bombs explode according to Hoyle!

H-bombs explode and each pretty wire basket
With bits of charred paper fly off through the air!
The question is answered, but who's there to ask it?
The man with the question is no longer there.

The question-man is somewhere in orbit;
He's calling—click-click—the whole human race.
A man in the moon, but no cow to jump over—
End of the poem . . . Space . . . Space . . . Space . . . Space . . .

WILLIAM JAY SMITH

ADMIRAL

Admiral, the prisoner of your giant's
Strength, I spent my leisure in the brig,
Devising arms against your eminence
And arsenal of law, absurdly bent
To open war on my inconsequence.

Your might, the quarry of my rich abuse,
Refused to settle in a human face,
But rose in visionary interviews
To constellate my firmament with bright
Insignia whose stars shone to accuse.

But when, as though in parody of grace,
The amnesty of your indifference
Fell upon my crime, how commonplace
That long impenitence appeared!   How dull
The sulky freedom yawning in my face!

Now, compounded by neglect, my debts
Assail their creditors, and, Admiral,
Your far agenda, year by year, forgets
My reckoning, though each oblivious night
Shoulders aloft your golden epaulets.

JOHN ALEXANDER ALLEN

UNDER THE HILL

Suppose your eyes
Stared into time's heart for a moment
Finding under the hill
The cavern where he drowses still
Beneath the heather roots, hearing the centuries run slow;

Suppose that what you saw
Among lost rivers, stony trees,
Was the old veritable king,
Gold-helmeted, the great cross-hilted sword
Quiet on his knees,
His iron peers round him in a ring;

Taught by this vision,
Suppose you grope your way
Through pot-hole and dripping vein
To his sunk monarchy,

And put the question, is not our ill day
Dark enough yet to call him out again—

Do not imagine he will let you know
More than you know now
Which way the dice will fall.
He will choose his own day,
Not yours or mine; waken to the call
Not of yours or mine but his own passion,
Know his own enemies, not yours or mine,
Order the battle after his own fashion.

What if he cares no more for such posterity
As you and I?
Maybe it is for the badger and the water-rat,
Mirkwood again and the encroaching salt-flat,
That he spells victory.

GRAHAM HOUGH

THE SECOND COMING

Turning and turning in the widening gyre
The falcon cannot hear the falconer;
Things fall apart; the center cannot hold;
Mere anarchy is loosed upon the world,
The blood-dimmed tide is loosed, and everywhere
The ceremony of innocence is drowned;
The best lack all conviction, while the worst
Are full of passionate intensity.

Surely some revelation is at hand;
Surely the Second Coming is at hand.
The Second Coming!   Hardly are those words out
When a vast image out of *Spiritus Mundi*
Troubles my sight: somewhere in sands of the desert
A shape with lion body and the head of a man,
A gaze blank and pitiless as the sun,
Is moving its slow thighs, while all about it

Reel shadows of the indignant desert birds.
The darkness drops again; but now I know
That twenty centuries of stony sleep
Were vexed to nightmare by a rocking cradle,
And what rough beast, its hour come round at last,
Slouches towards Bethlehem to be born?

W. B. YEATS

FROM ANCIENT FANGS

(*The Three Impacts of Auschwitz: II*)

(*the time of this poem is in the far future, shortly after peace and love return to earth*)

i

Like lamp of intricate stained-glass which hangs
        From curved blue ceiling,
A fat bright-bellied insect hangs up there.
        At night, on traveler,
It drops like rich and heavy poison welling
        From ancient fangs.

ii

That insect's not the only thing which falls.
So many things must fall in their short day.
Careers and wine-cups; bombs and tennis-balls.
Even the sun. But sky? The sky must stay.

But now the sky itself is caving in.
O good old sky, O lid that keeps us snug,
Dear blue in which we always used to trust
As in the nurse our childhood bullied so,
When comfort was to see her loyal grin,
Ugly and safe, beam down on us below:
Dear sky, we pray to you, hold on, you must!
Hold tighter, sky. Be roof to us, not rug.

iii

"It seems I'm being prayed to; I
    Am sky,
Older than hours and than miles more far,
    Your spectator.
When worlds grow honest, noble, clean, or clever,
    I fall and smother them forever.
To keep your high roof high, stop being good.
    All sights bore Me now but blood.
The main thing is to kill. And kill. And kill.
    First with your bullets. Then with steel.

"And when steel breaks, with hands and stumps of hands.
And when you've killed all strangers, kill your friends.
And if you've used up humans, stone a rat.
Call it a whim—I like My world like that.
It's your world, too. The only world you'll get."

iv

"At school they never used to talk like You."
    "No, not like Me."
"People back home don't want such things to do."
    "Perhaps. We'll see."
"Men won't splash harmless blood just for Your thirst."
    "No, not at first."

PETER VIERECK

THE BLACK TOWER

Say that the men of the old black tower,
Though they but feed as the goatherd feeds,
Their money spent, their wine gone sour,
Lack nothing that a soldier needs,
That all are oath-bound men:
Those banners come not in.

*There in the tomb stand the dead upright,
But winds come up from the shore:*

They shake when the winds roar,
Old bones upon the mountain shake.

Those banners come to bribe or threaten,
Or whisper that a man's a fool
Who, when his own right king's forgotten,
Cares what king sets up his rule.
If he died long ago
Why do you dread us so?

There in the tomb drops the faint moonlight,
But wind comes up from the shore:
They shake when the winds roar,
Old bones upon the mountain shake.

The tower's old cook that must climb and clamber
Catching small birds in the dew of the morn
When we hale men lie stretched in slumber
Swears that he hears the king's great horn.
But he's a lying hound:
Stand we on guard oath-bound!

There in the tomb the dark grows blacker,
But wind comes up from the shore:
They shake when the winds roar,
Old bones upon the mountain shake.

W. B. YEATS

TRIUMPHAL MARCH

Coriolan: I

Stone, bronze, stone, steel, stone, oakleaves, horses' heels
Over the paving.
And the flags. And the trumpets. And so many eagles.
How many? Count them. And such a press of people.
We hardly knew ourselves that day, or knew the City.
This is the way to the temple, and we so many crowding the
way.

So many waiting, how many waiting? what did it matter, on
     such a day?
Are they coming? No, not yet. You can see some eagles.
     And hear the trumpets.
Here they come. Is he coming?
The natural wakeful life of our Ego is a perceiving.
We can wait with our stools and our sausages.
What comes first? Can you see? Tell us. It is
   5,800,000 rifles and carbines,
     102,000 machine guns,
      28,000 trench mortars,
      53,000 field and heavy guns,
I cannot tell how many projectiles, mines and fuses,
      13,000 aeroplanes,
      24,000 aeroplane engines,
      50,000 ammunition waggons,
now 55,000 army waggons,
      11,000 field kitchens,
       1,150 field bakeries.

What a time that took. Will it be he now? No,
Those are the golf club Captains, these the Scouts,
And now the *société gymnastique de Poissy*
And now come the Mayor and the Liverymen. Look
There he is now, look:
There is no interrogation in his eyes
Or in the hands, quiet over the horse's neck,
And the eyes watchful, waiting, perceiving, indifferent.
O hidden under the dove's wing, hidden in the turtle's breast,
Under the palmtree at noon, under the running water
At the still point of the turning world. O hidden.

Now they go up to the temple. Then the sacrifice.
Now come the virgins bearing urns, urns containing
Dust
Dust
Dust of dust, and now
Stone, bronze, stone, steel, stone, oakleaves, horses' heels
Over the paving.

That is all we could see. But how many eagles! and
    how many trumpets!
(And Easter Day, we didn't get to the country,
So we took young Cyril to church. And they rang a bell
And he said right out loud, *crumpets*.)
                        Don't throw away that sausage,
It'll come in handy. He's artful. Please, will you
Give us a light?
Light
Light
Et les soldats faisaient la haie?   ILS LA FAISAIENT.

T. S. ELIOT

STREETS TOO OLD

I walked among the streets of an old city and the streets were
    lean as the throats of hard seafish soaked in salt and kept
    in barrels many years.
How old, how old, how old, we are:—the walls went on say-
    ing, street walls leaning toward each other like old women
    of the people, like old midwives tired and only doing
    what must be done.
The greatest the city could offer me, a stranger, was statues of
    the kings, on all corners bronzes of kings—ancient bearded
    kings who wrote books and spoke of God's love for all
    people—and young kings who took forth armies out across
    the frontiers splitting the heads of their opponents and en-
    larging their kingdoms.
Strangest of all to me, a stranger in this old city, was the mur-
    mur always whistling on the winds twisting out of the
    armpits and fingertips of the kings in bronze:—Is there no
    loosening? Is this for always?
In an early snowflurry one cried:—Pull me down where the
    tired old midwives no longer look at me, throw the bronze
    of me to a fierce fire and make me into neckchains for
    dancing children.

CARL SANDBURG

AMERICAN PRIMITIVE

Look at him there in his stovepipe hat,
His high-top shoes, and his handsome collar;
Only my Daddy could look like that,
And I love my Daddy like he loves his Dollar.

The screen door bangs, and it sounds so funny—
There he is in a shower of gold;
His pockets are stuffed with folding money,
His lips are blue, and his hands feel cold.

He hangs in the hall by his black cravat,
The ladies faint, and the children holler:
Only my Daddy could look like that,
And I love my Daddy like he loves his Dollar.

WILLIAM JAY SMITH

THE FATHERS

Our fathers all were poor,
Poorer our fathers' fathers;
Beyond, we dare not look.
We, the sons, keep store
Of tarnished gold that gathers
Around us from the night,
Record it in this book
That, when the line is drawn,
Credit and creditor gone,
Column and figure flown,
Will open into light.

Archaic fevers shake
Our healthy flesh and blood
Plumped in the passing day

And fed with pleasant food.
The fathers' anger and ache
Will not, will not away
And leave the living alone,
But on our careless brows
Faintly their furrows engrave
Like veinings in a stone,
Breathe in the sunny house
Nightmare of blackened bone,
Cellar and choking cave.

Panics and furies fly
Through our unhurried veins,
Heavenly lights and rains
Purify heart and eye,
Past agonies purify
And lay the sullen dust.
The angers will not away.
We hold our fathers' trust,
Wrong, riches, sorrow and all
Until they topple and fall,
And fallen let in the day.

EDWIN MUIR

THE MAGI

Now as at all times I can see in the mind's eye,
In their stiff, painted clothes, the pale unsatisfied ones
Appear and disappear in the blue depth of the sky
With all their ancient faces like rain-beaten stones,
And all their helms of silver hovering side by side,
And all their eyes still fixed, hoping to find once more,
Being by Calvary's turbulence unsatisfied,
The uncontrollable mystery on the bestial floor.

W. B. YEATS

THE COUNCIL

In gorgeous robes befitting the occasion,
For weeks their spiritual and temporal lordships met
To reconcile eternity with time and set
Our earth of marriage on a sure foundation.
The little town was full of spies: corrupt mankind
Waited on tenterhooks.

                    With ostentation
Doors were at last flung back; success had been complete:
The formulae essential to salvation
Were phrased for ever and the true relation
Of Agape to Eros finally defined.
The burghers hung out flags in celebration;
The peasants danced and roasted oxen in the street.

Into their joy four heralds galloped up with news.
'Fierce tribes are moving on the Western Marches.
Out East a virgin has conceived a son again.
The Southern shipping-lanes are in the hands of Jews.
The Northern Provinces are much deluded
By one who claims there are not seven stars but ten.'

Who wrote upon the council-chamber arches
That sad exasperated cry of tired old men:
Postremum Sanctus Spiritus effudit?

                       W. H. AUDEN

THE AWAKENING
    (The Kid: VII)

Dark was the forest, dark was the mind:
dark the trail that he stooped to find:
dark, dark, dark, in the midnight lost,
in self's own midnight, the seeking ghost.
Listen to the tree, press leaves apart:
listen to the blood, the evergreen heart:

deep, deep, deep, the water in the soul,
there will I baptize, and there be whole.
Dark, dark, dark, in this knowledge immersed,
by filth, by fire, and by frost aspersed,
in horror, in terror, in the depths of sleep,
I shudder, I grow, and my roots are deep.
The leaf is spoken: the granite is said:
now I am born, for the king is dead:
now I awake, for the father is dead.
Dark is the forest when false dawn looms—
darkest now, when the true day comes.
Now I am waking: now I begin:
writhe like a snake from the outworn skin:
and I open my eyes: and the world looks in!

CONRAD AIKEN

"IGNORANT OF SOURCE"

Ignorant of source,
Of consequence,
Love does not know
Its cause, its end,

Instinctually goes
About its business, opening
For a dozen minutes, maybe more,
The almost unendurable
Delight before
The closing once again
Of its blazing door.

Last night it opened as it had
Fifteen years ago.
That supersensual light
Made me father then,
And now we know
It's on our Father's errand
That we come and go.

Lovers into parents, we
Were transformed by love
Yet are the same.
Those who deeply think have said
That by the action of
A divine Love
The Unmoved Mover made the world.
Ever unchanged,
He must be changed thereby, begetting

New loves, new
Ways of loving, being loved.
Such reciprocities
Between what love creates and love
Were unforetold.
How could He know
His children would become the world?

DANIEL HOFFMAN

EXHORTATION TO THE ARTISTS

> (*Rabbi Elazer once became sick. Rabbi Jochanan came
> to visit him. . . . Rabbi Elazer was weeping. "Why do
> you weep?" asked Rabbi Jochanan. . . . "I weep," said
> Rabbi Elazer to him, "for the beauty which will decay in
> the earth." "For that indeed," Rabbi Jochanan said, "you
> ought to weep," and both wept.*
>
> —The Talmud)

Two weeping for beauty perished, husband
And wife, lover and mistress, friend and friend,
    Shall mark the world's end.

As I was spinning a fable for this page,
There came ghosts weeping, two and two,
    In pity, dolor, or in rage.

Against the pillars of the heartless temple
Throw, whom knowledge blinded, your brute skill
　Though it is yourself you kill.

He crushes the sparrow fallen among the rocks;
The hunter is trapped with his quarry: the man and the fox—
　Even the little mouse on the hill.

HYAM PLUTZIK

PIED BEAUTY

Glory be to God for dappled things—
　　For skies of couple-colour as a brinded cow;
　　　　For rose-moles all in stipple upon trout that swim;
Fresh-firecoal chestnut-falls; finches' wings;
　　Landscape plotted and pieced—fold, fallow, and plough;
　　　　And áll trádes, their gear and tackle and trim.
All things counter, original, spare, strange;
　　Whatever is fickle, freckled (who knows how?)
　　　　With swift, slow; sweet, sour; adazzle, dim;
He fathers-forth whose beauty is past change:
　　　　　　Praise him.

GERARD MANLEY HOPKINS

BECAUSE THE RED OSIER DOGWOOD

Because the red osier dogwood
Is the winter lightning,
The retention of the prime fire
In the naked and forlorn season
When snow is winner
(For he flames quietly above the shivering mouse
In the moldy tunnel,
The eggs of the grasshopper awaiting metamorphosis
Into the lands of hay and the times of the daisy,
The snake contorted in the gravel,

His brain suspended in thought
Over an abyss that summer will fill with murmuring
And frogs make laughable: the cricket-haunted time)—
I, seeing in the still red branches
The stubborn, unflinching fire of that time,
Will not believe the horror at the door, the snow-white worm
Gnawing at the edges of the mind,
The hissing tree when the sleet falls.
For because the red osier dogwood
Is the winter sentinel,
I am certain of the return of the moth
(Who was not destroyed when an August flame licked him),
And the cabbage butterfly, and all the families
Whom the sun fathers, in the cauldron of his mercy.

                    HYAM PLUTZIK

❧ TWO ❦

Conflict

Conflict is implicit in the very concept of the Father. He is the image of authority and therefore attracts, if he does not incite, rebellion; he reflects the fractious two-fold nature of man—cruelty and loving-kindness, reason and imagination, ego and id; he becomes identified with the Establishment and stands in the way of necessary change; his creative power is inseparable from violence, suffering, and destruction. The history of the gods, like that of mankind, is in large measure a chronicle of savage power politics: Cronus castrates and deposes his father, Uranus. Zeus, in his turn, usurps the throne of Cronus and thereafter rules uneasily, challenged successively by the Titans and the Giants, always alert to the threat of conspiracy against his throne. For Shelley, in *Prometheus Unbound*, Jupiter's tyranny is epitomized by his cruel persecution of Prometheus, whose only offense is to have befriended an oppressed mankind; and Blake never tires of castigating quasi-deities, like Tiriel and Urizen, who represent, in his invented pantheon, the faculty of reason grown perverse and dedicated to the enslavement of the imagination.

Everyone, at some time, has experienced the mingled awe and terror that the deity inspires in the speaker of Blake's poem, "The Tyger." The exuberant energy of the creator at his work provokes both wonder and a fearful sense of a titanic ruthlessness and cruelty. Regarding the Tyger and his maker, we are also moved to ask, "Did

he who made the Lamb make thee?" How are these violent op-
posites to be reconciled?

The conception of the Father as raw sexual energy is implicit
in the amorous adventures of Zeus. The "feathered glory" of that
deity in the form of a swan descends upon the helpless Leda, and
from the divine lust thus satisfied upon a mortal woman, Helen is
engendered—she whose beauty will enchant the eyes of men and set
in motion the chain of events which burns the topless towers of
Ilium and, with the murder of Agamemnon, brings about the bloody
cycle of revenge and counterrevenge that Aeschylus chronicles in
his trilogy, the *Oresteia.* The "brute blood" of divine power sets
human history in motion and creates supernal beauty and the havoc
which must necessarily attend it. It is experienced by the human
spirit in brief flashes, but cannot be fully grasped by mortal under-
standing. The infusion of divine energy into the affairs of man can
issue in the rule of law:

> *Peace between tribe and tribe, converse of merchants,*
> *Trust, the squared stone, the ordered grave procession.*

> (Graham Hough, "Children of Zeus")

Or it can result in the madness, the orgiastic frenzy and fury which
is typified by Dionysus and is experienced as that force which
"Hounds us from rest in city or in grassland," and drives us forth
upon our travels in the worlds of nightmare and of vision.

The Father as the source of order in the universe and in the
society of men is forever in conflict with the necessity for all things
in the temporal world to change. If sexual morality, for instance,
is essential to the civilized order of mankind, it can also harden into
a life-defeating Puritanism. No poet is more keenly aware of this
than Blake, who characteristically embodies pseudo-righteousness
in Father-figures like the one who represses and distorts the innocent
love of the children in the poem, "A Little Girl Lost." The Father,
in the context of organized religion, is the exemplar of all that is
righteous, and the righteousness which he demands, when it is codi-
fied by Scribes and Pharisees, becomes the refuge of the timid and
the servile. The protagonist of W. S. Merwin's "Sea Wife" fears
and is secretly jealous of the life that she imagines the sea-faring men

of her community to lead when their vocation takes them beyond the sound of church bells to the open ocean, where all is ruled by a licentious changefulness and "doom calls like women."

Domestically, it is, in the nature of things, the Father's role eventually to be superseded by his offspring—an event which has been anatomized by Sophocles in *Oedipus Rex* and by Freud in his formulation of the Oedipus complex. While her engagement party is in progress, the affianced girl in Chester Kallman's "Party Bird" informs her intended bridegroom that she has discovered, in a downstairs room, the body of her father, partially consumed by a large carrion bird. But the infatuated youth does not heed the warning that this message holds for him, although "the nubile remainder of Daddy" tells him plainly that "If you want the park, you just have to expect a zoo. . . ." The battle of the generations, as no one in this day needs to be reminded, is often a savage one. "The Colossus" (Sylvia Plath) is a virtuoso exercise in grotesque sarcasm at the expense of the Father who will not yield his daughter to a younger rival. In this poem, he is envisioned as the ruined statue of a god. The daughter, torn between a lingering allegiance and revulsion, has inhabited the nooks and crannies of her father's shattered immensity for thirty dreary years, attempting somehow to repair the oracular voice and reap the benefits of its wisdom. But she is none the wiser. The Father has become her prison, and she grows familiar with the unhappy fact that no hero-suitor ever will appear at this late date to liberate her. The opposite case is put in "Homecoming" (Peter Viereck), where the complacent Father's offspring, led by an irrepressible warlock, utterly shatter their parent's " 'civilized' hedonism" and exile him to an Indonesian Eden where his cozy moral isolation is revealed in all of its debilitating emptiness.

The immemorial history of authority and rebellion is, in some degree, relived by every politician. The Father as king, as one learns from turning the pages of Sir James Frazer's *The Golden Bough*, was faced, in ancient times, with an uncomfortable dilemma: On the one hand, he was accorded the honor and authority of a god incarnate; and on the other, he was executed at the end of a set period of time, to prevent the immortal spirit from inhabiting a body that had passed the prime of life. One of the basic drives in man, as Adler tells us, is the urge to power; and the person in authority clings to his power with a tenacity equaled only by that

of the rivals whose machinations are designed to pluck him down.
All that remains of Shelley's Ozymandias, king of kings, are the
fragments of his enormous statue, including the "shattered visage,"
on which can still be seen the "frown, / And wrinkled lip, and sneer
of cold command."

The relationship between the immortal Father and the time-
bound creatures whom he has created is an inexhaustible source of
irony—one which the modern poet mines assiduously. Impelled by
paternal love for a mortal, the Father may wish to inspire in him a
reverence for truth, only to find, like Auden's Zeus, in "Ganymede,"
that the youth in question has no interest in that subject but is fas-
cinated by the deity's sometime specialty of exercising power through
destruction. If, again, the Father is conceived of as a being with the
singleness of purpose and the infallibility of a machine (vide David
Wagoner's "The Man from the Top of the Mind"), then he will not
respond to our prayer that he "Love us, hold us fast," but will look
upon our "horrible shapes" with loathing as the dregs of nightmare,
and perceive that we are good for nothing but to be "slaughtered
backward into time." Conversely, if the Father is indeed in love
with the works of time, then (as John Wain suggests in "Poem") to
observe human suffering cannot fail to constitute "the burden of his
divinity," for a god, unlike a human, "has no ignorance to hold him
separate"; his knowledge must be absolute and eternal; and therefore,
perpetually beholding the agony of the race that they have pro-
duced, "The gods are desperate."

As it happens, the Hero is not much given to speculation of a
theological kind. Heracles, Odysseus, Theseus, and Aeneas are ex-
emplars of a largely unreflecting love of action; and this, perhaps, is
a clue to their success. The hero's strength reposes in a faith which
may or may not be attached to a particular god, but always, with
regard to life itself, is firm and constant. When Noah had witnessed
the destruction of the world by an angry Lord, he sailed the flood
as he was bidden. If he wondered at the ways of the Lord, we are
not told of it. But when the ark was safe on Ararat and the Lord
displayed his rainbow in a cloud as a sign of peace between himself
and the earth, that covenant was Noah's just reward; and all men, as
Richard Wilbur wrote, are Noah's sons.

THE TYGER

Tyger! Tyger! burning bright
In the forests of the night,
What immortal hand or eye
Could frame thy fearful symmetry?

In what distant deeps or skies
Burnt the fire of thine eyes?
On what wings dare he aspire?
What the hand dare seize the fire?

And what shoulder, & what art,
Could twist the sinews of thy heart?
And when thy heart began to beat,
What dread hand? & what dread feet?

What the hammer? what the chain?
In what furnace was thy brain?
What the anvil? what dread grasp
Dare its deadly terrors clasp?

When the stars threw down their spears,
And water'd heaven with their tears,
Did he smile his work to see?
Did he who made the Lamb make thee?

Tyger! Tyger! burning bright
In the forests of the night,
What immortal hand or eye,
Dare frame thy fearful symmetry?

WILLIAM BLAKE

DESIGN

I found a dimpled spider, fat and white,
On a white heal-all, holding up a moth

Like a white piece of rigid satin cloth—
Assorted characters of death and blight
Mixed ready to begin the morning right,
Like the ingredients of a witches' broth—
A snow-drop spider, a flower like a froth,
And dead wings carried like a paper kite.

What had that flower to do with being white,
The wayside blue and innocent heal-all?
What brought the kindred spider to that height,
Then steered the white moth thither in the night?
What but design of darkness to appall?—
If design govern in a thing so small.

ROBERT FROST

LEDA AND THE SWAN

A sudden blow: the great wings beating still
Above the staggering girl, her thighs caressed
By the dark webs, her nape caught in his bill,
He holds her helpless breast upon his breast.
How can those terrified vague fingers push
The feathered glory from her loosening thighs?
And how can body, laid in that white rush,
But feel the strange heart beating where it lies?

A shudder in the loins engenders there
The broken wall, the burning roof and tower
And Agamemnon dead.
                          Being so caught up,
So mastered by the brute blood of the air,
Did she put on his knowledge with his power
Before the indifferent beak could let her drop?

W. B. YEATS

PASIPHAE

There stood the mimic cow; the young bull kept
Fast by the nose-ring, trampling in his pride,
Nuzzled her flanks and snuffed her naked side.
She was a queen: to have her will she crept

In that black box; and when her lover leapt
And fell thundering on his wooden bride,
When straight her fierce, frail body crouched inside
Felt the wet pizzle pierce and plunge, she wept.

She wept for terror, for triumph; she wept to know
Her love unable to embrace its bliss
So long imagined, waking and asleep.
But when within she felt the pulse, the blow,
The burst of copious seed, the burning kiss
Fill her with monstrous life, she did not weep.

A. D. HOPE

CHILDREN OF ZEUS

Ageless, lusty, he twists into bull, ram, serpent,
Swan, gold rain; a hundred wily disguises
To catch girl, nymph or goddess; begets tall heroes,
Monsters, deities, gets Troy's fall and the long history
Of many a wandering after, pestilence, death in exile,
Founding of hearths and cities.   All that scribe or sculptor
Chronicle is no more than fruit of his hot embraces
With how many surprised recumbent breasts and haunches.

His legend tells that from a summer encounter
With a mild girl along the shores of the tousled
Sea was engendered once the sagest of judges,
Made for his endless wisdom the strong doomster
Of earth and hades.
Look, they say, from his play is law begotten,

Peace between tribe and tribe, converse of merchants,
Trust, the squared stone, the ordered grave procession.
Maybe it is so.
All he knew was the law that stiffened his members
Seeing a girl's soft hair curled down on her shoulders.
A tale more likely.

To one he came in thunder and raging glory,
Dropped like a bolt to impregnate her hapless
Womb before his extravagant fire consumed her;
And of that blazing
The child was madness, wine, was tragic fury,
Sleeps long years, but wakes again, immortal;
And even sleeping
Troubles the well-turned acres and the grassland,
Haunts the straight road and whispers in the city,
Breathes through the forge, reddens the pale hearth-smoke;
His dream creates the landscape of our travel,
Hounds us from rest in city or in grassland,
Fires the walled homestead, turns the forehead seaward.

GRAHAM HOUGH

GANYMEDE

   (*Sonnets from China: IX*)

He looked in all His wisdom from His throne
Down on the humble boy who herded sheep,
And sent a dove. The dove returned alone:
Song put a charmed rusticity to sleep.

But He had planned such future for this youth:
Surely, His duty now was to compel,
To count on time to bring true love of truth
And, with it, gratitude. His eagle fell.

It did not work: His conversation bored
The boy, who yawned and whistled and made faces,
And wriggled free from fatherly embraces,

But with His messenger was always willing
To go where it suggested, and adored,
And learned from it so many ways of killing.

W. H. AUDEN

A LITTLE GIRL LOST

Children of the future Age
Reading this indignant page,
Know that in a former time
Love! sweet love! was thought a crime.

In the Age of Gold,
Free from winter's cold,
Youth and maiden bright
To the holy light,
Naked in the sunny beams delight.

Once a youthful pair,
Fill'd with softest care,
Met in garden bright
Where the holy light
Had just remov'd the curtains of the night.

There, in rising day,
On the grass they play;
Parents were afar,
Strangers came not near,
And the maiden soon forgot her fear.

Tired with kisses sweet,
They agree to meet
When the silent sleep
Waves o'er heaven's deep,
And the weary tired wanderers weep.

To her father white
Came the maiden bright;

But his loving look,
Like the holy book,
All her tender limbs with terror shook.

"Ona! pale and weak!
To thy father speak:
O, the trembling fear!
O, the dismal care!
That shakes the blossoms of my hoary hair."

WILLIAM BLAKE

SEA WIFE

There must be so many souls washing
Up and down out there just out of sight,
You would think the sea would be full; one day
It will surely be full and no more sea.
We will not live to see it. You can see
That the eyes of fish, used to staring at souls,
Can never believe us: standing up and breathing air.
So much the sea changes things. Husbands
Maybe you never know, but sons, fathers,
Above all brothers—they are fished from us
And gone in the holds of boats, and only
Strangers come in to us from the sea, even
If sometimes they be the same strangers.
Or else their names, sounding like strangers, on
The church wall. Us too it changes; just
With hating it our eyes take on its distance
And our hair its blowing whiteness. But we
Are the same, here with God and the bells. And the boats,
Maybe they are the same when we see them.
But we were never close to them, they were always
Untouchable as though in bottles. Do not learn it
From us; the bells are old and impartial
And upright and will tell you: beyond
The last channel nun and the cape horn
God is not righteous, doom calls like women,

The fish wait for friends. God is our rock here
In His goodness. The bells tell where He is.
They tell of His righteousness, and they moan seaward
Mourning for the souls, the souls, that are lost there.

W. S. MERWIN

THE COLOSSUS

I shall never get you put together entirely,
Pieced, glued, and properly jointed.
Mule-bray, pig-grunt and bawdy cackles
Proceed from your great lips.
It's worse than a barnyard.

Perhaps you consider yourself an oracle,
Mouthpiece of the dead, or of some god or other.
Thirty years now I have labored
To dredge the silt from your throat.
I am none the wiser.

Scaling little ladders with gluepots and pails of lysol
I crawl like an ant in mourning
Over the weedy acres of your brow
To mend the immense skull plates and clear
The bald, white tumuli of your eyes.

A blue sky out of the Oresteia
Arches above us. O father, all by yourself
You are pithy and historical as the Roman Forum.
I open my lunch on a hill of black cypress.
Your fluted bones and acanthine hair are littered

In their old anarchy to the horizon-line.
It would take more than a lightning-stroke
To create such a ruin.
Nights, I squat in the cornucopia
Of your left ear, out of the wind,

Counting the red stars and those of plum-color.
The sun rises under the pillar of your tongue.
My hours are married to shadow.
No longer do I listen for the scrape of a keel
On the blank stones of the landing.

SYLVIA PLATH

PARTY BIRD

From the ballroom window the park lay in excellent view,
And the room (except for one yielding section of floor
      That the guests in their measured frivolity
Instinctively circled) was tastefully solid though new.
It was the kind of party that had often been given before:
      Which gave it its particular quality.

Across the park in the diamond-blue dusk fresh lights
Bared the ceilings of other lives or their shades;
      And though everyone apprehended
An underfoot stillness that spurred the dance to new heights,
Few looked when (the trap-door flaps opened by two of the
      maids)
      Our coming-out heiress descended

To a leathery den and the couch a carrion bird
Hid with his crooknecked poise and the scholarly back
      Of an old petitioner hatless:
With one slow red dispeptic glance he stirred
And glided into the dusk from his casual snack
      She had beaten him off with an atlas.

"Oh, Daddy's down there; he's been dead for a while, it's true,
But he'd die if he missed my party; and as for his guest,
      He hadn't got much of him, had he?
If you want the park, you just have to expect a zoo . . ."
Then off with her partner who clutched to himself like
      possessed
      The nubile remainder of Daddy.

CHESTER KALLMAN

FATHER WHO ENTERS INTO MY REST

I dream in the womb where he imprisons me,
His fury up from twenty years of death,
Till ghostly love gives birth and sets me free,
My lungs remembering from her screams to breathe.

Before his threat I tremble from fear to rage
But schooled in the love he buried in his wife
I hone my frenzy down to skill and edge
And fall from careful ambush upon his life.

Awake, I cry for torches on the tale's intent
Like those who in old tragedies survive,
And, see, she rises skyward, indifferent,
Where he lies pleading the love my guilt must give.

But sleeping I'm far from safe enough to love,
Being too poor, in the dark, for such expense,
For he still raves, pounding the dream alive
Where she still screams in a shame of innocence.

ERNEST SANDEEN

HOMECOMING

*(a charade on "civilized" hedonism and its
eventual purgatory through moral isolation)*

My seven sons came from Indonesia.
Each had ruled an atoll twenty years alone.
Twenty years of loneliness, twenty years of craziness,
Of hell's and Eden's silence on an exiled coral throne.
My six grunting sons had forgotten what a language is;
My seventh was a warlock, chanting every language known.

My seven sunburnt sons arrived at the airport.
The airport had a banner up. Its words were "WELCOME HOME."
The mayor made a speech, and the virgins rainbowed over
     them

The many-tongued hooray of confetti's polychrome.
But, though seven new Rolls-Royces sped them richly to my
  parlor,
They only filed their long sharp teeth; the warlock's were
  afoam.

The day before my seven sons returned from atoll-loneliness,
The butler starched his livery to welcome them in style;
"*Thé dansant* for the young masters?" gushed the housemaid,
  strewing doilies;
I bought my sons a set of Proust to titillate their guile.
My seven Dresden China cups were waiting, hot with tea;
And all was ready as my sons tramped in. They didn't smile.

"You homesick boys from far-off Indonesia,
Relax and romp," I said, "and know you're loved,
It's true that twenty years alone with coral
Is not God's hand at its most velvet-gloved.
But let's test your sense of humor; don't be morbid;
I'll get tantrums if my welcome is rebuffed."

Did they listen? No, they only watched the seventh . . .
Till he made a kind of signal. Then they roared and went
  amok.
Two swung from chandeliers and pounced on the butler.
Two held the maid down, and clawed off her smock;
Two ate the Proust set. "Be careful, kids," I wheedled;
"Romp all you like but spare my teacups any shock.

"I can buy you chubby housemaids by the dozen.
You can eat a butler, even eat a book.
But whoever chips—no matter who—my china,
He'll get magicked back to nature's loneliest nook."
"No matter who?" the warlock asked—and tripped me
Right across my magic teacups. I awoke

On this hellish, Eden-beautied reef of coral
In a perfect climate full of perfect food,
Where my sense of humor's tested by the silence

And I've nothing else to do but fish and brood.
"Sons, come back and get me out of Indonesia!"
But, of course, they couldn't hear me. No one could.

PETER VIERECK

DADDY

You do not do, you do not do
Any more, black shoe
In which I have lived like a foot
For thirty years, poor and white,
Barely daring to breathe or Achoo.

Daddy, I have had to kill you.
You died before I had time—
Marble-heavy, a bag full of God,
Ghastly statue with one grey toe
Big as a Frisco seal

And a head in the freakish Atlantic
Where it pours bean green over blue
In the waters off beautiful Nauset.
I used to pray to recover you.
Ach, du.

In the German tongue, in the Polish town
Scraped flat by the roller
Of wars, wars, wars.
But the name of the town is common.
My Polack friend

Says there are a dozen or two.
So I never could tell where you
Put your foot, your root,
I never could talk to you.
The tongue stuck in my jaw.

It stuck in a barb wire snare.
Ich, ich, ich, ich,
I could hardly speak.
I thought every German was you.
And the language obscene

An engine, an engine
Chuffing me off like a Jew.
A Jew to Dachau, Auschwitz, Belsen.
I began to talk like a Jew.
I think I may well be a Jew.

The snows of the Tyrol, the clear beer of Vienna
Are not very pure or true.
With my gypsy ancestress and my weird luck
And my Taroc pack and my Taroc pack
I may be a bit of a Jew.

I have always been scared of *you*,
With your Luftwaffe, your gobbledygoo.
And your neat moustache
And your Aryan eye, bright blue.
Panzer-man, panzer-man, O You—

Not God but a swastika
So black no sky could squeak through.
Every woman adores a Fascist,
The boot in the face, the brute
Brute heart of a brute like you.

You stand at the blackboard, daddy,
In the picture I have of you,
A cleft in your chin instead of your foot
But no less a devil for that, no not
Any less the black man who

Bit my pretty heart in two.
I was ten when they buried you.
At twenty I tried to die.
And get back, back, back to you.
I thought even the bones would do.

But they pulled me out of the sack,
And they stuck me together with glue.
And then I knew what to do.
I made a model of you,
A man in black with a Meinkampf look

And a love of the rack and the screw.
And I said I do, I do.
So daddy, I'm finally through.
The black telephone's off at the root,
The voices just can't worm through.

If I've killed one man, I've killed two—
The vampire who said he was you
And drank my blood for a year,
Seven years, if you want to know.
Daddy, you can lie back now.

There's a stake in your fat black heart
And the villagers never liked you.
They are dancing and stamping on you.
They always *knew* it was you.
Daddy, daddy, you bastard, I'm through.

SYLVIA PLATH

OZYMANDIAS

I met a traveller from an antique land
Who said: "Two vast and trunkless legs of stone
Stand in the desert. . . Near them, on the sand,
Half sunk, a shattered visage lies, whose frown,
And wrinkled lip, and sneer of cold command,
Tell that its sculptor well those passions read
Which yet survive, stamped on these lifeless things,
The hand that mocked them and the heart that fed:
And on the pedestal these words appear—
'My name is Ozymandias, king of kings:
Look on my works, ye Mighty, and despair!'

Nothing beside remains. Round the decay
Of that colossal wreck, boundless and bare
The lone and level sands stretch far away."

PERCY BYSSHE SHELLEY

THE PLEASURE OF PRINCES

What pleasures have great princes?   These: to know
Themselves reputed mad with pride or power;
To speak few words—few words and short bring low
This ancient house, that city with flame devour;

To make old men, their father's enemies,
Drunk on the vintage of the former age;
To have great painters show their mistresses
Naked to the succeeding time; engage

The cunning of able, treacherous ministers
To serve, despite themselves, the cause they hate,
And leave a prosperous kingdom to their heirs
Nursed by the caterpillars of the state;

To keep their spies in good men's hearts; to read
The malice of the wise, and act betimes;
To hear the Grand Remonstrances of greed,
Led by the pure; cheat justice of her crimes;

To beget worthless sons and, being old,
By starlight climb the battlements, and while
The pacing sentry hugs himself for cold,
Keep vigil like a lover, muse and smile,

And think, to see from the grim castle steep
The midnight city below rejoice and shine:
"There my great demon grumbles in his sleep
And dreams of his destruction, and of mine."

A. D. HOPE

THE MAN FROM THE TOP OF THE MIND

From immaculate construction to half death,
See him: the light bulb screwed into his head,
The vacuum tube of his sex, the electric eye.
What lifts his foot? What does he do for breath?

His nickel steel, oily from neck to wrist,
Glistens as though by sunlight where he stands.
Nerves bought by the inch and muscles on a wheel
Spring in the triple-jointed hooks of his hands.

As plug to socket, or flange upon a beam,
Two become one; yet what is he to us?
We cry, "Come, marry the bottom of our minds.
Grant us the strength of your impervium."

But clad in a seamless skin, he turns aside
To do the tricks ordained by his transistors—
His face impassive, his arms raised from the dead,
His switch thrown one way into animus.

Reach for him now, and he will flicker with light,
Divide preposterous numbers by unknowns,
Bump through our mazes like a genius rat,
Or trace his concentric echoes to the moon.

Then, though we beg him, "Love us, hold us fast,"
He will stalk out of focus in the air,
Make gestures in an elemental mist,
And falter there—as we will falter here

And turns in rage upon our horrible shapes—
When the automaton pretends to dream
Those nightmares, trailing shreds of his netherworld,
Who must be slaughtered backward into time.

DAVID WAGONER

POEM

> Hippolytus: *Do you see my plight, Queen, stricken as
> I am?*
> Artemis: *I see. But my eyes are not permitted to shed
> tears.*
>
> —Euripides, *Hippolytus*, 1395–96.

Like a deaf man meshed in his endless silence
the earth goes swishing through the heavens' wideness.

Doubtless some god with benign inquiring brow
could lean over and let his brown eye so true

play over its whirling scabby hide with a look of searching
till suddenly, with eye and bland forefinger converging

he points to a specially found spot. *Here, this moment*
he might say, *I detect it; this is the locus of torment:*

This spot is the saddest on the earth's entire crust.
A quaint fancy?   Such gods can scarcely exist?

Still, the fact outlives the metaphor it breeds;
whether or not the god exists, the scored earth bleeds.

There must be a point where pain takes its worst hold.
One spot, somewhere, holds the worst grief in the world.

Who would venture a guess as to where this grief lies cupped?
Ah, from minute to minute it could never be mapped.

For trouble flies between molecules like a dream.
It flowers from the snapped edge of bones like sour flame.

Who knows what child lies in a night like a mine-shaft
unblinking, his world like a fallen apple mashed and cleft?

Or what failed saint plummets into his private chasm
having bartered all Heaven for one stifling orgasm?

Or perhaps it is even an animal who suffers worst,
gentle furry bundle or two-headed obscene pest.

But where pain's purest drop burns deep no one could say,
unless it were this god with benign brown eye.

Some would curse this god for doing nothing to help.
But he has knowledge like cold water on his scalp.

To perceive that spirit of suffering in its raging purity
is to a god the burden of his divinity.

O then, if he exists, have pity on this god.
He is clamped to that wounded crust with its slime of blood.

He has no ignorance to hold him separate.
Everything is known to a god.   The gods are desperate.

JOHN WAIN

❧ THREE ❦

Atonement

Change is the key to Atonement with the Father, and the Hero reaches it by accepting death and thus, paradoxically, assuring the rebirth of the body and the spirit. "Verily, verily," said Jesus to the questioning Nicodemus, "I say unto thee, Except a man be born again, he cannot see the kingdom of God." But Nicodemus answered, "How can these things be?" (John: 3.3,9). Rebirth of the spirit will not come because we desire it, but only by a special grace, a seeming accident. One does not change, but rather he is changed. When Adam and Eve had eaten of the Forbidden Fruit and had learned the meaning of alienation from their maker, each accused the other of betrayal, and of their dispute there seemed no end. But Eve, seized by the first impulse to moral heroism ever to visit the human heart, found herself asking leave of Adam to take all of the blame for their trespass upon herself ("on mee, mee only"); then the barrier between them lifted, and their repentance could begin.

Everyone would willingly be reconciled with the Father, but shame and pride and fear and anger stand in the way. John Donne, in his fourteenth Holy Sonnet, boldly prays to be changed—not patched with virtue but utterly shattered and burned like metal in a furnace in order to be made new. Donne deals in paradox, the kind of riddle which abounds in relationships with the Father: He cannot be free until the Lord enthralls him, nor chaste until the Lord has ravished him.

Why must one change? The question takes us back to the Call and to the fact that not to change can issue only in a kind of living death—Stagnation. Not to achieve Atonement with the Father is to cut one's self off from the source of energy which is the fuel for all existence. In Elizabeth Bishop's poem, "The Prodigal Son," the title figure is caught in the familiar trap: He has squandered his resources and cannot, by himself, replenish them; but shame and pride prevent him from returning home to the Father whose forgiveness alone can free him from the prison of his wounded ego. He would rather live with pigs and day by day become more fully inured to "The brown enormous odor he lived by" and more compatible with his companions, who "stuck out their little feet and snored." But his increasing degradation has not quite defeated his humanity; he is touched by "shuddering insights, beyond his control," and at last can "make up his mind to go home."

The exchange of forgiveness between father and child is essential to the child, because only by forgiving can he hope, when his time comes, to be himself forgiven; and it is essential to the father, because he cannot, in good conscience, yield his place to a successor who does not understand the sacrificial role that he inherits. As the Lord of creation, the Father demands complete obedience. He calls upon Abraham to sacrifice his only child, Isaac; but, when Abraham meets the test, the Lord blesses him, saying that he will multiply his seed "as the stars of the heaven, and as the sand which is upon the sea shore" (Gen.: 23.17). Nevertheless, no blessing is without its sacrifice: The child, in the course of time, becomes the Father's executioner; and, in the myth and ritual of many peoples in all ages, the sacrifice of the Hero as incarnate god assures mankind of physical regeneration and a share in immortality. When the will of the Hero is atoned with that of the Father, the Hero's Boon is self-transcendence, which delivers him from the snare of egocentricity and from the fear, hostility, and desire that it entails. Eternity is not to be measured by minutes, hours, and years; its proper measure is qualitative. The hero enters the timeless world at the moment when he commits himself to a love unshakeable by mortal accident, one which "does not alter when it alteration finds . . . But bears it out even to the edge of doom" (Shakespeare, Sonnet CXVI).

The Atonement that occurs in George Garrett's poem, "Abraham's Knife," has an authentic ring, because the father who speaks has made his commitment secretly and in the spirit of sacrificial love, not only to his mortal father, but to his "old father" Abraham as well, and to his children, in whose eyes he reads his murder. This being so, we can believe in the "fountains of foolish tears"—that is, tears of reconciliation—which the father sheds, and we can believe that they have power to "flood and green the world again." Quite a different feeling is generated by Stanley Kunitz' "Father and Son," where the speaker runs like a child to beg instruction in love from a father "whose indomitable love," he says, "Kept me in chains." From the details of the son's life we can infer the childish ignorance of his incapacity for love, and we realize that it is too late now for the father to liberate the son, or the son the father. When at last the ghostly parent turns to his son, the latter may or may not recognize, in the father's face, "The white ignorant hollow" of his own.

Through Atonement with the Father, time and eternity are reconciled. The son who visits his father's deathbed in "After Night Flight . . ." (Robert Penn Warren) finds that his past—"all joy and the hope that strove"—is snatched from him by the "black blast" of his dying parent's love. But the final gesture of the father's hand, reaching "like law . . . from History / To claw at a star," is also a link between the present and the past, the dead and the world of time which is their legacy to the living. The search for the father's spirit in "I Fellowed Sleep" (Dylan Thomas) results in the rediscovery of the father, not in "the upward sky" but on "the hours' ladder to the sun," which the ghost of the "old, mad man" is climbing still in the rain. And the son who speaks in "A Word to a Father, Dead" (John Alexander Allen) is content in his turn "to do the worrying" of which the father tired, and he finds no reason for the father to be sorry for passing along to him the burden of the world's grief and anxiety, but spends his days "getting the hang of time / In time for what comes next." From the female point of view (*vide* Julia Randall's "Danaë"), the Father as divine lover— Zeus, whose love for the imprisoned Danaë expressed itself as a shower of gold—is not difficult to reconcile with mortal love. Divine love, the speaker tells the father of her son, "is no soft dream, / But that by which I love, and I am."

Love is the link between the eternal world and the temporal one, which are finally and mysteriously the same. "Amor vincit omnia" reads the medallion on the rosary of Chaucer's Prioresse.

Nothing is impossible to love. It can heal the breach between
enemies who have sought each other's death in "this soil'd world"
(*vide*, Whitman, "Reconciliation"). It can choose the unlikeliest of
mouthpieces, causing a goatish evangelist preacher to babble wisely,
while "God springs from [his] lips like a snowy dove" (George
Garrett, "Holy Roller"). Chaucer's Pardoner could not be more
candid in assuring his companion pilgrims that he is "a full vicious
man," yet the eloquence of his sermons can save souls; and when he
has quarreled with the Host, who is infuriated by the notion of a
man of God who is also a con-man and a fraud, the kiss of peace that
effects their reconciliation is a token of the common purpose which
the world's mixed bag of pilgrims share.

When all that is grim and even brutal about the way of the
Father with his creatures has been taken into account, there remains
a saving grace—a kind of indulgence which can be descried, like the
towers of the City of God, rising above the waste land of our night-
mares. The beard of the austere Father may, on occasion, shake out
a feast of little mice for his congregation of errant cats (*vide* A. D.
Hope, "The House of God"). All who enter the kingdom enter it
unworthy; and when the weak there become strong, the whores
become maidens, then oily love, brought to perfection, can an-
nounce: "I obeyed / Necessity, who blessed me. / God possessed
me" (Julia Randall, "A Scarlet Letter about Mary Magdelene").
The warfare between father and son, which seems unappeasable,
proves after all to mask a secret oneness:

> *king and rebel are like brother and brother,*
> *Or father and son, co-princes of one mind,*
> *Irreconcilables, their treaty signed.*

(Edwin Muir, " The Trophy")

HOLY SONNETS (XIV)

Batter my heart, three person'd God; for, you
As yet but knocke, breathe, shine, and seeke to mend;
That I may rise, and stand, o'erthrow mee, 'and bend

Your force, to breake, blowe, burn and make me new.
I, like an usurpt towne, to'another due,
Labour to'admit you, but Oh, to no end,
Reason your viceroy in mee, mee should defend,
But is captiv'd, and proves weake or untrue.
Yet dearely'I love you,'and would be loved faine,
But am betroth'd unto your enemie:
Divorce mee,'untie, or breake that knot again,
Take mee to you, imprison mee, for I
Except you'enthrall mee, never shall be free,
Nor ever chast, except you ravish mee.

JOHN DONNE

THE PRODIGAL

The brown enormous odor he lived by
was too close, with its breathing and thick hair,
for him to judge.   The floor was rotten; the sty
was plastered halfway up with glass-smooth dung.
Light-lashed, self-righteous, above moving snouts,
the pigs' eyes followed him, a cheerful stare—
even to the sow that always ate her young—
till, sickening, he leaned to scratch her head.
But sometimes mornings after drinking bouts
(he hid the pints behind a two-by-four),
the sunrise glazed the barnyard mud with red;
the burning puddles seemed to reassure.
And then he thought he almost might endure
his exile yet another year or more.

But evenings the first star came to warn.
The farmer whom he worked for came at dark
to shut the cows and horses in the barn
beneath their overhanging clouds of hay,
with pitchforks, faint forked lightnings, catching light,
safe and companionable as in the Ark.
The pigs stuck out their little feet and snored.
The lantern—like the sun, going away—

laid on the mud a pacing aureole.
Carrying a bucket along a slimy board,
he felt the bats' uncertain staggering flight,
his shuddering insights, beyond his control,
touching him.   But it took him a long time
finally to make his mind up to go home.

ELIZABETH BISHOP

THE COLLAR

I struck the board, and cry'd, No more.
                    I will abroad.
   What? shall I ever sigh and pine?
My lines and life are free; free as the rode,
   Loose as the winde, as large as store.
            Shall I be still in suit?
      Have I no harvest but a thorn
      To let me bloud, and not restore
      What I have lost with cordiall fruit?
            Sure there was wine
Before my sighs did drie it: there was corn
         Before my tears did drown it.
   Is the yeare onely lost to me?
         Have I no bayes to crown it?
No flowers, no garlands gay? all blasted?
            All wasted?
   Not so, my heart: but there is fruit,
            And thou hast hands.
   Recover all thy sigh-blown age
On double pleasures: leave thy cold dispute
Of what is fit, and not.   Forsake thy cage,
            Thy rope of sands,
Which pettie thoughts have made, and made to thee
   Good cable, to enforce and draw,
            And be thy law,
   While thou didst wink and wouldst not see.
            Away; take heed:
            I will abroad.

Call in thy deaths head there: tie up thy fears.
    He that forbears
    To suit and serve his need,
    Deserves his load.
But as I rav'd and grew more fierce and wilde
    At every word,
Me thoughts I heard one calling, *Child!*
    And I reply'd, *My Lord.*

GEORGE HERBERT

ABRAHAM'S KNIFE

Where hills are hard and bare,
rocks like thrown dice, heat
and glare that's clean and pitiless,
a shadow dogs my heels, limp
as a drowned man washed ashore.
True sacrifice is secret, none
to applaud the ceremony, nor
witness to be moved to tears.
No one to see. God alone
knows, Whose great eye winks not,
from Whom no secrets are hid.

My father, I have loved you,
love you now, dead twenty years.
Your ghost shadows me home.
Your laughter and your anger still
trouble my scarecrow head like wings.
My own children, sons and daughter,
study my stranger's face. Their flesh,
bones frail as a small bird's,
is strange, too, in my hands.
What will become of us?
I read my murder in their eyes.

And you, old father, Abraham,
my judge and executioner, I pray

bear witness for me now. I ask
a measure of your faith. Forgive
us, Jew and Gentile, all
your children, all your victims.
In the naked country of no shadow
you raise your hand in shining arc.
And we are fountains of foolish tears
to flood and green the world again.
Strike for my heart. Your blade is light.

GEORGE GARRETT

A SONG FOR SIMEON

Lord, the Roman hyacinths are blooming in bowls and
The winter sun creeps by the snow hills;
The stubborn season has made stand.
My life is light, waiting for the death wind,
Like a feather on the back of my hand.
Dust in sunlight and memory in corners
Wait for the wind that chills towards the dead land.

　　Grant us thy peace.
I have walked many years in this city,
Kept faith and fast, provided for the poor,
Have given and taken honour and ease.
There went never any rejected from my door.
Who shall remember my house, where shall live my children's
　　children
When the time of sorrow is come?
They will take to the goat's path, and the fox's home,
Fleeing from the foreign faces and the foreign swords.

　　Before the time of cords and scourges and lamentation
Grant us thy peace.
Before the stations of the mountain of desolation,
Before the certain hour of maternal sorrow,
Now at this birth season of decease,
Let the Infant, the still unspeaking and unspoken Word,

Grant Israel's consolation
To one who has eighty years and no to-morrow.

   According to thy word.
They shall praise Thee and suffer in every generation
With glory and derision,
Light upon light, mounting the saints' stair.
Not for me the martyrdom, the ecstasy of thought and prayer,
Not for me the ultimate vision.
Grant me thy peace.
(And a sword shall pierce thy heart,
Thine also.)
I am tired with my own life and the lives of those after me,
I am dying in my own death and the deaths of those after me.
Let thy servant depart,
Having seen thy salvation.

T. S. ELIOT

FATHER AND SON

Now in the suburbs and the falling light
I followed him, and now down sandy road
Whiter than bone-dust, through the sweet
Curdle of fields, where the plums
Dropped with their load of ripeness, one by one.
Mile after mile I followed, with skimming feet,
After the secret master of my blood,
Him, steeped in the odor of ponds, whose indomitable love
Kept me in chains.   Strode years; stretched into bird;
Raced through the sleeping country where I was young,
The silence unrolling before me as I came,
The night nailed like an orange to my brow.

How should I tell him my fable and the fears,
How bridge the chasm in a casual tone,
Saying, "The house, the stucco one you built,
We lost. Sister married and went from home,
And nothing comes back, it's strange, from where she goes.

I lived on a hill that had too many rooms:
Light we could make, but not enough of warmth,
And when the light failed, I climbed under the hill.
The papers are delivered every day;
I am alone and never shed a tear."

At the water's edge, where the smothering ferns lifted
Their arms, "Father!" I cried, "Return! You know
The way. I'll wipe the mudstains from your clothes;
No trace, I promise, will remain. Instruct
Your son, whirling between two wars,
In the Gemara of your gentleness,
For I would be a child to those who mourn
And brother to the foundlings of the field
And friend of innocence and all bright eyes.
O teach me how to work and keep me kind."

Among the turtles and the lilies he turned to me
The white ignorant hollow of his face.

STANLEY KUNITZ

AFTER NIGHT FLIGHT

(*Mortmain: I*)

After Night Flight Son Reaches Bedside of Already Un-
conscious Father, Whose Right Hand Lifts in a Spasmodic
Gesture, as Though Trying to Make Contact: 1955

In Time's concatenation and
Carnal conventicle, I,
Arriving, being flung through dark and
The abstract flight-grid of sky,
Saw rising from the sweated sheet and
Ruck of bedclothes ritualistically
Reordered by the paid hand
Of mercy—saw rising the hand—

Christ, start again! What was it I,
Standing there, travel-shaken, saw
Rising? What could it be that I,
Caught sudden in gut- or conscience-gnaw,
Saw rising out of the past, which I
Saw now as twisted bedclothes? Like law,
The hand rose cold from History
To claw at a star in the black sky,

But could not reach that far—oh, cannot!
And the star horribly burned, burns,
For in darkness the wax-white clutch could not
Reach it, and white hand on wrist-stem turns,
Lifts in last tension of tendon, but cannot
Make contact—*oh, oop-si-daisy*, churns
The sad heart, *oh, atta-boy, daddio's got
One more shot in the locker, peas-porridge hot—*

But no. Like an eyelid the hand sank, strove
Downward, and in that darkening roar,
All things—all joy and the hope that strove,
The failed exam, the admired endeavor,
Prizes and prinkings, and the truth that strove,
And back of the Capitol, boyhood's first whore—
Were snatched from me, and I could not move,
Naked in that black blast of his love.

ROBERT PENN WARREN

I FELLOWED SLEEP

I fellowed sleep who kissed me in the brain,
Let fall the tear of time; the sleeper's eye,
Shifting to light, turned on me like a moon.
So, planing-heeled, I flew along my man
And dropped on dreaming and the upward sky.

I fled the earth and, naked, climbed the weather,
Reaching a second ground far from the stars;

And there we wept, I and a ghostly other,
My mothers-eyed, upon the tops of trees;
I fled that ground as lightly as a feather.

"My fathers' globe knocks on its nave and sings."
"This that we tread was, too, your fathers' land."
"But this we tread bears the angelic gangs,
Sweet are their fathered faces in their wings."
"These are but dreaming men. Breathe, and they fade."

Faded my elbow ghost, the mothers-eyed,
As, blowing on the angels, I was lost
On that cloud coast to each grave-gabbing shade;
I blew the dreaming fellows to their bed
Where still they sleep unknowing of their ghost.

Then all the matter of the living air
Raised up a voice, and, climbing on the words,
I spelt my vision with a hand and hair,
How light the sleeping on this soily star,
How deep the waking in the worlded clouds.

There grows the hours' ladder to the sun,
Each rung a love or losing to the last,
The inches monkeyed by the blood of man.
An old, mad man still climbing in his ghost,
My fathers' ghost is climbing in the rain.

DYLAN THOMAS

A WORD TO A FATHER, DEAD

Whatever it was that went wrong—the stove aflame
In the kitchen with a sudden rage to burn
The house down; or the shower madly bent
On flooding us out, when stubbornly the drain
Backed up and nothing you did could shut the water
Off—whatever it was, it worried you;
And though your faith was perfect, in your hand
Buckets wickedly would turn to sieves.

I believe you were ready to call it quits
When something in your heart, a part of you not
To be gotten along without, went wrong. I believe
You were ready then, when all was said and done,
For death, unsent-for though it was, to come;
Willing, as anyone might have been, for someone
Different, in event of fire and flood,
To be on hand, to do the worrying.

Familiar now with death, whatever it is,
You will have forgotten the old bizarre concoction
Of the kitchen, the old routine of plumbing's
Comic imperfection. Still, I've not
Forgotten how you told me, in a dream,
"I'm sorry, sorry," and I knew your flesh
Had only pity for its own, and held
Itself alone accountable for grief.

But no. I've kept my hand in, in the kitchen;
Being a tenant, needn't worry my head,
Though a rusty pool appear beside the grumbling
Water heater. What's a landlord for?
Whatever it is that's happened since we met,
You're used to it. I'm getting the hang of time
In time for what comes next. Whatever it is,
Don't worry. Don't, whatever it is, be sorry.

JOHN ALEXANDER ALLEN

DANAË

This love I make
Alone, and for my sake,
In a room of the summer town
Where you have never been.
I call his name a god,
His shape gold;
Since the sun cannot fall,
He comes glittering small,

Coining the air bright;
Finches in flight
He may be, or the great
Acacia falling over me.
I am laved
In radiance, each sense clean,
Loud awake in the dream
Where at last I know my name
Is Danaë, Danaë.

Oh when you speak that name,
My love, or one day when the little son
Crawls on his mother's breast, and I cannot tell
Myself from Rachel or Anna at the well,
One day when I chatter over my chores
And the light is late,
If there is a sudden glint
In my eyes, or a softening
Of habit-hard attendance, it is no soft dream,
But that by which I love you, and I am.

JULIA RANDALL

HOLY ROLLER

Nothing so white as he is
(not lazy lily nor unlikely unicorn)
when, shirt sweatstained, flapping like
a luffing sail around his ploughboy muscles,
arms outspread like airplanes taking off,
he grins (old piano keys) and hollers:
        "Let us pray!"

I know *your* prayers, brother. I know
why they ran you out of Plant City on a rail.
I know your whiteness is used—
eggsmooth jowls, fishbelly hands, ram's hair—
to trouble young virgins where they kneel

and sweetly press their hairless thighs together.
It's your *voice*, dark and hoarse
as a clarinet in lowest register,
that tickles the goodwives where they live.
      Oh, I know you of old, brother.

I know this too:
the ways of God are crazy, daze
a skeptic mind like summer lightning.
Others false and foolish as you (and I)
have been chosen and, so chosen,
babbled more wisely than they knew.
You bow your handsome goathead and
God springs from your lips like a snowy dove.

                              GEORGE GARRETT

RECONCILIATION

Word over all, beautiful as the sky,
Beautiful that war and all its deeds of carnage must in time be
      utterly lost,
That the hands of the sisters Death and Night incessantly
      softly wash again, and ever again, this soil'd world;
For my enemy is dead, a man divine as myself is dead,
I look where he lies white-faced and still in the coffin—I draw
      near,
Bend down and touch lightly with my lips the white face in the
      coffin.

                      WALT WHITMAN

THE HOUSE OF GOD

Morning service! parson preaches;
People all confess their sins;
God's domesticated creatures
Twine and rub against his shins;

Tails erect and whiskers pricking,
Sleeking down their Sunday fur,
Though demure, alive and kicking,
All in unison they purr:

Lord we praise Thee; hear us Master!
Feed and comfort, stroke and bless!
And not too severely cast a
Glance upon our trespasses:

"Yesterday we were not able
To resist that piece of fish
Left upon the kitchen table
While You went to fetch the dish;

"Twice this week a scrap with Rover;
Once, at least, we missed a rat;
And we *do* regret, Jehovah,
Having kittens in Your hat!

"Sexual noises in the garden,
Smelly patches in the hall—
Hear us, Lord, absolve and pardon;
We are human after all!"

Home at last from work in Heaven,
This is all the rest God gets;
Gladly for one day in seven
He relaxes with His pets.

Looking down He smiles and ponders,
Thinks of something extra nice:
From His beard, O Joy, O wonders!
Falls a shower of little mice.

                                        A. D. HOPE

A SCARLET LETTER ABOUT MARY MAGDALENE

If I asked you to look out
The back window, where the crumbs are spread,
And asked you who was king
Of the sparrows, you would say the red
Bird, not a sparrow, and not because
He has manners, or is larger than them all.
He is not more virtuous:
He is more beautiful.

It is hard to conceive
A god irrational as man,
But we believe
In the image, patch it as we can.
We fall in love
Not with the best or brightest in the nest
Of reason, but some light in the heart's cave.

And that, perhaps, my dear, is how we save
Ourselves. How after a life of sin,
We say "I love you," and we enter in
Unworthy, to the kingdom which he made,
Where weak are strong, whores maid,
And oily love announces: I obeyed
Necessity, who blessed me.
God possessed me.

JULIA RANDALL

THE TROPHY

The wise king dowered with blessings on his throne,
The rebel raising the flag in the market place,
Haunt me like figures on an ancient stone

The ponderous light of history beats upon,
Or the enigma of a single face
Handed unguessed, unread from father to son,
As if it dreamed within itself alone.

Regent and rebel clash in horror and blood
Here on the blindfold battlefield.   But there,
Motionless in the grove of evil and good
They grow together and their roots are twined
In deep confederacy far from the air,
Sharing the secret trophy each with other;
And king and rebel are like brother and brother,
Or father and son, co-princes of one mind,
Irreconcilables, their treaty signed.

                              EDWIN MUIR

❧ VI ❧

THE END
AND
THE BEGINNING

Happy endings always have been popular. We like to see things come out right: for every Jack to have his Jill, for good to be rewarded and evil punished, for desires to be fulfilled—all with sufficient ease to harmonize with a summer afternoon in the hammock or the after-dinner haze when we turn the TV on as an aid to unreflective relaxation. But the quasi-Hero's triumph over cardboard villains grows monotonous. The way of the genuine Hero is far more interesting and essentially more realistic. A child's belief that Mommy and Daddy can be relied upon to banish every threatening bogey must be left behind at the threshold of adulthood. The happy ending of the Quest is a world transfigured—and that is not to be achieved by clinging to the archaic past. The dreams of the Hero lead him forward into a world where all things are uncertain, unfamiliar, threatening. Yet, on the farther side of the dark wood, at the mountain's top, or beyond the waste land lies a realm where fear and desire are forgotten and the spirit delights in the music of the spheres, eternal light, the love that moves the sun and the other stars. Dante rightly called his greatest work a comedy, for the beatitude of the blessed is the final and, in a sense, the only happy ending. The souls which form the mystic rose in Dante's Paradise have escaped from time forever; however, Dante himself must return to earth, for he has reached only the midpoint in the pathway of his life; and, if Dante the poet may be equated with Dante the pilgrim, he has a book to write.

The Hero may at last be granted immortality, but the prayers of mankind will seek him out. The link between the gods and man is indissoluble. The Buddha and the Holy Spirit continue to lend their vision to assist the blind in the unenlightened world of time. For every hero, the Quest is incomplete until he has made the journey home. He may bring back with him the Golden Fleece, the gift of fire, the Apples of the Hesperides; and if he has nothing more to show for his adventures than a glittering eye and a tale to tell, then he will stop the unwilling wedding guest and tell that tale. The return is often no less difficult than the outward journey. After rigorous training in the House of Holiness, Spenser's Redcrosse Knight (*The Faerie Queene*, Book I) at last is strong enough to reach the top of a high hill, where he finds a solitary holy man named Heavenly Contemplation. From his lofty vantage point, the old man shows the visitor the distant walls and towers of the New

Jerusalem. So enchanting is the sight that Redcrosse gladly would forget that the world still has a claim on him:

> 'O let me not,' quoth he, 'then turn again
> Back to the world, whose joys so fruitless are;
> But let me here for aye in peace remain,
> Or straightway on that last long voyage fare,
> That nothing may my present hope impair.'

(X.63.1-5)

But the joys of contemplation and the Heavenly City must be put aside until his mission is completed: the dragon (Satan) must be slain and the parents of Una (Adam and Eve) released from imprisonment. He has no choice but to get on with the task in hand. The Boon cannot be truly won until he has shared it with mankind; and if he fails, they must remain in bondage.

Happily, man, no less than the gods, has a durable affection for the time-bound world. As the U.S. astronauts sped away from the earth in December, 1968, on man's first flight to the moon, their conversation came to be salted with the expression, "the good old earth"; and editorials in newspapers everywhere remarked that space travel has contributed to the world a sense of our planet's oneness and of the essential triviality of the quarrels which divide it. Years ago, in a prophetic poem "The Explorers," Adrienne Rich imagined a pair of spacemen seated beside the Mare Crisium, "that sea / Where water never was." The clockwork of the starry systems "blazes overhead," but they have seen enough of that. They only want to talk of the familiar places of the earth; and, imagining that they hear the "far-off echo of a cattle bell / Against the cratered cliff of Arzachel," they weep "to think no sound can ever come / Across that outer desert" from their home. The returning hero accepts and even celebrates the imperfections of the world, and it is proper that he should, for without those imperfections there could be no life at all. Hawthorne puts the matter cogently in "The Birthmark," where a scientist named Aylmer suffers from an irresistible desire to remove a birthmark from the cheek of his beautiful wife. Too late, he discovers that, as this "token of imperfection" fades, so does her life.

The dominant mood of poems that deal with the Hero's Boon—

the new vitality and understanding that are the fruit of a successful Quest—is one of celebration. Curiously enough, their metaphors are often similar to those of poems about Stagnation, but the connotations alter with the shift in context. For example, in Stagnation, Uncle Dan, who died before his death, lies unlamented in his coffin while the world around him relishes the spring (John Alexander Allen, "The Death of Uncle Dan"), whereas the Boon permits Giselle, at the touch of a wand, to leap from her grave and dance (Randall Jarrell, "The Girl Dreams that She Is Giselle"). Those who journey in Stagnation, as in "The Snow," by Clifford Dyment, make their way through a trackless waste in pursuit of a vague and unattainable objective, and the protagonist of E. L. Mayo's "The Uninfected" is unaware that he is either diseased or mad or both; but at the end of the journey in "Psychiatrist's Song" (Louise Bogan), the patient stands on "firm dry land" and can say, "Farewell, phantoms of flesh and ocean! Vision of earth / Heal and receive me!"

Loving kindness and delight to the point of ecstasy predominate in the transfigured world of the Boon, and even death holds no terrors for the enlightened. In tragedy, the shattering of a life, as Aristotle duly noted, is accompanied by purgation of pity and fear and by an enhanced regard for the dignity of mankind. Perhaps the greatest moments in Shakespearian drama are those in which the imminence of death makes possible a love which is as disinterested and guileless as a child's. When he approaches Juliet in the tomb of the Capulets, Romeo says of that dark place that it is "a feasting presence full of light." Cleopatra, when she comes to die, puts all her wiles behind her, saying of the countryman who brings the deadly asp:

> *He brings me liberty.*
> *My resolution's placed, and I have nothing*
> *Of woman in me. Now from head to foot*
> *I am marble-constant; now the fleeting moon*
> *No planet is of mine.*

> (V.ii.237–41)

Such passages convey a somber joy which gains a great part of its effect by combining opposites in a grandly mythic manner: light with darkness, death with life, and constancy with change. The antidote to death is metamorphosis: "Except ye be converted and become as little children, ye shall not enter into the kingdom of heaven" (Matthew: 18.3).

In *Gawain and the Green Knight*, the final reckoning between the title figures is not wholly a triumph for Gawain's purity of spirit. In secret, against the rules of the game, he has accepted from the Lady of the Castle the gift of a green girdle which, she assures him, will protect his life. For this reason, when he lays his neck on the block, in keeping with his bargain with the Green Knight, his willingness to be sacrificed is flawed. In a sense, the talisman lives up to the Lady's claim for it, as the Giant, instead of severing Gawain's head from his shoulders, gives him only a token nick and sends him on his way. Gawain has escaped with his life, but the Lady's gift is properly ambiguous: It signifies the indestructibility of life, which informs the endless rounds of change; but, at the same time, it is a reminder of the mortal imperfection of mankind. Gawain is perhaps the greater hero because he does not rise superior to the love of life; and he wears the badge of his mortality with pride.

The Refusal

If the Hero sets out into the dark woods, or up the high mountain, or takes ship upon the wine-dark sea and simply vanishes without a trace, we may assume that his adventure has, in some sense, been a failure. The pattern of the Quest, like that of history for Arnold Toynbee, is one of withdrawal and return; it is neither a straight line nor an arc, but a complete circle. Had Odysseus not come home to rocky Ithaca at last after his years of wandering, it would not have been surprising; his path was strewn with formidable dangers and temptations. But he was well equipped to meet the tests. The dangers he could overcome by means of courage, strength, and a deep-devising intellect; and the temptations had no power over him so long as he saw them truly for what they were: the seductive charm of Circe as the lure of self-indulgent pleasure; the euphoria of the Lotos-eaters as a brutish lethargy, disguised as an epicurean feast for the mind and senses. And if one asks why a man is not entitled to take surcease from care, John Donne supplies the answer:

> *No man is an island, entire of itself; every man*
> *is a piece of the continent, a part of the main . . .*
> *Any man's death diminishes me, because I am involved in man-*
> *kind.*

The dictum, "Troll, be unto thyself—enough" may have the sound of manly individualism, but he who follows it becomes a troll himself, as Peer Gynt found to his sorrow, and that should be enough to give us pause. The goal of the Hero's Quest is not satisfaction of the individual will, but escape from the imprisoning ego. Ideally, the Buddhist discipline frees the initiate from desire, hostility and delusion. In *The Republic*, Plato likens men to prisoners in a dark cave who can see no object truly as it is, but mistake for reality the flickering shadows which are projected onto the wall before them. In order to find the true source of light, they must escape the cave, laboriously climb upward toward the sun, and, in the upper world, accustom their eyes to the blinding radiance of the Good, which is "the universal author of all things beautiful and right." One must not be surprised, says Plato, "that those who attain to this beatific vision are unwilling to descend to human affairs"; nevertheless, descend they must, for only they can hope to dissuade the mass of men from perpetually fighting over shadows.

These considerations may appear to have little to do with Everyman's experience; and, to be sure, few of us are likely to attain Nirvana. Our acquaintance with false Nirvanas, however, is extensive. Like the commuter in Richard Wilbur's "In the Smoking Car," we daydream of Elysiums where all are solicitous for our welfare "And the whole air is full of flower-smells." Thurber has immortalized the dream of glory in the timid Walter Mitty, whose swashbuckling exploits unfold at every street corner but are known to no one but himself. Prince Charming's proper role is to re-create the sleeping world by awakening the Sleeping Beauty with a kiss; but it could be more convenient for the Prince to let the lady sleep while he occupies his fancy with imaginary brides (John Alexander Allen, "A Kind of Quest, a Sort of Briar Rose") or decides to sleep forever at her side and thus preserve "the last long world" of her discovery— the kingdom of the hunter, Death (Randall Jarrell, "The Sleeping Beauty: Variation of the Prince"). It is possible that world-weariness may persuade the heroine to remain bewitched, though the kingdom has been purged of her wicked stepmother and she is invited to become a princess once again ("The Laily Worm and the Machrel of the Sea"); it may induce Odysseus to abandon his return to patient Penelope, because he has "grown old / in the wrong world" and must bury the future together with his companions of the past (John Ciardi, "Ulysses"). But these alternatives are hardly calculated to transform the world.

Sleep, silence, stone, dry rustling leaves—a deadly pall hangs

over the country of the unreturning Hero. The coats of the com-
pany of silent soldiers in "The Constant Bridegrooms" (Kenneth
Patchen) "Flap idly in the wind" while they await the command
that will never come; not a living thing is to be found in the great
house of "Beyond the Hunting Woods" (Donald Justice): the
ladies, old and young, have vanished, together with the men who
went forth to pursue "the mythic beast," and none can tell what has
become of ladies, hunters, hounds, and "the beast in view." These
poems have an eerie quality which results from bringing together
suggestions of intense action (warfare, hunting) in the past and an
utter lack of purpose, communion, and vitality in the present. The
emotional effect is not one of nostalgia but of something very like
despair for the defeat of life itself. The Hero heart has gone out of
the world, and we are left to mourn its absence. Something similar
happens in the elegiac world of Homer when Helen, thinking of her
brothers, the bright young warriors Castor and Polydeuces, looks
out from the battlements of Troy and wonders where they may be,
not knowing that they have met their deaths and have long lain
buried in the teeming earth. One of the finest passages in Keats
occurs in "Ode on a Grecian Urn," when the description of the
priest and villagers, leading a sacrificial beast to slaughter, is followed
by reference to the town which has been deserted on this festive
occasion:

> *And, little town, thy streets for evermore*
> *Will silent be; and not a soul to tell*
> *Why thou art desolate, can e'er return.*

The festive procession and the intended sacrifice convey a ceremo-
nial sense of life going on, but the eerie silence of the empty village
strikes the note of death.

Escape from time may appeal to the imagination, but it tends
to leave the emotions chilled. "Bright Star," by Keats, like his
chronicle of that unreturning hero, Endymion, combines suggestions
of a timeless realm with those of a breathing sensuality imagined
as perpetual in time. But the two cannot be harmonized. The
speaker of the poem cannot attain the purity and constancy of the
star, nor can he wake forever upon his "fair love's ripening breast."
The one has an inhuman coldness, and the other a human warmth
which is by definition subject to the rule of time and change. Emily

Dickinson's description of the "meek members of the resurrection" ("Safe in Their Alabaster Chambers") consciously suggests the coffined dead and makes them seem the deader by contrasting them with images from living nature. If to be immortal is only to be oblivious of time, then one may well exclaim, "Ah, what sagacity perished here!" What the world needs, it would seem, is not dead saints but living heroes. Andrew Marvell's drop of dew may strike one as a little priggish in its disdain for physical nature and its terror of impurity, but it is redeemed at the close of the poem by a reference to "Manna's sacred Dew,"which brings to mind the miraculous food which heaven provided for the hungering Israelites in the wilderness. The angel who appears, in *The Divine Comedy*, to assist the almost-despairing Dante at the gates of the City of Dis displays an understandable repugnance toward the noisome realm of Satan. Nevertheless, he does his duty at the Lord's command and speeds the travelers on their way. The Hero's task is a doubly difficult one: He must avoid the pitfalls of blind appetite on the one hand, and on the other must preserve his willingness to soil his hands, for mankind's good, with even the basest tasks. Heracles could clean the Augean stables, and of Prince Arthur, Spenser admiringly remarks, in *The Faerie Queene*,

> *Neither darkness foul nor filthy bands*
> *Nor noyous smell his purpose could withhold—*
> *Entire affection hateth nicer hands.*

(I.viii.40)

This is the kind of rescuer the Hero needs when the giant Pride has locked him away in a prison tended by a man called Ignorance.

Only a hero-god can be forever simultaneously immersed in time and freed from time in the immortal void. The experience for Everyman is limited to occasional "Bright shoots of everlastingness," but this may be enough to assist him in conceiving of a deity who is both immanent and transcendent, such as Vishnu-Narayana in May Sarton's poem, "The Sleeping God." This God, as he is described, has an astounding delicacy; he sleeps and dreams by daylight; although he is utterly disarmed, relaxed, and at rest, perpetually he "renews all within his fertile reign." He is "A human Heaven," and if he does not return in the way we expect of a less exalted

Hero, it is because he has never taken leave. In him all opposites meet and are in harmony, and it is not to be wondered at that "anguish flowed away under his rule."

CHORIC SONG

from The Lotos-Eaters (V–VII)

V

How sweet it were, hearing the downward stream,
With half-shut eyes ever to seem
Falling asleep in a half-dream!
To dream and dream, like yonder amber light,
Which will not leave the myrrh-bush on the height;
To hear each other's whisper'd speech;
Eating the Lotos day by day,
To watch the crisping ripples on the beach,
And tender curving lines of creamy spray;
To lend our hearts and spirits wholly
To the influence of mild-minded melancholy;
To muse and brood and live again in memory,
With those old faces of our infancy
Heap'd over with a mound of grass,
Two handfuls of white dust, shut in an urn of brass!

VI

Dear is the memory of our wedded lives,
And dear the last embraces of our wives
And their warm tears; but all hath suffer'd change;
For surely now our household hearths are cold,
Our sons inherit us, our looks are strange,
And we should come like ghosts to trouble joy.
Or else the island princes over-bold
Have eat our substance, and the minstrel sings
Before them of the ten years' war in Troy,

And our great deeds, as half-forgotten things.
Is there confusion in the little isle?
Let what is broken so remain.
The Gods are hard to reconcile;
'T is hard to settle order once again.
There *is* confusion worse than death,
Trouble on trouble, pain on pain,
Long labor unto aged breath,
Sore task to hearts worn out by many wars
And eyes grown dim with gazing on the pilot-stars.

VII

But, propt on beds of amaranth and moly,
How sweet—while warm airs lull us, blowing lowly—
With half-dropt eyelid still,
Beneath a heaven dark and holy,
To watch the long bright river drawing slowly
His waters from the purple hill—
To hear the dewy echoes calling
From cave to cave thro' the thick-twined vine—
To watch the emerald-color'd water falling
Thro' many a woven acanthus-wreath divine!
Only to hear and see the far-off sparkling brine,
Only to hear were sweet, stretch'd out beneath the pine.

ALFRED, LORD TENNYSON

AMITABHA'S VOW
    (*Burning: 10*)

"If, after obtaining Buddhahood, anyone in my land
    gets tossed in jail on a vagrancy rap, may I
    not attain highest perfect enlightenment.

    wild geese in the orchard
    frost on the new grass

"If, after obtaining Buddhahood, anyone in my land
    loses a finger coupling boxcars, may I
    not attain highest perfect enlightenment.

Mare's eye flutters
jerked by the lead-rope
stone-bright shoes flick back
ankles trembling: down steep rock

"If, after obtaining Buddhahood, anyone in my land
    can't get a ride hitch-hiking all directions, may I
    not attain highest perfect enlightenment.

wet rocks buzzing
rain and thunder southwest
hair, beard, tingle
wind whips bare legs
we should go back
we don't

GARY SNYDER

IN THE SMOKING-CAR

The eyelids meet.   He'll catch a little nap.
The grizzled, crew-cut head drops to his chest.
It shakes above the briefcase on his lap.
Close voices breathe, "Poor sweet, he did his best."

"Poor sweet, poor sweet," the bird-hushed glades repeat,
Through which in quiet pomp his litter goes,
Carried by native girls with naked feet.
A sighing stream concurs in his repose.

Could he but think, he might recall to mind
The righteous mutiny or sudden gale
That beached him here; the dear ones left behind . . .
So near the ending, he forgets the tale.

Were he to lift his eyelids now, he might
Behold his maiden porters, brown and bare.
But even here he has no appetite.
It is enough to know that they are there.

Enough that now a honeyed music swells,
The gentle, mossed declivities begin,
And the whole air is full of flower-smells.
Failure, the longed-for valley, takes him in.

RICHARD WILBUR

A KIND OF QUEST,
SORT OF BRIAR ROSE

After the windy sighs were done, for once
And all, the pigeons on the gritty sill
Bemoaned, or so it seemed, in monotones,
Illicit pleasure in the city's tall
Hotels, and pain in broken assignations.

He, for whom the service elevator,
Rising, should have quelled a miracle
Of continence too long preserved by war
And angels, waited faithfully, but hall
And stolid door purveyed no paramour.

Still, the midget citizens pursued
Their paths of fretted industry below,
As though precipitated down a chute;
And only he, beneath a laden bough,
Had leisure to regret the wasted fruit.

No stranger to that insulated room,
He rang the changes on a message meant
For every solitary girl whose name
His wish had conjured with; but discontent
Eschewed the pigeons roosting in the grime.

He took the wedded pigeons to betoken
Pleasure, waiting in the wings to heed
An honest suit. How sweet to lie forsaken
Yet a while, and contemplate the bride
No prince could fail, nor any kiss awaken!

JOHN ALEXANDER ALLEN

THE SLEEPING BEAUTY:
VARIATION OF THE PRINCE

After the thorns I came to the first page.
He lay there gray in his fur of dust:
As I bent to open an eye, I sneezed.
But the ball looked by me, blue
As the sky it stared into . . .
And the sentry's cuirass is red with rust.

Children play inside: the dirty hand
Of the little mother, an inch from the child
That has worn out, burst, and blown away,
Uncurling to it—does not uncurl.
The bloom on the nap of their world
Is set with thousands of dawns of dew.

But at last, at the center of all the webs
Of the realm established in your blood,
I find you; and—look!—the drop of blood
Is there still, under the dust of your finger:
I force it, slowly, down from your finger
And it falls and rolls away, as it should.

And I bend to touch (just under the dust
That was roses once) the steady lips
Parted between a breath and a breath
In love, for the kiss of the hunter, Death.
Then I stretch myself beside you, lay
Between us, there in the dust, His sword.

When the world ends—it will never end—
The dust at last will fall from your eyes
In judgment, and I shall whisper:
"For hundreds of thousands of years I have slept
Beside you, here in the last long world
That you had found; that I have kept."

When they come for us—no one will ever come—
I shall stir from my long light sleep,
I shall whisper, "Wait, wait! . . . She is asleep."
I shall whisper, gazing, up to the gaze of the hunter,
Death, and close with the tips of the dust of my hand
The lids of the steady—
                  Look, He is fast asleep!

               RANDALL JARRELL

THE LAILY WORM AND THE MACHREL OF THE SEA

'I was bat seven year alld
    Fan my mider she did dee,
My father marrëd the ae warst woman
    The wardle did ever see.

'For she has made me the lailly worm
    That lays att the fitt of the tree,
An o my sister Meassry
    The machrel of the sea.

'An every Saterday att noon
    The machrl comes to me,
An she takes my laylë head,
    An lays it on her knee,
An keames it we a silver kemm,
    An washes it in the sea,

'Seven knights ha I slain
    Sane I lay att the fitt of the tree;
an ye war na my ain father,
    The eight an ye sud be.'

'Sing on your song, ye l[a]ily worm,
    That ye sung to me;'
'I never sung that song
    But fatt I wad sing to ye.

'I was but severn year aull
    Fan my mider she [did] dee,
My father marrëd the a warst woman
    The wardle did ever see.

'She changed me to the layel[y] worm
    That layes att the fitt of the tree,
An my sister Messry
    [To] the makrell of the sea.

'And every Saterday att noon
    The machrell comes to me,
An she takes my layly head,
    An layes it on her knee,
An kames it weth a siller kame,
    An washes it in the sea.

'Seven knights ha I slain
    San I lay att the fitt of the tree;
An ye war na my ain father,
    The eight ye sud be.'

He sent for his lady
    As fast as sen cod he:
'Far is my son,
    That ye sent fra me,
And my daughter
    Lady Messry?'

'Yer son is att our king's court,
    Sarving for meatt an fee,
And yer daugh[t]er is att our quin's court,
    A mary suit an fre.'

'Ye lee, ye ill woman,
    Sa loud as I hear ye lea,

For my son is the layelly worm
    That lays at the fitt of the tree,
An my daughter Messry
    The machrell of the sea.'

She has tain a silver wan
    An gine him stroks three,
An he started up the bravest knight
    Your eyes did ever see.

She has tane a small horn
    An loud as shill blue she,
An a' the fish came her tell but the proud machrell,
    As she stood by the sea:
'Ye shaped me once an unshemly shape,
    An ye's never mare shape me.'

He has sent to the wood
    For hathorn an fun,
And he has tane that gay lady,
    An ther he did her burne.

                ANONYMOUS

ULYSSES

At the last mountain I stood to remember the sea
and it was not the sea of my remembering
but something from an augur's madness:
sheep guts, bird guts, ox guts, smoking
in a hot eye. Was this my life? Dull red,
dull green, blood black, the coils still writhing
the last of the living thing: a carnage
steaming into the smokes of a sick dawn.

I had planted the oar at the crossroads, there in the goat dust
where the oaf waited, chewing a stalk of garlic.
"Stranger," he said, "what have you on your shoulder?"
"A world," I said, and made a hole for it,

watched by the oaf and his goats. I gave him money
for the fattest goat and asked to be alone,
and he would not leave me. I gave him money again
for a peace-parting, and he would not go.
"Stranger," I said, "I have sailed to all lands,
killed in all lands, and come home poor. I think
blood buys nothing, and I think it buys
all that's bought. Leave me this goat and go."
Why should I want his blood on me? The goat
stared at me like an old man, and the oaf
sat chewing garlic. This much had been commanded.
Was the rest commanded, too? Was it my life
or the god's laughter foresaw me?

                      I prayed in anger:
"O coupling gods, if from your lecheries
among the bloods of man, a prayer may move you
to spare one life, call off this last sad dog
you have set on me. Does Heaven need such meat?"
The heavens lurched on unheeding. The fool stayed:
would not be scared off, and would not be whipped off.
Then he raised his staff against me.

                   Was it my life
or the gods' laughter answered? I hacked him sidearm
across the middle: almost a stunt for practice—
dead level, no body weight to it, all in the shoulder
and wrist, and not three feet to the whole swing.
But it halved him like a melon! A chop
the ships would have sung for a century!
. . . But there were no ships, and the oar was planted unknown
in a country of garlic and goat turds,
and what lay fallen was rags and bones.

                    "Take him, then!" I cried.
"Who else could stomach such a dusty tripe?"
I made the pyre with the planted oar at its center,
and as it flamed, I raised the libation cup,
but mouthed the wine and spat it at the blaze.
The fire roared up like Etna. "At your pleasure!"

I shouted back, and threw the dead clown in,
first one piece, then the other. The horns of the flame
raped him whole and blew for more. The goats
stood watching, huddled like old crazy men
in a chorus round the fire, and one by one
I slit their throats and threw them to their master.
I say those goats were mad: they waited there
as if the fire were Medusa: the blood of the dead
ran down the legs of the living and they did not move,
not even to turn their heads. And in the center
the flame went blood-mad in a shaft to Heaven.

It was dark when I turned away. I lost my road
and slept the night in a grove. When I awoke
I found a shrine to Apollo, a marble peace
leaned on by cypresses, but across his belly
a crack grinned hip to hip, and the right hand
lay palm-up in the dust. On the road back
I came on many such, but that was the first
of the cracked gods and the dusty altars.

I returned to the sea, and at the last mountain
I stood to remember, and the memory
could not live in the fact. I had grown old
in the wrong world. Penelope wove for nothing
her fabric and delay. I could not return.
I was woven to my dead men. In the dust
of the dead shore by the dead sea I lay down
and named their names who had matched lives with me,
and won. And they were all I loved.

JOHN CIARDI

THE CONSTANT BRIDEGROOMS

Far down the purple wood
Coats of a company
Of silent soldiers
Flap idly in the wind

There they have stood

Since early day
Faces turned incuriously to the sound
Of the dry rustling
Of leaves in the wind

No command has reached

Them there
All silent have they stood
As
Though they were asleep
Now night darkens their coats
Far away
Their names are spoken
Somewhere at world's end

KENNETH PATCHEN

BEYOND THE HUNTING WOODS

I speak of that great house
Beyond the hunting woods,
Turreted and towered
In nineteenth-century style,
Where fireflies by the hundreds
Leap in the long grass,
Odor of jessamine
And roses, canker-bit,
Recalling famous times
When dame and maiden sipped
Sassafras or wild
Elderberry wine,
While far in the hunting woods
Men after their red hounds
Pursued the mythic beast.

I ask it of a stranger,
In all that great house finding
Not any living thing,
Or of the wind and the weather,
What charm was in that wine
That they should vanish so,
Ladies in their stiff
Bone and clean of limb,
And over the hunting woods
What mist had maddened them
That gentlemen should lose
Not only the beast in view
But Belle and Ginger too,
Nor home from the hunting woods
Ever, ever come?

DONALD JUSTICE

THE UNRETURNING HOSTS

Supreme in the distance, veiled
As one's own horizon,
The ancients stand,
Immutably shadowless in lengthening obliquity.

Stone is the rain

That falls on
Them. Panthers of frozen gold pad
Soundlessly round their shrouded
Immobility, while history's piping flutes

Shred hollowly against their

Stone music.
Honey-combed with shadow, great
Unsorrowing

Roses garland their sleep.
And stone is the air . . .
Of stone,
Their sea . . . *Dreamers lost*

In an unrotting solemnity.

KENNETH PATCHEN

THE COUNTRY OF A THOUSAND YEARS OF PEACE

Here they all come to die,
Fluent therein as in a fourth tongue.
But for a young man not yet of their race
It was madness you should lie

Blind in one eye, and fed
By the blood of a scrubbed face;
It was madness to look down
On the toy city where

The glittering neutrality
Of clock and chocolate and lake and cloud
Made every morning somewhat
Less than you could bear;

And makes me cry aloud
At the old masters of disease
Who dangling high about you on a hair
The sword that, never falling, kills

Would coax you still back from that starry land
Under the world, which no one sees
Without a death, its finish and sharp weight
Flashing in his own hand.

JAMES MERRILL

BRIGHT STAR

[*Written on a Blank Page in Shakespeare's Poems,
facing 'A Lover's Complaint.'*]

Bright star, would I were stedfast as thou art—
    Not in lone splendour hung aloft the night
And watching, with eternal lids apart,
    Like nature's patient, sleepless Eremite
The moving waters at their priestlike task
    Of pure ablution round earth's human shores,
Or gazing on the new soft-fallen mask
    Of snow upon the mountains and the moors—
No—yet still stedfast, still unchangeable,
    Pillow'd upon my fair love's ripening breast,
To feel for ever its soft fall and swell,
    Awake for ever in a sweet unrest,
Still, still to hear her tender-taken breath,
And so live ever—or else swoon to death.

                   JOHN KEATS

SAFE IN THEIR ALABASTER CHAMBERS

Safe in their alabaster chambers,
Untouched by morning and untouched by noon,
Sleep the meek members of the resurrection,
Rafter of satin, and roof of stone.

Light laughs the breeze in her castle of sunshine;
Babbles the bee in a stolid ear;
Pipe the sweet birds in ignorant cadence,—
Ah, what sagacity perished here!

Grand go the years in the crescent above them;
Worlds scoop their arcs, and firmaments row,
Diadems drop and Doges surrender,
Soundless as dots on a disk of snow.

                 EMILY DICKINSON

NEWS FOR THE DELPHIC ORACLE

I

There all the golden codgers lay,
There the silver dew,
And the great water sighed for love,
And the wind sighed too.
Man-picker Niamh leant and sighed
By Oisin on the grass;
There sighed amid his choir of love
Tall Pythagoras.
Plotinus came and looked about,
The salt-flakes on his breast,
And having stretched and yawned awhile
Lay sighing like the rest.

II

Straddling each a dolphin's back
And steadied by a fin,
Those Innocents re-live their death,
Their wounds open again.
The ecstatic waters laugh because
Their cries are sweet and strange,
Through their ancestral patterns dance,
And the brute dolphins plunge
Until, in some cliff-sheltered bay
Where wades the choir of love
Proffering its sacred laurel crowns,
They pitch their burdens off.

III

Slim adolescence that a nymph has stripped,
Peleus on Thetis stares.
Her limbs are delicate as an eyelid,
Love has blinded him with tears;
But Thetis' belly listens.
Down the mountain walls
From where Pan's cavern is
Intolerable music falls.

Foul goat-head, brutal arm appear,
Belly, shoulder, bum,
Flash fishlike; nymphs and satyrs
Copulate in the foam.

                              W. B. YEATS

ON A DROP OF DEW

See how the Orient Dew,
    Shed from the Bosom of the Morn
    Into the blowing Roses,
Yet careless of its Mansion new;
For the clear Region where 'twas born
    Round in its self incloses:
    And in its little Globes Extent,
Frames as it can its native Element.
    How it the purple flow'r does slight,
        Scarce touching where it lyes,
    But gazing back upon the Skies,
        Shines with a mournful Light;
            Like its own Tear,
Because so long divided from the Sphear.
    Restless it roules and unsecure,
        Trembling lest it grow impure:
    Till the warm Sun pitty it's Pain,
And to the Skies exhale it back again.
        So the Soul, that Drop, that Ray
Of the clear Fountain of Eternal Day,
Could it within the humane flow'r be seen,
    Remembring still its former height,
        Shuns the sweat leaves and blossoms green;
        And, recollecting its own Light,
Does, in its pure and circling thoughts, express
The greater Heaven in an Heaven less.
    In how coy a Figure wound,
        Every way it turns away:
    So the World excluding round,
        Yet receiving in the Day.
            Dark beneath, but bright above:

Here disdaining, there in Love.
How loose and easie hence to go:
How girt and ready to ascend.
Moving but on a point below,
It all about does upwards bend.
Such did the Manna's sacred Dew destil;
White, and intire, though congeal'd and chill.
Congeal'd on Earth: but does, dissolving, run
Into the Glories of th'Almighty Sun.

ANDREW MARVELL

THE SLEEPING GOD

Vishnu-Narayana, Katmandu

High in Nepal, the lock sprang at last:
There Vishnu lies entranced upon his pool,
And there I was touched deeply and held fast,

Was dreamed and delved, each nerve put to school,
Dreamed by this fertilizing power at rest
While anguish flowed away under his rule.

God, flower-fragile, open to the least,
Naked to every pulse of air and light,
More vulnerable in fact than any beast,

Young man relaxed in beauty, and so slight
He seems to float upon his dangerous sleep,
Daring to dream, exposed to the daylight.

He lies there on the coil, the massive loop
Of the eternal snake, a sovereign
Disarmed, without a wall, without a keep,

And renews all within his fertile reign,
And so, become the master of all space,
Is pure creation that can know no pain.

I saw him, naked, as a holy place,
A human Heaven which had learned to float
The universe upon a sleeping face.

And I, the Western one, was lost in thought,
Felt the lock spring, demons fly out,
And, all cracked open as the image caught,

Knew I was dreamed back to some ancient school
Where we are held within a single rule:
True power is given to the vulnerable.

                             MAY SARTON

❧ TWO ✿

The Return

The Return is an event that everyone is well acquainted with from his daily round of sleep and waking, solitude and sociability, wordless dreaming and attempts to communicate the dream. The homecoming Hero may receive a triumphal welcome, or he may be greeted by indifference and hostility. Persons who have tried to tell their dreams will understand how Rip Van Winkle felt when he returned from the mountains with remarkable adventures to recount, and none would listen. "Men always descend to meet," says Emerson, and everyone has suffered the frustration of knowing something which he cannot express, or of finding that his words have fallen on deaf ears. Cassandra was endowed by the gods with the gift of prophecy, but this power was canceled out by the provision that no one would believe what she predicted. "Wisdom crieth without; she uttereth her voice in the streets," but "fools hate knowledge" (Prov: 1.20,22). St. Paul was acutely aware of the problem:

> . . . *the natural man receiveth not the things*
> *of the Spirit of God: for they are foolishness*
> *unto him.*
>
> (I Cor: 2.14)

Daniel Hoffman's adventurer, in "Another Country," has discovered a land where "darkness . . . is brighter than familiar noon," but his words, when he would tell of it, are like mutters of thunder "When the bolt's dazzle has come, and gone." Patience and more patience is required of the returning voyager who finds, like Lazarus, that he is an alien in the world of time. The poet in May Sarton's "Lazarus" comes back from "distant and strange lands," bearing a store of "calm and hoarded powers" which are all but lost in the routine of daily living. But in time "The buried self" breaks through, and the design of the poem which she would write, with "the living beat," emerges like the dance of one who moves "On weightless feet."

Not every Hero, when he returns, brings with him the understanding which he sought. Walt Whitman asks, "where is what I started for so long ago? / And why is it yet unfound?," and the hero of "μῆτις . . . οὖτις," having made his journey in disguise and escaped its dangers by unscrupulous trickery, returns to his native "No Man's land," only to find that water cannot wash the guilt from his hand, and that his reflection shows him nothing more than his "old face." Swift's Gulliver believes that he has learned among the Houyhnhnms—a race of entirely reasonable horses—to live superior to the ugly Yahoos, whom he now perceives beneath the thin veneer of supposedly civilized mankind; but his rejection of his unenlightened brethren is ironic, for it springs from a spiritual pride which is itself a symptom of acute irrationality.

Perhaps the wisest travelers, or at any rate the sanest ones, are those, like Robert Graves' Alice and George Garrett's miners ("Underworld"), who realize that the two worlds of their knowledge must be kept distinct. If Alice were to rationalize the Red Queen as, after all, only a kitten, she would not explain, but merely explain away, the land behind the looking glass; and if one returns from the underworld inspired to give his soul, "like a careless saint," to God, he is sure to join the martyred ranks of those whose "flesh belongs to furies." Whatever can be told with "simple honesty" is a lie, says the speaker in "The Third Dimension" (Denise Levertov). Love has split her open "from / Scalp to crotch," and she walks about, "pleased with / the sun and all / the world's bounty"; yet she hesitates to tell of the experience: "the words / change it." Bottom, in *A Midsummer Night's Dream*, awakens from "a most rare vision" which he would recount, but he recognizes that it is "past the wit of man to say what dream it was" and concludes that "Man is but an ass if he go about to expound this dream." Nevertheless, like Plato's chosen few who receive enlightenment and descend once more to lead the shadow-bound in the cave, the Hero as teacher, philosopher, artist, preacher, or saint will never truly be satisfied until he has made his vital message known.

The returning Hero, with his treasure of enlightenment from a timeless world, must be the agent of that treasure's incarnation in the world of time. The poet's instinct is a deeply humanistic one, and he is likely to be sceptical of the "sensible emptiness" which is said to be the source of bliss for the mystic, the Buddha, and the Bodhisattvas. The Word of God put on the flesh for the redemption of mankind, and the meaning of the Buddhist phrase, "The jewel is in the lotos," is that eternity exists in, and is revealed through, time. For Richard Wilbur's traveler ("A World without Objects . . ."), the aureole of sainthood is best observed in "light incarnate," "the hills' bracken tiaras made / Gold in the sunken sun." The antagonist in William Stafford's lively parable, "The Animal that Drank Up Sound," is an animal which serves the cold and silent perfection of the moon. When the world has become "just like the moon, shining back that still / silver," it possesses an unearthly beauty—and is dead. Under the circumstances, the earth's savior is the sole remaining cricket, whose small voice triggers the return of "the kind of world we know"—a richly noisy one, full of vitality.

The issue of the Hero's journey may not be transfiguration of the world so much as an understanding of its somehow endearing imperfection. The spirits that give praise to heaven in Delmore Schwartz's "The Fulfillment" long, amid the "action of joy" which they experience there, for

> *the dear dark hooded mortality*
> *Which we had been and never known, which we resisted, de-*
> *tested, feared and denied, the rocks and flowers and the faces*
> *of the needs and hopes which had given us our reality!*

Curiously enough, to be in easy command of miracles is not as satisfying as our wish-fulfilling dreams would lead us to believe. The will, when it is fully gratified, though it offend no man, awakens to find itself imprisoned in a dark tower, a moated castle, desperate to be liberated from its "holy spell" (Julia Randall, "Miracles"). Almost perversely, the spirit demands the right to sacrifice, to be a

Noah, serving the Lord's compassion for mankind. No sooner does
Shakespeare's Prospero, by exercise of magic art, contrive to get his
enemies fully in his power than he discovers, after all, that

> *The rarer action is*
> *In virtue than in vengeance. They being penitent,*
> *The sole drift of my purpose doth extend*
> *Not a frown further.*
>
> (The Tempest: V.i.27–30)

He surrenders superhuman power and prepares to reassume his
responsibilities as Duke of Milan, announcing cheerfully that "Every
third thought," in his native city, "shall be my grave." It is not the
philosophical Duke Senior who refuses, at the end of *As You Like
It,* to abandon the quasi-paradise of Arden, but the sour Jaques
whose delight it is, living among exiles, to "suck melancholy out of
a song as a weasel sucks eggs" (II.v.10–11).

"Love Calls Us," the title of Richard Wilbur's poem an-
nounces, "to the Things of This World." Certainly, love would
seem to be the motivating force of the returning Hero. But it is not
love of life alone which makes him fully human. Freud maintains
that the world, both within the individual psyche and outside of it,
is kept in motion by a balance of the libido and the death-wish.
Before they can resume their lives and destinies, Aeneas and Dante
are obliged to visit the world of the dead. Christ harrows hell.
Persephone is ravished away by gloomy Dis to be the queen of the
underworld, and while she is in exile there, winter prevails on earth.
But when at last the messenger, Hermes, comes to release her from
imprisonment, as A. D. Hope imagines, "Looking her last on her
grim ravisher / For the first time she loved him from her heart"
("The Return of Persephone"). Death and the renewal of life are
inseparable, and, more mysteriously still, prove in the end to be
actually the same. The riddle lies at the heart of the birth and
ministry and crucifixion of the Son of Man. His death on the cross
was, from the first, implicit in his life and was, indeed, the purpose
of his incarnation. T. S. Eliot ("Journey of the Magi") lets his
travelers to Bethlehem remember that "This Birth was / Hard and
bitter agony for us, like Death, our death." When they returned to

their several kingdoms, they were "no longer at ease . . . With an alien people clutching their gods." For all the pain of the experience he has undergone, the spokesman voices the paradox which every Hero, in his fashion, tries to convey to a world which sometimes listens: "I should be glad of another death."

FACING WEST FROM CALIFORNIA'S SHORES

Facing west from California's shores,
Inquiring, tireless, seeking what is yet unfound,
I, a child, very old, over waves, towards the house of maternity, the land of migrations, look afar,
Look off the shores of my Western sea, the circle almost circled;
For starting westward from Hindustan, from the vales of Kashmere,
From Asia, from the north, from the God, the sage, and the hero,
From the south, from the flowery peninsulas and the spice islands,
Long having wander'd since, round the earth having wander'd,
Now I face home again, very pleas'd and joyous,
(But where is what I started for so long ago?
And why is it yet unfound?)

WALT WHITMAN

μῆτις · · · οὖτις
For R. M. Powell

He fed them generously who were his flocks,
Picked, shatterbrained, for food. Passed as a goat
Among his sheep, I cast off. Though hurled rocks

And prayers deranged by torment tossed our boat,
I could not silence, somehow, this defiant
Mind. From my fist into the frothed wake ran
The white eye's gluten of the living giant
I had escaped, by trickery, as no man.

Unseen where all seem stone blind, pure disguise
Has brought me home alone to No Man's land
To look at nothing I dare recognize.
My dead blind guide, you lead me here to claim
Still waters that will never wash my hand,
To kneel by my old face and know my name.

W. D. SNODGRASS

ANOTHER COUNTRY

Coming to a cavern in a valley,
Who would not explore?
His pineknot lit, he thrust a way
Past droppings on the mossy floor,
Past walls that gleamed and streamed with waters
Into a chamber none had known before
Save who drew in colors deep as blood
The great creatures on that sacred dome
—Horned Huntsman, and the Woman, Moon—
It was then he found the doorway
To another country. Darkness
There is brighter than familiar noon.
The light that lights that land's like lightning.
Its sudden crackle rends the skies.
                                        He tries
To tell a prospect of that country,
His words as much like lightning as the mutter
Of seared cloud
When the bolt's dazzle has come, and gone.

DANIEL HOFFMAN

ALICE

When that prime heroine of our nation, Alice,
Climbing courageously in through the Palace
Of Looking Glass, found it inhabited
By chessboard personages, white and red,
Involved in never-ending tournament,
She being of a speculative bent
Had long foreshadowed something of the kind,
Asking herself: 'Suppose I stood behind
And viewed the fireplace of Their drawing-room
From hearthrug level, why must I assume
That what I'd see would need to correspond
With what I now see?   And the rooms beyond?'

Proved right, yet not content with what she had done,
Alice decided to prolong her fun:
She set herself, with truly British pride
In being a pawn and playing for her side,
And simple faith in simple stratagem,
To learn the rules and moves and perfect them.
So prosperously there she settled down
That six moves only and she'd won her crown—
A triumph surely!   But her greater feat
Was rounding these adventures off complete:
Accepting them, when safe returned again,
As queer but true—not only in the main
True, but as true as anything you'd swear to,
The usual three dimensions you are heir to.
For Alice though a child could understand
That neither did this change-discovered land
Make nohow or contrariwise the clean
Dull round of mid-Victorian routine,
Nor did Victoria's golden rule extend
Beyond the glass: it came to the dead end
Where empty hearses turn about; thereafter
Begins that lubberland of dream and laughter,
The red-and-white-flower-spangled hedge, the grass
Where Apuleius pastured his Gold Ass,

Where young Gargantua made whole holiday. . . .
But farther from our heroine not to stray,
Let us observe with what uncommon sense—
Though a secure and easy reference
Between Red Queen and Kitten could be found—
She made no false assumption on that ground
(A trap in which the scientist would fall)
That queens and kittens are identical.

ROBERT GRAVES

UNDERWORLD

You've seen coalminers coming up
for air, all in blackface like
no minstrel show comedian,
but bent over, seamed by the danger
and the darkness they must bear,
at once a badge and a wound.

Or maybe a diver on the deck,
his heavy helmet cast aside,
blinking in the hard bright light
where each breath is a gust of fire.
It is no laughing matter
to live in two strange worlds.

So it is with certain myths and dreams.
The songs of Orpheus never were the same
after he had seen hell.   They roused
nothing but rage and madness; yet,
after such vision and total loss,
who wouldn't change his tune?

Oh, you will descend, all right,
dream into the fiery darkness or
stumble, awkward among the deep sea
shiftings, troubled by bones

and voiceless cries. And then
you wake and wonder what is real. . . .

Better to come back grinning,
scrub the darkness off yourself,
wisecrack with the ordinary seamen,
unless, like a careless saint,
you can give your soul to God.
And then your flesh belongs to furies.

GEORGE GARRETT

THE LOST MUSIC

In the underworld, O Orpheus,
How strangely sounded string and voice
Before the midnight throne of Dis.
In gardens of Persephone
Where ghosts of flowers that bloomed above
Blossom again all winter long,
How strangely living was your song!
The Queen embraced Eurydice,
Homesick for summer and for love,
And both stood unbelieving there
To hear your music from afar.

O Orpheus, on your return
How strangely sounded voice and string
Along the beams of living spring.
Those were your lyre when you were young;
But birds and beasts now shunned the sound
That once had charmed them, for the tone
Held echoes from a world unknown.
Eurydice, still lost among
The wandering shadows underground,
Heard nothing now; and daylight spurned
Dead music from the past returned.

ROBERT HILLYER

RETURN

Sometimes the moment comes for the return,
the drawing-back-again into the known:
the remembered room, the loved face, the accepted idea.
Even Ulysses knew that secret magnet
which through the years of sea and island wanderings gave him
    no rest.
Nymphs were not beautiful enough,
nor the salt waves
so bright and daunting as to bar the way.
The Circe islands might delay his coming
but could not stop him.   The loud-voiced gulls
in vain cried Freedom on the veering winds.
The sirens sang to deaf ears, even Polyphemus,
the stupid, lovesick, man-devouring shepherd,
had not the wits in his thick ogre's skull
to match Ulysses' homeward-tending will.
There comes the time for each and every one
to be Ulysses. Somewhere the tapestry
is woven and unwoven. Somewhere the dog
lies blind and listening in the familiar sun.

ELIZABETH COATSWORTH

THE THIRD DIMENSION

Who'd believe me if
I said, 'They took and

split me open from
scalp to crotch, and

still I'm alive, and
walk around pleased with

the sun and all
the world's bounty.' Honesty

isn't so simple:
a simple honesty is

nothing but a lie.
Don't the trees

hide the wind between
their leaves and

speak in whispers?
The third dimension

hides itself.
If the roadmen

crack stones, the
stones are stones:

but love
cracked me open

and I'm
alive to

tell the tale—but not
honestly:

the words
change it. Let it be—

here in the sweet sun
—a fiction, while I

breathe and
change pace.

DENISE LEVERTOV

LAZARUS

(*Anglo-Saxon*, A.D. *1000*, *Chichester Cathedral*)

I

From the rock and from the deep
The sculptor lifts him out aware.
This is the dead man's waking stare.
This is a man carved out of sleep.
The grave is hard; the walls are steep.

The sculptor lifts him out aware
From the rock and from the deep.
We watch with awe; we watch and keep
The heavy world he has to bear.
The sculptor lifts him out, aware.
Huge forlorn eyes open from sleep.
When morning comes, what do we keep?

The heavy world he has to bear.
He comes from the unconscious deep
With what to give and what to keep?
Lazarus lifts huge hands in prayer.
He turns the world round in his stare.

He sees his late death everywhere.
It hurts his eyes; he has to care.

Now broken from the rock of sleep,
He comes toward us from the deep

To face once more the morning star,
To see us desperate as we are.

And Lazarus relearns despair.
His look is grave; his gaze is deep

Upon us, men carved out of sleep
Who wish to pray but have no prayer.

2

A weightless traveler, I too come back
From miles of air, from distant and strange lands,
Put on my house again, my work, my lack,
And looking down at my own clumsy hands,
Feel courage crack.

How can I answer all these needs at once?
Letters and friends and work and flowers?
They sweep me back in their devouring glance
To carry off my calm and hoarded powers
In a huge pounce.

That heavy thickness as of new-mown hay
Flung down in heaps over a tentative fire—
How lift my smothered flame up to the day?
Have I come back depleted of desire,
To tire and fray?

At last I hear the silence in the room:
The buried self is breaking through to be,
And Lazarus is calling me by name.
At last I slowly lift the poem free,
One-pointed flame.

I hear, "to live as one already dead"—
A voice heard in Japan long months ago.
The sweat of *muga* starts on my forehead.
It is the sweat poets and dancers know,
In joy and dread.

Images flow together in that heat,
And confused numbers thread a single line.
Detached from all except the living beat,
I dance my way into complex design
On weightless feet.

MAY SARTON

THE CIRCUS ANIMALS' DESERTION

I

I sought a theme and sought for it in vain,
I sought it daily for six weeks or so.
Maybe at last, being but a broken man,
I must be satisfied with my heart, although
Winter and summer till old age began
My circus animals were all on show,
Those stilted boys, that burnished chariot,
Lion and woman and the Lord knows what.

II

What can I but enumerate old themes?
First that sea-rider Oisin led by the nose
Through three enchanted islands, allegorical dreams,
Vain gaiety, vain battle, vain repose,
Themes of the embittered heart, or so it seems,
That might adorn old songs or courtly shows;
But what cared I that set him on to ride,
I, starved for the bosom of his faery bride?

And then a counter-truth filled out its play,
The Countess Cathleen was the name I gave it;
She, pity-crazed, had given her soul away,
But masterful Heaven had intervened to save it.
I thought my dear must her own soul destroy,
So did fanaticism and hate enslave it,
And this brought forth a dream and soon enough
This dream itself had all my thought and love.

And when the Fool and Blind Man stole the bread
Cuchulain fought the ungovernable sea;
Heart-mysteries there, and yet when all is said
It was the dream itself enchanted me:
Character isolated by a deed
To engross the present and dominate memory.
Players and painted stage took all my love,
And not those things that they were emblems of.

III

Those masterful images because complete
Grew in pure mind, but out of what began?
A mound of refuse or the sweepings of a street,
Old kettles, old bottles, and a broken can,
Old iron, old bones, old rags, that raving slut
Who keeps the till.   Now that my ladder's gone,
I must lie down where all the ladders start,
In the foul rag-and-bone shop of the heart.

WILLIAM BUTLER YEATS

"A WORLD WITHOUT OBJECTS IS A SENSIBLE EMPTINESS"

The tall camels of the spirit
Steer for their deserts, passing the last groves loud
With the sawmill shrill of the locust, to the whole honey of
the arid
Sun.   They are slow, proud,

And move with a stilted stride
To the land of sheer horizon, hunting Traherne's
Sensible emptiness, there where the brain's lantern-slide
Revels in vast returns.

O connoisseurs of thirst,
Beasts of my soul who long to learn to drink
Of pure mirage, those prosperous islands are accurst
That shimmer on the brink

Of absence; auras, lustres,
And all shinings need to be shaped and borne.
Think of those painted saints, capped by the early masters
With bright, jauntily-worn

Aureate plates, or even
Merry-go-round rings.   Turn, O turn

From the fine sleights of the sand, from the long empty oven
Where flames in flamings burn

Back to the trees arrayed
In bursts of glare, to the halo-dialing run
Of the country creeks, and the hills' bracken tiaras made
Gold in the sunken sun,

Wisely watch for the sight
Of the supernova burgeoning over the barn,
Lampshine blurred in the steam of beasts, the spirit's right
Oasis, light incarnate.

RICHARD WILBUR

THE ANIMAL THAT DRANK UP SOUND

I

One day across the lake where echoes come now
an animal that needed sound came down. He gazed
enormously, and instead of making any, he took
away from, sound: the lake and all the land
went dumb. A fish that jumped went back like a knife,
and the water died. In all the wilderness around he
drained the rustle from the leaves into the mountainside
and folded a quilt over the rocks, getting ready
to store everything the place had known; he buried—
thousands of autumns deep—the noise that used to come there.

Then that animal wandered on and began to drink
the sound out of all the valleys—the croak of toads,
and all the little shiny noise grass blades make.
He drank till winter, and then looked out one night
at the stilled places guaranteed around by frozen
peaks and held in the shallow pools of starlight.
It was finally tall and still, and he stopped on the highest
ridge, just where the cold sky fell away

like a perpetual curve, and from there he walked on silently,
and began to starve.

When the moon drifted over that night the whole world lay
just like the moon, shining back that still
silver, and the moon saw its own animal dead
on the snow, its dark absorbent paws and quiet
muzzle, and thick, velvet, deep fur.

2

After the animal that drank sound died, the world
lay still and cold for months, and the moon yearned
and explored, letting its dead light float down
the west walls of canyons and then climb its delighted
soundless way up the east side. The moon
owned the earth its animal had faithfully explored.
The sun disregarded the life it used to warm.

But on the north side of a mountain, deep in some rocks,
a cricket slept. It had been hiding when that animal
passed, and as spring came again this cricket waited,
afraid to crawl out into the heavy stillness.
Think how deep the cricket felt, lost there
in such a silence—the grass, the leaves, the water,
the stilled animals all depending on such a little
thing. But softly it tried—"Cricket!"—and back like a river
from that one act flowed the kind of world we know,
first whisperings, then moves in the grass and leaves;
the water splashed, and a big night bird screamed.

It all returned, our precious world with its life and sound,
where sometimes loud over the hill the moon,
wild again, looks for its animal to roam, still,
down out of the hills, any time.
But somewhere a cricket waits.

It listens now, and practices at night.

WILLIAM STAFFORD

THE FULFILLMENT

"Is it a dream?" I asked. To which my fellow
Answered with a hoarse voice and dulled insistence:
"Dream, is it a dream? What difference
Does it make or mean? If it is only a dream
It is the dream which we are. Dream or the last resort
Of reality, it is the truth of our minds:
We are condemned because this is our consciousness."

Where we were, if we were there, serene and shining
Each being sang and moved with the sleekness of rivers,
United in a choir, many and one, as the spires of flames in fire,
Flowing and perfected, flourishing and fulfilled forever,
Rising and falling as the carousel and palace of festival and
    victory.

"I was told often enough," my fellow said—
"You were told too—and you as little believed—
'Beware of all your desires. You are deceived.
(As they are deceived and deceptive, urgent and passing!)
They will be wholly fulfilled. You will be dead.
They will be gratified. And you will be dead!' "

In a fixed fascination, wonderstruck, we gazed,
Marveling at the fulfillment so long desired and praised.
There, effort was like dancing's its own pleasure.
There, all things existed purely in the action of joy—
Like light, like all kinds of light, all in the domination of cele-
    bration existed only as the structures of joy!

Then, as we gazed in an emotion more exhausting than moun-
    tains,
Then, when at last we knew where we had come,
It was then that we saw what was as lost as we knew where we
    had been
(Or knew where we had been as we saw all that was lost!)
And knew for the first time the richness and poverty
Of what we had been before and were no more,

The striving, the suffering, the dear dark hooded mortality
Which we had been and never known, which we resisted,
    detested, feared and denied, the rocks and the flowers and
    the faces of the needs and the hopes which had given us
    our reality!

DELMORE SCHWARTZ

MIRACLES

I said to the stream, Be still, and it was still.
I walked across the water like a fool.
Such ease—you'd think a man had never tried
The simple miracles, but lived and died
Sweating at wood and steel: chop, forge, bend, bind,
Get up the armory, don't trust humankind,
They were damned from the start.

                            I said to the mineral hill,
Lie down, and the hanging rocks and the canyons fell
As soft as smoke. It was quiet. I called out
Some friends to look. For a while they walked about
Uncomfortably, I thought, and one picked up
A fragment for the Museum. Envy? Fear?
I don't know what. I kept on all that year.
Wherever I went, the trees bowed down; the fruit
Rolled like obedient coins to my feet,
And so on. Late one night I tried to command—
How shall I say?—my holy spell to end,
Break, blast, unmagic me here in the dark
Tower I'd built. I wanted a horn to knock
The cullis in, and the crazy ditch to rise.
Oh god, for the need of nails, for the wild eyes
Of Noah with creation in his hold
Stampeding. But I'd sold
My Ararat for meadows. Oh, the flowers!
Too deep, too deep.
I said, accept my tears.

JULIA RANDALL

LOVE CALLS US TO THE THINGS OF THIS WORLD

The eyes open to a cry of pulleys,
And spirited from sleep, the astounded soul
Hangs for a moment bodiless and simple
As false dawn.
                    Outside the open window
The morning air is all awash with angels.

Some are in bed-sheets, some are in blouses,
Some are in smocks: but truly there they are.
Now they are rising together in calm swells
Of halcyon feeling, filling whatever they wear
With the deep joy of their impersonal breathing;

Now they are flying in place, conveying
The terrible speed of their omnipresence, moving
And staying like white water; and now of a sudden
They swoon down into so rapt a quiet
That nobody seems to be there.
                              The soul shrinks
    From all that it is about to remember,
From the punctual rape of every blessèd day,
And cries,
            "Oh, let there be nothing on earth but laundry,
Nothing but rosy hands in the rising steam
And clear dances done in the sight of heaven."

Yet, as the sun acknowledges
With a warm look the world's hunks and colors,
The soul descends once more in bitter love
To accept the waking body, saying now
In a changed voice as the man yawns and rises,

"Bring them down from their ruddy gallows;
Let there be clean linen for the backs of thieves;
Let lovers go fresh and sweet to be undone,

And the heaviest nuns walk in a pure floating
Of dark habits,
                    Keeping their difficult balance."

                    RICHARD WILBUR

THE RETURN OF PERSEPHONE

Gliding through the still air, he made no sound;
Wing-shod and deft, dropped almost at her feet,
And searched the ghostly regiments and found
The living eyes, the tremor of breath, the beat
Of blood in all that bodiless underground.

She left her majesty; she loosed the zone
Of darkness and put by the rod of dread.
Standing, she turned her back upon the throne
Where, well she knew, the Ruler of the Dead,
Lord of her body and being, sat like stone;

Stared with his ravenous eyes to see her shake
The midnight drifting from her loosened hair,
The girl once more in all her actions wake,
The blush of colour in her cheeks appear
Lost with her flowers that day beside the lake.

The summer flowers scattering, the shout,
The black manes plunging down to the black pit—
Memory or dream?   She stood awhile in doubt,
Then touched the Traveller God's brown arm and met
His cool, bright glance and heard his words ring out:

"Queen of the Dead and Mistress of the Year!"
—His voice was the ripe ripple of the corn;
The touch of dew, the rush of morning air—
"Remember now the world where you were born;
The month of your return at last is here."

And still she did not speak, but turned again
Looking for answer, for anger, for command:
The eyes of Dis were shut upon their pain;
Calm as his marble brow, the marble hand
Slept on his knee. Insuperable disdain

Foreknowing all bounds of passion, of power, of art,
Mastered but could not mask his deep despair.
Even as she turned with Hermes to depart,
Looking her last on her grim ravisher
For the first time she loved him from her heart.

A. D. HOPE

JOURNEY OF THE MAGI

"A cold coming we had of it,
Just the worst time of the year
For a journey, and such a long journey:
The ways deep and the weather sharp,
The very dead of winter."
And the camels galled, sore-footed, refractory,
Lying down in the melting snow.
There were times we regretted
The summer palaces on slopes, the terraces,
And the silken girls bringing sherbet.
Then the camel men cursing and grumbling
And running away, and wanting their liquor and women,
And the night-fires going out, and the lack of shelters,
And the cities hostile and the towns unfriendly
And the villages dirty and charging high prices:
A hard time we had of it.
At the end we preferred to travel all night,
Sleeping in snatches,
With the voices singing in our ears, saying
That this was all folly.

Then at dawn we came down to a temperate valley,
Wet, below the snow line, smelling of vegetation,

With a running stream and a water-mill beating the darkness,
And three trees on the low sky.
And an old white horse galloped away in the meadow.
Then we came to a tavern with vine-leaves over the lintel,
Six hands at an open door dicing for pieces of silver,
And feet kicking the empty wine-skins.
But there was no information, and so we continued
And arrived at evening, not a moment too soon
Finding the place; it was (you may say) satisfactory.

All this was a long time ago, I remember,
And I would do it again, but set down
This set down
This: were we led all that way for
Birth or Death?   There was a Birth, certainly,
We had evidence and no doubt, I had seen birth and death,
But had thought they were different; this Birth was
Hard and bitter agony for us, like Death, our death.
We returned to our places, these Kingdoms,
But no longer at ease here, in the old dispensation,
With an alien people clutching their gods.
I should be glad of another death.

T. S. ELIOT

THREE

The Boon

The Hero's Boon, the goal and product of the Quest, is always self-transcendence. The moment of enlightenment may be as swift and fleeting as a lightning stroke, but it has power to transform his life. Job's vision of the Lord may well have taken place between a breath and breath, yet it repaired the ravages of his long doubt and suffering. The restoration of his health, and goods and family was to follow, but the essential Boon was spiritual and occurred when Job answered the Lord and said,

> *I have heard of thee by the hearing of the ear:*
> *but now mine eye seeth thee. Wherefore I abhor*
> *myself, and repent in dust and ashes.*
>
> (42.5–6)

Job at last is able to accept his place in the universal scheme of things, to humble himself before an inscrutable power whose terror, might, and joy have made his individual will a part of the eternal one: a death that coincides with an ennobling second birth. As Dante says at the end of his long pilgrimage,

> *already my desire and will were rolled—even*
> *as a wheel that moveth equally—by the Love*
> *that moves the sun and the other stars.*

Presumably, he returns to earth and takes up his mortal existence
where he left it, but he is not the same man who, at the midpoint in
his life, came to himself in a dark wood and realized that he had al-
together lost his way.

The heroes of Greek and Roman myth may seem to display a
hardy independence which sets them apart from those of the Judeo-
Christian tradition, but the impression is deceptive. Homer and
Vergil are at pains to show that the remarkable achievements of
Odysseus and Aeneas are made possible by the advice and inspiration
of the gods. In times of crisis, the former turns to his patroness,
Athene; and the latter is assisted by his mother, Venus, though she
is sometimes obliged to yield to the higher purposes of Jupiter.
Both Odysseus and Aeneas are destined for political roles, in which
the gifts of the gods can be put to work for the good of civilization
and mankind, and it should be borne in mind that kingship requires
the subordination of the self to an office and a purpose larger than
the individual who serves them.

The Hero's Boon is a gift, not a reward. The youngest son
of three who is typically the protagonist in fairy tales is an unlikely
specimen, so undistinguished as to become a common laughing stock;
and, to make the matter worse, he has a penchant for disregarding
sage advice, and often does precisely what his counselors tell him
not to do. Yet he somehow manages to win the princess, while the
abler aspirants fail. "Many be called, but few chosen"; and the
seeming unworthiness of the successful Hero suggests the depen-
dence of Everyman upon the inscrutable generosity of the gods:

> *The stone which the builder refused is become*
> *the head stone of the corner. This is the Lord's*
> *doing; it is marvelous in our eyes.*
>
> (Psalms: 118.22–23)

So long as he relies upon his own inadequate powers, the bumbling
Redcrosse Knight of Spenser's *Faerie Queene* (Book I) falls ever
more deeply into error. At last he is rescued from despair by the
Grace of God and triumphs over the dragon (Satan) through the
timely agency of water from the Well of Life (baptism) and balm
from the Tree of Life (Holy Communion). No one can say that
Coleridge's Ancient Mariner *deserved* the access of love which en-

abled him to bless the water-snakes and thus to end his ordeal of
spiritual isolation; and he does not pretend that he deserved it:

> *A spring of love gushed from my heart,*
> *And I blessed them unaware:*
> *Sure my kind saint took pity on me,*
> *And I blessed them unaware.*

In short, one never is certain when (or if) the Boon is to be be-
stowed, and this lends a certain piquancy to the Quest of Everyman,
the progress of which, whatever else one may say of it, is sure to be
incalculable.

To descend to the realm of everyday affairs, we have all at
some time been recipients of the Hero's Boon; and we have gener-
ally found ourselves, on those occasions, caught off guard, surprised
by joy. No one can will himself to fall in love. This is the gift of
Aphrodite. A young poet may belabor his head for days without
producing so much as a couplet worth preserving; then, on impulse,
he may scribble something inattentively, and learn, to his astonish-
ment, that he has the germ of an authentic poem. This is the gift
of the Muse. Paradoxically, such visitations of unexpected power
are likeliest to occur when "fierce vexation" holds us most tightly
in its grip. After their night of rampant misadventure in the wood
near Athens, Shakespeare's lovers in *A Midsummer Night's Dream*,
awakening, discover that their animosities have somehow vanished
while they slept. Duke Theseus looks in wonder at Lysander and
Demetrius:

> *I know you two are rival enemies.*
> *How comes this gentle concord in the world*
> *That hatred is so far from jealousy*
> *To sleep by hate and fear no enmity?*

> (IV.i.141–44)

And Demetrius can only say that "by some power" a miracle has
come to pass.

Joy, generosity, enfranchisement, and ecstasy are keynotes in
the poems whose subject is the Boon. The note of irony, so ubiqui-
tous elsewhere in the progress of the Quest, has little relevance here.

Light, song, flowers, dance, bright colors, feasting, and ascent are the predominant images. However, these suggestions of the festive mood more often than not proceed from equally potent evocations of frustration, violence, failure, suffering, and grief. The farmer in Julia Randall's parable ("The Farmer's Tale") is "ruined" before his dance upon a stone brings forth the "lusty flower" which is "The glory of the town." Giselle, in the poem by Randall Jarrell, is dead and in the grave when the ominous black queen appears, "Her wands quiver," and the limbs of the girl remember how to dance. It is the grinding misery of mankind which moves the "son of heaven" to say "The world's been crucified / long enough" and to undo the "hard fact" of Hell (Jerome Rothenberg, "A Bodhisattva Undoes Hell"). In tragedy, the world is restored at the very moment of its violent death. The cry of "Love" is evoked, in David Wagoner's "The Eye of the Storm," from mariners who have only now recovered from a "battering night, rack and distress" and are hurtling once again into a storm whose fury promises to rend and rip and crush their vessel into kindling.

The life that is utterly shattered may mysteriously be the one that is enabled to put itself, and the world as well, together again. The crucifixion must precede the ascension. While the "small war for her beauty / Is stitched out of sight and lost," the title figure of James Dickey's "The Scarred Girl" is constantly aware that "the bright, fractured world," which suffered just as she did when her accident occurred, "Burns and pulls and weeps / To come together again." When her bandages are removed, her beauty is gone, but "The pastures of earth and heaven" are "restored and undamaged," and all things "in the seamless sunlight" wear "a newborn countenance." At the other end of the mortal life span, a death "slow, grotesque and hard" comes to a venerable Pope (A. D. Hope, "Ode on the Death of Pius the Twelfth"). But even while he was dying, he experienced

> *A strange illumination of the heart,*
> *Voices and visions such as mark the man*
> *Chosen and set apart.*

His "triumphant death" is exactly comparable to that of the leaves on Autumn's "fire-enchanted trees"; the beauty of both has no purpose in nature except to be glorious; and none can fail to read the

message, either in the trees or in the death of the holy Hero, of
"that immense / Epiphany of light."

THE THING MADE REAL

The thing made real by
a sudden twist of the mind:
relate the darkness to a face
rather than
impose a face on the darkness
which has no face, in reality.

The Daisy made recognisable
suddenly
by a flash of
magic light, the tongue
of fire, Pentecost.

The ox made real
in its own essence
without change or pollution . . .
waking up in the cellar to find
him, rusty & contemplative, staring
me in the face
. . . the thing in its own essence
outside the confines of those
perfunctory fields, in the unlimited
environment of the imagination—

till it thunders into
the consciousness
in all its pure & beautiful
absurdity,
like a White Rhinoceros.

RON LOEWINSOHN

THE BUTTON

I wake each morning to a different set
Of threats in the mail: eviction notices
And bills marked "Please!" in red.
A pale bridge partner twitters by my chair,
Where the radio ruminates unsavory news.
Each night, in a different way unmade,
I try to sleep in a different unmade bed.

Why then, dead in the dead of night, last night,
Did I walk the halls, long after my eyes
Had set?   Why poke in closet and trunk?
Because, in a wilderness of bric-a-brac,
I lacked the wherewithal to sew a button on;
And found, in a bureau drawer, a needle; sunk
To the bottom of a chest, a spool of thread.

Into my lap I took my coat of no particular
Color, tied a knot in the thread, and thought:
I cannot make my bed, yet I can lie in it!
With that, between two stitches, like an angel
Rose my heart and chanted: Bill collectors,
Though you dun for nothing less than all
I own, blest be your unforgivingness!

While neat and strong I sewed, it seemed
The daughters of the morning sang, at dawn,
My husbandry.   And though the grave
Antagonist, whose only trump is doom,
Appeared, when the sun was high, to press my bell,
He could not repossess that handiwork!
In time, a stitch in time will save us all.

                    JOHN ALEXANDER ALLEN

I COULD GIVE ALL TO TIME

To Time it never seems that he is brave
To set himself against the peaks of snow

To lay them level with the running wave,
Nor is he overjoyed when they lie low,
But only grave, contemplative and grave.

What now is inland shall be ocean isle,
Then eddies playing round a sunken reef
Like the curl at the corner of a smile;
And I could share Time's lack of joy or grief
At such a planetary change of style.

I could give all to Time except—except
What I myself have held. But why declare
The things forbidden that while the Customs slept
I have crossed to Safety with? For I am There,
And what I would not part with I have kept.

ROBERT FROST

A BLESSING

Just off the highway to Rochester, Minnesota,
Twilight bounds softly forth on the grass.
And the eyes of those two Indian ponies
Darken with kindness.
They have come gladly out of the willows
To welcome my friend and me.
We step over the barbed wire into the pasture
Where they have been grazing all day, alone.
They ripple tensely, they can hardly contain their happiness
That we have come.
They bow shyly as wet swans. They love each other.
There is no loneliness like theirs.
At home once more,
They begin munching the young tufts of spring in the dark-
    ness.
I would like to hold the slenderer one in my arms,
For she has walked over to me
And nuzzled my left hand.
She is black and white,
Her mane falls wild on her forehead,

And the light breeze moves me to caress her long ear
That is delicate as the skin over a girl's wrist.
Suddenly I realize
That if I stepped out of my body I would break
Into blossom.

JAMES WRIGHT

THE FARMER'S TALE

Farmer, farmer, tell me,
My crop is slow to make,
Your wagon goes to market
Seven days a week.

You've melon for your daughter
And berry for your son.
Now by the rain that falls the same,
Why have I none?

Because the rain is equal,
Because the seed is true,
It is not every husbandman
His pulse and pastures grow.

Who sows a marble acre
Six of his seeds will die,
Let him hoe and shelter,
Let him weep and pray,

Let him shield the seventh,
Though market be there none,
Neither maize nor melon,
Neither daughter nor son.

There comes a lusty flower,
But rare, rare.

I cannot tell the color
But people at the Fair

Recall a ruined farmer
Who danced upon a stone
Until it bore that wonder,
The glory of the town,

The envy of the country.
But none could buy that bloom.
He flung it to the farmer's boy
And struck up harvest home.

JULIA RANDALL

THE DREAM

In a dream I was in a tunnel struggling
A chalky tunnel, and torturous place,
With at the end a suggestion of light,
A space of light and gruff old optimistic strokes
For though convulsed, frisked, I felt I would reach the light

And as in a dream things happen without pain,
In a childhood sequence of untractable reality,
In this pleasurable though unpredictable predicament
I struggled, drawn directly by the great light,
The tunnel was merely there, exfoliating.

Then as if angels whisked you, an unseen force
Yet seemingly not a force, for all was fervent balance,
I was in high regions of beautiful world and life,
I visited the extreme palaces, stroked the glowing air,
Went up through hitched forests to a gold plateau

And all was triumph, magnitude, deep vistas,
All was largess of harmonies, freedom of form,
Luminous periodicities in a static realm,

The unimaginable godhead, divine peculiarity,
The child's, the death's-head's unconquerable vanity.

RICHARD EBERHART

ADVENT POEMS, 1963 (7–8)

7

And who shall walk the tides of time
And lift the gates of Paradise?
One with swords upon his tongue
Or one with lilies in his eyes?

A heavy blade lay in a tree.
The legend ran: "Who takes me up
Shall fear no other enemy.
I cut the death-worm from the crop.

I spear the moth.   I shave the rust.
I scatter every sandy house.
I flatten all the heads of lust.
I blind the little eyes of grass."

A child who could not read came by
And laid his hand upon my hand.
Inseparable, then and now,
We walked away across that land,

And begged at many a battened door,
And sang at many a sun-go-down,
Slept once on sand, and once on flower,
And finally, upon a tomb,

I traced this legend: Season me,
Thou Lord who counts the sparrow's quill,
Raise me in time bloom, bird, or tree,
Unsevered from my blood, thy will.

8

This was a dream. I drew that sword,
A feather, from the airy wood,
And walked with peace in all my blood.

The grass stood up along my way
The hawk, with pity in his eye,
Fed, phoenix-like, upon his prey.

This was the sword that cut the dream
Of self, the knife at my birth-string.
By blood alone I walk in time,
Weeping and praising.

JULIA RANDALL

THE GIRL DREAMS THAT SHE IS GISELLE

Beards of the grain, gray-green: the lances
Shiver. I stare up into the dew.
From her white court—enchantress—
The black queen, shimmering with dew,

Floats to me. In the enchainment
Of a travelling and a working wing
She comes shying, sidelong, settling
On the bare grave by the grain.

And I sleep, curled in my cold cave. . . .
Her wands quiver as a nostril quivers:
The gray veilings of the grave
Crumple, my limbs lock, reverse,

And work me, jointed, to the glance
That licks out to me in white fire
And, piercing, whirs *Remember*
Till my limbs catch. Life, life! I dance.

RANDALL JARRELL

THE EYE OF THE STORM

After the battering night, rack and distress—
The waves like monuments above the mast,
Ruin in wind, the flocking of the stays,
And spray dark with the fallen dark—our ship
Careened from the haze, and came to calm at last.

In the storm's eye, all of us breathed again,
Felt the salt sunlight cleaving lip to lip,
Watched water shrink to a circle where the rain
Raised the horizon like a single shore.
We fished our luck out of the morning air.

What place was this?   Whose garden in the sea?
What tiller of foam had plunged his rudder here?
We leaned against the taffrail, and we saw
Blossoms along the keel, an anchorage
For the sea-laid, star-crossed flowers of his rage.

The garland spread behind us and turned white,
And, like a wing, water to starboard rose
And hovered in long streamers, and its mate,
Grown huge to larboard, gathered for a stroke.
Slowly, the bowsprit lifted like a beak.

And while the mock suns wheeled from east to west,
Our lanyards tautened and gave way, and soared,
The skysail mounted to the gulls, the crest
Of the billowing deck came past us, and the strakes
Sprang from themselves like petals to the light,

And the deadlights skimmed astern, and the ripped shrouds
Fluttered beyond the yardarms toward the sun.
Here in the calm, here in our drying hoods,
Athwart the center and the furrow of noon,
We leaped above the water and cried, Love.

DAVID WAGONER

MARINA

Quis hic locus, quae regio, quae mundi plaga?

What seas what shores what grey rocks and what islands
What water lapping the bow
And scent of pine and the woodthrush singing through the fog
What images return
O my daughter.

Those who sharpen the tooth of the dog, meaning
Death
Those who glitter with the glory of the humming-bird, mean-
ing
Death
Those who sit in the stye of contentment, meaning
Death
Those who suffer the ecstasy of the animals, meaning
Death

Are become unsubstantial, reduced by a wind,
A breath of pine, and the woodsong fog
By this grace dissolved in place

What is this face, less clear and clearer
The pulse in the arm, less strong and stronger—
Given or lent? more distant than stars and nearer than the eye

Whispers and small laughter between leaves and hurrying
feet
Under sleep, where all the waters meet.

Bowsprit cracked with ice and paint cracked with heat.
I made this, I have forgotten
And remember.
The rigging weak and the canvas rotten
Between one June and another September.
Made this unknowing, half conscious, unknown, my own.
The garboard strake leaks, the seams need caulking.

This form, this face, this life
Living to live in a world of time beyond me; let me
Resign my life for this life, my speech for that unspoken,
The awakened, lips parted, the hope, the new ships.

What seas what shores what granite islands towards my tim-
   bers
And woodthrush calling through the fog
My daughter.

                              T. S. ELIOT

PSYCHIATRIST'S SONG

Those
Concerning whom they have never spoken and thought never
   to speak;
That place
Hidden, preserved,
That even the exquisite eye of the soul
Cannot completely see.
But they are there:
Those people, and that house, and that evening, seen
Newly above the dividing window sash—
The young will broken
And all time to endure.

Those hours when murderous wounds are made,
Often in joy.

I hear.
But far away are the mango trees (*the mangrove swamps, the
   mandrake root* . . .)
And the thickets of—are they palms?
I watch them as though at the edge of sleep.
I often journey toward them in a boat without oars,
Trusting to rudder and sail.
Coming to the shore, I step out of the boat; I leave it to its
   anchor;

And I walk fearlessly through ripples of both water and sand.
Then the shells and the pebbles are beneath my feet.

Then these, too, recede,
And I am on firm dry land, with, closely waiting,
A hill all sifted over with shade
Wherein the silence waits.

Farewell, phantoms of flesh and of ocean!
Vision of earth
Heal and receive me.

LOUISE BOGAN

DUNS SCOTUS

Striking like lightning to the quick of the real world
Scotus has mined all ranges to their deepest veins:
But where, oh, on what blazing mountain of theology
And in what Sinai's furnace
Did God refine that gold?

Who ruled those arguments in their triumphant order
And armed them with their strict celestial light?
See the lance-lightning, blade-glitter, banner-progress
As love advances, company by company
In sunlit teams his clean embattled reasons,

Until the firmament, with high heavenly marvel
Views in our crystal souls her blue embodiment,
Unfurls a thousand flags above our heads—
It is the music of Our Lady's army!

For Scotus is her theologian,
Nor has there ever been a braver chivalry than his precision.
His thoughts are skies of cloudless peace
Bright as the vesture of her grand aurora
Filled with the rising Christ.

But we, a weak, suspicious generation,
Loving emotion, hating prayer,
We are not worthy of his wisdom.
Creeping like beasts between the mountain's feet
We look for laws in the Arabian dust.
We have no notion of his freedom

Whose acts despise the chains of choice and passion.
We have no love for his beatitude
Whose act renounces motion:
Whose love flies home forever
As silver as felicity,
Working and quiet in the dancelight of an everlasting arrow.

Lady, the image of whose heaven
Sings in the might of Scotus' reasoning:
There is no line of his that has not blazed your glory in the
    schools,
Though in dark words, without romance,
Calling us to swear you our liege.

Language was far too puny for his great theology:
But, oh!   His thought strode through those words
Bright as the conquering Christ
Between the clouds His enemies:
And in the clearing storm and Sinai's dying thunder
Scotus comes out, and shakes his golden locks
And sings like the African sun.

THOMAS MERTON

A BODHISATTVA UNDOES HELL

Because he saw the men of the world
ploughing their fields, sowing the
seed, trafficking, huckstering,
buying and selling, and at the end
winning nothing but bitterness,
For this he was moved to pity . . .

To the figures bathing at the river
Jizo appeared

The sky was full of small fishes
The bodies of the men
twisted in an afternoon
when earth and air were one

With Hell a hard fact
the double lotus
brought the son of heaven
down among us
And the bathers showed their hands
that bore the marks of nails

What Jizo said
was this

Let's bury their lousy hammers
My people
are tired of pain
The world's been crucified
long enough

The rain fell gently on their wounds
The women lugged
big platters of shrimp
to the bathers
when Jizo's diamond
caught the sun

The rest of us
sat at the stone windows
overlooking the river
We saw him climb the hill
and disappear
behind the guardhouse

What he told the guards
was this

Your bosses are men
who darken counsel
with words
But the white sun
carries love
into the world

When Jizo leaned on his stick
the blue lines on his face
were shining with tears
We followed him
into the city
where lilies bled beside a lake

He said

The heart's
a flower
Love
each other
Keep the old
among you

Write the poem
The image
unlocks Hell
Man's joy
makes
his gods

For those who heard him
hatred fell away

We spent the night
with angels
Fishing in the ponds
of Hell

JEROME ROTHENBERG

THE SCARRED GIRL

All glass may yet be whole
She thinks, it may be put together
From the deep flashing of her face.
One moment the windshield held

The countryside, the green
Level fields and the animals,
And these must be restored
To what they were when her brow

Broke into them for nothing, and began
Its sparkling under the gauze.
Though the still, small war for her beauty
Is stitched out of sight and lost,

It is not this field that she thinks of.
It is that her face, buried
And held up inside the slow scars,
Knows how the bright, fractured world

Burns and pulls and weeps
To come together again.
The green meadow lying in fragments
Under the splintered sunlight,

The cattle broken in pieces
By her useless, painful intrusion
Know that her visage contains
The process and hurt of their healing,

The hidden wounds that can
Restore anything, bringing the glass
Of the world together once more,
All as it was when she struck,

All except her. The shattered field
Where they dragged the telescoped car

Off to be pounded to scrap
Waits for her to get up,

For her calm, unimagined face
To emerge from the yards of its wrapping,
Red, raw, mixed-looking but entire,
A new face, an old life,

To confront the pale glass it has dreamed
Made whole and backed with wise silver,
Held in other hands brittle with dread,
A doctor's, a lip-biting nurse's,

Who do not see what she sees
Behind her odd face in the mirror:
The pastures of earth and of heaven
Restored and undamaged, the cattle

Risen out of their jagged graves
To walk in the seamless sunlight
And a newborn countenance
Put upon everything,

Her beauty gone, but to hover
Near for the rest of her life,
And good no nearer, but plainly
In sight, and the only way.

JAMES DICKEY

THE HEROES

When these in all their bravery took the knock
And like obedient children swaddled and bound
Were borne to sleep within the chambered rock,
A splendour broke from that impervious ground,
Which they would never know.   Whence came that greatness?
No fiery chariot whirled them heavenwards, they

Saw no Elysium opening, but the straitness
Of full submission bound them where they lay.

What could that greatness be?   It was not fame.
Yet now they seemed to grow as they grew less,
And where they lay were more than where they had stood.
They did not go to any beatitude.
They were stripped clean of feature, presence, name,
When that strange glory broke from namelessness.

EDWIN MUIR

ODE ON THE DEATH OF PIUS THE TWELFTH

To every season its proper act of joy,
To every age its natural mode of grace,
Each vision its hour, each talent we employ
    Its destined time and place.

I was at Amherst when this great pope died;
The northern year was wearing towards the cold;
The ancient trees were in their autumn pride
    Of russet, flame and gold.

Amherst in Massachusetts in the Fall:
I ranged the college campus to admire
Maple and beech, poplar and ash in all
    Their panoply of fire.

Something that since a child I longed to see,
This miracle of the other hemisphere:
Whole forests in their annual ecstasy
    Waked by the dying year.

Not budding Spring, not Summer's green parade
Clothed in such glory these resplendent trees;
The lilies of the field were not arrayed
    In riches such as these.

Nature evolves their colours as a call,
A lure which serves to fertilize the seed;
How strange then that the splendour of the Fall
        Should serve no natural need

And, having no end in nature, yet can yield
Such exquisite natural pleasure to the eye!
Who could have guessed in summer's green concealed
        The leaf's resolve to die?

Yet from the first spring shoots through all the year,
Masked in the chlorophyll's intenser green,
The feast of crimson was already there,
        These yellows blazed unseen.

Now in the bright October sun the clear
Translucent colours trembled overhead
And as I walked, a voice I chanced to hear
        Announced: The Pope is dead!

A human voice, yet there the place became
Bethel: each bough with pentecost was crowned;
The great trunks rapt in unconsuming flame
        Stood as on holy ground.

I thought of this old man whose life was past,
Who in himself and his great office stood
Against the secular tempest as a vast
        Oak spans the underwood;

Who in the age of Armageddon found
A voice that caused all men to hear it plain,
The blood of Abel crying from the ground
        To stay the hand of Cain;

Who found from that great task small time to spare:
—For him and for mankind the hour was late—
So much to snatch, to save, so much to bear
        That Mary's part must wait,

Until in his last years the change began:
A strange illumination of the heart,
Voices and visions such as mark the man
    Chosen and set apart.

His death, they said, was slow, grotesque and hard,
Yet in that gross decay, until the end
Untroubled in his joy, he saw the Word
    Made spirit and ascend.

Those glorious woods and that triumphant death
Prompted me there to join their mysteries:
This Brother Albert, this great oak of faith,
    Those fire-enchanted trees.

Seven years have passed, and still, at times, I ask
Whether in man, as in those plants, may be
A splendour, which his human virtues mask,
    Not given to us to see?

If to some lives at least there comes a stage
When, all the active man now left behind,
They enter on the treasure of old age,
    This autumn of the mind.

Then, while the heart stands still, beyond desire
The dying animal knows a strange serene:
Emerging in its ecstasy of fire
    The burning soul is seen.

Who sees it? Since old age appears to men
Senility, decrepitude, disease,
What Spirit walks among us, past our ken,
    As we among these trees,

Whose unknown nature, blessed with keener sense
Catches its breath in wonder at the sight
And feels its being flood with that immense
    Epiphany of light?

A. D. HOPE

LAPIS LAZULI

(For Harry Clifton)

I have heard that hysterical women say
They are sick of the palette and fiddle-bow,
Of poets that are always gay,
For everybody knows or else should know
That if nothing drastic is done
Aeroplane and Zeppelin will come out,
Pitch like King Billy bomb-balls in
Until the town lie beaten flat.

All perform their tragic play,
There struts Hamlet, there is Lear,
That's Ophelia, that Cordelia;
Yet they, should the last scene be there,
The great stage curtain about to drop,
If worthy their prominent part in the play,
Do not break up their lines to weep.
They know that Hamlet and Lear are gay;
Gaiety transfiguring all that dread.
All men have aimed at, found and lost;
Black out; Heaven blazing into the head:
Tragedy wrought to its uttermost.
Though Hamlet rambles and Lear rages,
And all the drop-scenes drop at once
Upon a hundred thousand stages,
It cannot grow by an inch or an ounce.

On their own feet they came, or on shipboard,
Camel-back, horse-back, ass-back, mule-back,
Old civilisations put to the sword.
Then they and their wisdom went to rack:
No handiwork of Callimachus,
Who handled marble as if it were bronze,
Made draperies that seemed to rise
When sea-wind swept the corner, stands;
His long lamp-chimney shaped like the stem

Of a slender palm, stood but a day;
All things fall and are built again,
And those that build them again are gay.

Two Chinamen, behind them a third,
Are carved in lapis lazuli,
Over them flies a long-legged bird,
A symbol of longevity;
The third, doubtless a serving-man,
Carries a musical instrument.

Every discoloration of the stone,
Every accidental crack or dent,
Seems a water-course or an avalanche,
Or lofty slope where it still snows
Though doubtless plum or cherry-branch
Sweetens the little half-way house
Those Chinamen climb towards, and I
Delight to imagine them seated there;
There, on the mountain and the sky,
On all the tragic scene they stare.
One asks for mournful melodies;
Accomplished fingers begin to play.
Their eyes mid many wrinkles, their eyes,
Their ancient, glittering eyes, are gay.

WILLIAM BUTLER YEATS

❧ FOUR ❧

Change

The rule of the universe is constancy in Change. Every end is
a beginning. We are familiar with the signs: day follows night, and
night the day; the moon waxes and wanes; winter follows autumn,
and if winter comes, can spring be far behind?; youth grows to
maturity and age, and age gives way to youth; civilizations rise and
fall; The king is dead! Long live the king! The Hero has no sooner
returned from his journey and taken a deep breath than he is off
again, for not to change perpetually is to be stagnant—"the cistern
contains; the fountain overflows." The serpent, time, with its tail
in its mouth, becomes eternity; the more things change, the more
they remain the same; the old patterns persist and recur, there is
nothing new under the sun; and the inexhaustible and indestructible
stuff of life is everywhere to be found in the stream that, while it
slides away, provides. At the end of the fragmentary seventh book
of Spenser's *The Faerie Queene*, the goddess Nature rejects the claim
of the Titaness Mutability to rule over the gods as well as man:

> "*I well consider all that ye have sayd;*
> *And find that all things stedfastnes doe hate*
> *And changed be; yet, being rightly wayd,*
> *They are not changed from their first estate;*
> *But by their change their being doe dilate;*
> *And turning to themselves at length againe,*
> *Doe worke their owne perfection so by fate:*

Then over them Change doth not rule and raigne:
But they raigne over Change, and doe their states maintaine."

Eternity is known to us only through epiphanies in time, and these epiphanies are points on the perfect circle of eternity, which has no beginning and no end.

The paradox of constancy in Change is superbly dramatized in two great myths: that of Demeter and Persephone, and that of the Phoenix. The story of Demeter and Persephone which was once canonical in the Mysteries of Eleusis, deals with a mother and daughter who, as a double character, represent all birth and all destruction, and the balance that must be maintained between them. As a young girl (Kore), Persephone is picking spring flowers in the fair fields of Enna, when she is ravished away by Dis (Hades), the brother of Zeus and the ruler of the underworld. Her mother, Demeter, who is the principle of fertility in all growing things on earth, is frantic with grief at the loss. It is significant and touching that, although she is a goddess, she cannot remember that she has suffered this same sorrow and rage many times before. She cannot understand why her daughter, the vehicle of her own regeneration, has been violently taken from her, and she blames the disaster on the brutal authority of the male, and, in particular, of Zeus, the ruler of the gods and men. Zeus has indeed given his assent to the abduction, for his brother, Hades, loves the girl and longs to have her rule beside him as the Queen of the Underworld. But Zeus cannot permit mankind to die, and he would restore Persephone to Demeter permanently; unfortunately, he finds that she has eaten the Food of the Dead and has therefore unwittingly established an indissoluble link between herself and the Kingdom of the Dead. The best he can do is to permit Persephone's return to the upper world for half or a third of every year. The compromise is effected; Persephone is again the virgin Kore, and her joyous reunion with Demeter brings warm sunlight and life-giving showers to the withered earth. All sorrow is forgotten; but soon the child will be tempted once again to gather flowers in the fields of Enna where her once and future bridegroom, loving her still, again will ravish her away.

The cycle of death and rebirth is eloquently dramatized in an anonymous Old English poem, "The Phoenix," which explicitly links the marvelous bird's life history with the life, death on the cross, and resurrection of the Lord. The home of the Phoenix is a beautiful garden in the East, were "Plants do not perish, / the bright blooms, but the trees ever / stand green, as God bade them." Here the solitary bird lives for a thousand years, greeting the sun each morning with ecstatic song. At the end of this time, the Phoenix becomes aged and gray, and it flies away to the waste land of the earth, where for a time it assumes lordship over the race of birds. Then it seeks out a great tree, far in the West, and high in the branches builds itself a nest of fragrant herbs. In summer, when "the sky's gem," the sun, is at its hottest, the nest is ignited by the "brightness of the sky," and both nest and Phoenix burn to ashes. But the ashes gather into a ball and soon develop into a glorious fledgling, "renewed altogether, again created, / sundered from sin." The reborn Phoenix gathers its own ashes and flies away with them to its native garden, where it buries them. Then it returns triumphantly to earth and, in its "adornments fair beyond birdkind," is the subject of universal praise and song, "the loved first-of-people," until it flies away once again to its fatherland to pass another thousand years in blissful worship of the sun. The second coming of the Phoenix to the earth is by far more joyful than the first, because its own regeneration has in the interim purged and regenerated the earth and its inhabitants. The tree in the West, where the immolation occurs, suggests the Tree of Life in the biblical Eden and, at the same time, the Holy Rood, the Tree on which Christ suffered death to redeem mankind. "About its neck, like the sun's circuit," the rejuvenated Phoenix wears "the brightest of rings woven of feathers." It is, in fact, the sun itself, which is immortal, though it dies in the winter of every year and is reborn in the spring. The ashes of its former self repose in the eternal garden of the East, for its death and everlastingness are inseparable, different aspects of a single abiding power that perpetually changes form and lives, world without end.

Metamorphosis as a natural phenomenon and as metaphor is frequently a vehicle for poems that deal with constancy in Change. Howard Nemerov's dragonfly is "the aged one / imprisoned in the dying child"; and the "brown old man with a green thumb," in Richard Wilbur's "He Was," lives again in the new leaves of the orchard which he had planted with such care, and finds his voice "in the sparrowy air." One is reminded of Ariel's song in *The Tempest*. It is sung to young Prince Ferdinand, who believes that his father, Alonso, has met death by drowning. Literally, he is mistaken, for Alonso is alive and well in another part of the island. But the guilty spirit of the king is being transformed, through the agency of Prospero, into something new and shining:

> *Nothing of him that doth fade*
> *But doth suffer a sea-change*
> *into something rich and strange.*

In the end, having repented for the ills he has done Prospero, the father will be restored to the son, and the son will not only be restored to the father but will bring Miranda with him as a bride-to-be, promising both physical continuity and succession to the throne of Alonso's kingdom.

The concept of the sacrificial female, in the tradition of the Demeter-Persephone story, appears in "In Defense of Felons" (Robert Mezey), "Altarpiece" (R. H. W. Dillard), and "Selene Afterwards" (Archibald MacLeish). In Mezey's poem, the "Cruel hands" of winter, after all, are sweet, "and death is worth / The green and giant labor of the earth." When the priestess La is symbolically sacrificed in "Altarpiece," it would appear that "The sun can never / Rise again," but, to the sound of cymbal and horn, the priestess smiles, and dawn restores the light of day to the world. Again, the lovers of the world are told, in "Selene Afterwards," that "The moon is dead"; and indeed she seems to be so: She has withered in the shriveling cold of space and is reduced to "A Woman's skull," which crumbles, year by year; she lies, as though under water, deep in the "Night shadows of the world." But it would be rash to imagine that the thing that makes us love is truly dead. If ever myth had meaning, it has that meaning still; it is civilizations which crumble, not the experience which their myths distill: "The low moon / Moves in the elms. It will be summer soon. . . ."

The triumph of death (*vide* the poem by Barbara Howes) is to trick us into life again and again. When the sacrificial lamb has been wept for, "Washed and risen / To its own demand / For a defense-less death," its flesh is Easter (John Ciardi, "The Lamb"). Through Holy Communion, or some lay equivalent thereof, we share as best we can in Christ and the Resurrection; every spring, we gather June and store "a heap of fodder in a bin" against the winter (Julia Randall, "The Silo under Angel's Gap"); and when the mountains of the gods sink out of sight at sunset, they have gone into "the fallow dark where blood and dreams / Refashion all the populace of day"; watching the seasons turn and each new day arise from shadow, our bones "Rehearse the garland rising in their clay." Nothing is more fragile than a daisy, and nothing more fiercely determined than the "Heads of the characters," the biological force which sees to the replenishment of the species. Dylan Thomas said it; it is true: "And death shall have no dominion."

THE DRAGONFLY

Under the pond, among rocks
Or in the bramble of the water wood,
He is at home, and feeds the small
Remorseless craving of his dream,

His cruel delight; until in May
The dream transforms him with itself
And from his depths he rises out,
An exile from the brutal night.

He rises out, the aged one
Imprisoned in the dying child,
And spreads his wings to the new sun:
Climbing, he withers into light.

HOWARD NEMEROV

HE WAS

a brown old man with a green thumb:
I can remember the screak on stones of his hoe,
The chug, choke, and high madrigal wheeze
Of the spray-cart bumping below
The sputtery leaves of the apple trees,
But he was all but dumb

Who filled some quarter of the day with sound
All of my childhood long.   For all I heard
Of all his labours, I can now recall
Never a single word
Until he went in the dead of fall
To the drowsy underground,

Having planted a young orchard with so great care
In that last year that none was lost, and May
Aroused them all, the leaves saying the land's
Praise for the livening clay,
And the found voice of his buried hands
Rose in the sparrowy air.

RICHARD WILBUR

IN DEFENSE OF FELONS

Winter will not let go of earth.   The lust
Of a listless sun finds April difficult,
Weakly astonished that frost fights so hard.
The black earth still is tough in my back yard,
The brittle stubble has not begun to melt,
And in the shed, my frozen spade turns rust.

Possibly Winter is afraid of what
The softening soil might turn up to sight—
Perhaps my spade would scrape against a bone,
Perhaps some half-starved animal would moan,
Having endured the long, relentless night—
Possibly Winter is ashamed of that.

How many stiff-furred bodies has she buried,
How many coverts converted into graves
About my house?   All that I want to know
Is underground or underneath of snow.
But circumstantial icicles plunge from the eaves.
I know that Winter is at large, and worried.

Well, late or soon, the sun will have his day
And drive her into hiding, in the north.
And when that trouble's over, there will come
Swallows venturing back to their summer home,
And many citizen flowers will step forth
In the green wake of Winter's getaway.

And what of this felon who is doomed to be
The hack and executioner of Time?
Her cruel hands are sweet, and death is worth
The green and giant labor of the earth—
I call her conscience clear, her breath sublime,
Striving with heat for balance, harmony.

Sometime, not now, in bloody boot and glove,
Stirred by compulsive memories, she will turn
Back to these fields, again and again, until
The earth be driven against heaven's will
To its old asylum, where the sun would burn
Winter and earth to ashes with its love.

ROBERT MEZEY

ALTARPIECE
for Monica

The stone steps, red,
The setting sun and La,
The priestess, robed
In white, the butcher's
Knife, cruel priest,
And—BOOM— the sun,
The drum, the sounding
Gong, the rising knife
Descends.

Her hair was blond,
Long was La's hair

Spread on her shoulders,
Clip, the knife, the grinning
Priest, the swaying
Crowd, the ooh
And ah, a shout:

He has cut her hair.

The dark descends,
The knife, the littered
Stones, her fallen hair,
A tear.

The low chant
Becomes a wail:
The sun can never
Rise again, the drum,
The cymbal and the horn,
The priestess in the night,
The cries, her eyes,
The dawn, she smiles.

R. H. W. DILLARD

MAYAN FESTIVAL

The small pale flower of May
curls her lips with music
and movement of festival.

As long as the Mayas is May,
catching castanet snaps
and feet on clay.

Fiesta day falls, piñatas break open
in the marketplace, and Guatemala in May
burns with toes on red stone clay.
The Mayan crab taps his way in streets,
a blind beggar of many red canes.

He snaps at toes to castanet tunes,
while clicking fingers of Mayan girls
beg monedas on red clay streets.

Mayas last as long as May
and tappings on the clay
of crustacea and cucaracha.

Money clatters on the streets of clay,
silver and copper clink around the niña—
cracks of clay are walkways of the crabs.
They lead Mayas near the coast by tappings,
red canes, clicking fingers,
niñas jingle in festival swaying,
all their pockets lined in silver.
The Mayas last as long as May.

Water is playing about their feet.
Castanets click together,
sounds of crabs and cucaracha.

Mayas last as long as May
the festival moves along the clay
to walkways in the water.

GAYLE JOHNSON

SELENE AFTERWARDS

The moon is dead, you lovers!

She who walked
Naked upon the dark Ægean, she
Who under Ida in the beach groves mocked
The rutting satyrs, she who secretly,
Leaving below her the slow lifting sea,
Climbed through the woods of Latmos to the bed
Of the eternal sleeper—she is dead,

Dead, you lovers!   I have seen her face.
The sun rose by St.-Etienne.   She fled
Half turning back (as though the plunge of space
Over the world's rim frightened her) her head
And stared and stared at me.   Her face was dead.
It was a woman's face but dead as stone
And leper white and withered to the bone.

It was a woman's skull the shriveling cold
Out there among the stars had withered dry
And its dry white was mottled with dry mould.
It was a long dead skull the caustic lye
Of time had eaten clean, and in the sky
As under the cold water of a lake
Lay crumbling year by year, white flake by flake,

Scabious, scurfy.   Oh, look down, look down
You lovers, through that water where there swing
Night shadows of the world.   Look deep, deep.
     Drown
Your eyes in deepness.   Look!   There lies the thing
That made you love, that maddened you!
                            Oh sing,
Sing in the fields, you lovers.   The low moon ·
Moves in the elms.   It will be summer soon.   . . .

ARCHIBALD MAC LEISH

THE CAT AND THE MOON

The cat went here and there
And the moon spun round like a top,
And the nearest kin of the moon,
The creeping cat, looked up.
Black Minnaloushe stared at the moon,
For, wander and wail as he would,
The pure cold light in the sky
Troubled his animal blood.
Minnaloushe runs in the grass

Lifting his delicate feet.
Do you dance, Minnaloushe, do you dance?
When two close kindred meet,
What better than call a dance?
Maybe the moon may learn,
Tired of that courtly fashion,
A new dance turn.
Minnaloushe creeps through the grass
From moonlit place to place,
The sacred moon overhead
Has taken a new phase.
Does Minnaloushe know that his pupils
Will pass from change to change,
And that from round to crescent,
From crescent to round they range?
Minnaloushe creeps through the grass
Alone, important and wise,
And lifts to the changing moon
His changing eyes.

WILLIAM BUTLER YEATS

THE TRIUMPH OF DEATH

Illusion forms before us like a grove
Of aspen hazing all the summer air
As we approach a new plateau of love.

With discs of light and shade, vibration of
Leaf-candelabra, dim, all-tremulous there,
Illusion forms before us like a grove

And bends in welcome: with each step we move
Nearer, quick with desire, quick to dare.
As we approach a new plateau of love,

New passion, new adventure wait above
And call to our drumming blood; all unaware
Illusion forms before us like a grove

In a mirage, we reach out to take Love
In our arms, compelled by one another's stare.
As we approach a new plateau of love

The aspen sigh in mockery: then have
We come this way before? Staining the air,
Illusion forms before us like a grove
As we approach a new plateau of love.

BARBARA HOWES

THE SECOND TRY

> Goethe: "The eternal feminine draws us onward."

I

Make me a world, girl; make as terra made;
Be she, be starting over what went stale.
One fingertip of femininity—
To pat what musses and to flounce what twirls—
Could spruce whole planets up. The god-spell then:
One minute's spell you have to groom a globe
Any old kind of way. Start fussing, wish.
Your slightest fidget reigns; I don't know why
Except that life's been loaned a second try.

2

A coaxing of cupped palms—just so—from clay,
Dark sting of cheeks, strict wildness of the voice,
And now all's underway. Already swamp
Twists free—all palm and saurian—out of sea;
Your reeking, waddling firstlings play. Enough!
Now sponge the slate, make room for—use your fancy
What to make room for. Monsters cleared away,
Build phoenix, pegasus, and unicorn;
Hurry, don't waste brief godhood; build them, plan
Such symbols of your role as Muse to man.

3

At once kaleidoscopes of matter rattle
A second chance the second time around.
Swamps groan, hills labor, new life comes to life
Beyond old dowdy domesticities.
But what familiar sound is this (cluckcluck)?
Incredible priestess, stop!—what have you loosed?
With housewife-fingers, buxom terra tidies
A landscape for gallina of the roost.

PETER VIERICK

THE LAST ARRIVAL

The last arrival in the furthest country,
All he saw he saw as mystery.
He to doorknob, counterpane and incised stone
That chanced to notice him appeared
Too familiar for comment.

And so they got used to one another,
The mysteries and the familiar.
In time all mysteries became familiars.
He in long familiarity
Disowned their secrets of their mystery.

Ceasing to notice him, they left as though
By prearrangement for the nearest country.
Someone will be the first to find that country,
In reciprocity for its reality
Will learn new names of all the mysteries

And write such full particulars in letters home
Unlike all correspondence known,
Since he with counterpane, doorknob and cut stone
Will parse that language of their own
To blurt out mysteries in ours, where all's familiar.

DANIEL HOFFMAN

THE SILO UNDER ANGEL'S GAP

The silo under Angel's Gap
Through garland orchards breaks in the morning light.
Forty times by the sun
My eyes have gathered June
And stored a heap of fodder in a bin.

Stalk over stalk, the green turned down to gold:
Whatever beat once on the bloody field,
Or split the roof of air.
Dido is there,
And the rag doll I murdered in the cold.

All mountains shrivel to some sort of food,
Eryx and Andes, Ida, Otter Peaks.
Mad David helps his eyes
To Adam's husbandries.
A tortured Jew translated by the Greeks

Leans out from heaven in pitiless mockery
Of the coarse bread and the raw dreggy wine,
Shadows that fire the gut
Until death puts them out
To feed the shadowy fish and Circe's swine.

I take these shadowy hills to fill my eye.
Shadow on shadow falls till it come night.
Helicon, Everest,
And Woody's barn at last
Ride with the moonless meadow out of sight

Into the fallow dark where blood and dreams
Refashion all the populace of day.
And forty bones that shook
When Eden's summer broke
Rehearse the garland rising in their clay.

JULIA RANDALL

THE LAMB

A month before Easter
Came the time of the lamb
Staked on my lawn
To frisk and feed and be
My tenderest playmate,
Sweeter for being
Sudden and perilous.

Fed from my hand,
Brushed by my love,
An acrid and tangled wool
Grew clumsy and cardinal.
The lamb is a beast of knees.
A thin and tipsy chant
Quavers in it.

Year by year the lamb
Danced the black lenten season.
On the Thursday of sorrow
It disappeared.
On the Friday of blood I knew
What business was in the cellar
And wept a little.

But ah came Easter
My lamb, my sufferer, rose,
Rose from the charnel cellar,
Glowed golden brown
On religious plenty.
How gravely he was broken,
Sprigged for a bridal.

I praise the soil
In the knuckle and habit
Of my feeding parents
Who knew anciently
How the holy and edible

Are one, are life, must be loved
And surrendered.

My tears for the lamb
Were the bath it sprang from
Washed and risen
To its own demand
For a defenseless death.
After the lamb had been wept for
Its flesh was Easter.

JOHN CIARDI

COME GREEN AGAIN

If what heals can bless
Can what blesses heal?
And all come green again
That was bodied forth
Years and years ago?
Years before my time.

Yet things I deepest learned
Turn into memory
As though no man's creation
But enlarges mine;
As though no man's existence
But was also mine
In its lonesomeness.

Henry Thoreau bent
In his boat on Walden Pond
Whistling his wooden flute
Under midnight stars
Across the stars in the water.

Hawthorne and Melville parting
At night in Liverpool,
Parting on a rainy corner
For the final time,
Something unsaid between them.

Mark Twain in moonlight
Standing in his Hartford house,
That wounded, beautiful man,
His hands at his white hair
While he sang "Nobody knows
The troubles I see but Jesus."

Then in broad daylight
The ladies of Camden drawing
Their skirts and kids aside
To avoid the dirty man
As Whitman hobbled past,
His basket on his arm
Filled with his book for sale.

Can such existences
Help but heal our hearts
Or such lonesomeness
Help but bless in us
That everlasting change
Which is our changelessness
And our humbleness?
And all come green again.

What I have learned enough
To have as air to breathe
Returns as memory
Of undiminished love:
That no man's creation
But enlarges me
O all come green again.

WINFIELD TOWNLEY SCOTT

BIRD AND BEAR

I looked through my black window into black
And saw the great bear on his endless track

That leads him round the pole, back to his start,
Until the hatching sun shall break his heart

He paces in his circle through our sleep
Restless for his own that's long and deep,
Stays till the sky becomes a cave of light,
Retreats into his blazing, brilliant night.

Now comes the golden bird which flies its way
As if a thousand years were but a day,
Whose eye sheds light in watching busy men
And molting, drops to feed its fire again,

In the tall tree of its death and birth,
That stands in Memphis underneath the earth,
It finds the silence of the song it sings
And into ashes folds its glistening wings.

Then from the winter of cold hungry rest
The bear will rise as from a flaming nest
To transfix with a bright but lightless eye
The dreaming men who sleep beneath the sky;

Not as the bird in seeing to create
But, watching through the dark half of their fate,
To see that sleeping eyes shall always find
The black beast at the bottom of the mind.

The bird can keep the dream that is the day,
But when its time is run, it cannot stay.
Behind the daylight sky I see in black
The bear careening slowly on his track.

                                                    JANE GENTRY

DIRECTIVE

Back out of all this now too much for us,
Back in a time made simple by the loss
Of detail, burned, dissolved, and broken off

Like graveyard marble sculpture in the weather,
There is a house that is no more a house
Upon a farm that is no more a farm
And in a town that is no more a town.
The road there, if you'll let a guide direct you
Who only has at heart your getting lost,
May seem as if it should have been a quarry—
Great monolithic knees the former town
Long since gave up pretense of keeping covered.
And there's a story in a book about it:
Besides the wear of iron wagon wheels
The ledges show lines ruled southeast-northwest,
The chisel work of an enormous Glacier
That braced his feet against the Arctic Pole.
You must not mind a certain coolness from him
Still said to haunt this side of Panther Mountain.
Nor need you mind the serial ordeal
Of being watched from forty cellar holes
As if by eye pairs out of forty firkins.
As for the woods' excitement over you
That sends light rustle rushes to their leaves,
Charge that to upstart inexperience.
Where were they all not twenty years ago?
They think too much of having shaded out
A few old pecker-fretted apple trees.
Make yourself up a cheering song of how
Someone's road home from work this once was,
Who may be just ahead of you on foot
Or creaking with a buggy load of grain.
The height of the adventure is the height
Of country where two village cultures faded
Into each other.   Both of them are lost.
And if you're lost enough to find yourself
By now, pull in your ladder road behind you
And put a sign up CLOSED to all but me.
Then make yourself at home.   The only field
Now left's no bigger than a harness gall.
First there's the children's house of make-believe,
Some shattered dishes underneath a pine,
The playthings in the playhouse of the children.
Weep for what little things could make them glad.

Then for the house that is no more a house,
But only a belilaced cellar hole,
Now slowly closing like a dent in dough.
This was no playhouse but a house in earnest.
Your destination and your destiny's
A brook that was the water of the house,
Cold as a spring as yet so near its source,
Too lofty and original to rage.
(We know the valley streams that when aroused
Will leave their tatters hung on barb and thorn.)
I have kept hidden in the instep arch
Of an old cedar at the waterside
A broken drinking goblet like the Grail
Under a spell so the wrong ones can't find it,
So can't get saved, as Saint Mark says they mustn't.
(I stole the goblet from the children's playhouse.)
Here are your waters and your watering place.
Drink and be whole again beyond confusion.

ROBERT FROST

ON THE BEACH AT NIGHT

On the beach at night,
Stands a child with her father,
Watching the east, the autumn sky.

Up through the darkness,
While ravening clouds, the burial clouds, in black masses
    spreading,
Lower sullen and fast athwart and down the sky,
Amid a transparent clear belt of ether yet left in the east,
Ascends large and calm the lord-star Jupiter,
And nigh at hand, only a very little above,
Swim the delicate sisters the Pleiades.

From the beach the child holding the hand of her father,
Those burial-clouds that lower victorious soon to devour all,
Watching, silently weeps.

Weep not, child,
Weep not, my darling,
With these kisses let me remove your tears,
The ravening clouds shall not long be victorious,
They shall not long possess the sky, they devour the stars only
    in apparition,
Jupiter shall emerge, be patient, watch again another night, the
    Pleiades shall emerge,
They are immortal, all those stars both silvery and golden shall
    shine out again,
The great stars and the little ones shall shine out again, they
    endure,
The vast immortal suns and the long-enduring pensive moons
    shall again shine.

Then dearest child mournest thou only for Jupiter?
Considerest thou alone the burial of the stars?

Something there is,
(With my lips soothing thee, adding I whisper,
I give thee the first suggestion, the problem and indirection,)
Something there is more immortal even than the stars,
(Many the burials, many the days and nights, passing away,)
Something that shall endure longer even than lustrous Jupiter,
Longer than sun or any revolving satellite,
Or the radiant sisters the Pleiades.

WALT WHITMAN

AND DEATH SHALL HAVE NO DOMINION

And death shall have no dominion.
Dead men naked they shall be one
With the man in the wind and the west moon;
When their bones are picked clean and the clean bones gone,
They shall have stars at elbow and foot;
Though they go mad they shall be sane,
Though they sink through the sea they shall rise again;
Though lovers be lost love shall not;
And death shall have no dominion.

And death shall have no dominion.
Under the windings of the sea
They lying long shall not die windily;
Twisting on racks when sinews give way,
Strapped to a wheel, yet they shall not break;
Faith in their hands shall snap in two,
And the unicorn evils run them through;
Split all ends up they shan't crack;
And death shall have no dominion.

And death shall have no dominion.
No more may gulls cry at their ears
Or waves break loud on the seashores;
Where blew a flower may a flower no more
Lift its head to the blows of the rain;
Though they be mad and dead as nails,
Heads of the characters hammer through daisies;
Break in the sun till the sun breaks down,
And death shall have no dominion.

DYLAN THOMAS

Bibliography

Background Reading

The most important sources of contemporary poetry in the mythic tradition are Greek and Roman myth, the Bible, and certain works of elder poets in the western literary tradition. The following lists of background materials are offered for the convenience of instructors who may wish to precede or accompany study of *Hero's Way* with readings in myth and earlier literature. Of course, the lists given below are highly selective and include only those items which (1) seem most useful to literary study in general, and (2) have particular relevance to the poems and thematic structure of *Hero's Way*.

Figures of Greek and Roman Mythology

AENEAS (cf. Cumaean Sibyl, Dido, Turnus)
APHRODITE (Venus; cf. Adonis)
APOLLO (cf. Asclepius, Phaethon, Daphne)
ARES (Mars)
ARTEMIS (Diana, Hecate; cf. Actaeon, Endymion)
ATALANTA
ATHENE (Minerva)
CASSANDRA
CENTAURS

TEREUS (cf. Philomela)

THESEUS (cf. Ariadne, the Minotaur, Phaedra, Hippolyta, Hippolytus)

TIRESIAS

TITHONUS

TRITON

URANUS

ZEUS (Jupiter, Jove; cf. Leda, Europa, Danaë, Semele)

Biblical Materials

Abraham and Isaac

Adam and Eve (the creation, naming of the animals, temptation and fall)

Cain and Abel

Daniel in the lion's den

David (cf. Goliath, Saul, Bathsheba)

Ecclesiastes

Jacob (cf. Esau, Laban, wrestling with the angel)

The Book of Job

The Gospel According to St. John

Jonah

Lazarus

The Gospel According to St. Luke

Mary Magdalene

The Magi

The Gospel According to St. Matthew

Moses (cf. the burning bush, manna, striking water from stone, the epiphany on Mount Sinai)

Nebuchadnezzar

Noah and the flood

St. Paul: *The First Epistle to the Corinthians*

The prodigal son

The Proverbs

The Book of Psalms

The Revelation of St. John the Divine

The Book of Ruth

Samson and Dalilah

The Song of Solomon

Works of Literature

Aeschylus. *The Oresteia*

Anonymous. *Beowulf, The Phoenix, Sir Gawain and the Green Knight, The Pearl, Everyman*

Blake, William. *The Marriage of Heaven and Hell, The Mental Traveller, Songs of Innocence and Experience, The Book of Thel, Tiriel*

Boethius. *The Consolation of Philosophy*

Browning, Robert. *The Ring and the Book*

Bunyan, John. *Pilgrim's Progress*

Carroll, Lewis. *Alice in Wonderland* and *Through the Looking Glass*

Chaucer. *The Canterbury Tales* (especially, *The General Prologue, The Wife of Bath's Prologue* and *Tale, The Pardoner's Prologue* and *Tale, The Clerk's Tale*), *Troilus and Criseyde*

Conrad, Joseph. *Heart of Darkness, The Secret Sharer*

Coleridge, S. T. *Cristabel, The Rime of the Ancient Mariner*

Dante. *La Vita Nuova, The Divine Comedy*

Eliot, T. S. "The Love Song of J. Alfred Prufrock," *The Waste Land*

Euripides. *Hippolytus*

Goethe. *Faust* (Parts One and Two)

Golding, William. *Lord of the Flies*

Grimm, Jacob and Wilhelm. *Cinderella, The Frog Prince, Little Briar Rose*

Hesiod. *Theogony*

Homer. *The Iliad, The Odyssey*

Kafka, Franz. *The Castle, The Trial*

Keats, John. *Hyperion, Lamia,* "Ode on a Grecian Urn"

Malory. *Morte d'Arthur*

Melville, Herman. *The Confidence Man, Mardi, Moby Dick, The Piazza Tales*

Milton. *Paradise Lost, Samson Agonistes*

Ovid. *Metamorphoses*

Plato. *The Apology, The Republic, The Symposium*

Salinger, J. D. *The Catcher in the Rye*

Shakespeare. *Antony and Cleopatra, As You Like It, Hamlet, King Lear, Macbeth, Measure for Measure, The Merchant of*

Venice, A Midsummer Night's Dream, Much Ado about Nothing, Othello, Romeo and Juliet, The Sonnets, The Tempest, "Venus and Adonis," *The Winter's Tale*

Shelley, Percy B. *Prometheus Unbound*

Sophocles. *Oedipus, Antigone, Oedipus at Colonus*

Spenser, Edmund. *The Faerie Queene*

Stevenson, R. L. *The Strange Case of Dr. Jekyll and Mr. Hyde*

Swift, Jonathan. *Gulliver's Travels*

Tennyson, Lord Alfred. *The Idylls of the King,* "Merlin and Vivien," "Tithonus"

Tolkien, J. R. R. *The Lord of the Rings*

Twain, Mark. *Huckleberry Finn*

Virgil. *The Aeneid*

White, T. H. *The Once and Future King*

Whitman, Walt. *Leaves of Grass*

Wilde, Oscar. *The Portrait of Dorian Gray*

Wordsworth. "Ode on Intimations of Immortality," *The Prelude*

REFERENCE WORKS

Readers will find it interesting and profitable, in connection with poetry and fiction in the mythic tradition, to look into certain works of mythography, anthropology, literary criticism, and psychology. The list that follows consists largely of books which have proven useful to the editor and his students in literature and writing classes. Most of the titles are available in paperback.

Bettelheim, Bruno. *Symbolic Wounds: Puberty Rites and the Envious Male.* (Collier Books.) New York: The Macmillan Company, 1962.

Bodkin, Maud. *Archetypal Patterns in Poetry: Psychological Studies of Imagination.* (Oxford Paperbacks.) London: Oxford University Press, Inc., 1960.

    One of the first books, and still one of the best, to examine in detail certain mythic patterns in poetry and to consider their counterparts in the unconscious mind.

Campbell, Joseph. *The Flight of the Wild Gander: Explorations in the Mythological Dimension.* New York: The Viking Press, Inc., 1969.

——. *The Hero with a Thousand Faces.* Bollingen Series, No. 17. (Meridian Books.) New York: World Publishing Company, 1956.
The best available introduction to representative myths of all ages and cultures, the mythic pattern to which they are all related, and their significance to human experience. Recommended for use in conjunction with *Hero's Way.*
All books in the Bollingen Series are available from Princeton University Press; however, I have listed paperback editions issued by other publishers where these are obtainable.

——. *Primitive Mythology.* Vol. I of *The Masks of God.*   4 vols. New York: The Viking Press, Inc., 1959.

——. *Oriental Mythology.* Vol. II of *The Masks of God.*   4 vols. New York: The Viking Press, Inc., 1962.

——. *Occidental Mythology.* Vol. III of *The Masks of God.*   4 vols. New York: The Viking Press, Inc., 1964.

——. *Creative Mythology.* Vol. IV of *The Masks of God.*   4 vols. New York: The Viking Press, Inc., 1968.
"How modern mythology has discarded conventional symbols and adopted new ones arising from the unconscious."

——, ed. *Pagan and Christian Mysteries: Papers from the Eranos Yearbooks.* Bollingen Series, No. 30. (Harper Torchbooks.) New York: Harper & Row, Publishers, 1963.

Cassirer, Ernst. *Language and Myth.* Translated by Susan Langer. New York: Dover Publications, Inc., 1946.

——. *Mythical Thought.* Translated by Ralph Manheim. Vol. II of *The Philosophy of Symbolic Forms.*   3 vols. (Yale Paperbacks.) New Haven: Yale University Press, 1955.

Eliade, Mircea. *Cosmos and History: The Myth of the Eternal Return.* Translated by Willard R. Trask. Bollingen Series, No. 46. (Harper Torchbooks.) New York: Harper & Row, Publishers, 1959.

——. *Images and Symbols.* Translated by Philip Mairet. New York: Sheed & Ward, 1961.

——. *Myth and Reality.* Translated by Willard R. Trask. (Harper Torchbooks.) New York: Harper & Row, Publishers, 1963.

——. *Myths, Dreams, and Mysteries: The Encounter Between Contemporary Faiths and Archaic Realities.* Translated by Philip Mairet. (Harper Torchbooks.) New York: Harper & Row, Publishers, 1961.

————. *Rites and Symbols of Initiation: The Mysteries of Birth and Rebirth.* Translated by Willard R. Trask. (Harper Torchbooks.) New York: Harper & Row, Publishers, 1965.

————. *The Sacred and the Profane: The Nature of Religion.* Translated by Willard R. Trask. (Harper Torchbooks.) New York: Harper & Row, Publishers, 1961.

Fordham, Frieda. *Introduction to Jung's Psychology.* (Pelican Books.) Baltimore: Penguin Books, Inc., 1953.

Frazer, Sir James G. *The Magical Origin of Kings.* New York: Barnes & Noble, Inc., 1968.

————. *The New Golden Bough.* Edited by Theodor H. Gaster. (Mentor Books.) New York: New American Library, Inc., n.d.
    A condensation of the classical study of sacred kingship and of the persistence of the tradition in folk observances to the present day. Essential to studies of the Father in myth and literature.

————. *Psyche's Task: A Discourse Concerning the Influence of Superstition on the Growth of Institutions.* New York: Barnes & Noble, Inc., 1968.

Freud, Sigmund. *On Creativity and the Unconscious: Papers on the Psychology of Art, Literature, Love, Religion.* (Harper Torchbooks.) New York: Harper & Row, Publishers, 1958.

————. *On Dreams.* Edited and translated by James Strachey. (Norton Library.) New York: W. W. Norton & Company, Inc., 1962.

————. *The Ego and the Id.* Translated by Joan Riviere. Edited by James Strachey. (Norton Library.) New York: W. W. Norton & Company, Inc., 1961.

————. *General Selection from the Works of Sigmund Freud.* Edited by John Rickman. (Anchor Books.) New York: Doubleday & Company, Inc., 1957.

————. *The Interpretation of Dreams.* Translated by James Strachey. (Discus Books.) New York: Avon Books, 1965.
    Still a good and indispensable introduction to the subject.

————. *Totem and Taboo.* Edited and translated by James Strachey. (Norton Library.) New York: W. W. Norton & Company, Inc., 1952.
    The subtitle of the original edition was *Concepts of Agreement Between the Mental Lives of Savages and Neurotics.* Useful for studies of the father-son relationship.

Fromm, Erich. *The Dogma of Christ and Other Essays on Religion, Psychology and Culture.* (Anchor Books.) New York: Doubleday & Company, Inc., 1966.

――――. *The Forgotten Language: An Introduction to the Understanding of Dreams, Fairy Tales, and Myths.* (Evergreen Books.) New York: Grove Press, Inc., 1957.
An interesting and readable account of metaphor as language in dream and story (*e.g., Little Red Riding Hood*).

――――. *Psychoanalysis and Religion.* (Yale Paperbacks.) New Haven: Yale University Press, 1950.

Frye, Northrop. *The Anatomy of Criticism: Four Essays.* New York: Atheneum Publishers, 1966.
An absorbing book which has formed the basis for modern archetypal criticism of literature.

――――. *Fables of Identity: Studies in Poetic Mythology.* (Harbinger Books.) New York: Harcourt, Brace & World, Inc., 1963.
Includes essays on *The Winter's Tale, Lycidas, Finnegan's Wake*, Stevens, Blake, Dickinson.

――――. *The Return of Eden: Five Essays on Milton's Epics.* Toronto: University of Toronto Press, 1965.

――――, Knights, L. C., *et al. Myth and Symbol: Critical Approaches and Applications. 15 Essays.* (Bison Books.) Omaha: University of Nebraska Press, 1963.

Gaster, Theodor H. *Thespis: Ritual, Myth and Drama in the Ancient Near East.* (Harper Torchbooks.) New York: Harper & Row, Publishers, 1966.

――――. *The Oldest Stories in the World.* (Beacon Paperbacks.) Boston: Beacon Press, 1958.
The myths and legends here included—Babylonian, Hittite, Canaanite—are not only ancient but extremely interesting. Helpful background comments and notes by the author.

Gennep, Arnold von. *The Rites of Passage.* Translated by M. Vizedom and G. Caffee. (Phoenix Books.) Chicago: University of Chicago Press, 1960.

Ghiselin, Brewster, ed. *The Creative Process.* (Mentor Books.) New York: New American Library, Inc., n.d.

Graves, Robert. *Adam's Rib and Other Anomalous Elements in the Hebrew Creation Myth.* New York: Thomas Yoseloff, Inc., 1958.

————. *The Greek Myths.* 2 vols. Baltimore: Penguin Books, Inc., 1955.

A well-organized, learned, and somewhat eccentric work. It is worth reading, if only for the introduction, the bibliographical references, and the entertaining retelling of the mythic stories. As in all of Graves' work, emphasis falls upon the role of the Lady Goddess.

————. *The White Goddess: A Historical Grammar of Poetic Myth.* (Noonday Press.) New York: Farrar, Straus & Giroux, Inc., 1966.

A rambling and eclectic treatise which graphically conveys Graves' quasi-religious view of the Lady Goddess as Muse.

Guerard, A. J., ed. *Stories of the Double.* (Preceptor Books.) Philadelphia: J. B. Lippincott Co., 1967.

A handy basic collection of stories in a genre which invites study by persons interested in myth and literature.

Hamilton, Edith. *Mythology.* (Mentor Books.) New York: The New American Library, 1953.

Probably the best inexpensive handbook of mythology. Recommended for use with *Hero's Way.*

Harrison, Jane Ellen. *Ancient Art and Ritual.* New York: Henry Holt & Co., 1913.

————. *Mythology.* (Harbinger Books.) New York: Harcourt, Brace & World, Inc., 1963.

————. *Prolegomena to the Study of Greek Religion.* (Meridian Books.) New York: World Publishing Company, 1955.

————. *Themis: A Study of the Social Origins of Greek Religion.* (Meridian Books.) New York: World Publishing Company, 1962.

Henderson, Joseph L. *Thresholds of Initiation.* Middletown, Connecticut: Wesleyan University Press, 1967.

————, and Oakes, Maud. *The Wisdom of the Serpent: The Myths of Death, Rebirth, and Resurrection.* ("Patterns of Myth" Series.) New York: George Braziller, Inc., 1963.

Herzog, Edgar. *Psyche and Death: Archaic Myths and Modern Dreams in Analytical Psychology.* (Jung Foundation Books.) New York: G. P. Putnam's Sons, 1967.

Hoffman, Daniel. *Barbarous Knowledge: Myth in the Poetry of Yeats,*

Graves and Muir. (Oxford Paperbacks.) London: Oxford University Press, Inc., 1967.

Hoffman, Frederick J. *Freudianism and the Literary Mind.* Baton Rouge: Louisiana State University Press, 1957.

————. *Imagination's New Beginning: Theology and Modern Literature.* South Bend, Indiana: University of Notre Dame Press, 1967.

————. *The Mortal No: Death and the Modern Imagination.* Princeton: Princeton University Press, 1964.

Hooke, Samuel Henry. *In the Beginning.* London: Oxford University Press, Inc., 1947.

————. *The Labyrinth: Further Studies in the Relation Between Myth and Ritual in the Ancient World.* New York: The Macmillan Company, 1935.

————, ed. *Myth, Ritual, and Kingship: Essays on the Theory and Practice of Kingship in the Ancient Near East and in Israel.* London: Oxford University Press, Inc., 1958.

————. *The Resurrection of Christ: As History and Experience.* New York: Hillary House Publishers, 1967.

Hughes, Pennethorne. *Witchcraft.* (Pelican Books.) Baltimore: Penguin Books, Inc., 1965.

Jacobi, Jolande. *Complex / Archetype / Symbol in the Psychology of C. G. Jung.* Bollingen Series, No. 57. (Pantheon Books.) New York: Random House, Inc., 1959.

————. *The Psychology of C. G. Jung.* Translated by Ralph Manheim. New Haven: Yale University Press, 1963.

————. *The Way of Individuation.* New York: Harcourt, Brace & World, Inc., 1967.
      An explanation of the Jungian concept, "the achievement of wholeness."

James, E. O. *The Cult of the Mother Goddess.* New York: Barnes & Noble, Inc., 1961.

————. *Seasonal Feasts and Festivals.* (University Paperbacks.) New York: Barnes & Noble, Inc., 1963.

Jung, Carl G. *Aion: Researches into the Phenomenology of the Self.* Translated by R. F. C. Hull. Vol. IX, Pt. 2 of *Collected Works.*

Edited by G. Adler, *et al.* 17 vols. Princeton: Princeton University Press, 1968.

———. *The Archetypes and the Collective Unconscious.* Translated by R. F. C. Hull. Vol. IX, Pt. 1 of *Collected Works.* Edited by G. Adler, *et al.* 17 vols. Princeton: Princeton University Press, 1968.

———. *Man and His Symbols.* New York: Dell Publishing Co., Inc., 1968.

———. *Psyche and Symbol.* Edited by Violet S. de Laszlo. (Anchor Books.) New York: Doubleday & Company, Inc., 1958.
An excellent introductory selection of Jung's writings. Cf., especially, the opening selection from *Aion.*

———. *Psychology and Alchemy.* Translated by R. F. C. Hull. Vol. XII of *Collected Works.* Edited by G. Adler, *et al.* 17 vols. Princeton: Princeton University Press, 1968.
A fascinating study of science and symbolism.

———. *Psychology and Religion: West and East.* Vol. XI of *Collected Works.* (Yale Paperbacks.) New Haven: Yale University Press, 1960.

———. *The Spirit in Man, Art, and Literature.* Translated by R. F. C. Hull. Vol. XV of *Collected Works.* Edited by G. Adler, *et al.* 17 vols. Princeton: Princeton University Press, 1966.

———. *Symbols of Transformation: An Analysis of the Prelude to a Case of Schizophrenia.* Vol. V of *Collected Works.* 2 vols. (Harper Torchbooks.) New York: Harper & Row, Publishers, 1962.
Perhaps the most coherently detailed account ever made of a long sequence of dreams.

———. *Two Essays on Analytical Psychology.* Vol. VII of *Collected Works.* (Meridian Books.) New York: World Publishing Company, 1956.
An introduction to, among other things, the theory of the introvert and the extrovert.

———, and Kerényi, C. *Essays on a Science of Mythology. The Myths of the Divine Child and the Divine Maiden.* Bollingen Series, No. 22. (Harper Torchbooks.) New York: Harper & Row, Publishers, 1963.

The essays on the Kore-Demeter myth are of particular interest, as this myth is prototypically feminine and provides a needed counterbalance to the usual emphasis upon the male hero as protagonist.

————, and Pauli, W. *The Interpretation of Nature and the Psyche.* Bollingen Series, No. 51. (Pantheon Books.) New York: Random House, Inc., 1955.

Kerényi, Carl. *The Heroes of the Greeks.* (Evergreen Books.) New York: Grove Press, 1952.

————. *Prometheus: Archetypal Image of Human Existence.* Translated by Ralph Manheim. Vol. I of *Archetypal Images in Greek Religion.* 3 vols. Bollingen Series, No. 65. (Pantheon Books.) New York: Random House, Inc., 1963.

Lesser, Simon O. *Fiction and the Unconscious.* (Vintage Books.) New York: Random House, Inc., 1962.

Long, Charles H. *Alpha: The Myths of Creation.* ("Patterns of Myth" Series.) (Collier Books.) New York: The Macmillan Company, 1969.

Lucas, F. L. *Literature and Psychology.* (Ann Arbor Paperbacks.) Ann Arbor, Michigan: University of Michigan Press, 1957.

Malin, Irving, ed. *Psychoanalysis and American Fiction.* (Dutton Paperback.) New York: E. P. Dutton & Co., Inc., 1965.

Mullahy, Patrick. *Oedipus: Myth and Complex. A Review of Psychoanalytic Theory.* (Evergreen Books.) New York: Grove Press, 1955.

Murray, Gilbert. *Five Stages of Greek Religion.* (Anchor Books.) New York: Doubleday & Company, Inc., 1955.

Murray, Henry A., ed. *Myth and Myth-Making: A Symposium of Mythology in Religion, Literature, Psychology, Politics, and Other Aspects of Society.* (Beacon Paperback.) Boston: Beacon Press, Inc., n.d.
    Includes essays by Kluckhohn, Rieff, McLuhan, and others.

Murray, Margaret. *The God of the Witches.* London: Oxford University Press, 1952.
    This and the following work present a detailed account of the pre-Christian cult which survived into Christian times and, according to Miss Murray, claimed adherents in high places.

————. *The Witch-Cult in Western Europe: A Study in Anthropology.* London: Oxford University Press, 1962.

Neumann, Erich. *Amor and Psyche: The Psychic Development of the Feminine. A Commentary on the Tale by Apuleius.* Princeton: Princeton University Press, 1956.
　　The story of Cupid and Psyche, from Apuleius' *The Golden Ass*, is reprinted here and analyzed in detail as a metaphoric embodiment of feminine psychology. A good story and a cogent analysis.

————. *Art and the Creative Unconscious: Four Essays.* Bollingen Series, No. 61. Princeton: Princeton University Press, 1959.

————. *The Great Mother. An Analysis of the Archetype.* Bollingen Series, No. 47. Princeton: Princeton University Press, 1964.
　　An exhaustive study of the Mother and a valuable presentation of the immense complex of symbols that is associated with her.

Norton, Dan S., and Peters Rushton. *Classical Myths in English Literature.* New York: Rinehart & Co., 1952.
　　An excellent survey, in handbook form, of the mythic tradition in the work of major English authors—especially poets. The style is lively and invigorating.

Ohmann, Richard M., ed. *The Making of Myth.* New York: G. P. Putnam's Sons, 1962.

Otto, Walter F. *Dionysus: Myth and Cult.* Translated by R. B. Palmer. (Midland Books.) Bloomington, Indiana: Indiana University Press, 1965.

————. *The Homeric Gods: The Spiritual Significance of Greek Religion.* Translated by Moses Hadas. (Beacon Paperback.) Boston: Beacon Press, 1964.
　　An extraordinarily fine work, full of insights which bring the principal gods to life and give them meaning. A good starting point for an intensive study of any major Greek god or goddess.

Perry, John Weir. *Lord of the Four Quarters: Myths of the Royal Father.* ("Patterns of Myth" Series.) New York: George Braziller, Inc., 1966.

Raglan, Fitzroy Richard Somerset, 4th Baron. *The Hero: A Study in Tradition, Myth, and Drama.* (Vintage Books.) New York: Random House, Inc., 1956.
　　A pioneering work which makes up in simplicity and coherence what it may lack in modern scholarly technique.

Rank, Otto. *The Myth of the Birth of the Hero and Other Essays.* Edited by P. Freund. (Vintage Books.) New York: Random House, Inc., 1959.

———, and Hanns Sachs, *et al. Psychoanalysis as an Art and a Science.* Detroit: Wayne State University Press, 1968.

Róheim, Géza. *The Eternal Ones of the Dream: A Psychoanalytic Interpretation of Australian Myth and Ritual.* New York: International Universities Press, 1945.

   A work, as Joseph Campbell has demonstrated, of far broader significance than its special focus of attention might suggest.

Rose, Herbert J. *A Handbook of Greek Mythology.* (Dutton Paperbacks.) New York: E. P. Dutton & Co., Inc., 1959.

Royce, Joseph R., ed. *Psychology and the Symbol: An Interdisciplinary Symposium.* New York: Random House, Inc., 1965.

Ruitenbeck, Hendrik M., ed. *The Creative Imagination: Psychoanalysis and the Genius of Inspiration.* New York: Quadrangle Books, Inc., 1965.

   Twenty eminent psychoanalysts investigate the phenomena of creativity.

———, ed. *Psychoanalysis and Literature.* (Dutton Paperbacks.) New York: E. P. Dutton & Co., Inc., 1964.

Sebeok, Thomas A., ed. *Myth: A Symposium. Nine Essays.* Bloomington, Indiana: Indiana University Press, 1955.

Seznec, Jean. *The Survival of the Pagan Gods: The Mythological Tradition and Its Place in Renaissance Humanism and Art.* Translated by Barbara F. Sessions. Bollingen Series, No. 38. (Harper Torchbooks.) New York: Harper & Row, Publishers, 1961.

Tymms, Ralph. *Doubles in Literary Psychology.* London: Bowes and Bowes, 1949.

   Cites and analyzes works in this genre, drawn from relatively unfamiliar continental fiction.

Watts, Alan W. *The Joyous Cosmology: Adventures in the Chemistry of Consciousness.* (Vintage Books.) New York: Random House, Inc., 1969.

———. *The Two Hands of God: Myths of Polarity.* ("Patterns of Myth" Series.) (Collier Books.) New York: The Macmillan Company, 1969.

An interesting treatment of a pattern that lies near the heart of all mythology—and of poetry.

Wechsler, Herman Joel. *Gods and Goddesses in Art and Legend*. New York: Washington Square Press, 1961.

Weston, Jessie L. *From Ritual to Romance: An Account of the Holy Grail from Ancient Ritual to Christian Symbol*. (Anchor Books.) New York: Doubleday & Company, Inc., 1957.

The book which Eliot frequently recalled in writing *The Waste Land*. It convincingly illustrates the process by which myth passes into literature, retaining the essentials of its religious significance.

Zimmer, Heinrich. *The King and the Corpse: Tales of the Soul's Conquest of Evil*. Edited by Joseph Campbell. Bollingen Series, No. 11. (Meridian Books.) New York: World Publishing Company, 1960.

Analyses which are penetrating both as literary criticism and as psychological commentary. The final section—"*Four Episodes from the Romance of the Goddess*"—is an absorbing and invaluable introduction to the Lady as she appears in the mythologies of the East.

Acknowledgments

Grateful acknowledgment is made to the following publishers, agents, and individuals who have granted permission to reprint copyrighted selections included in this book.

ATHENEUM HOUSE, INC.
"Cinderella," "The Girl Dreams that She is Giselle," and "In Those Days," from Randall Jarrell, *The Woman at the Washington Zoo.* Copyright © 1949, © 1960 by Randall Jarrell, © 1952 by the Curtis Publishing Co. "The Girl Dreams that She is Giselle" appeared originally in *The Nation,* and "In Those Days" in the *Ladies Home Journal.* "In the Night Fields," from W. S. Merwin, *The Moving Target.* Copyright © 1961, 1963 by W. S. Merwin. Originally appeared in *The Nation.* "Callers," from Robert Watson, *A Paper Horse.* Copyright © 1960, 1961, 1962 by Robert Watson.

THE BELOIT POETRY JOURNAL
"Heard in Old Age," by Babette Deutsch.

THE BOBBS-MERRILL COMPANY, INC.
"From Ancient Fangs," "Homecoming," and "The Second Try," from Peter Viereck, *New and Selected Poems, 1932–1967.* Copyright © 1967 by Peter Viereck.

CHATTO AND WINDUS LTD.
"The Dream," from Richard Eberhart, *Collected Poems 1930–1960.*

JOHN CIARDI
"Ulysses," from *39 Poems.* Copyright 1959 by Rutgers, The State

JOHN CIARDI (CONT.)
University. "Song for an Allegorical Play," and "Damn Her," from *In the Stoneworks*. Copyright 1961 by Rutgers, The State University. "The Lamb," from *As If: Poems New and Selected*. Copyright 1955 by the Trustees of Rutgers College in New Jersey.

ELIZABETH COATSWORTH
"Return," from *Southwest Review* (Spring, 1957).

COLLINS-KNOWLTON-WING, INC.
"The Witches' Cauldron," "The White Goddess," "Nobody," "The Troll's Nosegay," "Alice," and "Beware, Madam," from Robert Graves, *Collected Poems*. Copyright © 1955, 1963 by Robert Graves.

CORINTH BOOKS
"Amitabha's Vow" (Burning: 10), from Gary Snyder, *Myths & Texts*. Copyright © 1960 by Gary Snyder.

DELACORTE PRESS
"Funeral," and "Tune for the Teletype," from William Jay Smith, *The Tin Can*. Copyright © 1966 by William Jay Smith. A Seymour Lawrence Book/Delacorte Press.

J. M. DENT & SONS LTD.
"The Snow," from Clifford Dyment, *Poems 1935–1948*. "Love in the Asylum," "I Fellowed Sleep," and "And Death Shall Have No Dominion," from Dylan Thomas, *Collected Poems*. Reprinted by permission of the Trustees for the copyrights of the late Dylan Thomas.

JAMES DICKEY
"Orpheus before Hades," from *Into the Stone* (*Poets of Today: VII*).

THE DOLMEN PRESS, LTD.
"Another September," from Thomas Kinsella, *Another September* (1958).

DOUBLEDAY & COMPANY INC.
"In a Dark Time," by Theodore Roethke, copyright © 1960 by Beatrice Roethke as Administratrix to the Estate; "I Knew a Woman," by Theodore Roethke, copyright 1954 by Theodore Roethke; both from Theodore Roethke, *The Collected Poems of Theodore Roethke*. "The Fulfillment," from Delmore Schwartz, *Summer Knowledge: New & Selected Poems 1938–1958*. Copyright 1954 by Delmore Schwartz.

DUFOUR EDITIONS, INC.

"The Image," from Roy Fuller, *Collected Poems.* "The Rebirth of Venus," from Geoffrey Hill, *For the Unfallen: Poems, 1952–1958.* "The Fox-Coloured Pheasant Enjoyed His Peace," from Peter Levi, S.J., *Water, Rock and Sand.*

E. P. DUTTON & COMPANY, INC.

"The Known World," from Brewster Ghiselin, *Against the Circle.* Copyright 1946 by E. P. Dutton & Co., Inc.

FABER & FABER LIMITED

"Atlantis," "Lady, Weeping at the Crossroads," "The Council," and "Ganymede" (Sonnets from China: IX), from W. H. Auden, *Collected Shorter Poems 1927–1957.* "La Figlia Che Piange," "Gerontion," "Animula," "Marina," "A Song for Simeon," "Triumphal March," "Journey of the Magi," from T. S. Eliot, *Collected Poems 1909–1962.* "The Corridor," from Thom Gunn, *A Sense of Movement.* "Perdita," from Louis MacNeice, *Collected Poems of Louis MacNeice.* "Horses," "The Bridge of Dread," "The Fathers," "The Trophy," "The Return," and "The Heroes," from Edwin Muir, *Collected Poems.* "Polar Exploration," from Stephen Spender, *Collected Poems 1928–1953.*

JEAN FARLEY

"Prodigal Son," and "Korê to Coed."

FARRAR, STRAUS & GIROUX

"The Dream," "A Tale," "Medusa," "Psychiatrist's Song," and "The Cupola," from Louise Bogan, *Collected Poems.* "Cupidon," and "The Dream" from William Jay Smith, *Celebration at Dark.* "The Prodigal," from Elizabeth Bishop, *The Complete Poems.* Copyright 1951 by Elizabeth Bishop. "Jack," "The Snow Leopard," "Dummies," and "The Sleeping Beauty: Variation of the Prince," from Randall Jarrell, *Complete Poems,* copyright © 1942, 1945, 1955.

JOSEPH FRANK

"Mirage" (Sea Island Miscellany: IX), from Richard Blackmur, *From Jordan's Delight.* Reprinted by permission of the executor of the estate of Richard Blackmur.

DON GEIGER

"Love Song by Husband after Being Buried with Wife One Night," from *Fiddlehead,* 1958.

JANE GENTRY

"Henry Griffith." "Bird and Bear," from *The Sewanee Review,* copyright by the University of the South.

GERALD DUCKWORTH & CO. LTD.
"Diana and Actaeon," "Andromeda," "Under the Hill," and "Children of Zeus," from Graham Hough, *Legends and Pastorals* (1961).

MADELINE GLEASON
"Once and Upon," from *Botteghe Oscure*.

THE GOLDEN QUILL PRESS
"Whirlwind," "The Death of Uncle Dan," "A Dream of the Consumer," "To a Young Woman, Entering a Formal Garden," "Admiral," "A Word to A Father, Dead," "A Kind of Quest, a Sort of Briar Rose," "The Button," "A Vision of the Goddess Kali as a Childhood Sweetheart," and "On the Lean Divider," from John Alexander Allen, *The Lean Divider*. "Ex-Surrealist," from Jeanne de Longchamps, *Eden under Glass*.

HARCOURT BRACE JOVANOVICH, INC.
"Journey of the Magi," "La Figlia Che Piange," "Gerontion," "Animula," "Marina," "A Song for Simeon," and "Triumphal March," from T. S. Eliot, *Collected Poems 1909–1962*. Copyright 1936 by Harcourt Brace Jovanovich, Inc. Copyright © 1963, 1964 by T. S. Eliot. "Streets Too Old," from Carl Sandburg, *Smoke and Steel*. Copyright 1920 by Harcourt Brace Jovanovich, Inc.; Copyright 1948 by Carl Sandburg. "Beowulf," "A World without Objects," and "He Was," from Richard Wilbur, *Ceremony and Other Poems*, copyright © 1948, 1949, 1950 by Richard Wilbur. "Beasts," by Richard Wilbur, copyright 1955 by Pantheon Books; "Love Calls Us to the Things of this World," by Richard Wilbur, © 1956 by Richard Wilbur; from Richard Wilbur, *Things of This World*. "She," by Richard Wilbur, © 1958 by Richard Wilbur; "In the Smoking Car," by Richard Wilbur, © 1960 by Richard Wilbur; from Richard Wilbur, *Advice to a Prophet and Other Poems*. "In the Smoking Car" was first published in *The New Yorker*.

HARPER & ROW, PUBLISHERS, INC.
"Daddy," from Sylvia Plath, *Ariel*. Copyright © 1963 by Ted Hughes. "The Begetting of Cain," and "Exhortation to Artists," from Hyam Plutzik, *Aspects of Proteus*. Copyright 1949 by Hyam Plutzik. "Lying Awake," from W. D. Snodgrass, *After Experience*. Copyright © 1959 by W. D. Snodgrass. Originally appeared in *The New Yorker*. "In the Museum," from William Stafford, *Traveling through the Dark*. Copyright © 1958 by William Stafford. "The Animal that Drank up Sound," from William Stafford, *The Rescued Year*. Copyright © 1964 by William E. Stafford.

HART-DAVIS LTD.
"Cape Dread," "Sea Monster," "Odysseus," and "Sea Wife," from W. S. Merwin, *The Drunk in the Furnace.*

DAVID HIGHAM, ASSOCIATES
"The Sphinx," from John Heath-Stubbs, *The Blue-Fly in His Head: Poems.* "Cape Dread," "Sea Monster," "Odysseus," and "Sea Wife" from W. S. Merwin, *The Drunk in the Furnace.*

HOLT, RINEHART AND WINSTON, INC.
"The Sound of Trees," "For Once, Then, Something," "Neither Out Far Nor in Deep," "Provide, Provide," "The Most of It," "The Witch of Coös," "Desert Places," "Design," "I Could Give All to Time," "Directive," from *The Poetry of Robert Frost,* edited by Edward Connery Lathem. Copyright 1916, 1923, 1947, © 1969 by Holt, Rinehart and Winston, Inc. Copyright 1936, 1942, 1944, 1951 by Robert Frost. Copyright © 1964, 1970 by Lesley Frost Ballantine.

HOUGHTON MIFFLIN COMPANY
"The Minotaur," from Isabella Gardner, *Birthdays from the Ocean.* Copyright 1955 by Isabella Gardner McCormick. "The Night Dream," "The Revenant," and "Selene Afterwards," from Archibald MacLeish, *Collected Poems.* Copyright 1952 by Archibald MacLeish. "The Starry Night," from Anne Sexton, *All My Pretty Ones.* Copyright © 1962 by Anne Sexton. "Her Kind," from Anne Sexton, *To Bedlam and Part Way Back.* Copyright © 1960 by Anne Sexton.

OLWYN HUGHES
"Lorelei," "The Bull of Bendylaw," "Strumpet Song," "Full Fathom Five," and "The Colossus," from Sylvia Plath, *The Colossus.* Copyright by Ted Hughes. "Daddy," from Sylvia Plath, *Ariel.* Copyright © 1963 by Ted Hughes. Published by Harper & Row and Faber & Faber. All poems used with the permission of the representative of the estate of Sylvia Plath.

INDIANA UNIVERSITY PRESS
"Meeting," from Josephine Miles, *Prefabrications.* Copyright © 1955 by Josephine Miles. "The Savages," from Josephine Miles, *Poems: 1930–1960.* Copyright © 1960 by Indiana University Press. "The Hero with One Face," "Words above a Narrow Entrance," "The Man from the Top of the Mind," and "The Eye of the Storm," from David Wagoner, *A Place to Stand.* Copyright © 1958 by Indiana University Press.

GAYLE JOHNSON
"Mayan Festival."

DENISE LEVERTOV
"The Third Dimension," from *Here and Now.*

LITTLE, BROWN AND COMPANY
"The Thing that Eats the Heart," by Stanley Kunitz, copyright 1958 by Stanley Kunitz, first appeared in *New World Writing #9;* "The Dark and the Fair," by Stanley Kunitz, copyright 1957 by Stanley Kunitz, first appeared in *Poetry;* "Father and Son," by Stanley Kunitz, copyright 1958 by Stanley Kunitz; from Stanley Kunitz, *Selected Poems 1928–1958.* "The Ten," by William Jay Smith, copyright © 1957 by William Jay Smith, and "American Primitive," by William Jay Smith, copyright © 1953 by William Jay Smith, from William Jay Smith, *Poems: 1947–1957.*

RON LOEWINSOHN
"The Thing Made Real," from *Watermelons.* Copyright 1959 by Ron Loewinsohn.

LOUISIANA STATE UNIVERSITY PRESS
"A Blind Man Locking His House," from Henry Taylor, *The Horse Show at Midnight.*

THE MACMILLAN COMPANY
"The Voice," from Thomas Hardy, *Collected Poems.* Copyright 1925 by The Macmillan Company. "Cape Dread," "Sea Monster," "Odysseus," and "Sea Wife," from W. S. Merwin, *The Drunk in the Furnace.* Copyright © 1956, 1957 by W. S. Merwin. "The Difference," "Come Green Again," "Merrill's Brook," and "William Primrose Gets His Guarnerius," from Winfield Townley Scott, *Collected Poems.* Copyright © 1953, 1956, 1957, 1959 by Winfield Townley Scott. "In Waste Places," from James Stephens, *Collected Poems.* Copyright 1915 by The Macmillan Company, renewed 1943 by James Stephens. "The Second Coming," by William Butler Yeats, copyright 1924 by The Macmillan Company, renewed 1961 by Bertha Georgie Yeats; "Her Triumph," by William Butler Yeats, copyright 1933 by The Macmillan Company, renewed 1961 by Bertha Georgie Yeats, and "Leda and the Swan," by William Butler Yeats, copyright 1928 by The Macmillan Company, renewed 1956 by Bertha Georgie Yeats; "The Cap and Bells," copyright 1916 by The Macmillan Company, renewed 1934 by William Butler Yeats; "The Magi," copyright 1916 by The Macmillan Company, renewed 1944 by Bertha Georgie Yeats; "The Cat and the Moon," copyright 1919 by The Macmillan Company, renewed 1947 by

THE MACMILLAN COMPANY (CONT.)

Bertha Georgie Yeats; "Lapis Lazuli," "News for the Delphic Oracle," "The Circus Animals' Desertion," and "The Black Tower," copyright 1940 by Georgie Yeats, renewed 1968 by Bertha Georgie Yeats, Michael Butler Yeats, and Anne Yeats; from William Butler Yeats, *Collected Poems*.

MACMILLAN & COMPANY LTD.

"Poem," from John Wain, *Weep before God*. Reprinted by permission of The Macmillan Company of Canada Limited and Macmillan & Company Ltd., London.

THE MACMILLAN COMPANY OF CANADA LIMITED

"The Voice," from Thomas Hardy, *Collected Poems*. Reprinted by permission of the Trustees of his Estate; Macmillan & Company Ltd., London; and The Macmillan Company of Canada Limited. "In Waste Places," from James Stephens, *Collected Poems*. Reprinted by permission of Mrs. Iris Wise; Macmillan and Company Ltd., London; and The Macmillan Company of Canada Limited.

MARGOT JOHNSON AGENCY

"A Predecessor of Perseus," "Maiden with Orb and Planets," "De Anima," and "The Dragonfly," from Howard Nemerov, *The Next Room of the Dream*. Copyright 1962 by Howard Nemerov. "Limits," and "Lore," from Howard Nemerov, *Mirrors and Windows*. Copyright 1958 by Howard Nemerov.

MARVIN JOSEPHSON ASSOCIATES, INC.

"The Minotaur," from Muriel Rukeyser, *Beast in View*. Copyright 1944 by Muriel Rukeyser. "Crayon House," from Muriel Rukeyser, *The Green Wave*. Copyright 1948 by Muriel Rukeyser.

THE MARVELL PRESS

"Poetry of Departures," from Philip Larkin, *The Less Deceived*. Copyright © 1955, 1969.

HAROLD MATSON COMPANY, INC.

"Nearing Again the Legendary Isle," by C. Day-Lewis. Copyright 1967 by C. Day-Lewis.

E. L. MAYO

"The Uninfected," and "The Diver," from *The Diver*. Reprinted by permission of the author and *Poetry*.

ROBERT MEZEY

"In Defense of Felons," from *The Lovemaker*.

UNIVERSITY OF MINNESOTA PRESS
"The Sleeping Beauty," and "The Loss," from E. L. Mayo, *Summer Unbound and other Poems*. Copyright © 1958 by University of Minnesota.

NEW DIRECTIONS PUBLISHING CORPORATION
"The Goddess," from Denise Levertov, *With Eyes at the Back of Our Heads*. Copyright © 1959 by Denise Levertov Goodman. "Ariadne," "Ariadne at the Labyrinth," and "Duns Scotus," from Thomas Merton, *Selected Poems*. Copyright © 1963 by the Abbey of Gethsemani, Inc. "The Constant Bridegrooms," and "The Unreturning Hosts," from Kenneth Patchen, *Collected Poems*. Copyright 1952 by Kenneth Patchen. "Love in the Asylum," "I Fellowed Sleep," and "And Death Shall Have No Dominion," from Dylan Thomas, *Collected Poems*. Copyright 1943 by New Directions Publishing Corporation, copyright 1953 by Dylan Thomas.

W. W. NORTON & COMPANY, INC.
"Lazarus," and "The Sleeping God," from May Sarton, *A Private Mythology*. Copyright © 1966 by May Sarton.

UNIVERSITY OF NOTRE DAME PRESS
"The Improvement of Prayer," and "Father Who Enters Into My Rest," from Ernest Sandeen, *Children and Older Strangers*, 1961.

OHIO STATE UNIVERSITY PRESS
"Love among the Manichees," from William Dickey, *Interpreter's House*, *1963*. Copyright © 1961 by William Dickey. It first appeared in *New World Writing 18* (J. B. Lippincott Company, 1961).

OHIO UNIVERSITY PRESS
"Hunter, Immobile," from Josephine Jacobsen, *The Animal Inside*.

OXFORD UNIVERSITY PRESS, INC.
"The Awakening" (The Kid: VII), from Conrad Aiken, *Collected Poems*. Copyright 1953 by Conrad Aiken. "The Dream," from Richard Eberhart, *Collected Poems*, *1930–1960*. Copyright © 1960 by Richard Eberhart. "In Cytherea," from Daniel Hoffman, *A Little Geste*. Copyright © 1960 by Daniel G. Hoffman. "The Line," "The City of Satisfactions," and "The True Testament of Thomas the Rhymer," from Daniel Hoffman, *The City of Satisfactions*. Copyright © 1963 by Daniel Hoffman. "A Visitation," "When my wiser brother," "Ignorant of source," "Another Country," and "The Last Arrival," from Daniel Hoffman, *Striking the Stones*. Copyright © 1968 by Daniel Hoffman. "Perdita," from Louis MacNeice, *Collected Poems*, edited by E. R. Dodds. Copyright © 1966 by The Estate of Louis MacNeice. "Horses," "The

OXFORD UNIVERSITY PRESS, INC. (CONT.)
Bridge of Dread," "The Fathers," "The Trophy," "The Return," and "The Heroes," from Edwin Muir, *Collected Poems.* Copyright © 1960 by Willa Muir.

LeRoy P. PERCY
"Medusa," from William Alexander Percy, *Selected Poems.*

PRINCETON UNIVERSITY PRESS
The Hero with a Thousand Faces, Joseph Campbell, Bollingen Series XVII (Princeton University Press, rev. ed., 1968). Copyright 1949 by Bollingen Foundation: quotes from pp. 15, 17, and 23.

RANDOM HOUSE, INC.
"Atlantis," "Lady, Weeping at the Crossroad," and "Ganymede," copyright 1945 by W. H. Auden; "The Council," copyright © 1966 by W. H. Auden; and "The Old Man's Road," copyright © 1960 by W. H. Auden; from W. H. Auden, *Collected Shorter Poems 1927–1957.* "The Lost Music," from Robert Hillyer, *The Relic and Other Poems.* Copyright 1957 by Robert Hillyer. "The Country of a Thousand Years of Peace," from James Merrill, *The Country of a Thousand Years of Peace.* Copyright 1958 by James Merrill. Originally appeared in *The New Yorker.* "The Bull of Bendylaw," by Sylvia Plath, Copyright © 1962 by Sylvia Plath; "Strumpet Song," by Sylvia Plath, Copyright © 1957 by Sylvia Plath; "Full Fathom Five," by Sylvia Plath, Copyright © 1961 by Sylvia Plath; "The Colossus," by Sylvia Plath. Copyright © 1961 by Sylvia Plath; "Lorelei," by Sylvia Plath, Copyright © 1959 by Sylvia Plath; reprinted from Sylvia Plath, *The Colossus and Other Poems,* by permission of Alfred A. Knopf, Inc. "The Ring," from Julia Randall, *Adam's Dream.* Copyright 1969 by Julia Randall. "Captain Carpenter," from John Crowe Ransom, *Selected Poems.* Copyright 1924 by Alfred A. Knopf, Inc., and renewed 1952 by John Crowe Ransom. "Orpheus," by W. D. Snodgrass, Copyright © 1956 by W. D. Snodgrass; and "μῆτις . . . οὖτις," by W. D. Snodgrass, Copyright © 1954 by W. D. Snodgrass; from W. D. Snodgrass, *Heart's Needle.* "Polar Exploration," from Stephen Spender, *Selected Poems.* Copyright 1942 by Stephen Spender. "Pursuit," and "Original Sin: A Short Story," by Robert Penn Warren, Copyright 1942 by Robert Penn Warren; "Eidolon," and "To a Face in the Crowd," by Robert Penn Warren, Copyright © 1966 by Robert Penn Warren; "After Night Flight . . . ," by Robert Penn Warren, Copyright © 1960 by Robert Penn Warren; and "Keepsakes," by Robert Penn Warren, Copyright © 1957 by Robert Penn Warren; from Robert Penn Warren, *Selected Poems: New And Old, 1923–1966.*

RUTGERS UNIVERSITY PRESS
"Fairy Tale," from John Frederick Nims, *Knowledge of the Evening: Poems 1950–1960.*

ST. MARTIN'S PRESS, INC.
"Poem," from John Wain, *Weep before God.*

ELEANOR M. SCOTT
"The Far-Off Man," from Winfield Townley Scott, *To Marry Strangers.* Published by Thomas Y. Crowell Company, 1945. Reprinted by permission of the administratrix of the estate of W. T. Scott.

CHARLES SCRIBNER'S SONS
"The Traveller," "I Know a Man," "The Hero," and "The Door," from Robert Creeley, *For Love.* Copyright © 1962 Robert Creeley. "The Sirens," from Donald Finkel, *The Clothing's New Emperor and Other Poems (Poets of Today: VI).* Copyright © 1959 by Donald Finkel. "The Quest," from George Garrett, *The Reverend Ghost: Poems (Poets of Today: IV).* Copyright © 1956, 1957 by George Garrett. "The Man Who Lost His Vision," from Robert Pack, *The Irony of Joy: Poems (Poets of Today: II).* Copyright © 1955 by Robert Pack. "Journey," from Kenneth Pitchford, *The Blizzard Ape: Poems (Poets of Today: V).* Copyright © 1958 by Kenneth Pitchford. "In Praise of Her," and "Climate," from Jon Swan, *Journeys and Return: Poems (Poets of Today: VII).* Copyright © 1960 by Jon Swan. "Hypnotist," from May Swenson, *To Mix with Time.* Copyright © 1963 by May Swenson.

WILLIAM JAY SMITH
"Cupidon," "Dream," and "Nukuhiva," from *Poems, 1947–1957.*

TROBAR
"A Bodhisattva Undoes Hell," by Jerome Rothenberg. Reprinted by permission of the author and publisher.

THE VIKING PRESS, INC.
"The End of a Journey," "Conquistador," "The House of God," "The Pleasure of Princes," "Circe," "The Return of Persephone," "Coup de Grâce," "Crossing the Frontier," and "Ode on the Death of Pius the Twelfth," by A. D. Hope, Copyright 1963, 1966 in all countries of the International Copyright Union by A. D. Hope; "Pasiphae," by A. D. Hope, Copyright © 1960 by A. D. Hope; from A. D. Hope, *Collected Poems: 1930–1965.* All rights reserved.

UNIVERSITY OF NORTH CAROLINA PRESS

"Tartar Horsemen," "Tanjong Malim: 1934," "Why Were the Bandit's Eyes Hidden behind a Green Mask?," "The Gullet of the Crocodile," "An Amoretti for Annie," "Altarpiece," and "Out of Sight, Out of Mind," from R. H. W. Dillard, *The Day I Stopped Dreaming about Barbara Steele*. "Figure Study," "A Modern Fiction," "Don Juan, Old," "Abraham's Knife," and "Holy Roller," from George Garrett, *Abraham's Knife*. "Boundbrook," "Journey," "A Ballad of Eve," "A Scarlet Letter about Mary Magdalene," "Danaë," "Miracles," "The Farmer's Tale," "Advent Poems, 1963: 7,8," and "The Silo under Angel's Gap," from Julia Randall, *The Puritan Carpenter*.

UNIVERSITY OF TEXAS PRESS

"The Cage," "Narcissus," and "Underworld," from George Garrett, *The Sleeping Gypsy and Other Poems, 1958*.

ROBERT A. WALLACE

"Song of a Journey," from *This Various World* (*Poets of Today: IV*). Copyright © 1957 by Robert Wallace.

J. P. WARD

"The Burglar," from *Times Literary Supplement* (London), May 26, 1965.

A. P. WATT & SON LTD.

"The Cap and Bells," "The Magi," "The Cat and the Moon," "Lapis Lazuli," "News for the Delphic Oracle," "The Circus Animals' Desertion," "The Black Tower," "The Second Coming," "Her Triumph," and "Leda and the Swan," from William Butler Yeats, *Collected Poems*. Permission to reprint given by Mr. M. B. Yeats and Macmillan Canada.

WESLEYAN UNIVERSITY PRESS

"The Scarred Girl," from James Dickey, *Helmets*. Copyright © 1963 by James Dickey. This poem was first published in *The New Yorker*. "In the Dark," from David Ferry, *On the Way to the Island*. Copyright © 1959 by David Ferry. "City Afternoon," "Chimera," and "The Triumph of Death," from Barbara Howes, *Light and Dark*. Copyright © 1955, 1959 by Barbara Howes. "Beyond the Hunting Woods," from Donald Justice, *The Summer Anniversaries*. Copyright © 1956 by Donald Justice. This poem was first published in *The New Yorker*. "Party Bird," from Chester Kallman, *Absent and Present*. Copyright © 1963 by Chester Kallman. "Because the Red Osier Dogwood," from Hyam Plutzik, *Apples from Shinar*. Copyright © 1950 by Hyam Plutzik.

WESLEYAN UNIVERSITY PRESS (CONT.)
"Grabbling in Yokna Bottom," and "The Majorette on the Self-Rising Flour Sign," from James Seay, *Let Not Your Hart.* Copyright © 1969 by James Seay. "A Blessing," from James Wright, *The Branch Will Not Break.* Copyright © 1961 by James Wright. This poem was first published in *Poetry.*

YALE UNIVERSITY PRESS
"Exploration over the Rim," from William Dickey, *Of the Festivity.* Copyright © 1959 by Yale University Press. "December: Of Aphrodite," and "Proteus," from W. S. Merwin, *The Dancing Bears.* Copyright © 1954 by Yale University Press.

Poems in Public Domain

Grateful acknowledgment is made to the following publishers for the use in this book of poems which are in the public domain.

APPLETON-CENTURY-CROFTS
"Childe Roland to the Dark Tower Came," from Robert Browning, *The Shorter Poems of Robert Browning,* 1937.

DOUBLEDAY & COMPANY, INC.
"When I Heard the Learn'd Astronomer," "Darest Thou Now O Soul," "Reconciliation," "On the Beach at Night," and "Facing West from California's Shores," from Walt Whitman, *Leaves of Grass,* 1929.

DOVER PUBLICATIONS, INC.
"Tam Lin," "Thomas Rhymer," "Kemp Owyne," and "The Laily Worm and the Machrel of the Sea," from *English and Scottish Popular Ballads,* 1965, ed., Francis J. Child.

HOUGHTON MIFFLIN COMPANY
"Ozymandias," from Percy B. Shelley, *Complete Poetical Works,* 1892. "Ulysses," and "Choric Song from The Lotos Eaters," from Alfred, Lord Tennyson, *Works,* 1904.

LITTLE, BROWN & COMPANY
"Safe in Their Alabaster Chambers," from Emily Dickinson, *Poems,* 1936.

THE MACMILLAN COMPANY
"Past and Present," from Thomas Hood, *Golden Treasury of Songs and Lyrics,* 1943.

WILLIAM MORROW & COMPANY, INC.
"Ulysses and the Siren," from Samuel Daniel, *Elizabethan Lyrics,* 1949, ed. Norman Ault.

OXFORD UNIVERSITY PRESS
"Holy Sonnets (XIV)," from John Donne, *Poems,* 1929. "The Collar," from George Herbert, *Works,* 1941. "The Sea and the Skylark," and "Pied Beauty," from Gerard Manley Hopkins, *Poems,* 1967. "La Belle Dame Sans Merci," and "Bright Star," from John Keats, *Poems,* 1956. "On a Drop of Dew," from Andrew Marvell, *Metaphysical Lyrics and Poems,* 1921. "The Retreat," and "Joy of My Life! While Left Me Here," from Henry Vaughan, *Works,* 1914. "The World Is Too Much with Us," from William Wordsworth, *Works,* 1936.

RANDOM HOUSE, INC.
"A Little Girl Lost," and "The Tyger," from William Blake, *Complete Works,* 1958.

Index of Authors